Indian Economy

Issues and Concerns

K.R. Gupta

ATLANTIC
PUBLISHERS & DISTRIBUTORS (P) LTD

Published by
ATLANTIC
PUBLISHERS & DISTRIBUTORS (P) LTD
7/22, Ansari Road, Darya Ganj, New Delhi-110002
Phones : +91-11-40775252, 23273880, 23275880, 23280451
Fax : +91-11-23285873
Web : www.atlanticbooks.com
E-mail : orders@atlanticbooks.com

Branch Office
5, Nallathambi Street, Wallajah Road, Chennai-600002
Phones : +91-44-64611085, 32413319
E-mail : chennai@atlanticbooks.com

Printed in India at Nice Printing Press, A-33/3A, Site-IV, Industrial Area, Sahibabad, Ghaziabad, U.P.

Preface

India's economy is the sixth-largest in the world measured by nominal GDP, and the third-largest by purchasing power parity (PPP). India is recognized as a newly industrialized country, and one of the G-20 major economies, with an average growth rate of approximately 7% over the last two decades.

The long-term growth prospective of the Indian economy is positive due to its young population, corresponding low dependency ratio, healthy savings and investment rates, and increasing integration into the global economy. The Indian economy has the potential to become the world's third-largest economy by the next decade and one of the two largest economies by mid-century. India had over US$ 600 billion worth of retail market in 2016 and one of world's fastest growing e-commerce markets. India has become a major exporter of IT services, Business Process Outsourcing (BPO) services, and software services with nearly US$ 170 billion worth of services exports. India is the third-largest start-up hub in the world with over 4750 technology start-ups as on February 2017. India ranks second worldwide in farm output. The industry sector has held a steady share of its economic contribution (29.2% of GDP in 2016-17). The Indian automobile industry is one of the largest in the world with an annual production of 25.03 million vehicles in 2016-17. India's two largest stock exchanges, Bombay Stock Exchange and National Stock Exchange of India, had a market capitalization of US$ 1.94 trillion and US$ 1.41 trillion, respectively, as of March 2016.

The International Monetary Fund (IMF) described the Indian economy as the "bright spot" in the global landscape. India topped the World Bank's growth outlook for the first time in fiscal year 2015-16, during which the economy grew 7.6%. The World Bank has projected that India's economic growth will accelerate to 7.3% in 2018-19 and 7.5% in 2019-20. According to the IMF, India's growth is expected to rebound to 7.2% in the 2017-18 fiscal and 7.7% in 2018-19. However, the figures were subsequently revised to 6.7% and 7.4 for 2017-18 and 2018-19, respectively, by IMF.

The book studies various aspects of Indian economy and analyzes the growth prospects in different sectors and segments on all the important parameters. The subject matter is divided into 8 chapters, each highlighting an important topic, with all the pertinent issues.

India's economic history has been taken up in the first chapter, which studies the condition of India's economy under British rule. It explains how the British, through their exploitative rule, drained India of its wealth. An analysis of the position of India's Industry has been made. The causes of decline of handicraft industry, stagnation of agriculture, recurring famines, the policies of the British during the two World Wars, permanent settlement, ryotwari system, growth of tenancy and tenancy act, provincial autonomy, rampant rural indebtedness—all have been discussed in detail.

Chapter 2 gives an overview of Indian economy. Economic reforms of the 1990s, growth in major sectors, like agriculture, industry and services, and other sectors like telecommunication, civil aviation, and tourism have been discussed. India's GDP growth in recent years, the components of GDP, capital market, social infrastructure, skill development, sustainable development, and the future outlook of Indian economy have been discussed, giving latest facts and figures.

India's economy is in a transition stage. From a developing economy, it has become an emerging economy. It has shown great progress in many parameters of development, like an improved level of infrastructure, more initiative in enterprise, better standard of living, fast human development, and better utilization of natural resources, among others. All these have been taken up in chapter 3 on features of Indian economy.

India's demography, with all its key statistics based on 2011 population census and analysis thereon, have been given in chapter 4. The large size of India's population, high rate of growth of population and the consequences thereof on employment and development, density of population, low sex ratio, large household size, and India's demographic dividend have been discussed in this chapter.

Chapter 5 takes up agriculture and food security. Although agriculture is not contributing as much to GDP growth as do services or industry, it provides livelihood to a very high proportion of working population in India. Important factors influencing Indian agriculture, the second green revolution, emerging areas in agriculture, genetically modified crops, allied sectors in agriculture, agriculture extension services, the effect of climate change, and challenges in maintaining food security in India, form part of this chapter.

Chapter 6 discusses various aspects of food inflation and public distribution system (PDS). It provides information on urban and rural sector inflation in India, minimum support price, origin and significance of PDS in India, food subsidy, agriculture marketing reforms, and buffer stock, among other pertinent issues.

In chapter 7, India's industry has been discussed in detail. The progress of India's industry after the achievement of independence, in the post-liberalization period, and during more recent period has been explained. The progress of various types of industries, both under public sector and private sector, have been presented. Major sectors of industry, like engineering, heavy electrical, iron and steel, automotive, petroleum and gas, civil aviation, shipping, IT, etc. have also been dealt with.

The last chapter of the book deals with Indian public finances. Covered in this chapter are, India's taxation policy, direct and indirect taxes, tax reforms, including the latest reform in bringing Goods and Services Tax (GST), corporate tax, expenditure tax, taxation on agriculture, revenues of the central government and the state government, public expenditure in India, pubic debt, and fiscal deficit.

The book presents latest available data on all the topics chosen in the chapters. The latest facts and figures have been taken from authentic sources, mostly from the data provided by relating ministries. It includes a large number of tables on various parameters of economy. The data has been analyzed so that readers are able to draw proper conclusions. The structure and presentation of the book are highly accessible for easy understanding by the readers. Some latest policies in the pertinent fields brought by the government have been given as appendices in a few chapters. Many sources have been drawn upon to prepare the book, which have been acknowledged in the notes. If some source has been left out, it is unintentional.

The book will be useful for the students and teachers of economics and researchers in this field. It will also help economists, policymakers, parliamentarians and legislators in making effective policies. The book will also prove beneficial for those preparing for various competitive examinations for lucrative positions.

K.R. Gupta

Contents

1

Economic History of India

INDIAN ECONOMY UNDER THE BRITISH RULE: INDUSTRIAL DEVELOPMENT

We can discuss the industrial development under the British rule as follows:

I. The East India Company and Early British Rule

Although India has never been an industrialized country in the Western sense, or modern sense (large-scale industries, factories, factory laws, division of labour, etc.), yet numerous varieties of goods have been manufactured in India since time immemorial. Muslin of Dacca, woollen shawls of Kashmir, marble work of Jaipur, perfumes, ivory works, art works, etc. were sold to many foreign traders, including European traders. In spite of predominantly agricultural character, India produced a large variety of industrial goods.

The main purpose of East India Company or the Britishers for coming over to India was to trade in those manufactured goods, which were in large demand in European countries. They were attracted by the value and variety of its manufactures and crafts. When in 1600 the East India Company obtained a charter (or sought permission) from Queen Elizabeth to trade with East India, it was "to carry the manufactures and commodities of India to Europe". At the end of 17th century, cheap and graceful Indian calicoes (cotton fabrics of Calicut), muslin and woollen fabrics found such favour in England that the manufacturers of those fabrics in England were seriously alarmed. Acts were passed in 1700 prohibiting the use of Indian printed or dyed calicoes in England. By a subsequent Act, the wearing of silken fabrics imported from India was also banned and a penalty of £200 was imposed on the persons selling the printed fabrics from India, China and Persia. However, the East India Company was allowed to sell it in other countries. Thus, up to 19th century, Indian manufacturers were excluded from the British market by law.

The huge amount of wealth exports from India was less by trade and more by plunder. From 1757 (Battle of Plassey) onwards, the direct plunder of Indian economy began with the import of raw material from India at cheap rates in large quantities, which prepared the ground for industrial revolution to take place first in England (around 1760).

But once the revolution began, it changed the whole outlook of England. The manufacturers and traders of England first broke the monopoly of the East India Company in 1813. Then they systematically encouraged the import of manufactured goods into India and the export of raw materials (raw silk, raw cotton, raw jute, coal, etc.) from India. The East India Company had to oblige the English manufacturers even if that meant a decline in the profit of East India Company.

II. The Early 19th Century

From 1813, when East India Company's monopoly of trade with India was broken by the British manufacturers, India became suddenly an importing country from an exporting one. And this was brought about, not on the basis of technical superiority of British industries, but on the basis of direct state assistance in the form of one-way forced trade.

After the removal of international restrictions by the Charter of 1813, Indian trade expanded substantially and over the long term showed an upward trend.[1] The result was a significant transfer of capital from India to England, which, due to the colonial policies of the British, led to a massive drain of revenue rather than any systematic effort at modernization of the domestic economy.[2]

This resulted in ruining of a large number of artisans and craftsmen, spinners, weavers, potters, etc. from the towns or from the villages, as they had no alternative employment. As the deterioration of industries set in, more and more people fell on agriculture. In 1872, the total number of dependents on agriculture was 61 per cent of the total population. After fifty years, i.e. in 1921, it became 73 per cent. However, foreign capital began to be invested in extracting industries, like rubber, tea and coffee plantation. Foreign capital, notably from Britain, was also invited to build railways. This capital was assured a return of 5 per cent which was disproportionately higher than the rate of interest at that time.

Progress up to the First World War

Around 1860, a modest beginning of modern Indian industries was made. This period witnessed the establishment of three cotton mills in Bombay, two jute mills in Bengal, and coal mining industry at Raniganj. While the cotton mills were owned and managed by Indians (who were later on constantly harassed and discriminated against), the jute mills and coal mines were owned and managed by the British and the Scottish capitalists. The same period saw the beginning of railways. The first railway line, between Bombay and Thane, was opened in 1853 and the period 1860-70 saw a remarkable growth of 5000 miles.

Thus, by and large, consumption goods industry dominated the Indian scene. Basic and key industries were perfectly absent. The only important exception was the inauguration of the Tata Iron and Steel Company at Jamshedpur. This commenced its production in 1912. The large organized industries on a stable footing were three in number: the cotton industry of Bombay, the jute industry of Bengal and the coal mining industries of Bihar, Orissa and Bengal.

This period (up to 1914) was marked by two important features—(1) the opposition of the British manufacturers to the starting of new industries in India, and (2) the spread of Swadeshi Movement in 1905.

Opposition of British Interests

The British manufacturers tried their best to destroy India's new industries, especially cotton textile industry. When in 1853, cotton textile factories were being started in India, the Manchester Chamber of Commerce insisted that the Government of India should identify themselves "with the cause of civilization, justice and Christianity by helping them to destroy new industry". In December 1894, when financial consideration forced the GOI to impose a general import duty of 5 per cent, a 'countervailing' cotton excise of 5 per cent was imposed upon all Indian mill-made yarn which exempted the imports from Manchester when in 1896, import duty was reduced to 3.5 per cent. Similarly, in the last quarter of the century, there was an agitation in Dundee (England) against Indian jute manufacturing. Fortunately for India, Dundee was not as strong as Manchester, and Indian jute manufacturing had been Scottish-owned rather than Indian. The Scots of Calcutta took up the challenge and defeated the sinister move of Dundee. Insofar as coal industry was concerned, it was actively supported by the Government to enable it to meet the demand from railways.

Swadeshi Movement

The next landmark in the history of Indian industries was the Swadeshi Movement of 1905. From the last two decades of 19th century, the economic backwardness of India began to attract the attention of patriots and economists like Dadabhai Naoroji and Ranade. The industrial backwardness was rightly held responsible for the recurrent famines and poverty from which the country suffered. The achievements of Japanese Government in bringing their country into the forefront of industrial nations within a very short period stood in contrast with unsympathetic attitude of the government in our country. The much hated cotton excise duties confirmed the suspicion of the people that the government was deliberately inhibiting the industrial development. Therefore, it is not surprising that the economic discontentment due to the poverty of the masses, and the lack of employment opportunities of the educated middle-class youth began to assume a political colour. The Swadeshi Movement called upon people to buy indigenous goods and to boycott imported goods. This caught the imagination of the people and a great wave of industrial enthusiasm (Indian market establishing more and more industry) spread throughout the country. Between 1890 and 1914, when the number of cotton and jute mills increased three-four times, railways (in the hands of British) continued to expand at the rate of 800 miles per annum.

Further, apart from the existing three major industries, numerous factories for the manufacture of small items like pencils, matches, glassware, etc. were started. But, because of the lack of experience and training, these industries had to suffer.

III. The First World War (1914-18)

Up to the First World War, the opposition of the Britishers to industrial development in India was open, and unconcealed. But the First World War proved an eye-opener to the people. When the war broke out, imports from foreign countries, particularly enemy countries were completely stopped. This revealed our miserable dependence on imports even for the basic necessities. From strategic military angle, this was even more serious. So, for the defence of British Empire, India had to be industrialized. Secondly, it was necessary for the foreign rulers to make certain political and economic concessions and promises of concessions to secure cooperation of the Indian people during the war and in the disturbed period following the war. The Government announced that industrialization will be promoted by all means in future. Thirdly, foreign competition (notably from Japan) had been affecting British import in India. It was felt that growth of some industries within India was better than foreign competition displacing British imports.

Industrial Commission (1916)

All the above considerations resulted in the appointment of the Industrial Commission in 1916, with Sir Thomas Holland as Chairman. The aim was to examine the whole question of industrial development in India, and to indicate new openings for the profitable employment of Indian capital.

Indian Munitions Board

While the report of the Commission was still pending, the Indian Munitions Board was set up as an emergency measure in 1917 "to control and develop Indian resources with special reference to the needs created by the war, and to apply the manufacturing resources of India to war purposes with the special object of reducing demands on shipping".[3] The Board helped the progress of indigenous industries in various ways such as the following:

(a) Direct purchase of Indian-made articles and materials of all kinds needed for the army, the civil departments, and the railways;

(b) The diversion of all orders from the U.K. and elsewhere to manufacture in India;

(c) Assistance to Indian firms in importing industrial plants or technical experts from abroad. In fact, it gave considerable stimulus to certain established industries, e.g. cotton, jute, iron and steel, leather, etc.

Industrial Progress During the Period

During the war period, cotton and jute industries worked at full capacity, thus earning large profits. Steel production increased from 19,000 tonnes in 1913 to 1,24,000 tonnes in 1918 (i.e. 7 times). Due to the cutting off of import from abroad, the production of some consumer goods also developed. Many articles, like chemicals, minerals, acids, cements, fertilizers, cutlery, etc. for which India relied on foreign countries were manufactured for the first time in India. However, the lack of basic industries prevented the consumer goods industries from taking full advantage of the temporary protection accorded by the war to these industries.

It has been rightly observed by Professor Jather and Beri that the success of this new departure of the Government from the traditional policy of *laissez-faire* showed how much could be done in the sphere of industrial development with the active cooperation of the Government. But once the war and the fear of it on the British Empire was over, the concessions in favour of Indian industries were also withdrawn. The First World War provided only temporary gains to the established industries. And it did nothing to set the country firmly on the road to industrialization.

IV. Inter-War Period (1918-39)

Report of the Industrial Commission

In 1918, the Industrial Commission presented its report which stressed that, in future, the Government must extend active assistance in industrializing the country with a view to making India self-sufficient. The report also recognized the fact that the Government cannot do much in this direction unless it is equipped with (i) adequate administrative machinery, and (ii) trained, technical and scientific experts. Therefore, the Commission recommended (i) the creation of special industrial and chemical services and (ii) the establishment of Board of Industries.

But the elaborate scheme of Indian Industrial Commission for the rapid industrialization of the country came to nothing. Under the GOI Act 1919, industries became a provincial subject, and following the recommendations of the Industrial Commission, a Provincial Department of Industries was established in each province. The main work of these departments was (i) promotion of technical and industrial education, (ii) supply of industrial intelligence, and (iii) financial assistance to industries and holding of industrial exhibitions for popularizing their products. But nothing substantial was achieved because of lack of funds. The constitutional transfer of industries to the Provinces also handicapped the evolution of a comprehensive industrial policy.

Discriminating Protection

The period after the war was followed by a short period of prosperity brought by the rising income and unfulfilled demand of the preceding period. It was a short period of great prosperity for the existing manufacturing industries, such as jute, cotton, iron and steel, etc. But by the middle of 1920, Indian industries were again subjected to the full force of foreign competition, and the long-standing demand for protection of India industries became more powerful and vocal. This eventually led to the appointment of the Fiscal Commission in October 1921. The Commission recommended (1922) a policy of discriminating protection to be administered through an expert body called the Tariff Board. This policy was accepted by the Government in 1923 and a Tariff Board was constituted to examine the claims for the protection of several industries. As many as 13 industries received protection and this enabled a few of them, like steel, cotton, sugar, paper and matches to establish themselves in social sector. But the lack of genuine concern on the part of the Government to industrialize the country hampered the progress of many industries. In fact, protection was given grudgingly and only to face foreign competition. Protection was never used as an instrument of industrialization.

The triple formula evolved to decide about granting protection was rightly called as discrimination and no protection because the Government could refuse protection on any of the three grounds mentioned in the triple formula. These were:

(1) The industry must have natural advantages which would facilitate its growth. These included abundant supply of raw materials, cheap power, a sufficient supply of labour and a large home market.

(2) The industry must be such as is not likely to develop at all, or at least not as rapidly as desirable in the interests of the country, unless it was given protection.

(3) The industry must be one which would ultimately be able to face world competition, without the help of protection.

This triple formula meant that the protection would be temporary, and given only when it was indispensable for the permanent development of a particular industry. Moreover, this was not a permanent Tariff Board. For each case, a separate Board was constituted. This resulted in inordinate delays. Lastly, the effectiveness of protection was reduced in some cases by excise duties on the production of sugar, matches, steel, etc. in 1943.

Another noteworthy feature of industrialization during this period was the institution of 'imperial preferences'.

Export of British Capital to India

During the period following the war, large amount of British capital was brought to India. This was largely encouraged by huge projects earned by the British and Indian firms during and after the war. The total of British capital investment in India which was roughly £400 million just before the war reached £1000 million by 1933. From the Indian share of 11 per cent of the total of British capital investment throughout the world, it reached 25 per cent of the total of British investment. For the Indian industries this was an extremely difficult period. The difficulty aggravated when the Tariff Board turned down the applications of many vital industries for protection.

Imperial Preference

Imperial preference, a tariff policy, which gave British products an advantage over non-empire products in the Indian markets and Indian products an advantage over non-empire product in the empire market now became the keynote of the tariff system. Though originally proclaimed as a means for promoting Indian industrialization, in reality it was a system which assisted British industry to compete in the Indian market while India got the privilege of reduced rates for the sake of raw materials in the British market. The continuation of this policy of exploitation was naturally opposed by the rising class of industrialists of India. The clash of interests between British and Indian industrialists found expression in the Indian Legislative Assembly when the Trade Agreement between England and India, based on Ottawa Agreement, was defeated. But even in the face of the adverse vote of the Assembly, the Trade Agreement (Imperial Preference) was thrust upon India.

Political Inspiration

Another significant development in the inter-war industrial history of Indian was the move of Indian National Congress for industrial planning for India. Experiences of other countries, notably Japan, had made it clear to the educated sections of people that with proper guidance of the Government, substantial progress in industrialization can be achieved within a comparatively short time. Remarkable results achieved by the USSR through a system of planning also raised new hopes and strengthened the faith in planning for solving economic problems of poverty and unemployment. The Indian National Congress, which was generally opposed to industrialization, particularly large-scale mechanization, also modified its policy in 1938. Under the leadership of Subhas Chandra Bose, an ex-Congress President, a Conference of Industries Ministers, from the 'Congress Provinces' was held in October 1938. The conference came to the conclusion that the problems of poverty and unemployment, of defence and economic development in general could not be generally solved without industrialization. The conference emphasized the urgency of taking steps to start 'key' industries of national importance, and appointed a National Planning Committee under the Chairmanship of Pandit Jawaharlal Nehru to draw up a comprehensive scheme of national planning. The National Planning Committee appointed 29 sub-committees which submitted their reports. But no concrete action could be taken as the Congress Ministries had to resign in September 1939 following the outbreak of the Second World War. The war and the consequent change in political situation in the country relegated the problems of industrialization to the background.

Industrial Progress during Inter-war Period

In spite of the difficulties and obstacles which Indian industries had to face, there was considerable industrial development during the inter-war period. Between 1922 and 1939, the production of cotton piece goods increased two and a half (2½) times, that of steel nearly eight times, and paper nearly two and a half times. In the case of sugar, India became self-sufficient and its production increased nearly 12 times. From a zero-start, the cement industry produced nearly 95 per cent of total requirements. The production of matches, glass, soap, vanaspati and a number of engineering industries also recorded large increases. By 1938-39, the manufacturing of electric equipment and goods also started. The total number of factories increased 4 times and the number of workers employed in them increased 40 per cent. It means, by and large, the new industries were small-scale industries.

In spite of considerable expansion of industrial production during the period, the overall picture suggested a very slow rate of development. As already said, by and large, new establishments were small scale, catering mostly to the demand for consumer goods. Although some protected industries expanded considerably and India became independent of foreign countries for the supply of machinery and other capital goods without which the establishment of new industries would be impossible, yet full-fledged industrialization was not still achieved. Even *The Economist*, *Indian Supplement* published from London, in its survey of India's industrialization at the end of 1936 observed, "The proportion of the population dependent upon industry as a whole has tended to decline. Although India has begun to modernize her industries, it can hardly be said that she is as yet being industrialized."

V. The Second World War (1939-45)

In spite of the life and death situation in which England found herself in the Second World War, the industrialization of India was knowingly discouraged. This was particularly true during the initial years, but the exigencies of war compelled the Government to take up some positive steps for industrialization. Nazi Germany was threatening the vast Empire of the Britishers. Their ships were being sunk. Near India, Japan had occupied Burma and was threatening to enter India. This revealed the total lack of military base in India. In short, the World War II created a more urgent demand for the rapid growth of 'heavy and key' industries in India than the war of 1914-18.

Further, apart from the needs of the Allies (the forces which constituted to fight Nazi Germany) for the war purposes, there were other important factors which favoured industrial development during this period.

(1) Drastic curtailment of imports and restrictions on imports created near monopoly conditions in the home market.

(2) The assurance given by the Government that industries which are required for war purposes would be given protection after the war is over provided great incentives to start new industries.

(3) In 1940, Board of Scientific and Industrial Research (BSIR) was started at Calcutta partly for training war technicians. The Board provided training to Indian technicians. The British also offered stipends for training Indian technicians in British industries.

All this greatly increased the supply of skilled labour and technicians. BSIR found a number of indigenous substitutes for import and developed the use of vegetable oil, lubricants, drugs, dyes, plastics, etc.

Progress of Industries

A number of industries were benefited in different degrees by the conditions created by the war. The existing large and organized industries such as the iron and steel, jute, cotton, leather and tanning, woollen, sugar, paper and cement industries made considerable progress. Production increased by increasing the time and number of shifts or by improving methods. Wherever feasible, new plants were also added. Some new large-scale industries also started production for the first time. They were:

(a) Heavy chemical industries like caustic soda, bleaching powder, soda ash, superphosphate, etc.

(b) Ferrous-alloys (Ferro-manganese) and non-ferrous metals like aluminum, copper-wires, cables, etc.

(c) New branches of engineering industry including diesel engines, pumps, bicycles, sewing machine tools, etc.

Thus, compared with the First World War, new capital and intermediate goods industries also received stimulus. A number of medium and large-scale industries were also established during the World War II as compared with small-scale industries during the First World War.

The trend of industrial activity during the war and the major large-scale industries can be studied from their performances. For example, before the war, India was entirely dependent on foreign sources for high grades steel. But during the war, the production of high grade steel, pig iron, etc. picked up. Fifty-four firms began to manufacture more tools. Armaments work, explosive plants and small arm factories were expanded. The Hindustan Aircraft Company at Bangalore assembled its first plane in August 1941 from imported parts. Iron and steel industries and consumer goods industries, like cotton goods, also recorded a sizeable growth. There was a great demand for clothes from the Allies. Within one year during 1943-44, the production of cotton clothes increased by 30 per cent. So were other industries like sugar and jute. Jute which had depressed earlier established fresh records in production and exports.

Critical Estimate of Progress

As already stated, as far as possible the British Government discouraged industrialization in India. The establishment of certain key industries was their war compulsion. It never wanted to lose India as the supplier of raw materials and the market for British goods. When the Eastern Group Conference was held in New Delhi in October 1940, India was recognized as the leader of the Eastern Group Commonwealth Countries. The main object of the conference was to make the countries of the Eastern Group, especially India, as far as possible, self-supporting for war purposes. But the recommendations of the conference were never published in India—the country where the conference was held. When the question of manufacturing aeroplanes came up, it was simply set aside on the ground that it would be a duplication of what other parts of the Empire (viz. Australia) were doing.

Similarly, the American Technical Mission, headed by Dr. Henry Grady, which visited India in April 1942, carried out an investigation into India's war production possibilities. It recommended the establishment of some new industries for which the country was fully equipped. It also recommended an increase in training facilities. But all its elaborate schemes came to nothing. For safeguarding the interest of British industrialists, the Government avoided the development of key industries even at the risk of losing the war. British capital further strengthened its grip over Indian enterprises. The giant British concerns like Lever Brothers, Dunlop, Imperial Chemicals, etc. started their Indian subsidiaries. The number of these 'India Limited' companies was daily growing and within 5 years (period ending 1943-44) their number grew to 108. These limited concerns concentrated on the production of matches, cigarettes, soaps, rubber, chemicals, etc. But the proposal for the establishment of an automobile industry—owned and managed by Indians, was rejected on the ground of difficulties created by war. It was the time when the GOI was placing orders for the import of automobiles from other countries. Australia and Canada were manufacturing aeroplanes with the help of England. But when Indian industrialists showed their interest to do so, without any subsidy, the request was turned down. Same was the fate of shipbuilding industry.

Thus, in spite of the extremely favourable environment created by the war and India's large metallurgical resources, it still lagged behind in basic and 'key' industries. It is true that India became self-sufficient in respect of something like 90 per cent of its military supplies, but it must also be remembered that the supplies in respect of which India became self-sufficient, consisted mainly of clothing, small ammunition, foodstuffs, tents and blankets. Only those basic and key industries were started for which abundant raw material was available. But not much was done to reverse the shortage of capital and trained personnel.

Adverse Effects

What is worse, the limited industrial progress which was achieved during the war period led to undesirable trends:

(1) As already stated, the increase in production was primarily achieved through intensive use of existing machinery, with the result that after the war, the machinery was worn out and needed urgent repair which was neglected.

(2) War time inflation sidetracked the economic factors like availability of raw materials, location of industry, proper financial management, etc. These trends were not conducive for long-term industrialization.

(3) During the war, major emphasis was on defence goods industries. Consumer goods industries, like cotton clothes, cement, sugar, jute, paper, etc. were neglected. Thus, there was lopsided development in industry.

(4) The shortfall in the production of consumer goods industry compelled the Government to introduce rationing for their equitable distribution, but their continuous price rise made the controls ineffective. This led to corruption and blackmarketing.

Governments' Industrial Policy

While examining the growth of modern industries in India, a question which naturally comes up is what role did the Government play in this regard? The question is relevant because this would verify the claim of the British Government that it did a lot to lay the foundation of modern industries in India.

It is a well-known fact that during East India Company's tenure, several measures were taken to discourage our industries and to encourage the sale of British goods in India. For example, in 1869, the company's Director ordered the encouragement of production of raw silk in Bengal and discouragement of silk fabrics. In the same year, silk artisans were forced to work in the company's factories. When the company charter was renewed, the British Parliament enquired into the law whether Indian industrial products could be replaced by the British products. In this regard, the officials of the East India Company readily obliged the British manufacturers.

On the other hand, Indian handicraft products were shut out from England by high import duties varying from 67 per cent and going up to even 400 per cent. Not satisfied with high tariff, there was sometimes a complete ban on the import of Indian goods into England. But the British goods were forced on India free of duty. In this way, the process of political injustice was applied to kill Indian handicrafts.

When India came directly under the British crown after the Revolt of 1857, the attitude of the Government changed little. At best, it was a policy of absolute *laissez-faire*. And it served the British interest at the cost of Indian interest. For example, the Famines Commission of 1880 recommended encouragement to industries as the most important remedy for famines, but due to Government's pressure from Manchester, the centre of cotton mills in England, most of the import duties were removed by 1882. Manchester complained that cotton mills in India offered an 'unfair competition' since labour was relatively cheap in India. Consequently, Factory Acts of 1881 and 1891 were forced upon India, compelling the cotton manufacturers to provide more facilities to Indian labour and this increased their cost of production.

In December 1894, financial consideration forced the Government to impose a general import duty of 5 per cent, under the pressure of Manchester. A 'countervailing' cotton excise of 5 per cent was also imposed on Indian mill cloth when in 1896, import duty was reduced to 3.5 per cent, and excise duty was also cut to 3.5 per cent. Thus, excise duty greatly harassed the poor consumers demanding coarse cloth. It was only in 1926 that this much-hated 'countervailing' excise duty was removed.

What we needed at that time was protection for our infant industries. But what we received was one-way free trade which served the interest of the Britishers at the cost of Indians. It may be mentioned that some provincial governments tried to encourage the establishment of industries, but the European businessmen in India opposed this. Therefore, in 1910 Lord Morley, the Secretary of the State, reversed this policy. The indifference of Government to industrial development in India continued right up to the First World War.

On the whole, the attitude of the British Government towards industrialization in India was negative. It was only under certain compulsions that the British Government had to provide certain industries. It tried to retain India as a source of raw material for their industries in England and as a market for their manufacturers.

Indian Industries in the Past and their Decline or Decline of Handicrafts—Causes and Consequences

India was never an industrial country in the modern sense, yet Indian handicrafts before the British era were well known. These included cotton fabrics, silk fabrics, woollen fabrics, art products, timber (ship industry), and metal industries. Even the great iron pillars industries in India testifies that iron (melt) industry was quite developed at that time in India. Broadly, we can divide the Indian industries in three groups:

(1) Village & Cottage Industries,

(2) Urban Handicrafts, and

(3) Localized Industries.

(1) **Village & Cottage Industries.** There were self-sufficient villages. A large number of artisans existed in the village with certain amount of coarse weaving, grinding of grain flour mills, rice milling, sugar making, etc. Their organization was primitive and no division of labour or specialization existed. Often these industries were done along with agriculture.

(2) **Urban Handicrafts.** Urban handicrafts were better organized and confined more or less to higher class of products. These were organized into caste-based guilds. In certain industries, division of labour was practiced with same degree of localization.

(3) **Localized Industries.** Third group of industries, neither urban nor village, was highly localized because of the availability of raw material, for example, iron industry in Mysore, Chhotanagpur, and Central Provinces. Some of these industries were very important to the country. Although not highly developed, products were of fine quality. Their number was not very significant. But they soon decayed because of the unjust tariff and unhelpful attitude of the Government.

Causes of the Decline of Handicraft Industry

The main causes of the decline of handicraft industry in India are discussed below:

***Peculiar Nature of Demand*:** The artisans' excellence made their products luxury goods, but with growing poverty, the demand for such products declined. The final blow came from the products manufactured in factories in England, which were available at a lower price.

The Kashmiri shawls produced in Kashmir and some other parts of India (e.g. Amritsar) had been famous for centuries. But by 1850, the industry was rapidly declining and by the end of the century "the industry was already a mere tradition—a memory of the past". The first setback actually came in 1830, when a great famine broke out in Kashmir. This along with migration of the Kashmiri population to Punjab led to the extinction of Kashmiri shawls. Some unscrupulous manufacturers started producing low grade shawls. Around the middle of the 19th century, these shawls became very popular in France. The French traders had a monopoly over the shawl traders and asked the artisans to produce shawls to their order (already because of poverty, these artisans preferred to produce on order). The French traders introduced the European patterns with the result that artistic merit of the shawls greatly deteriorated. Then came France-German War which completely cut off the exports. Around this time fashion in France had also changed. To tide over this challenge, the industry adopted cheap dyes and stuff which further damaged the reputation. The final blow came from cheap factory products.

The gradual decline in demand, along with unfair competition from the side of supply can be considered the main causes of decline of Indian handicraft industry.

Disappearance of Princely Courts: The abolition of native Indian courts also meant stoppage of the main source of demand. For example, the prosperous muslin, cotton and silk industry of Bengal had largely depended on the existence of Mughal empire with courts in Agra, Lahore, Delhi, etc. There was a break-up of the Mughal empire and hence a decline in demand. Again, the Nawab of Oudh had patronized the dyeing industry in Lucknow, but after the accession of Oudh, this industry too declined. It is interesting to note that whereas handicrafts were still flourishing in princely states, they were dying in the British territory. With the gradual extension in the British empire, the decay of handicrafts further accelerated.

The disappearance of the Indian courts also led to the decay of handicrafts in another way. The princes used to hire best craftsmen to get the best quality goods because they had high salary. The craftsmen who had regular demand from the princes produced best quality handicrafts, not yielding to popular demand for cheaper goods. The stoppage of this patronage made the best artisans subject to popular tasks, not always the best, and they started making cheaper goods.

Hostile Policy of the East India Company and the British Parliament: The East India Company, in order to earn profits through trade, first gave encouragement to handicrafts. But that meant export of gold and silver from England to India which could not be tolerated. Incidentally, at that time industrial revolution took place in England which necessitated to convert the Indian market into the exporter of raw materials and importer of British factory goods. Tariff policy was changed. There was a prohibition of wearing Indian printed clothes. In short, the British manufacturers perpetrated political injustice to keep down the Indian handicrafts.

Alien (Foreign) Rule and Consequent Adverse Effects: The English Rule brought in English officers in place of Indian nawabs and nobles. Naturally they had different (European) tastes. Many Indians started imitating European way of life and suffered from inferiority complex. It became fashion to adopt and wear European designs. For example, in Punjab the demand to wear silken clothes was replaced by the demand for European printed clothes.

Apart from slavish mentality and the sense of inferiority, there were other reasons. For instance, Indian petty officials did not want to annoy their English officers by wearing Indian products. Sometimes, there were unwritten conventions and rules not to wear particular type of Indian products, such as no Indian could appear before their European officers wearing Indian embroidered shoes. They had to wear cheap factory boots.

Further, the Europeans naturally preferred imported goods from their own country. Indian craftsmen started imitating European designs. For example, Kashmiri shawls started using cheap dyes and cheap raw materials. This blind imitation destroyed the artistic value of handicrafts.

The alien rule also affected handicrafts in another way. It indirectly weakened the power of the caste-based guilds (because of de-industrialization artisans were fleeing to villages), which had hitherto regulated the quality of the product. This at once led to a decline in their value, both commercial as well as artistic. Further, some arms industries which owed their existence to princely courts and kingdoms had to be closed as people were no longer free to possess arms of their own.

Price Competition from Machine Made Goods: Finally, the most important reason of the decay of Indian handicrafts was that they could not withstand the foreign competition which derived its strength from the Industrial Revolution in England, based on large scale production and minute division of labour.

The invention of power loom in England completed the decline of the Indian textile industry. Though in the matter of quality Indian goods were still superior, in the matter of price they could not face the competition. Development of the means of transport and communication further opened up even the interior part of the country. The construction of Suez Canal further reduced the distance by thousand miles between India and England. This reduced the transport costs of British goods in India. In fact the development of the means of transport and communication was so quick that the urban handicrafts could not bear this sudden attack and disappeared quickly. This explains why some crafts noticed by some English historians in 1878 in Lahore were no more there after an interval of just 10 years.

Agriculture under the British Rule

During pre-British days there was a happy blend of agriculture and industry. Even in villages one could see urban handicrafts. As stated earlier, the policy of the Britishers was to turn India into an exporter of raw material for the British industries and an importer for the demand of manufactured goods produced in British factories. The proportion of population dependent on agriculture increased substantially from 61.7 per cent in 1891 to 73 per cent in 1921. Even in the face of growing population, the percentage as well as the absolute number of industrial workers declined.

Agriculture was the mainstay of the Indian economy as it is today. But unfortunately, it could not produce enough for its subsistence. Famines were frequent. There were imports of rice from Burma. Vicious circle—growing population—more dependence on agriculture—extension of cultivation through bullocks—more demand for fodder (i.e. there was a competition between man and animal population for subsistence) developed. The conditions of the Indian farmers deteriorated. Later on the farmer fell into the clutches of moneylender.

For convenience sake we can divide the study of agriculture during British regime in following periods:

1860-80	Period of stagnant agriculture
1881-95	Period of relative prosperity

1896-1914	Period of famines
1915-29	First World War up to the Depression
1930-39	The Depression and after
1940-47	Second World War and its consequences

I. Period of Stagnant Agriculture (1860-80)

Effects of the Permanent Settlement of 1793, began to be felt. Land became a scarce commodity which could be bought and sold. Because of the growing debt, the ownership of many pieces of land went from the cultivators to the moneylenders. Because of the decay of urban handicraft even the urban rich were turning to the agricultural sector. The actual cultivators were selling land to the moneylenders who were not agriculturists. The cultivators had to work for the moneylenders on share crop basis, i.e. part of the production being paid to the moneylender as the latter's share and partly to pay the interest. The cultivator found himself more and more at the mercy of moneylender after the hard work of one year.

Another characteristic of this period was the growing importance of cash crops, viz. jute and cotton. Jute cultivation for exports had already started in around 1833 in Bengal. The development of steam ships further accelerated the growth of jute. Cotton cultivation also picked up during this period. Till 1860, America was the chief supplier of raw cotton for the British mills in England. But the civil war in America interrupted this supply and the British industrialists had to turn towards India. Needless to say, the British Government in India provided the facilities to encourage cotton exports. A general prosperity, particularly of those engaged in cotton cultivation or cotton trade was seen.

But this prosperity was short-lived since it coincided with the period of revision of revenue assessment. The temporary prosperity was quite mistakenly considered as indicating the ability of the peasants to pay taxes. As a result, the assessments were heavier than what the peasants could bear. There was a sudden crash in cotton prices. Extravagant military expeditions and increasing establishment costs necessitated heavy taxes. All these factors compelled the cultivators to borrow more and more, and they fell victim to the moneylenders.

Revolt of the Peasantry

Bewildered by the growing indebtedness and cunningness of the moneylenders, the actual cultivators revolted. They started killing and looting the moneylenders. Broadly, they were satisfied by destroying the debt bonds. Although this riot was put down easily, this revealed the growing impoverishment of the cultivators. The growing poverty of the cultivators was attributed to the granting of free property right to the tillers who hitherto had not enjoyed it. Legal right was given to moneylenders to recover their loans by attaching the peasants' property. For this reason, the moneylender was very willing to lend money to the cultivators. Good crops encouraged the moneylender to lend still more. Bad crops compelled the cultivators to borrow more from him.

Dispossession of Land

Moneylenders were not interested in agricultural development. Even agriculturist moneylenders were not doing better. They tried to alienate and dispossess the peasantry from land.

Famines and their Consequences

During 1861-80 many famines took place. The effects of prosperity experienced during the American Civil War were short-lived. America soon resumed her cotton supply to Great Britain and the boom in the Indian cotton market came to a sudden end. Secondly, there were the following famines during this period:

1865	A mild famine in Madras
1868-69	Rajputana famine
1873-74	Bihar and Bengal famines

Famines increased the distress of farmers who became physically weak and financially they were destroyed. Agricultural progress was checked.

II. Period of Relative Prosperity (1881-95)

The period between 1881 and 1895 was one of comparative agricultural prosperity. There was a favourable rainfall and consequently absence of any major famines. Of course, local scarcity was there at some places. The relative abundance might have brought down the agricultural prices, but fortunately there was a rising demand for Indian agricultural produce—both within and outside the country. However, all categories of farmers were not benefited. Only large farmers who had more to sell (i.e. had marketable surplus) were the beneficiaries. This period was characterized by the following:

(1) Expansion of trade, mostly foreign.

(2) Extension of cultivation to meet the needs of growing population.

(3) Area under non-food crops which had started earlier picked up. Because of the development of means of transportation and communication, cash crops, like jute, cotton, sugarcane, oilseeds had a wider market.

(4) Greater regional specialization started developing. However, the proportion of area under food crops remained larger than the area under non-food or cash or industrial crops.

The Practice of Cultivation

Though cultivation remained traditional, yet in certain regions it was greatly developed. The practice of keeping the land fallow was abandoned because the farmers were too poor to leave the land uncultivated. Poverty forced the cultivators to cultivate whatever quality of land was available. But most of them had to turn towards moneylenders to buy seeds.

Thus, the period of prosperity did not alter the farmers' economic condition much.

III. Period of Famines (1896-1914)

The fifteen years of very limited prosperity came to a close. Once more the hands of the clock of agricultural progress were put back; the progress achieved during the previous period was lost throughout the country. The people of the country once more were in the grip of severe famines.

Famines and their Consequences

The famine of 1896-97 was more severe and widespread. The areas hitherto unknown or immune to famines also came in the grip of famines.

The famine of 1899-1900 was of lesser severity. It particularly was confined to cattle. Cattle population was reduced. Consequently, farmers became still poorer due to loss of valuable resources. This resulted in the following:

(a) Decline in double cropped area;

(b) Displacement of cash crops by food crops; and

(c) The decline in the total area under cultivation.

These two famines—one after the other—inflicted great misery on the farmers. They weakened the health of the people and broke their morale. These famines killed whatever small spirit of innovation might have been left.

IV. First World War up to the Depression (1915-29)

Famines continued unabated. The year 1918-19 witnessed very widespread and major famine calamity comparable in extent and severity with that of 1899-1900. Before the people could recover, monsoons failed in 1920-21. Although the famine of 1920-21 was of lesser severity, yet because of the growing poverty, the number of people accepting poor relief multiplied substantially. Since 1921 agricultural seasons had been, on the whole, good but periodic failure of monsoons continued to occur.

First World War and its Effects

The war years (as usual) were marked by rising prices. But increase in agricultural prices was less than the prices of imported goods such as cotton manufactures, metals, sugar, etc. So long as this unequal rise in prices continued, agriculture suffered. But by 1926, this disparity in rise in prices disappeared. Agricultural prices as well as manufactures rose by the same rate compared with 1914. But the period was short-lived. Again in 1929, agricultural prices crashed by 50 per cent, but the prices of manufactured articles did not experience similar declines.

During this period, the continuous competition between man and cattle reduced the area under fodder. Consequently, the number of cows and buffaloes decreased, bringing down the supply and availability of milk.

Growth of Rural Indebtedness and the Agricultural Labourers

Rural indebtedness continued to rise. Land continued to be transferred from the tillers to the moneylenders. During this period, laws were enacted to check this transfer. It was stipulated that only the agriculturalists would be allowed to hold land. But the term agriculturist was too vague to check this transfer.

Subdivision and Fragmentation of Holdings

Declining handicrafts and growing pressure of population on agriculture brought subdivision and fragmentation of existing land holdings. As a result, poverty continued during this period, and there was no positive change in the life of the farmers.

Extension of Irrigation

Some kinds of repair works had begun to revive the dying agricultural economy. Irrigation Commission, during this period recommended some large irrigation projects. However, the other areas continued to be neglected. No attention was paid to private wells with the result that the area irrigated through wells declined. However, canal colonies were developed in 1920.

V. The Great Depression (1930-39)

The Great Depression had twofold effects:

(a) Absolute fall in agricultural prices;

(b) Fall in agricultural prices vis-à-vis non-agricultural prices.

India at that time exported agricultural goods whose prices declined at much sharper rate than the prices of imported goods (which were basically manufactured goods and industrial goods).

The absolute fall in agricultural prices reduced the income of the cultivators. The official data showed that whereas in 1928-29, the value of agricultural crops was ₹ 10,340 million, it fell to ₹ 4,730 million in 1933-34—a fall of more than 50 per cent. Rural indebtedness increased. A notable feature of this period was that in spite of the 50 per cent fall in agricultural income, land revenue demand dropped by only 9 per cent. The inability to pay land revenue forced the cultivators in many provinces, notably in Bengal and the United Provinces, to surrender their lands.

Thus, the total area under cultivation decreased by 5.3 million acres. Out of this 0.3 million acres under food crops were shifted to cash crops.

The drop in agricultural income by 50 per cent meant 50 per cent increase in real debt, as well as more borrowings. It is estimated through official agencies that rural indebtedness increased from ₹ 900 crore in 1931 to ₹ 1,800 crore in 1937, i.e. doubled in just six years.

Pauperization of peasants continued. Relatively rich farmers were dispossessed of their gold. Gold worth 32 million ounce (more than England had it that time) was exported to England.

VI. Second World War and its Consequences (1940-47)

The agricultural economy of India suffered a severe blow during the war. After the entry of Japan into the war, the import of rice was stopped from Burma, and there was severe shortage of food. Mishandling of the situation resulted into a famine-like situation in the country. About 3 million people died in Bengal alone. Rural indebtedness increased. The profiteers and black-marketeers in urban areas made huge profits. To finance the war there was deficit financing or printing of money. Prices rose still higher. Economic conditions of the people in general and farmers in particular further deteriorated.

When India got independence on 15 August 1947, the country was partitioned and a new country Pakistan emerged. A major proportion of cultivated area went to Pakistan. Wheat-growing canal colonies (developed by the British) and many rice growing areas went to Pakistan. The proportion of population left in Indian side had greater problem of feeding millions.

Pakistan got 23 per cent of territory with wheat-cotton belt, but only 18 per cent of population. Rice-belt of Burma had already gone in 1937 (1st April 1937). India with 77 per cent of territory had to feed 82 per cent of population. India was a deficit country—that it remained more or less so until the mid-sixties when Green Revolution era—was ushered.

Agricultural Policy of the British Government

In a predominantly agricultural and backward country, Government's agricultural policy has a vital role to play. But under the British rule no concentrated and organized efforts were made in this direction.

I. Period 1860-80

Limited and Ineffective Action: Up to 1866, the only effort made was to start botanical gardens for introducing new plants or their varieties like tea, potato, etc. Then in 1870 came the Imperial Department of Agriculture, but it was abolished in 1878 on the ground that Provincial Government did not cooperate (in fact Provincial Government had no power at that time). In the same decade, some experimental farms were started to develop new varieties and new methods of production. But this too failed either because these farms were supervised by persons having no knowledge in agriculture, or that English scientists were limited to lead the experimental stations and the English people had no background of the Indian soil and other environmental conditions. In fact, the Indian peasants had a good knowledge of agricultural technique. What they lacked was irrigation and finance to farmers, which were completely ignored till that time. The Famine Commission of 1880 recommended that Government should immediately start Agricultural Department and collect agricultural statistics, but nothing was done.

II. Period 1881-95

In this period also there was a similar story of very limited or no action.

***Takavi Loans*:** The Acts passed in 1883 and 1884 re-introduced a very old method of encouraging agricultural improvements, i.e. to give small loans to farmers (called takavi loans) who repaid these loans in installments. This measure too did not succeed because the administration was faulty. The collector was made responsible to disburse these loans. These collectors were already overburdened with other administrative works. These loans were quite often untimely and the period of recovery was casually short. Rigidity in the collection of interest and principal further discouraged these loans. Up to 1900 only ₹ 6 crore was lent. However, in certain regions where the collectors were dynamic, these loans did make some progress.

In 1889 Dr. Volecker was appointed to suggest agricultural improvements. He toured throughout the country and submitted his report in 1893 but no action was taken on this report till 1900.

III. Period 1896-1914

During this period several beginnings and new type of action were initiated in several directions.

An Inspector-General of Agriculture was appointed in 1901. The Agricultural Research Institute and a few Provincial Agricultural Colleges and Schools were opened. More money was spent on Agricultural Department. But considering India's large size, neither the amount spent on the staff, nor for other agricultural activities was sufficient. Therefore, no substantial results were achieved.

To improve the quality of cotton, seed farms were started for producing and distributing better seeds. Research was also conducted in suitable regions for different varieties of wheat. New varieties of rice and groundnut were also introduced. In several parts of India improved implements were introduced, viz. light iron ploughs and small water pumps. Cooperative Credit Societies were started in 1904 and Non-credit Societies were formed in 1912.

To sum up, these improvements were limited in scope, wild in nature and did not always reach the farmers.

IV. Period 1915-29

The pace of agricultural improvement done by the Government remained slow, and the times of improvement were much the same as before. A large amount of work was done in introducing improved varieties. The major successes were wheat, cotton, jute, groundnut and sugarcane. To spread the knowledge of these varieties special seed farms were started. Arrangements were also made for the production and distribution of better seeds.

However, because of the fact that agricultural prices during this period rose less sharply than the prices of manufactured goods, agricultural sector had to suffer.

V. Period 1930-39

During Depression farmers suffered very severely. Their absolute as well as relative income declined and they had to sell gold to pay off debts and taxes. Gold worth 32 million ounces was exported. India was perhaps the only country in the world in which the Government did very little, rather nothing, to ameliorate the lot of farmers, whereas in many other countries the respective Governments tried to fight depression by positive price policies. However, the Government in India, particularly the Central Government remained a silent spectator.

Provincial Governments: By contrast, the Provincial Governments tried to do something. Payment of land revenue was suspended and in certain cases even some remission in land revenue was allowed. But the maximum reduction in land revenue did not exceed 9 per cent compared with more than 50 per cent decline in income. Nothing was done in respect of indebtedness, i.e. the farmers had to pay interest and the principal even in the face of their declining income. In some provinces Acts to regulate moneylenders were passed. In some provinces the Governments also tried to regulate the market for agricultural produce. In 1930s Tenancy Laws were also passed, but the problem of assuring security and justice to the cultivating tenant still remained. In the face of depression, the Cooperative Movement which was started in 1904 had to face a tough time. Many societies were wound up, recoveries fell and overdues increased. But no help came from the Government's side.

VI. Period 1940-47

War and Food Problem: During the Second World War, food problem arose with high prices and serious food shortages. Import of rice from Burma was cut and famine conditions existed in Bengal. But the Government had no well thought-out policy to execute.

In 1942, the Food Production Conference proposed a plan for increasing food production. "Grow More Food" campaign was launched. Then came the Bengal famine in 1943 in which 3 million people lost their lives and the Government was forced to act. A Foodgrain Policy Committee recommended measures for improving the procurement machinery, for extending rationing and food control and for changing the administrative machinery. Consequently, in January 1946, the policy announced was to supply the necessary quantity and quality of foodgrains. High priority was given to increase the yield of food crops. But the implementation was still left to provinces.

Meanwhile, prices continued to rise, which necessitated price control and food rationing. By September 1942, there were as much as six Price Control Conferences in quick succession. The last conference recommended the procurement of foodgrains by the Centre. Food was to be procured from the villages for the urban consumers. Rationing at the rate of 1 lb per day per head was introduced. Certain other articles were also provided at fixed prices. In villages also, ration cards were given to 74.5 million non-producers to buy cheaper foodgrains, but the Government had no obligation to supply them foodgrains. Several problems because of controls (blackmarketing, profiteering, etc.), did crop up, yet controls tried to keep the prices in check. The basic problem, however, was to increase production and distribute properly.

Consequences of Neglect of Agriculture

The British Government continued to neglect agriculture as it focused on increasing the wealth of their home country. The neglect of agricultural neglect led to the following:

(1) Growing pressure on land, low yields, shortage of food in general and famines if the crops failed.

(2) Rising unemployment and poverty;

(3) Export of raw material and import of manufactured goods, when farmers were asked to grow crops which the Britishers needed such as indigo, instead of foodgrain;

(4) Old village life was broken, i.e. integration of agriculture and industry was no longer followed;

(5) Industrial workers decreased in number and urban population declined.

While in England, in case of the loss of individual independence, workers were compensated by the growth of factories. No such thing happened in India. Workers continued to suffer.

LAND RELATIONS

Evolution of the Land Tenurial Systems during the British Regime

During the pre-British days in India land was aplenty and the rent was static. The main features of land relations were the following:

(1) Land belonged to the peasant who enjoyed hereditary occupancy right if he was a resident of the village. Rent was fixed and the Zamindars [who were responsible to pay a fixed amount as land revenue to the king (ruler)] could not raise this revenue beyond the customary level.

(2) Land was not a saleable commodity. No cultivator could be removed from land. But if a cultivator failed to cultivate a given piece of land, his eviction was possible but in that case his land had to be given to another cultivator. In short, land never passed out of the hands of the peasantry.

(3) The Zamindars whose tributes (or revenues) to the ruler were fixed were themselves petty rulers and had to perform the traditional duties of a ruler in relation to the development of agriculture.

CHANGES UNDER THE BRITISH RULE

The Early Phase

According to the legal form of land relations developed under the Mughal Empire, the right of a Zamindar (called tributary feudal landlord) could be obtained by assuring to pay a stipulated sum of revenue to the Emperor. The feudal landlord, apart from collecting his share in the total produce, could rule over the entire estate. With the decline in the influence of the emperor during the last days of Mughal rule, this right could be secured from the provincial (States) Governors (Subedars). The first decisive step on the part of the British East India Company was to secure Zamindari rights over Calcutta, Gobindapur and Sutanati in the year 1697.

In the prevailing system, apart from collecting revenue, the Zamindars provided social leadership in the villages. But the sole concern of the English Zamindars (or their agents) was money-making and with this the land relations in India entered a new phase.

After winning the Battle of Plassey in 1757, the East India Company threw the Zamindaries to public auction giving out the estate to the highest bidder. The bidders were mostly uprooted Nagar Seths and guilds (because of decline of urban handicrafts) and they turned out to be the Company's Banias. They, in fact, became second-rung robbers next to the East India Company in robbing the actual cultivators. Since the new Zamindars came from the urban rich, they were mostly interested in making money and were totally uninterested in agricultural improvement. The traditional rights of the peasants in cultivating the land were completely forgotten and land became a commodity.

Since the revenue hunger of the East India Company was unstable (which cannot be satisfied) the burden of land revenue increased from year to year. In case the actual cultivator could not pay the land revenue it was realized from the Zamindars. If he was in a position to pay, both the Zamindars and the East India Company exploited him. On occasions, he had to flee in order to avoid this heavy burden.

In the wake of this tyranny and plunder came the Bengal famine of 1770 which killed nearly 35 per cent of the total population. As a result, one-third of the cultivable area was laid waste. This figure increased to half in 1776. However, the famine of 1770 was just a beginning. It was quickly followed by famines in 1784, 1787 and 1790.

In certain parts, the cultivators even revolted against the collaborators and the foreign rulers. Although this movement remained localized, it revealed discontentment amongst the peasantry who were crying for a change.

Introduction of Permanent Settlement

Permanent settlement was an agreement between the East India Company and Bengali landlords to fix revenues to be raised from land. It had far-reaching consequences for both agricultural methods and productivity in the entire Empire and the political realities of the Indian countryside. Permanent settlement came in the background of an acute crisis in agrarian relations leading to periodic revolts of the peasantry. It was concluded in 1793, by the Company administration headed by Charles, the Earl Cornwallis. The Government demand was permanently fixed and at the time of settlement, it was 10/11 of the rental value. The Zamindars were recognized as the proprietors of land, and actual cultivators were left at the mercy of the new Zamindars. The cultivator lost his traditional status and was reduced to a virtual serf (bonded labour).

The introduction of Permanent Settlement had the following objectives:

(1) Stabilization of revenue.

(2) Creation of the loyal class.

(3) Zamindars would be an enlightened community and thus provide knowledge and sources for agricultural improvement.

(4) Agricultural improvement in return would provide flourishing trade i.e. India as a market for British manufactures and exporter of raw material and agricultural produce.

(5) The next and the most fundamental objective was to divert permanently the urban capital (accumulated into the hands of Nagar Seth, i.e. urban rich) into agricultural channels, and thereby check the growth of urban industrialization permanently. India was to be made to export raw material and agricultural produce and to import manufactured goods.

(6) There would be protection against famine. Land revenue being fixed will provide incentives for agricultural improvement. It is said that there were no major famines in Bengal after 1793.

(7) The arbitrary power of the revenue officers would be checked.

(8) There will less drain of country's resources, i.e. economical expenditure on reassessment would be avoided.

Abuses of Permanent Settlement

There were many abuses or disadvantages of permanent settlement, like the following:

(1) **Oppression of Tenants:** It was the Zamindars who benefited from the hard labour of actual tillers. The tenants were oppressed in many ways, until they received some relief from the various Rent Acts from 1859 onwards. As expected by Cornwallis, the Zamindars could not become the 'national leaders' of rural areas. The tenants, therefore, suffered from high rents, evictions (at will), absentee landlordism, unsympathetic agents and many middlemen. Rents increased more than threefold between 1793-1903, i.e. within 10 years of 1793.

(2) **Unfair Advantage to Rich Class:** Bengal had to sacrifice all future increase in land revenue. Bengal's income grew nearly four times by 1900, also there was a rapid increase in prices. Consequently, land revenue became a much smaller part of this income. Again, this income had grown not because of any land improvement but from social factors like the growth of population, development of the means of transport and communication, rise in prices, etc. But only the Zamindars, a well-to-do class, benefited from this development. Further, land resources in other Provinces had been growing, and also other taxes, so rich class in one Province obtained unfair advantage.

(3) **A Great Handicap for the Government:** At later stage when public expenditure needs of the Government multiplied this necessitated an elastic source of revenue. But land revenue under permanent settlement stood

in its way and seriously affected the developmental expenditure in Bengal.

(4) **Cost of Re-assessment:** While implementing Permanent Settlement it was stipulated that it would reduce the cost of re-assessment again and again, thus check the drain of revenue. But once the land records were completed (as they are now) the cost of reassessment cannot be formidable. Again, while reassessing the land revenue, cost of improvement can be deducted, thereby encouraging land improvement.

It may be mentioned that the Britishers tended to extend the permanent settlement in other parts of the country also. The desire was reinforced by the revolt of 1857 which confirmed the necessity of having dependable allies in the rural areas, i.e. Zamindars. But after 1857, having about 25 years of complete peace, the other considerations (viz. revenue needs) outweighed the above-mentioned one. In 1883, the idea of permanent settlement was formally abandoned. In the words of R.C. Dutt, "Never has the loyalty of a nation been worse rewarded, never has the peacefulness of a people led more clearly to the withdrawal of a boom proposed in years of trouble and anxiety. It is a bad lesson for a Government to teach and for the people to learn."[4]

Introduction of Ryotwari System

Permanent Settlement was introduced in Bengal, Bihar, Orissa, Banaras and North Madras and in some other areas. Temporary Zamindari settlements were made in Uttar Pradesh.

Ryotwari System was introduced in Southern Madras, Bombay, East Punjab, and some portions of Assam and Coorg. Under this type of settlement, the ryot directly worked under the State, and land revenue was assessed on each separate holding held by the ryot. He was recognized as the proprietor, i.e. he could sub-let, mortgage, transfer (by gift or buy/sell) the holding. He could be removed so long as he pays the land revenue.

Ryotwari Settlement was a temporary one. The period of settlement under the British rule varied between 20-40 years, and frequent revision were also there.

Although a proprietor, the peasant in the ryotwari area was no better than his counterpart in the Zamindari areas. Generally, the rents were high and uncertain. In every successive assessment, they were increased on one pretext or the other, like increase in productivity and rise in agricultural prices, etc. The ever-increasing greed of the British rulers ruined the ryots physically and economically. As R.C. Dutt has observerd, "Nature set a limit which the cultivators had not obtained from the moderation of their rulers. Population decreased in Bombay and still more in Central Provinces. Miles of cultivated land became waste. Jungle grew on homesteads, wheat lands and rice lands."[5]

No protection was extended to the ryot against the arbitrary powers of the settlement officers. In 1873, the High Court of Bombay gave ruling against the settlement queries and in favour of the ryots. Subsequently, in 1876, a law was enacted to bring the revenue assessments out of the purview of High Court.

Very often the revenue demands were excessive and sometimes were very close to total production. After meeting the cost of production and revenue requirements very little was left in the hands of the ryot to make further improvement in land. Small cultivators were the worst sufferers. Unable to meet the rising revenue requirements, they transferred their land to moneylenders. Their number declined from 54 per cent in 1891 to 45 per cent in 1900. A Land Alienation Act had to be enacted in 1901 to save the old tribes from a landless existence. The same was the process in other areas too (on land ownership).

Thus, the peasant proprietorship was very soon lost to the same elements who had become Zamindars in Bengal, Bihar, Orissa and in other permanent settlement areas. They were mostly urban rich. The result was that a new class of landlords, as much parasitic as the Zamindars of permanently settled areas, emerged. According to Famine Enquiry Commission (1945), "The tenant cultivator was insecure and therefore, had no permanent interest in lands." It further stated, "The absentee landlord earns only for his annual rent and takes no interest in the improvement of his land or the introduction of improved methods of cultivation".

The miseries of the tenant cultivator did not stop here. Taxes like land revenue and over surcharge on land revenue (to be paid by the Zamindars) were shifted onto him. Landlord being monopolist of land capital could succeed in doing this. And even courts upheld this action of the landlords.

The Mahalwari System was the indigenous system. Also called joint village system, it was first adopted in Agra and Audh (1833) and later extended to Punjab. Under this system, the villages concerned were jointly responsible for the payment of land revenue. The ownership was joint. And these villages or mahals were directly dealt with for the payment of land revenue. Of course, practically every individual has to pay his share of land revenue but they themselves were responsible for the payment of land revenue on behalf of the other cultivators. If a cultivator failed to pay his share, the other cultivator could acquire his piece of land.

It may be concluded that all these land relationships were new to India. Zamindari system was borrowed from the English pattern. Ryotwari system was copy of the French experience. Mahalwari was a modified form of early land relationship in India (Feudal lords had to pay tributes to the king—they were actually rulers). Whatever the system they adopted, the primary aim was to turn India into an exporter of raw material and agricultural produce. And net importer of food manufactured commodities.

Growth of Tenancy and Tenancy Act

Under the Zamindari system, almost all the lands were cultivated by the tenants. Even under the Ryotwari system, tenancy developed and sub-letting of land spread rapidly (through moneylenders). Sometimes there were as many as 50 intermediaries.

Under both the systems, intermediaries took the maximum from the man behind the plough. In certain cases such as in Bengal, there were as many as 50 and even more intermediaries. The tiller of the soil was, therefore, not left with anything to feed himself or his family. Even otherwise, the rents were very high and he had no incentive to make improvements. The position was made worse by insecurity of tenure. The tenants were always harmed by the fear of eviction from land. Apart from high rents, sometimes illegal premiums or personal services were obtained (free of charge from the tenants).

Tenancy Acts

Ultimately even the cruel and passive British Government in India had to take some steps and try to improve the position. The first Tenancy Act of 1859 was passed in Bengal—after 66 years of Permanent Settlement. It gave occupancy rights to tenants cultivating the same piece of land for 12 years. Their rents could not be increased except on reasonable and specific grounds. But the Act was ineffective as the Zamindars prevented a tenant from becoming an occupancy tenant cultivating the same piece of land for 12 years. Old tenants were removed, and thus rents continued to rise.

Considering the ineffectiveness of the 1859 Act, another Act was passed in 1885 which enabled the tenants to obtain the occupancy rights if he had cultivated any piece of land (not the same piece of land) for 12 years. Even this measure did not succeed, because of the rising land prices, growing pressure on land, transfer of land to non-agricultural classes, growing prestige attached to the ownership of land. Rents continued to rise and the occupancy rights were not honoured.

It was only in 1928 that occupancy holdings became transferable (i.e. the tenant could transfer his holding to new tenants or evicted holdings) that the plight of tenants was slightly improved. But a lot remained still to be done. And even today, the plight of tenants is not much better than the virtual serfs.

Effects of Tenancy Laws

Instead of improving the lot of tenants, the tenancy laws deteriorated it. The number of occupancy tenants decreased rapidly. And they scrolled the number of landless agricultural labourers. They, therefore, lost all incentives to improve the land or to put in hard work or use better methods. Thus, quality of land deteriorated, productivity declined and rents continued to rise. Intermediaries rose even in mahalwari and ryotwari systems. As much a 75 per cent of the land came to be cultivated by tenants.

Provincial Autonomy (1937-39)

Under Provincial Autonomy, popular Governments (democratic) came in power during 1937-39 and they naturally tried to redress the grievances of the tenants. The principal features of these measures were three Fs of Irish land registration:

(1) Fixing of tenure, i.e. no arbitrary removal of tenant;

(2) Fair rents, i.e. limit on rent, without which fixing of tenure would not be of much use;

(3) Freedom of transfer, i.e. making land inheritable and even sometimes transferable.

In addition, tenants were to get benefits for making improvement on land, reduction in rent in case of revision in land revenue and protection against personal service. Thus, landlord's privileges were curtailed. But as in the wake of the World War II, majority of the Provincial Governments resigned, and therefore many ideas could not be implemented. Even today, in spite of so much tall talk about land reforms and tenancy reforms, the plight of tenants is miserable.

Commercialization of Agriculture

In the pre-British days, village communities were self-sufficient. Apart from the portion of the output that had to be surrendered or sold in payment of land revenue, agricultural production had been largely for consumption within the village. Under the British rule, there was a consistent decline in village self-sufficiency. A growing production of output was now for sale in the market. For this reason, there was an important change in the character of agriculture. In the self-sufficient villages agriculture had been a way of life rather than business. It now began to be affected by commercial considerations. The growing cultivation of commercial crops, viz. cotton, jute, oilseed, sugarcane, tobacco, tea, indigo, etc. (commercial crops are those which by their very nature, are produced largely for sale and not for the producer's own consumption, like food crops, wheat, rice, maize, etc.) indicated a growing trend in this direction. The increased cultivation of such food crops as spices, fruits, vegetables (which were mostly grown now for sale) was another manifestation of this trend. In fact, in course of time, a substantial portion of even food grains like wheat came to be sold in the market. The commercialization trend attained its highest level of development from about the middle of the 19th century. Those were large-scale enterprises organized on commercial basis. The production was carried on by employing a large number of wage workers. Almost the entire output was marketed. Thus, commercialization was interwoven with the growth of the market economy.

Because of the American Civil War and suspension of supply of American cotton to English factories in England the cotton production picked up. There was encouragement of cotton growth and trade in India. Indigo cultivation was a traditional item of exports. Cultivation of tea was started later than indigo. In about 1820, after the discovery of tea plant in wild condition in Assam, the cultivation of tea on commercial basis started.

During 1880-95 there was a growth both in internal and external trade in respect of all commercial crops. The main causes of commercialization around that time are discussed below:

1. Political Unification of the Country

Before the British rule, India was a divided country. Therefore, different provinces or even villages had to be self-sufficient. But the near total unification of the country within 100 years after the Battle of Plassey, the independent rulers had either been eliminated or were made subordinate to the British Crown. About 75 per cent of the Indian population was directly under the British Crown. In rest of the country, the Indian states were preserved but they were no longer sovereign or independent states. They had only formal autonomy. British power was supreme.

A high degree of political unification of the country created favourable conditions for the growth of national market which in turn led to specialization of crops and commercialization of agriculture. The continuous wars and conflicts which were so common in the pre-British days came to an end. After the Crown took over the administration of the country (in 1858), for a long time the new regime was highly stable. It maintained peace and order with an iron hand. This situation was conducive to the growth of production, development of transport and communications, removal of physical and fiscal barriers to the movement of goods, creation of a single currency system, introduction and spread of modern banking, expansion of internal and external trade, etc. All this opened the way for market-oriented production both in the agricultural and non-agricultural sectors.

2. Centralized Administrative System

The British Government instituted a highly centralized administrative system. It altogether ignored and bypassed the village community and directly dealt with the individuals—Zamindars or Ryots (except a few cases of Mahalwari System). The decline and disintegration of the village community reduced the importance of custom. The market forces, viz. demand and supply became more relevant, paving the way for commercialization of agriculture.

3. Burden of Land Revenue

All the agrarian systems, viz. Zamindari, Ryotwari and Mahalwari led to incidence of heavy land revenue (except in case of Permanent Settlement that too in later years and the rigidity with which it was collected in cash and not in kind) and forced the agriculturists to bring their produce to the market.

In modern development economics, it is accepted that taxation of land and agriculture is a very important instrument in the hands of the State to compel the agriculturists to bring a large enough proportion of their produce to the market. Under the British rule, the stiff land revenue demand, payable in cash played this role.

4. Agricultural Indebtedness

The growth of agricultural indebtedness had a similar impact on production meant for the market. The agriculturist needed cash to meet his interest and repayment obligations. This was another factor that obliged him to produce for the market.

There was an unprecedented and continued growth in agricultural indebtedness under the British rule, due to (i) emergence of private property, (ii) rise in land value,

(iii) eagerness of the moneylender to lend more in order to acquire land, (iv) poverty, (v) famine, (vi) crushing burden of land revenue and rent, (vii) extravagance—socio-religious ceremonies, (viii) excessive litigation, (ix) borrowing sometimes even for productive purpose to buy seed, implements, land, etc.

Indian farmer was born in debt, lived in debt and died in debt. To pay off interest he had to sell his produce in the post-harvest season when prices were low (moneylenders were usually the traders so they were clearly benefited by receiving interest and purchase at low prices). The farmer had to buy again in the off season when prices were generally high. According to D.R. Gadgil, it was not a good sign of commercialization as most of the time, the farmers had sell to the moneylenders or traders right in the villages, where prices are not remunerative.

Once the peasant fell into indebtedness, he found it difficult to come out of it. The interest rates were very high and the debt continued to multiply endlessly because of the compound rate. The same factors which forced the agriculturist into debt prevented him from saving the necessary amount to clear his debt. Nor was the moneylender too keen to let the agriculturist debtor win back his freedom. He exploited the latter's helplessness, ignorance and illiteracy and indulged in malpractices. Since the emergence of private property in land, great prestige was attached to the ownership of land. The moneylenders tried to multiply debt by fair or foul means in order to grab the land of the ryots. On the death of the debtor, his obligations were often taken over by his heirs (children, sons and grandsons) who lacked proper consciousness, and considered it their religious duty to clear the debt of their forefathers. The ryot was often born in debt, lived in debt, and died in debt. The growing burden of interest charges compelled him to produce increasingly for the market.

5. Burden of Rent

Zamindari System or Permanent Settlement was introduced by Cornwallis in 1793. His expectations about the Zamindars were belied. The Zamindar was ruthless. He exploited the growing pressure of population and increased rent. If the rent was paid in cash, the tenant himself had to bring the produce in the market.

If, on the other hand, rent was in kind, the Zamindar sold the produce in the market. In either case, the produce was sold at the cost of actual cultivator who had to suffer.

Things were not better in ryotwari areas. Re-assessment here being higher and uncertain, the cultivator had to borrow money. Once in the grip of moneylender he became the tenant of moneylender who exploited the ryot in totality.

6. Replacement of Food Crops by Cash Crops

Even food crops tended to become cash crops. And regional specialization of crops took place bidding farewell to self-sufficiency.

7. Unified Monetary System

At the time of British conquest, a large number of currencies operated which discouraged the production on commercial basis. The Mughal rulers at various places issued both gold and silver coins. In addition, the independent and semi-independent rulers issued their own coins to prove their sovereignty. At that time as many as 994 different coins made of gold and silver and of varying weight and quality were in circulation. In such circumstances, no fixed exchange ratio was possible for different coins. The professional money-changers had a thriving business in converting the different coins. They affected trade and commerce greatly.

In 1806, the East India Company recognized the silver rupee as the standard coin. But rupees of different weights and qualities continued in circulation. It was in 1835 that for the first time the rupee of fixed weight and prescribed quality (11/12 purity) was declared as the legal tender money (official currency).

Since 1835, the country has had several distinct monetary systems as enumerated below:

1835-93 = Silver coin system

1893-99 = Gold exchange standard

1899-1916 = Wartime breakdown of the gold exchange standard

1916-25 = Return to gold exchange standard

1925-31 = Gold exchange standard

1931-47 = Sterling exchange standard

All through this period, British India had a single monetary system. It facilitated growth of domestic and foreign trade, fiscal integration, development of modern banking, etc. Without a unified monetary system, the market in general and commercialization in particular would never have grown the way it did.

8. Development of Modern Banking

In the beginning, the East India Company, like other European Trading Companies utilized the indigenous bankers to sell imported goods and to change different type of coins in order to purchase Indian goods, etc. However, after the Battle of Plassey, the English officials and traders set up their European Agency Houses with the help of their accumulated savings. This gave another blow to the indigenous bankers, and paved the way for the company to establish its own banks. With the growth of internal and external trade, the financial activities of the banks expanded which further encouraged trade, particularly external trade. External trade in its turn led to the development of commercial production, because banking, trade, currency, transport and communication, commercialization all are interrelated.

9. Growth of Organized Market

The growth of organized agricultural produce markets also led to commercialization of agriculture. Agricultural produce was brought from the villages to the town market from where it went to the ports (through well-developed railway system) to be exported to England. Expansion in the size of the market particularly for cash crop—jute, cotton, tea (export), sugarcane, oilseed (internal) was also responsible for this commercialization.

However, D.R. Gadgil has contested this point. According to him, commercialization of agriculture did not mean anything for the cultivator since he continued to sell his produce to the village trader or village moneylender. It was not that he had started producing on commercial lines. Most often the increasing marketed surplus amounted to distress sale in order to pay off rent, interest and the principal. However, it cannot be denied that because of growing market (particularly foreign export) for cash crops, notably, tea, jute, cotton, indigo, etc. production on commercial lines had started at the onset of British rule.

Consequences of Commercialization of Agriculture

There were following consequences of commercialization of agriculture in India:

1. ***Evolution of the Market Forces*:** Previously, there were self-sufficient villages. There was no outside contact. Farmers were unaware of the demand for different crops. But opening up of the villages and influence of foreign forces made demand and supply factors more dominant. For example, when export of tea from China to England was stopped, an alternative source of supply was found in India.

2. ***Localization or Specialization of Crops*:** Based on comparative advantage, localization or specialization of crops took place.

Rice	—	Burma
Wheat	—	Punjab
Cotton	—	Maharashtra
Sugarcane	—	Deccan
Jute	—	East Bengal

3. ***Growth in Farmer's Income*:** Every region did not try to produce its own food. The farmers grew the most profitable crops, sold them for cash and used it to buy food and other agricultural products needed by them. The growing of the most advantageous crops also increased the farmers' income.

4. ***Intensive Cultivation*:** In fact, important new crops like potatoes, groundnut, tea, coffee, rubber, etc. were introduced. With the extension of irrigation, the use of manure, better seeds, etc. became more widespread. The practice of keeping fallow land was abandoned and cropping intensity increased.

Rural Indebtedness

The Britishers exploited Indian farmers. Big cities and ports were the nerve centres of the colonial economy. The products of rural areas first found their way to these cities and ports from where they were exported to foreign countries mostly England.

In the cities and towns and ports along with the expansion of export and import trade there merged new institutions, viz. banking, insurance companies, firms, etc. Although in the initial stages they were mainly manned by the foreign experts, with the passage of time, indigenous expertise to grow out of it.

Lower down in the rural areas were the village moneylenders and traders (mostly one and the same person). Then there were small town moneylenders who in order to expand their business penetrated into the rural areas and for considerable time virtually ruled the rural areas. Slowly and steadily they got the land transferred to their names and looted the actual tillers through exorbitant rents and interest rates. In this plunder they were provided protection by law and were most often helped with police force to complete the plunder of the rural economy.

Rural Indebtedness in the Past

It must be understood that the moneylender and debt were not a new phenomenon in the old Indian society. It had existed even before the British rule. What was new was the role assumed by the moneylenders and consequent problems of rural debt under the British rule. In the pre-British Indian society, the peasant could borrow from moneylender only on his personal security. His property (land or the like, houses, animals, implements, etc.) could not be attached to debt. Under these circumstances, the business of moneylending was uncertain, often involving great risk. In fact, the trade of moneylending was looked down upon by the society (for example, according to Islamic laws taking and giving of interest is prohibited). Even in Hindu dominated areas, the village community acted as a check to charge the rate of interest beyond a particular limit. The principle of Damdupat (double money) was a common practice, limiting total interest equal to the total loan.

All these were changed during the British rule. No limit was prescribed for the rate of interest to be charged by the moneylenders. Rather the recovery of interest and principle was ensured through the legal machinery. And in case of default the peasant's land and other property could be attached. While the new economic system cut off the peasants from the seats of power and sources of finances, the moneylender was provided with all the power of police and law. Moneylender thus emerged as the pivotal force in the whole process of exploitation. He provided immoral services, suited to the plunder by the British Government and even collected land revenue on behalf of the British and mostly combined in himself the role of trader and the usurer (living on rate of interest). Often he advanced loans for seeds, implements and other inputs. Being disinterested in agriculture, his sole objective was to exploit the cultivators. It so happened that once the cultivators fell prey to him he had no chances to come out of his clutches. The process, according to R.C. Dutt, mostly ended with complete alienation of the actual tillers. They became landless labourers or share-croppers attached to the moneylenders. Such was the tragic outcome of the whole process of exploitation by the merchant-cum-usurious capital.

No wonder that quite often the exhausted peasants turned against the moneylenders and frequently murdered them. They even looted their property. But because of the widespread power and support of the moneylenders, such rebellions were often crushed.

Increase of Rural Indebtedness

Although indebtedness was not altogether a new thing in India, its increasing magnitude during the British rule owed its origin to direct colonial exploitation. As early as in 1911, Sir Edward Maclagan observed (appointed to examine the rural credit structure, particularly Cooperative Credit Societies), "It was long been recognized that indebtedness is no new thing in India.... But it is also acknowledged that the indebtedness has risen considerably during our rule, and more especially during the last half century."

As reported in 1880 by the Famine Commission, "The burden of debt had engulfed 2/3 of the land holding classes. In the subsequent period, especially during the first three decades of the present century, the burden of indebtedness further increased, and there was no evidence to indicate that this growth of debt was in proportion to the growing assets of the people. The fact that the total amount of rural credit increased from ₹ 900 crore in 1931 to ₹ 1800 crore in 1937 was really alarming."

Even in the wake of the Second World War, when prices were generally rising, the volume of indebtedness, contrary to expectations, increased except in case of the upper class of farmers. The Famine Enquiry Commission of 1945 reached the conclusion: "As a result of high prices of agricultural produce, there has been a substantial reduction in agricultural indebtedness. This appears to be particularly of cultivators with large holdings. It appears probable, however, that the indebtedness of small holders may not have been reduced substantially in any parts of the country."

The debt of the landless labourers increased faster than even that of the tenants. It may be added that the majority of rural population was composed of small tenants and agricultural labourers. In Punjab, it was estimated that only 17 per cent of the population was free from debt. Rate of interest being very high, they could not come out of debt. In the words of Professor D.R. Gadgil, it has been aptly remarked that the average cultivator in India during the British regime was born in debt, lived in debt and died in debt. Indebtedness, in fact, was hereditary.

Causes of Rural Indebtedness

1. Causes which compelled the farmers to borrow

(a) Poverty;

(b) Superfluous, socio-religious expenditure (D.R. Gadgil does not agree to this point. He stressed the point that why in the pre-British days in spite of the rigidity of customs and traditions people were free from debt.);

(c) Famines;

(d) Crushing burden of land revenue;

(e) Excessive litigation (sometimes forced upon by the moneylenders);

(f) Sometimes even for production purposes, plantations, seeds, etc.

2. Causes which enabled the cultivators to borrow liberally

(a) Emergence of private property—free purchase and sale of land;

(b) Encouragement to the moneylenders to lend liberally in order to acquire land;

(c) Rise in land values and ownership of land carried a status symbol.

3. System of money-lending and recovery of debts (no cooperative or Government credit)

Rates of interest on private lending were very high which the backward agriculture of India could not bear. They had to be put up with, because there was no Government system of easy credit. There was no check on the moneylender. Formerly, the village community acted as a check on the rate of interest. Damdupat (double money) was a common practice, limiting total interest to the amount of the loan. There was to be no transfer of land to the moneylender. Actually he was looked down upon. Under the British, the law gave the moneylender great powers over the debtor. Moneylenders manipulated the accounts and the debtors were cheated.

Consequences of Rural Indebtedness

Indebtedness mostly ended with completed exploitation, i.e. selling of land by the cultivators to the moneylenders. Thus, the farmer was completely alienated from land. In 1860, the process of alleviation started and during Great Depression the total rural debt increased from ₹ 900 crore in 1931 to ₹ 1800 crore in 1937.

The expropriation of farmers followed by indebtedness was universally acknowledged. In early 19th century when land was plentiful relative to labour, the moneylender had no inducement to take over the possession of land. By 1860, this was no longer the case, and land values began to increase. It was the beginning of the process of the alienation of land from the peasants into the hands of the moneylenders.

There is a consensus of opinion that the effects of this process of transference of land had been bad in India. In most parts of the country, the moneylender was not an agriculturist himself, it did not matter either if he was. Because the cultivation was usually carried on by the old cultivator, either as a tenant or as share-cropper working for the moneylender and paying over to him rent plus rate of interest which covered a greater proportion of the total produce. The position of the actual tiller thus became more precarious. On the other hand, the transference of land into the hands of the moneylender did not result, as it did in other parts of the world, in the consolidation of holdings (such as the Enclosure movement in England) or large-scale production. More striking was the fact that even long leasing of land was discouraged. Thus, there emerged a new class of cultivators called tenants-at-will.

It may be emphasized that as early as in 1892, the Deccan Commission on the working of the Agriculturists' Relief Act, which was earlier passed in 1879, observed with great concern, "the transfer of the land in an agricultural country to a body of rack-renting aliens, who do nothing for the improvement of the land". Various Commissions and the Committees appointed by the Government from time to time confirmed the fact that the non-agriculturist moneylender was the sole cause of the growing emergence of landless labourers and tenants. It may be mentioned here that although the British Government appointed agencies were sincere about their findings on the role of moneylender, yet these Commissions did not go deep to find out the causes (i.e. growing poverty) of growing indebtedness and the role of the Government in providing all sort of help, i.e. police, law, etc. to the moneylenders to recover their loans.

The world economic crisis of 1930s further deepened the crisis and the amount of indebtedness increased from ₹ 900 crore in 1931 to ₹ 1800 crore in 1937. In the wake of the World War II, when countrywide scarcity of foodgrains and famines were experienced, the rural indebtedness further increased.

The entire outcome of the process of expropriation of the peasantry was a catastrophic worsening of the status of the cultivator. They merely became a wage-labourers. The effects on the efficiency of cultivation were generally adverse; but now it was carried on without the incentive of the ownership of private property. The transfer of lands into the hands of the moneylender had not produced a class of agricultural entrepreneurs, not merely because the professional moneylender was not himself an agriculturist, even when lands were transferred to the agriculturist moneylender, the result was no different.

The growth of agriculturist moneylender was also an important development in Indian agriculture during the British period's later phase. The Rural Credit Survey reported that about 25 per cent of the loans to agriculturists had been supplied by the "agriculturist" moneylenders.

Thus, both the agriculturist as well as the non-agriculturist moneylenders failed to emerge as the agricultural entrepreneurs on the Indian scene and semi-moneylender turned out to be as much the exploiter as was the non-agriculturist moneylender. The whole system of land relations during the British opposed the modern (Capitalist) mode of production.

Government's Ameliorative Measures or Legislation to Check Indebtedness

Improvement of Civil Law: Changes in the Civil Procedure Code exempted the debtors from arrest and their cattle and implements from being attached. The debts could be rapid in installments. Under the Usurious Loans Act, 1918, the court could reopen the transaction and reduce the rate of interest if it was too high. But the act did not have much effect, mainly because the initiative was left to the court.

Under the Deccan Agriculturists Relief Act, 1879, arrest or imprisonment for debt was abolished. There was provision for complete insolvency so that the peasant could start on a clean state. Conciliatory machinery was appointed to settle the accounts. The courts were asked to go behind the contract (find reasons such as why the cultivator borrowed, how much he actually borrowed, what were the terms and conditions, etc.) and reduce an excessive rate of interest. Creditors (or moneylenders) had to furnish accounts and give receipts for all payments. But the Act was ineffective because no alternative source of credit was available, and even harmful as it put constraints on the moneylender and he refused to lend money. If he did, he resorted to certain illegal activities. He gave less but on the deed it was shown more as interest was deduced while lending, etc.—to bypass the law.

Restrictions on Land Transfer: The right to mortgage and sell land was a cause of increase in debts, which in turn led to land transfer. Therefore, laws were passed to restrict this right in many provinces. Non-agriculturists were not allowed to buy land from agriculturists, or to take it on mortgage for more than 20 years. But this did not cover agriculturist moneylenders. Nor were the debts checked much, as the farmers' need for credit remained unsatisfied. Moneylenders became more cautious and therefore, peasants found it more difficult to get loans.

Supply of Credit (Establishment of Cooperative Credit Societies): The crux of the problem was to supply loans to the farmer on suitable terms. The Government did try this (Takavi loans of 1883 and 1886). Cooperative Credit Societies were started in 1904 and Non-credit Societies in 1912, Land Mortgage Bank in 1920 (to provide long-term loans).

The Great Depression and the Provincial Autonomy

During the Great Depression, when prices of agricultural produce fell, indebtedness multiplied, which resulted in large numbers of suicides and forced sales of land. But the Central Government did nothing. It was only in 1937 when the Provincial Governments came into power that many Acts were passed to mitigate the evils of rural indebtedness.

Short-term Measures

Some of these were short-term measures which reduced the burden of debt. Interest dues were scaled down, the general principle being 'Damdupat' (double money), i.e. total interest was not to exceed loan. The courts had to reopen the cases and reduce the interest. In certain cases even principal was reduced. Although voluntary reductions of loans were welcomed, wherever necessary even compulsion was also used to reduce the debt burden.

Long-term Measures

Even if the above measures were successful, which they were not, they gave relief only for the time being. Therefore, there would still remain the need for permanent relief through long-term measures. These related to the control over money-lending.

Registration and licensing of moneylenders was made compulsory. They had to maintain accounts and give annual statements to debtors as also receipts for all payments made to them. The debtors were protected against threat and harassment and their property against attachment. Maximum rates of interest were fixed, being higher for unsecured loans. Again, simple rate of interest was higher than compound rate of interest.

But the popular ministries resigned after about two years in office (1939). They could not do much to ameliorate the lot of moneylenders. The moneylender remained by far the most important source of borrowings. A comprehensive and integrated programme of agricultural reform was urgently required. Since independence, various Land Reform Measures, Community Development Programmes, Integrated Area Development Programme, New Agricultural Technology, etc. have been adopted in this direction.

Population: A Historical View*

The role of quantity and quality of human power in economic development has been recognized since time immemorial. Both the high growth and low growth of population are considered harmful for economic development. A larger growing size of population apart from producing a growing supply of labour (both for industry and defense), also provides market for consumer goods. But a very high growth rate, i.e. disproportionate with the growth of capital, may retard economic development. With this background in mind, let us study the trends in population in the British India.

The first census in India was taken in 1871 when India's population was estimated at 25.4 crore. Even before 1871, some attempts were made to measure the size of India's population.

---

* Latest position in population is given in detail in Chapter 4, "India's Demography".

But because of the apathy of the people and their suspicions about the British Raj, those estimates are not much reliable. Anyway, from the different factors, viz. birth rate and death rate, affecting population, we can say that the size of Indian population remained stable for a considerable period.

Table 1.1 would explain the growth of population in the post-census period (i.e. 1871 onwards).

Table 1.1: Rate of Growth of Population in India with Causes

Period	Growth per cent	Causes of slow or rapid growth
1871-81	+1.5	Famines 1868-78
1881-91	+9.6	No famines
1891-1901	–0.2	Famines 1897-98 and 1899-1900
1901-11	+5.7	Hardly any famines
1911-21	–0.4	World War I, famines 1918-21 & Influenza, 1918
1921-31	+11.0	No famines
1931-41	+13.5	No famines
1941-51	+14.1	At some places, this rate to be lower than that of 1931-41 because of Partition and Famine of Bengal, 1943
1951-61	+21.0	From this year onward the rate of growth of population has been around 2.5 per cent, thus posing a serious problem.

Causes of Slow Growth Prior to 1921

Prior to 1921, the growth of population was not only slow but also fluctuating. In fact, periods of slight increase were followed by periods of actual decline. This is largely explained by recurrent famines and epidemics whose incidence was severe in some decades, but negligible in other. The great Bengal Famine of 1867-68 was followed by a comparatively normal decades of 1871-81 and 1881-91. Again the decade 1891-1901 saw the recurrence of severe famines in many parts of the country. Then there was an outbreak of plague in Bombay city in 1896, malaria and kala-azar (black fever) in the eastern part of the country. All these brought about an actual decline in the population during the decade 1891-1901. However, the comparatively normal decade of 1901-11 was followed by the great influenza epidemic of 1918. This decreased population by at least 12 to 13 million. Successive crop failures following the First World War and the epidemics of cholera, plague and malaria also contributed in the decline of population during 1911-21. In addition, the following factors greatly influenced the population growth:

1. Famines, war, crop failures, etc.;
2. Frequent epidemics (It must be stated that English population was more prone to such epidemics as the Indian population had developed immunity);
3. Migration to countries like Burma, Mauritius, Ceylon, Java, etc.

Causes of Steady and Accelerating Growth Since 1921

Since 1921, improvement of transport and communication and some extension of irrigation facilities, kept off any widespread famine except for the Bengal Famine of 1943 which involved, on a conservative estimate, a loss of nearly 3 million lives. Similarly, improvements in public health and sanitation have reduced (but not eliminated altogether) the dreadful fall of major epidemics. This resulted into a fairly steady growth of population till 1951. It must be noted that the population growth rate in India never exceeded 1.4 per cent per annum compared with 2 and 3 per cent in other developing countries like Egypt.

Birth Rates and Death Rates

Trends in population growth may be better studied by analyzing the trend in vital rates, i.e. birth rate and the death rate. Although information regarding both is inadequate, Dr. Kindley Davis' estimates which make necessary corrections in the census data, clearly brings out the trends:

Table 1.2: A Comparison of Birth Rates and Death Rates 1881-91 to 1951-61

Year	Estimated Birth Rate/1000	Estimated Death Rate/1000
1881-91	48.9	41.3
1891-1901	45.8	44.4
1901-11	48.1	42.6
1911-21	49.2	48.6
1921-31	46.4	36.3
1931-41	45.2	31.2
1941-51	39.9	29.4
1951-61	40.0	18.0

The death rate shows a high and little fluctuating trend until 1921, thereafter a continuous fall. Compared with death rates, birth rates show a uniform high level with minor fluctuations. There was some decline during 1941-51 but a further decline in the next decade.

Causes of High Death Rate (Before 1921)

The causes of the high death rate are diseases, lack of proper medical facilities, malnutrition (because of poverty and famine) and infant mortality. The diseases that occurred too often in an epidemic form and created maximum panic were plague, small pox and cholera. But taken together they hardly accounted for 5 to 10 per cent of total deaths. The most important single cause of high mortality in India was malaria which, according to Dr. Gyan Chand, accounted for roughly 20 per cent of all deaths in a year. It was an irony of fate that measures undertaken for famine relief, viz. construction of railways, road, canals, etc. led to breeding places for the mosquitoes, and hence malaria). Coale and Hoover put this death estimate at 2 million people per year. Other diseases which account for high mortality in India were, TB, dysentery and diarrhoea, respiratory infection and deficiency diseases due to malnutrition. The heavy incidence of all these diseases is partly due to severe exposure to infection because of unhygienic and unsanitary conditions of living, and partly due to dietary deficiencies and consequent low resistance of the people. In other words, poverty and ignorance are the main causes of high mortality rate. The other disturbing features of Indian mortality are the high infant and child mortality and the high female mortality rate. It has been estimated that before 1921 (during reproductive period) nearly 50 to 60 per cent of children born in India died before reaching the age of 20. Since 1921, the loss of life due to infant and child mortality had started declining but still it is very high (i.e. 40 per cent according to 1951 census). This heavy infant and child mortality implies that the country spends a considerable proportion of its resources every year on a batch of newly born population only to lose nearly half of them before they reach the age of 20 when they can be expected to make significant contribution to National Income.

Causes of Declining Death Rate

Although it is generally believed that the decline in death rate is directly associated with economic development, it was not so in case of India. Technological advancement in the sphere of medicine, viz. evolution of DDT, BCG vaccine, sulpha and antibiotic drugs, reduced the mortality rate directly. It is these quick and inexpensive means of fighting diseases which explain why countries like India, Ceylon (Sri Lanka) and Egypt achieved an improvement in the mortality rate in a quarter of a century after the World War II which took some of the advanced countries a long period of economic development. Various welfare measures adopted by the Government, vigorous public health drives including malaria eradication campaign adopted during and after the World War II, etc. reduced the death rate.

Causes of High Birth Rate

(1) Universal marriage; (2) Early marriage; (3) Grinding poverty (children are not liability rather than they are source of income); (4) Religious beliefs (children are the gifts of God), birth is outside the control of human beings; (5) Joint family system (no worry to bring up the children; (6) Inferior social status of women, i.e. women continue to bring up children. Had they been employed and gone outside the families, they would have naturally revolted and compelled the family to have lesser number of children; (7) High death rate particularly, high mortality rate amongst the children is also responsible for high birth rate. This would ensure that at least some of them would survive and live beyond 20 years (50-60 per cent died before they reached 20 years of age); (8) Lack of knowledge about family planning methods.

Forces Retarding/Reducing the Birth Rate

However, in India a large number of forces operated which reduced the birth rate such as:

(1) Prohibition on widow re-marriage;

(2) Poverty and malnutrition of women which reduced their capacity to bear children;

(3) Prolonged lactation period.

Since all these forces now are on the decline widow re-marriage is permissible, artificial feeding of children has replaced lactation, and poverty too, to some extent, has been removed. This has naturally affected the birth rate positively. However, at the same time new forces have emerged which have checked the positive impact of these forces. These new forces were urbanization, education and employment of women and consequently a rise in their social status. There was also a rise in the marriageable age amongst the educated class, and adoption of family planning measures, etc.

Relation between Population and Economic Development

Population and economic growth have always been taken to be interdependent variables, i.e. they are interrelated. The rapid growth of population in the West was not only an asset but also a cause of economic development. Similarly, a declining trend of population growth is generally considered to be one of the direct causes of a secular tendency towards stagnation in some mature economies.

Effect of Population on Economic Development

The size of population has a direct effect on the per capita income, an important indicator of economic development in a country. The problem of size had attracted Malthus to propound his theory of population. The same problem received more accurate treatment at the hands of optimum theorists, who clearly pointed out that man is not only a consumer but also a "producer", and, therefore, underpopulation is also as serious a problem as overpopulation. However, though this aspect of population is important, the rate of growth is far more important. A rapid growth of population in the West was not only an effect but also a cause of economic expansion. As J.M. Keynes has said, an expanding population will keep up the rate of growth of national income by increasing the effective demand for consumer goods and for houses and public utilities and increasing generally the marginal efficiency of capital. This is more so when the technical developments are leading more and more to capital saving inventions, as a nation becomes richer, its consumption tends to be directed towards these articles of consumption, particularly the services. Because of high marginal propensity to save (MPS), capital accumulation goes on increasing. If population fails to increase and new inventions fail to make use of increasing capital accumulation (which will be invariably the case), stagnation would come in. Thus, a declining trend of population growth is said to be one of the direct causes of secular stagnation in advanced capitalist countries.

In the developing countries the problem is reverse. Such countries are poor and here marginal propensity to consume (MPC) is very high so that very little is left for savings and investment. Thus, increasing population does not match with increasing investment, consequently national income declines.

Effects of an expanding population on the growth of national income, depends, mainly, on the ratio of population to other factors of production, like land, capital equipment and level of techniques. Where land is plenty and vast reserves await exploitation, an expanding population can keep up the rate of growth of national income by increasing demand for consumer goods and by encouraging proper division of labour. In this way, underdeveloped, underpopulated countries like Australia and South Africa have attained the present state of development. In such countries immigration was a boon because immigrants were generally able-bodied men of some productive capacity. But in densely populated underdeveloped countries (UDCs) where capital is less and resources fail to keep pace with population increase, an increasing population may aggravate the difficulties of achieving progress. The number of children, i.e. dependents increases, e.g. in India 50-60 per cent of children die before reaching the age of 20. Thus, it is a huge wastage of resources. Rising population apart from reducing servings, also creates serious food problem. Huge quantities of foodgrains may have to be imported, leading to loss of precious foreign exchange which otherwise would have been spent on capital imports.

A growing population can assist economic development only when capital accumulation, natural resources and level of technical efficiency can keep pace with population growth. Thus, high and rising level of technique and increasing capital accumulation are pre-conditions of economic development. It does not follow, however, that an increasing population is essential for progress. Progress can be achieved even when population is declining, if suitable fiscal policies to stimulate consumption and investment are adopted, and if the state is willing to fill up the gap (Y = C + I) by its own expenditure (G).

Thus, from a narrow economic point of view, "if a growing population has any advantages for the economic system, these can (unless the numbers are very small absolutely) nearly always be achieved by means other than expanding population". On the other hand, the disadvantages of an increasing population in a country already overpopulated are surely many.

Effects of Economic Development on Population

Professor Coale and Hoover's theory of demographic transition is largely based on the experience of the present industrialized countries of the world. It suggests that all countries passing through the process of economic development have to pass through three stages:

(1) The period of stability with rates of births and deaths both very high.

(2) Period of 'population explosion' characterized by declining death rates but stationary or slowly rising birth rates.

(3) The period when birth rates and death rates have both become stable at a low level.

Now, if we look to the demographic evolution historically, we find that the 'mature' industrialized countries of the world have passed through the first two stages and are now in the third stage. So far as India is concerned, it is in the second stage. As the figures of birth rates and death rates show that right up to 1921 both rates were very high because of a number of factors. In the post-1921 period while the death rates declined, birth rates did not decline much. Consequently, there is said to have occurred population explosion in India. But it must be understood that till recently fall in death rate did not correspond with economic development. It was rather due to the evolution of new technology in medicine, i.e. development of DDT, BCG, anti-cholera vaccines, antibiotics, etc. Thus, our demographic trends, strictly speaking, do not fall in the theory of demographic transition. It was incidental that a decline in death rate was achieved with zero or negative growth rate in national income.

Different Phases of British Rule in India

Before we come to the individual topics like population, decline of handicrafts, growth of agriculture industries, etc. let us have a brief look at the entire period [200 years of British Rule (1757-1947)].

India's size (land area) was 20 times the area of the Great Britain. At the time of World War II, India's colony was the largest colony which constituted more than half of the colonial population at that time. Almost all the European and other colonizing powers had set their eyes on the Indian wealth. They were making frantic efforts to find out new sea routes to India.

Key to British World Supremacy

The conquest of India by the British gave the later immense power and prestige. Britain became the world's largest power to be reckoned with. Behind the success struggle between England and other powers—France, Spain, Portugal, Holland, Russia and Germany, India was the main cause. Lord Curzon admitted in 1898, "If the Empire loses any other part of the domain, we can survive, but if we lose India the sun of our Empire will have set."

The Net Effect of the British Rule

It is generally believed that if a traditional economy comes into contact with an advanced country, its outlook is widened, technology is transferred, etc. It is totally incorrect. The British deliberately kept away Indians from new techniques of production. It was a paradox that there was poverty in the midst of plenty.

Travelers' accounts bear testimony to the fact that there was export surplus, and the demand of Indian products in foreign countries was huge. There were high natural resources. Even the American Technical Mission (1942) admitted that there was no proper exploitation of natural resources. There was loot and plunder of Indian economy, with the result that poverty increased.

Not to speak of clothing or shelter, even two times meals was a luxury. About the Bombay Textile workers (923) it is said that their ration was below the jail ration.

What was behind the poverty?

(1) Increase in population—No, the net increase in population was not more than the rate at which population grew in other countries. Even famines reduced population.

(2) Social backwardness—No, people were socially so previously also. Further social backwardness mostly follows economic backwardness and not vice versa.

Destructive Role of India

Whereas previous invaders or rulers settled here and adopted this culture, the English systematically ruined everything—economy, society, social values and relations. They thus played a destructive role.

I. Period of Merchant Capital up to the Year 1800 (East India Company)

Destruction of Indian Economy

(1) Direct plunder,

(2) Neglect of irrigation and public works,

(3) Introduction of English land system—private property ownership,

(4) Destruction of Indian handicrafts by unjustifiable tariff system.

The original aim of the East India Company was to trade in Indian goods. But the Battle of Plassey changed the scenario in 1757. In 1762, the Nawab of Bengal, Mir Kasim complained that the Company agents were forcibly buying goods from the bazars and the peasants by paying just one-fourth of their value. But they were forcing them to pay five times of what the English goods.

House of Commons (Parliament) condemned in 1784 the tactics adopted by East India Company to loot the Indian people. In 1858 one British M.P. remarked that, "I do most confidently maintain that no civilized government even existed on the face of this earth which was more corrupt than the Government of the East India Company from 1765 to 1784."

From a letter written by Lord Clive to the Directors of East India Company (1765) it becomes clear that the British looted India. The letter stated that out of the whole amount collected as revenue, one-fourth was sufficient to meet the expenditure needs. One-fourth was spent to please the native princes. Half of it was taken away as investment of his Company. It was a clear drain. The East India Company's dream was realized to draw wealth without paying for it.

There was complete neglect of irrigation, and a systematic destruction of industries drove the population to villages. Demand for land increased. There was a reckless collection of land revenue. More and more demand for revenue led to more exploitation and neglect of land and irrigation led to famines. In 1770, about 10 million people died in famine.

II. Period of Industrial Capital or the Industrial Devastation

Industrial Revolution in England (early 19th century) led to the demand for free trade. Initially there were objections by the East India Company. But other traders (jealous of East India Company) supported free trade. Adam Smith's *Wealth of Nations* (1776) explained the advantages of free trade. International division of labour and the theory of comparative advantage gained momentum.

In 1813, the monopoly of East India Company to trade with India was finally broken.

Tariff Policy of 1813

Before this, Indian goods (particularly cotton, silk fabrics) were selling in England at less than 50-60 per cent of the price of goods produced by English. So tariff rates were increased. In fact the wearing of printed Indian cotton fabric was banned under the law. But there was no tariff duty on British goods while entering India. In 1840 when because of revenue requirement, British cotton goods were imported by paying just 3 per cent, Indian goods were required to pay 10 per cent. Consequently,

British cotton export to India increased at a very high rate. By 1850, India which was net exporter of cotton fabrics became the importer and 25 per cent of English cotton clothes were exported to India.

The most questionable part in tariff history is the so-called countervailing duties imposed in 1896. In 1894, revenue requirement of the East India Company further increased. Import duty was increased generally by 50 per cent. There was a hue and cry by Manchester industrial capitalists. A countervailing duty on Indian goods was imposed.

Thus, political power was used to destroy Indian industries. The number of industrial workers decreased year after year—absolutely as well as relatively. The population of Dacca declined from 1,50,000 to 30,000, i.e. there was 80 per cent decline.

Effects of De-Industrialization

(1) Decline in industrial workers,

(2) Heavy dependence on agriculture,

(3) Growing poverty,

(4) Export of raw cotton, import of manufactured commodities,

(5) Famines were frequent. [While during 1800-1825 one million people died, during 1875-1900 as many as 15 million people died],

(6) Old village before had a combination of industries and agriculture. When the artisans lost their jobs they became dependent on agriculture.

III. Period of Financial Capital

British investment was a hoax. Resources were raised in India. In the name of home charges the British took away huge amount. In 1857, the so-called public debt was £70 million but it took away £150 million charges. When the British Crown took over from the East India Company, it declared a public debt of £70 million. Payment of interest, principal, etc. imposed a huge burden on Indian economy.

Public debt further increased by charging to the GOI every conceivable expenditure. If the Sultan of Turkey was given a reception in England, India had to bear its expenditure. Then expenditure of embassies was charged to India. The raising of Indian army to defend the British was financed by the Government of India.

When India was opened to private English capitalists, investment started flowing—first in banking industry, transport, plantation—tea, coffee, indigo. It was in no way related to industrial development. Its only purpose was the commercial exploitation of its natural resources.

The extent of financial capital before the First World War was 11 per cent of the total British investment in the world. But in 1933 it increased to 25 per cent.

Up to the First World War, exploitation was open and unconcealed. During the war it became difficult to import. Besides, the cooperation of nationalities was also required to run the Government. There was growing trend for freedom struggle.

However, this was a short-lived sympathy. The demand of iron and steel industry for protection was not acceded to. Subsidy was withdrawn. The value of the shares of the Tata Iron and Steel Industry fell from ₹ 100 to 10 and the company had to borrow from the Indian market.

During the depression of the thirties the value of Indian exports (agricultural goods) fell by 50 per cent. Gold worth 32 million ounces (more than the amount the British had it as reserves in England) was exported from Delhi during 1931-35.

During the War (1943-44) more than 108 foreign (English) business concerns had their branches in India—Dunlop, Lever Brothers, Imperial Chemicals.

In 1942, the American Technical Mission observed that in spite of the availability of all natural resources, industrialization did not take place. There was joint venture with Birla Brothers Ltd. and Nuffield Organization to manufacture cars, but only for assembling and under technical supervision of the English. Import of all spare parts continued. There were workshops for assembling and not for manufacturing.

Progressive Role and Contribution of the British Rule

(1) Education: Modern education, particularly foreign education was started in India.

(2) Free press (1835): The English who were used to democracy also popularized it in India.

(3) Means of transport and communication: Roads, railways, steamships, etc. led to the opening of villages and contact with the interaction of new ideas.

(4) Limited industrial development led to the division of labour. Caste system was broken.

(5) New land revenue system led to the emergence of the concept of private property. Land became a commodity. Collection of land revenue in cash led to more marketable surplus.

(6) Monetization of the rural economy broke the rigidities of barter system.

(7) New administration which was centralized led to the integration of the economy.

Notes

1. N.D. Shiva Kumar (23 June 2013). "Unemployment rate increases in India". *The Times of India.*
2. *Ibid.*
3. www.economicsdiscussion.net
4. Datt, E. Sundharam's *Indian Economy*, S. Chand Publishing, New Delhi.
5. *Ibid.*

2

An Overview of Indian Economy

India's economy is the sixth-largest in the world by nominal GDP and the third-largest by purchasing power parity (PPP). Classified as newly industrialized country, India is one of the G-20 major economies, a member of BRICS[1] and a developing economy with around 7% average growth rate for the last two decades. India's economy became the world's fastest growing major economy from the last quarter of 2014, replacing the People's Republic of China. The long-term growth prospective of the Indian economy is moderately positive due to its young population, corresponding low dependency ratio, healthy savings and investment rates, and increasing integration into the global economy.[2]

India is a member of the Commonwealth of Nations, the South Asian Association for Regional Cooperation (SAARC), the G20, the IMF, the World Bank, the World Trade Organization (WTO), the Asian Infrastructure Investment Bank (AIIB, the United Nations and the New Development BRICS Bank.

Indian economy has the potential to become the world's 3rd-largest economy by the next decade, and one of the largest economies by mid-century. According to IMF, the outlook for short-term growth of India's economy is also good and it is the "bright spot" in the global landscape. India also topped the World Bank's growth outlook for 2015-16 for the first time with the economy having grown 7.3% in 2014-15 and was expected to grow by 7.5% in 2015-16.

India has capitalized its economy based on its large educated English-speaking population to become a major exporter of information technology (IT) services, Business Process Outsourcing (BPO) services, and software services with US$ 167.0 billion worth of service exports in 2013-14. IT industry continues to be the largest private sector employer in the country. India is also the fourth largest start-up hub in the world with over 3,100 technology start-ups in 2014-15.

Agricultural sector is the largest employer in India's economy and contributes 17.4% share to its GDP (2014-15). In farm output, India ranks second in the world. The Industry sector has held a rather constant share of around 25% of GDP in economic contribution (2014-15). The Indian auto industry is one of the largest in the world with an annual production of 23.37 million vehicles during 2014-15. India had US$ 600 billion worth of retail market in 2015 and one of world's fastest growing e-commerce markets.

Economic Reforms in India

The liberalization of India's economic policies was initiated in 1991 with the aim of making the economy more market-oriented and expanding the role of private and foreign investment. Specific changes included a reduction in import tariffs, deregulation of markets, reduction of taxes, and clearance for greater foreign investment. This economic liberalization has been largely responsible for the country's high economic growth recorded by the country in the 1990s and 2000s. However, those who favour a balanced development of the people belonging to different regions and a focus inter alia on eradication of poverty and creation of more employment are against such liberalization which helps only elite business classes. They have even blamed it for increased poverty, inequality and economic degradation. The overall direction of liberalization has since remained the same, irrespective of the change in government at the centre, and no party has yet solved the politically difficult issues, like liberalizing labour laws and reducing agricultural subsidies.

Experts are of the view that economic liberalization is necessary for faster economic development. Barring the last couple of years, India has grown at a slower pace than China, because the latter has been liberalizing its economy since 1978. There is an ongoing debate around liberalization as an inclusive economic growth strategy. According to a *Times of India* review, the income inequality has deepened in India since 1992 with consumption among the poorest remaining stable and the wealthiest generating more and more consumption growth.

India's Gross Domestic Product (GDP) growth rate at 5.1% was the lowest in 2012-13 over a decade, which invited criticism of India's economic reforms alleging that they have failed to address employment growth, nutritional values in terms of food intake in calories, and also exports growth and has led to a worsening level of current account deficit compared to the period prior to the reforms. However, with the growth rebounding to 6.9% and 7.3% in 2013-14 and 2014-15, as a result of the reforms brought by the new government, the economy has looked like becoming healthy again.[3]

India's economic policy after the achievement of independence was protectionist in nature, with a strong emphasis on import substitution, industrialization under state monitoring, state intervention at the micro level in all businesses, especially in labour and financial markets, a large public sector, business regulation, and central planning. "There was a planning period resembling central planning in the Soviet Union. Steel, mining, machine tools, water, telecommunications, insurance, and electrical plants, among other industries, were effectively nationalised in the mid-1950s."[4]

There were attempts to liberalize the economy during the period 1966 and 1985, but the first attempt was reversed in 1967 following a strong bent towards socialism. The second major attempt was in 1985 by Prime Minister Rajiv Gandhi, whereby the government slightly reduced licence raj and promoted the growth of the telecommunications and software industries, but the process came to a halt in 1987. The governments of Vishwanath Pratap Singh (Dec. 1989 to Nov. 1990) and Chandra Shekhar Government (Nov. 1990 to June 1991) did not add to the reforms.

Position of Economy before Economic Liberalization

Before 1980, Indian economy registered slow growth, which stagnated around 3.5% from 1950s to 1980s. Per capita income averaged just 1.3%. Only four or five licenses were given for steel, electrical power and communications. License owners built huge powerful empires. A large private sector emerged. State-owned enterprises suffered big losses. However, since there was monopoly of public sector, investment in infrastructure remained poor. The country was in the grip of "irresponsible, self-perpetuating bureaucracy that still exists throughout much of the country", and there was widespread corruption.

Economic Liberalization and Thereafter

The economic liberalization initiated in 1991 started to make immediate impact. The major impacts are discussed below.

Increase in National Product

The Gross National Product (GNP) at factor cost registered a higher growth by 300% during the period 1990-91 to 1999-2000, as compared to 283% in the previous decade. Net National Product (NNP) at factor cost went up by 304% during the period as compared to 278% a year earlier. The increase in NNP at factor cost at current prices was 232% as against 206% in the previous decade. The absolute figures relating to National Product at factor cost at current prices are given in Table 2.1:

Table 2.1: Estimated National Product at Factor Cost at Current Prices

Item	1980-81	1990-91	2000-01
GNP (₹ crore)	122772	470269	1885713
NNP (₹ crore)	110685	418074	1687818
Per Capita NNP (₹)	1630	4983	16563
GNP Index (1980-81 = 100)	100	383	1536
NNP Index (1980-81 = 100)	100	378	1525
Per Capita NNP (1980-81=100)	100	306	1016

Source: Statistical Abstracts – India – 1997 and 2003 published by Central Statistical Organisation, Government of India.

It can be seen from the above table that GNP and NNP which were ₹ 1,22,772 crore and ₹ 1,10,685 crore respectively in 1980-

81, increased to ₹ 470 crore and 4,18,074 crore respectively in 1990-91, and ₹ 18,85,713 crore and 16,87,818 respectively in 2000-01. Other indicators like per capita NNP and GNP index also showed substantial increase.

Increase in the Production of Consumer Durables

There was a phenomenal increase in the production of consumer durables like fridges, TVs, cars, washing machines, music systems, DVDs, and other electronic gadgets. Since there was a stiff competition among the manufacturers and traders, the prices came down or remained static. India was turned into a consumer society and its economy became more dynamic.

Growth in Employment Opportunities

With an increase in production due to the abolishment of license raj, there came a growth in employment opportunities. Many new private companies came into being, creating more employment opportunities. As the terms for foreign companies, including multinational companies were made soft, they came to do business in India, giving further boost to employment. Besides, the pay packages of employees, especially those having technical skills in engineering, medicine, hospitality, etc. increased. The information technology (IT) sector in particular grew many-fold, creating vast employment opportunities.

Increase in Foreign Exchange Reserves

India's foreign exchange reserves grew significantly after the introduction of economic reforms in 1991. The reserves, which stood at US$ 5.8 billion at end-March 1991 increased gradually to US$ 25.2 billion by the end of financial year 1994-95, and further to US$ 38.0 billion by the end of March 2000. Subsequently, the reserves rose to US$ 54.1 billion by the end of March 2002, US$ 76.1 billion by end-March 2003, US$ 113.0 billion by end-March 2004 and further to US$ 141.5 billion by end-March 2005.

This was in contrast with the position before the ushering in of economic reforms, when, by the end of 1990, "the country's foreign exchange reserves had been reduced to such a point that India could barely finance three weeks' worth of imports which led the Indian government to airlift national gold reserves as a pledge to the International Monetary Fund (IMF) in exchange for a loan to cover balance of payment debts" (Rediff News).

In January 1991, India's foreign exchange reserves were merely US$ 1.2 billion, which further reduced to half by June 1991, and India was "only weeks away from defaulting on its external balance of payment obligations". The government had to secure an emergency loan of US$ 2.2 billion from IMF by pledging 67 tons of India's gold reserves as collateral.

India's foreign exchange reserves which started increasing after the introduction of reforms reached US$ 297 billion in December 2010, US$ 296 billion in December 2011, US$ 296 billion in December 2012, US$ 295 billion in December 2013, US$ 320 billion in December 2014, and US$ and stood at US$ 350 billion as on 1st Jan. 2016.

Boom in Telecommunication Sector

The economic reform agenda in telecommunications was addressed in National Telecom Policy 1994 and New Telecom Policy 1999.

The NTP 1994 was a major programme undertaken to expand and upgrade India's telecom network since 1991. It brought complete freedom of telecom equipment manufacturing, privatization of services, liberal foreign investment and new regulation in technology imports. The Department of Telecommunications (DoT) was restructured to remove its monopoly status as the service provider. Most value-added services, like cellular phones and radio pagers, which were virtually non-existent in the pre-reform era, grew rapidly thereafter.

In 1998, the government formed a high powered committee to develop the Internet Services Development Policy headed by the Chief Minister Chandrababu Naidu. The commitment of this committee and government's keenness in transforming the telecommunications sector gave birth the New Telecom Policy, 1999 (NTP 99).

It addressed the outstanding issues of telecommunications development and the challenges brought by modern telecommunications technology. It recognized the important role of private sector investment in the development process of telecom sector. The policy inter alia endorsed the policies under the following five policy frameworks:

(i) Framework for Services Deployment,

(ii) Framework for Licensing of Telecom Services,

(iii) Framework for Restructuring of Telecom Organizations,

(iv) Framework for Further Liberalization of Services, and

(v) Framework for Regulation.

Before 1989, a telecom board headed by Director General took all decisions on behalf of the central government. In 1986, the DoT corporatized two of its operational wings, viz. Videsh Sanchar Nigam Limited (VSNL) which looked after international operations, and Mahanagar Telephone Nigam Limited (MTNL) which had operational responsibility for providing telephone services in metropolitan Delhi and Mumbai; the rest of the country remained under the jurisdiction of the DoT. In May 1989, the Telecom Board was replaced by a Telecommunications Commission, whereby telecommunication operations were divided into five areas, each under the control of a full time member of the Commission. These areas were: telecom policy, regulation, technical research and development, design and manufacture of equipment, and provision of telecommunications services.

The NTP 99 brought a comprehensive programme of telecommunications policy reform in India. BSNL's share increased from 79 per cent to 86 per cent between March 1997 and June 2001, while the share for MTNL dropped from 21 per cent to below 13 per cent of the total connections. The basic telecom services expanded all over India except in Delhi and Mumbai, which is a clear indication that telecom services became more broad-based in India.

The number of licenses given to basic services was restricted in the early years of liberalization. The policy admitted one private operator in each circle to compete with the incumbent BSNL. New entrants were allowed to offer intra-circle long distance services, but the BSNL maintained its monopoly on inter-circle long-distance telephony. This policy was changed in 2001 to allow unlimited entry into each circle for basic services. As opposed to the fixed license fee regime based on which licenses were awarded earlier, fresh licenses were issued on the basis of a one-time entry fee and a percentage of revenue share that was linked to the area of operation.

Introduction of private service providers in the mobile market revolutionized the industry. The NTP 99 created an environment to expand the subscriber base. Many new operators came into being. Telecommunications regulatory reform began with the introduction of an independent regulatory agency, Telecom Regulatory Authority of India (TRAI) in March 1997. NTP 94 had a provision to introduce such an independent entity to regulate telecommunications in India. The need for such an authority was felt due to the on-going liberalization.

With the coming of new players in the telecom sector, not only the services have improved, but also the prices have reduced significantly.

Telephone connections are today affordable to everyone and are also easily available. The number of telephone connections which was 5.07 million (fixed lines) in 1991, went up to 54.62 million telephone connections in 2003 of which 41.33 million were fixed line telephone connections, and 12.69 million were cellular mobiles and the remaining 0.60 million were Wireless in Local Loop (WLL) telephones.

Growth in Civil Aviation

The civil aviation sector registered good growth after liberalization, as is evident from the fact that the number of hours flown under domestic services increased by 138 % during the period 1990-91 to 2002-03 as against a mere 27% during 1981 to 1990-91. The total number of hours in flight under domestic services was 98,000 in 1981, 1,24,000 in 1990-91, and 2,95,000 in 2002-03. The growth in the number of passengers carried in the domestic sector increased from 42% during 1981 to 1990-91 to 76% during the period 1990-91 to 2002-03. The number of passengers carried was: 55,60,000 in 1981, 79,12,000 in 1990-91 and 139,51,000 in 2002-03).

The civil aviation sector witnessed an improvement of 20.4 per cent in domestic traffic and 7.8 per cent in international passenger traffic during the first three quarters of 2015-16. During April-September 2015 cargo traffic at all ports increased by 1.1 per cent, while major ports reported an increase of 4.1 per cent and non-major ports a decline of 1.0 per cent as compared to the corresponding period in 2014-15. The performance of the telecommunication sector during 2015-16 was remarkable, with approximately 33.4 million new telephone connections added during April-October 2015, which was much higher than the 29.7 million new connections in the corresponding period of 2014-15.

At present, domestic airlines passenger traffic is increasing at the rate of 25%. India ranks fourth after US, China and Japan in terms of domestic passengers volume. The domestic aviation sector is expected to grow at the rate of 9-10 per cent to reach a level of 150 to 180 million passengers by the year 2020.

Fall in Poverty Ratio

Notwithstanding the charges by the detractors of economic reforms that it has perpetuated poverty, the statistics reveal that poverty ratio decreased from 36% in 1993 to 26% in 1999-2000. The earlier decreases were much smaller. For example, poverty ratio decreased from 51.3% in 1978 to 44.5% in 1983, and from 38.9% in 1988, to 36% in 1993.

The absolute number of poor remained around 320 million from mid-1980s to early 1990s, the number was reduced to 260 million by 1999-2000. The percentages of population below the poverty line for urban and rural areas are given in Table 2.2.

Table 2.2: Percentage of population below the poverty line in India

Year	Rural	Urban	Total
1973-74	56.4	49.0	54.9
1977-78	53.1	45.2	51.3
1983	45.7	40.8	44.5
1987-88	39.1	38.2	38.9
1993-94	37.3	32.4	36.0
1999-2000	27.1	23.6	26.1

Source: Selected Socio-Economic Statistics–India–2002, published by the Central Statistical Organisation, Govt. of India

Growth in Foreign Trade

External trade registered a remarkable improvement. The trade-GDP ratio increased only marginally from 13.6 to 14.2 per cent between 1980-1981 and 1989-1990, but shot up to 22.1% by 2000-2001. The declining trend in India's share of exports in world trade saw a reversal during 1990s. It increased from 05% to 06%. The total value of imports increased from ₹ 12,54,915 lakh in 1980-81 to ₹ 43,19,286 lakh in 1990-91 and to ₹ 297,20,587 lakh in 2002-03. The value of exports increased from ₹ 6,71,070 lakh in 1980-81 to ₹ 32,55,334 lakh in 1990-91 and to ₹ 255,13,728 lakh in 2002-03.

The other indicators of foreign trade also showed significant increase. The Unit Value Index (UVI) of imports rose by 278 points during 1990-91 to 2002-03 as against 134 points during 1980-81 to 1990-91. The Quantum Index (QI) of imports rose by 564 points during 1990-91 to 2002-03 as against 100 points during 1980-81 to 1990-91. The Unit Value Index of exports rose by 327 points during 1990-91 to 2002-03 as against 184 points during 1980-81 to 1990-91. The QI of exports jumped up by 528 points during 1990-91 to 2002-03 as against just 86 points during 1980-81 to 1990-91. These figures bear testimony to increase in foreign trade after the introduction of economic reforms.

Increase in Foreign Direct Investment (FDI)

There is no doubt that after liberalization, foreign investment as well as domestic private investment increased by leaps and bounds. During 1991-92 (August-March), the foreign direct investment (FDI) inflows were only ₹ 408 crore and the figure increased to ₹ 1094 crore during 1992-93. During 2003-04, the FDI inflows were ₹ 12,117 crore, which is more than ten times the figure of 1992-93. The FDI inflows during 2004-05 were ₹ 11,726 crore up to November 2004. Foreign investors are showing a keen interest in investing in India. A confidence survey by global consultancy AT Kearney rated India as the third most favored FDI destination, next only to China and the United States.[5]

Expansion of Tourism

Tourism industry in India expanded after the introduction of economic reforms. Tourism in India has a strong relevance to economic development, cultural growth and national integration. India is a vast country possessing rich biodiversity and beauty, almost every type of climate, rich cultural heritage manifest in its architectural wonders like palaces, forts, temples, mosques, etc. and varied topography ranging from the plains to the loftiest mountains of the world, beautiful long beaches on the sea coast, vast stretches of sands, tropical forests and above all, with great variety of the lifestyle, India offers an unending choice for the tourist.

Tourism industry in India expanded after the introduction of economic reforms. According to Central Statistical Organisation (CSO), the total number of tourists increased from 12,79,210 in 1981 to 16,77,508 in 1991 and 25,37,282 in 2001. This increased flow of foreign tourists has increased the country's foreign exchange earnings considerably.

Tourism in India is growing rapidly. According to The World Travel & Tourism Council, tourism generated US$ 94 billion or 6.6% of India's GDP in 2012. It supported 39.5 million jobs, 7.7% of its total employment. The sector is predicted to grow at an average annual rate of 7.9% till 2023 making India the third fastest growing tourism destination over the next decade. India has a large medical tourism sector which is expected to grow at an estimated rate of 30% annually and reached US$ 1.4 billion in 2015.

About 22.57 million tourists arrived in India in 2014, compared to 19.95 million in 2013. India occupies 38th country in the world in terms of foreign tourist arrivals.

Growth in the Corporate Sector

The corporate sector was the biggest gainer of economic reforms and experienced huge expansion in the 1990s and thereafter. Due to an increasing flow of foreign investment and enhanced domestic private investment, the number of industries in the corporate sector has gone up, as is evident from the following data: In 1980-81, there were only 62,714 companies with an aggregate paid up capital of ₹ 15,555 crore. In the year 2002-03, the number of companies rose to 6,12,155 with a total paid-up capital of ₹ 4,35,311 crore.

There were 8,21,212 companies at the end of 2009. According to MCA Annual Report 2012-13, as on 31.12.2012, a total of 12,89,229 companies were on the Register. Of these 11,67,226 were private limited companies and 1,22,003 public limited companies. Out of the above, 8,72,957 companies were at work, comprising 8,06,666 private limited and 66,291 public limited companies. A majority of the companies at work were operating in activities covered under four broad heads: (i) Financing, Insurance, Real Estate and Renting, Business Services (31.57%), (ii) Manufacturing (22.31%), (iii) Wholesale and Retail Trade, Restaurants and Hotels (15.85%), and (iv) Construction (10.74%) sectors. The sector is expected to grow in the coming years with some new initiatives being taken by the Modi government.

Improvement in the Position of Balance of Payments on Current Account

The position of balance of payments on current account was poor in the pre-reforms era. In 1980-81, there was a deficit of ₹ 2213.5 crore, which increased to ₹ 17,366 crore in 1990-91. There was a turnaround after 1991. In the year 2002-03, the balance of payments was favourable, and had a net earning of ₹ 19,987 crore. This was mainly because of earnings from export of services, remittances from Indian workers, income from financial assets and earnings from foreign tourists. The fast expansion of IT sector brought about by economic reforms, the earnings from export of services as well as from remittances made by Indian professionals employed abroad gave a big push to earnings.

India's balance of payments recorded a surplus for the sixth consecutive quarter, with Jan-Mar 2015 showing a US$ 30 billion surplus. It was more than double the accretion in the preceding quarter and almost four times of the reserves accrued in Jan-Mar 2014, signifying an increase in capital inflows and decrease in current account deficit.

GDP Growth in India

An overview of GDP growth in India presents a story of steady growth. The trigger was given by adopting a policy of liberalization in the 1990s. The fruits of liberalization reached their peak in 2006 when India achieved its highest GDP growth rate of 9.6%. The years 2005-06, 2006-07 and 2007-08 showed remarkable annual growth of 9.5%, 9.6%, and 9.3% respectively. The global economic slowdown had its effect on Indian economy, the GDP growth slipped to 6.7% which still was not bad considering the sharp decline in the economic growth of other countries. There was an uptrend in 2009-10, when the GDP growth was 8.6% and 8.9% in 2010-11. The downtrend returned in the subsequent years and the economy grew at 6.7%, 4.5% and 4.7% in 2011-12, 2012.13, and 2013-14, respectively.

The economy registered a growth of 7.3% growth in 2014-15, and 7.6% in 2015-16. With this, India became the fastest growing major economy in the world. However, there were periods of slow growth between 2007-08 and 2009-10 due to world economic recession triggered by subprime lending in America, and from first half of 2012 due to some other global factors. But overall, India's economy fared well as compared to most other countries, including the developed countries. A report by Organization for Economic Co-operation and Development (OECD) report states that the average growth rate 7.5% will double the average income in India in a decade's time, and more reforms would speed up the pace. The economy registered a growth of 7.3% growth in 2014-15, and 7.6% in 2015-16.

India has chosen a planned growth mode. According to Niti Aayog, the Twelfth Five Year Plan (2013-17) envisages an average annual growth target of 8 per cent. When the Plan was launched the economy was experiencing a slowdown on account of several domestic and global factors as shown above.

As per the Press Note on New Series Estimates of National Income, Consumption Expenditure, Saving and Capital Formation (Base Year 2011-12) released on 30th January 2015 by the Ministry of Statistics & Programme Implementation

(MOSPI), industry-wise estimates would be presented as the Gross Value Added (GVA) at basic prices. The use of Gross Domestic Product (GDP) growth rates at Factor Cost (GDPfc) would be discontinued. Also GDP at Market Prices (GDPmp) will now be referred to as GDP. The year-wise GDPfc and GDPmp (Base 2004-05) over the last six years along with GDP and GVA at 2011-12 prices for the last three years are given in Table 2.3 below:

Table 2.3: Growth Rates of GDP at Factor Cost & Market Prices at 2004-05 Prices

At 2004-05 prices			At 2011-12 prices	
Year	GDP_{fc}	GDP_{mp}	GDP	GVA at basic prices
2007-08	9.3	9.8	--	--
2008-09	6.7	3.9	--	--
2009-10	8.6	8.5	--	--
2010-11	8.9	10.3	--	--
2011-12	6.7	6.6	--	--
2012-13	4.5	4.7	5.1	4.9
2013-14	4.7	5.0	6.9	6.6
2014-15	--	--	7.4	7.5

Source: Central Statistics Office

Notes: 1. At 2004-05 prices: 2011-12 - Second Revised Estimates; 2012-13 First Revised Estimates; 2013-14 - Provisional Estimates as on 30.05.2014.

2. At 2011-12 prices: 2012-13 - Second Revised Estimates; 2013-14 - First Revised Estimates and 2014-15 - Advanced Estimates as on 09.02.2015.

As per the New Series Estimates of National Income, the growth rate of Gross Value Added (GVA) at constant (2011-12) basic prices increased from 4.9 per cent in 2012-13 to 6.6 per cent in 2013-14. GVA at basic prices is obtained by adding the net of production taxes and subsidies to GDP at factor cost.[6]

Contribution of Components to Real GDP Growth

The comparative position of contribution of components to India's GDP growth for the years 2013-14, 2014-15 and 2015-16 is given in Table 2.4 below:

Table 2.4: Contribution of Components to Real GDP Growth
Final expenditures Share in GDP Growth (in per cent) Contribution to GDP growth (in per cent)

	2011-12	2015-16	2013-14	2014-15	2015-16 (AE)	2013-14	2014-15	2015-16 (AE)
Private final consumption	56.2	59.8	6.8	6.2	7.6	57.1	48.3	55.9
Government final consumption	11.1	10.7	0.4	12.8	3.3	0.7	17.6	4.5
Fixed capital formation	34.3	29.4	3.4	4.9	5.3	17.5	22.1	22.4
Change in stock	2.4	1.7	-18.6	20.3	5.5	-6.0	4.6	1.4
Valuables	2.9	1.5	-42.2	15.4	13.3	-17.9	3.2	2.9
Net exports	-6.5	-2.6	70.0	11.7	6.1	67.4	2.9	1.2
GDP at constant market prices	100.0	100.0	6.6	7.2	7.6	100.0	100.0	100.0

Source: Central Statistics Office (CSO)

Note: AE—Advance Estimates. Shares/contributions may not add up to 100 due to errors and omissions.

Table 2.4 shows that the share of private final consumption has been the largest. It has increased from 48.3% in 2014-15 to 55.9% in 2015-16. The next highest share, i.e. that of fixed capital formation has also increased from 17.5% and 22.1% in 2013-14 and 2014-15 respectively, to 22.4% in 2015-16. It was aided by growth in capital. However, the share of government final consumption decreased from 17.6% in 2014-15 to 4.5% in 2015-16. We can see a substantial decrease in exports because of erosion of demand for our goods in the international market.

Indian economy was likely to grow between 7 and 7.5% in the year 2016-17, according to the Economic Survey. The survey had projected 7.6% economic growth rate in 2015-16. There are several favourable domestic factors. The three factors which can boost consumption are (i) increased spending from higher wages, (ii) allowances of government workers if the 7th Pay Commission is implemented and (iii) a normal monsoon. On the other hand, a slowdown in global economy could worsen the outlook of exports. If there is a rise in oil prices it would increase the drag from consumption. The most serious risk is combination of these two factors.

The country's macro-economy is stable, founded on the government's commitment to bring about fiscal consolidation and low inflation. India's economic growth is among the highest in the world, helped by a reorientation of government spending towards needed public infrastructure. Amidst volatile international environment, Indian economy stands "as a haven of stability and an outpost of opportunity".

Sectoral Composition of Growth

A look at the sectoral composition of growth will give a better picture of the areas where the economy is doing well and which areas need more attention so that no sector becomes a drag and brings the overall GDP growth. According to Niti Aayog, GDP growth rate for agriculture, industry and services sectors realized during the 11th Plan period (2007-12) were 4.1 per cent, 7.7 per cent and 9.4 per cent against the growth target of 4 per cent, 10-11 per cent and 9-11 per cent respectively. The 12th Plan (2013-17) targets growth rates of 4 per cent for agriculture, 7.6 per cent for industry and 9.0 per cent for services, thereby aiming at 8 per cent growth in overall GDP. The annual growth rates of GVA by economic activity at constant (2011-12) basic prices for 2012-13, 2013-14 and 2014-15 (AE) are given in Table 2.5 below:

Table 2.5: Annual Growth Rate of GVA by Economic Activity at Constant (2011-12) Basic Prices

(Unit: Per cent)

No.	Item	2012-13*	2013-14#	2014-15@
1	Agriculture, forestry & fishing	1.2	3.7	1.1
2	Mining & quarrying	-0.2	5.4	2.3
3	Manufacturing	6.2	5.3	6.8
4	Electricity, gas & water supply and other utility services	4	4.8	9.6
5	Construction	-4.3	2.5	4.5
6	Trade, hotels, transport, communication and services related to broadcasting	9.6	11.1	8.4
7	Financial services, real estate, ownership of dwellings and professional services	8.8	7.9	13.7

No.	Item	2012-13*	2013-14#	2014-15@
8	Public administration & Defence & other services	4.7	7.9	9
	Total GVA at Basic Prices	4.9	6.6	7.5
	Industry (2-5)	2.4	4.5	5.9
	Services (6-8)	8	9.1	10.6

Source: Central Statistics Office (CSO)

Note: * 2nd Revised Estimates; # 1st Revised Estimates; @ Advanced Estimates as on 9th February 2015.

Quarter-wise Growth

It is necessary to have a look at the quarter-wise growth to know the short-term growth patterns and near term outlook. The quarter-wise growth in GVA at 2011-12 basic prices of three major sectors, viz. agriculture, industry and services is shown in Table 2.6.

Table 2.6: Quarter-wise Growth in GVA at (2011-12) Basic Prices for 2014-15 and 2015-16

	2014-15				2015-16			
	Q1	Q2	Q3	Q4	Q1	Q2	Q3	Q4
Agriculture and allied	2.3	2.8	-2.4	-1.7	1.6	2.0	-1.0	2.6
Industry	8.0	5.9	3.8	5.7	6.8	6.4	9.0	7.3
Services	8.6	10.7	12.9	9.3	9.0	9.4	9.4	9.0
GVA at basic prices	7.4	8.1	6.7	6.2	7.2	7.5	7.1	7.4
Net indirect taxes	8.5	10.8	5.3	11.4	13.4	10.2	9.7	10.4
GDP	7.5	8.3	6.6	6.7	7.6	7.7	7.3	7.7

In the third quarter of 2014-15, a GVA growth of only 1.7% was realized in the manufacturing sector, adversely affecting industrial growth. The IIP data shows that the production of consumer durables plummeted by more than 20 per cent during this quarter. However, the GVA growth in the manufacturing sector bounced back in the fourth quarter to reach 6.6%. The industrial sector growth in the third and fourth quarter of 2015-16 showed a growth of 9.4% and 7.3%, respectively. Table 2.6 also shows that there was a steady growth in India's services sector. The growth of indirect taxes has also been quite steady except in the third quarter of 2014-15 when the growth decreased to 5.3% from 10.8% in the second quarter.

Performance of Agriculture, Industry, and Services

The performance of the three major sectors of agriculture, industry and services is discussed below:

Agriculture

Agriculture is the mainstay of Indian economy. It is the most important occupation for a majority of the Indian families. More than 60% of India's land area is arable, making it the second largest country in the world in terms of total arable land.

Agriculture and allied sectors like forestry, logging and fishing accounted for 17% of the GDP and employed 49% of the total workforce in 2014. As the Indian economy has diversified and grown, with more focus on industry, services, telecommunication, the contribution of agriculture to GDP has steadily declined over the years, but it is still the largest employment source and plays a significant role in the overall socio-economic development of India. Crop yield per unit area of all crops has grown significantly due to the special emphasis placed on agriculture in the five-year plans and steady improvements in irrigation, adoption of new methods of farming and provision of agricultural credit and subsidies.

India ranks second in the world in farm output. It produces a large quantity of food grains such as cereals, millets, pulses, etc. A major portion of the foodstuff produced is consumed within the country. Besides agriculture with a commercial bias, subsistence agriculture with its emphasis on the production of food for the cultivator's family is widespread in India. But this situation is changing with many more and more farmers taking their produce to the market and switching to non-traditional crops like vegetables, flowers, etc. rather than merely growing wheat and rice.

A large proportion of India's export trade is based on the agricultural products, like jute, tea, tobacco, coffee, spices, and sugar. It helps in earning valuable foreign exchange. India is ranked seventh in terms of agricultural exports. In 2013, India exported agricultural products valuing around 39 billion dollars.

Indian export of agro and allied products stood at $32 billion in FY 14. In FY 15, it is was around $30 billion, lesser by around 10% than the year before. India exports several agriculture products, such as Basmati rice, wheat, cereals, spices, fresh fruits, dry fruits, buffalo meat beef, cotton, tea, coffee and other cash crops, particularly to the Middle East, Southeast and East Asian countries. It earns about 10 per cent of its export earnings from this trade.

India is the largest producer in the world of milk, jute and pulses, and also has the world's second largest cattle population with 170 million animals. It is the second largest producer of rice, wheat, sugarcane, cotton and groundnuts, as well as the second largest fruit and vegetable producer, accounting for 10.9% and 8.6% of the occupation for majority of main-workers in India. A large number of rural women are also engaged in agriculture. According to 2011 census, over 55% of the main workers in India are engaged in agricultural and allied activities.

A number of industries are agro based industries, such as jute, cotton, sugar, tobacco, etc. Raw materials for such industries are supplied from agricultural produce. India's inland water resources including rivers, canals, ponds and lakes and marine resources comprising the east and west coasts of the Indian ocean and other gulfs and bays provide employment to nearly six million people in the fisheries sector. India has the world's sixth largest fishing industry.

The farming methods in India have improved over the last two-three decades. Farmers are using farm implements, high-yielding varieties of seeds, chemical fertilizers, pesticides and insecticides. With this, the per-acre yield in cereals, pulses and vegetables has increased. But there is scope for further improvement as in many crops our yield is still much lower than that in the developed countries.

Genetically Modified Crops in India

In agriculture, genetically modified crops (GM crops) refer to plants whose DNA has been modified using genetic engineering techniques. The aim is to introduce a new trait to the plant which does not occur naturally in the species. Examples in food crops include resistance to certain pests, diseases, or environmental conditions, reduction of spoilage, resistance to chemical treatments, or improving the nutrient profile of the crop. Examples in non-food crops include production of pharmaceutical agents, biofuels, and other industrially useful goods, as well as for bioremediation.

According to the International Service for the Acquisition of Agri-Biotech Applications (ISAAA), India has the fourth largest area planted under genetically modified (GM) crops. Farmers in India planted a total 11.6 million hectares (mh) under transgenics in 2014, behind the corresponding areas for Argentina (24.3 mh), Brazil (42.2 mh) and the US (73.1 mh).

Initially, Indian farmers and consumers were averse to GM crops thinking that they are not good to grow and that GM foods are dangerous for health. However, most such fears have been removed, and India has quietly changed course on GM field testing. In 2015, eight Indian states approved field trials of GM crops, between them allowing tests that include transgenic rice, cotton, maize (corn), mustard, brinjal and chickpea.

Industry

India's industrial sector has continued to perform well in the wake of various reform measures undertaken by the government recently. According to Economic Survey 2015-16, the growth of the industrial sector comprising mining and quarrying, manufacturing, electricity, gas, water supply and other utility services, and construction was 5.9 per cent during 2014-15, as against 5.0 per cent during 2013-14. The growth was expected to strengthen further to 7.3 per cent for 2015-16. Within the industrial sector, manufacturing was expected to register a growth of 9.5 per cent. In the first nine months of 2015-16, the growth rate in terms of the IIP was 3.1 per cent as compared to 2.6 per cent in the corresponding period of 2014-15. The rate of growth of gross capital formation (GCF) in industry registered a sharp rise from (–) 3.7 per cent in 2013-14 to 3.6 per cent in 2014-15.

India's eight industries—coal, crude oil, natural gas, refinery, fertilizers, steel, cement, and electricity are core infrastructure-supportive industries. Together they have a weightage of about 38 per cent in the IIP. They registered a cumulative growth of 1.9 per cent during April-December 2015-16 as compared to

5.7 per cent during April-December 2014-15, showing a sharp decline. Measures are being taken to achieve higher growth in the coming and subsequent years.

According to Economic Survey 2015-16, in the corporate sector, the growth of sales has been contracting since the third quarter of 2014-15. There was a steep contraction in raw material expenses in the last four successive quarters since the third quarter of 2014-15. Year-on-year growth in interest expenses moderated during 2014-15 as compared to 2013-14. There was a further decline in the growth of interest expenses from 9.4 per cent in the first quarter of 2015-16 to 4.2 per cent in the second quarter of 2015-16. Other income, which was contracting since the third quarter of 2014-15, grew by 12.5 per cent in the second quarter of 2015-16. However, net profit grew by 19.8 per cent in the second quarter of 2015-16, after a contraction in three successive quarters. Growth in credit flow to the industrial sector, including mining and manufacturing, also slowed down in 2015-16 as compared to 2014-15. Growth of credit flow to the manufacturing sector was 2.5 per cent in the first three quarters of 2015-16 as compared 13.2 per cent in the corresponding period of 2014-15.

Services Sector

The services sector remains one of the key drivers of India's economic growth. The global growth of services in the post-global slowdown period (2010-14) at 2.5% was lower than the 3% per cent growth in the pre-global slowdown period (2001-08). India's services sector growth in the pre-crisis period was as high as 9.3 per cent which declined marginally to 8.6 per cent in the post-crisis period.

The global financial crisis adversely affected the services trade, with the Compound Annual Growth Rate (CAGR) of world commercial services exports during the post-crisis period going down to 6.4% as compared to 15% during the pre-crisis period. The corresponding growth for India in the pre-crisis and post-crisis periods was 30.1% and 7.5% respectively. In 2015, world's services trade growth was in negative territory from first quarter to third quarter as was also the case with India.

According to Economic Survey 2015-16, services sector growth in India went up to 10.3 per cent in 2014-15 from 7.8 per cent in the previous year, on account of higher growth in services sub-sectors like trade, repair, hotels and restaurants (10.7 per cent), financial services (7.9 per cent), public administration and defence (9.8 per cent), and other services (11.4 per cent). As per advance estimates given by Central Statistical Office), in 2015-16, the services sector registered a growth of 9.2 per cent (constant prices), mainly due to the lower growth of 6.9 per cent in public administration, defence and other services vis-à-vis 10.7 per cent growth achieved in 2014-15.

In India, the share of services in the Gross State Domestic Product (GSDP) varies across states. During 2014-15, the services sector accounted for 87.5% of Delhi's GSDP, followed by Maharashtra at 63.8%, with growth rates of 8.2% and 5.7% respectively. The services sector accounted for only 30.2 per cent of the GSDP in Arunachal Pradesh in 2014-15, which is the lowest in all the 23 states and union territories for which the data was available. In 2014-15, the total FDI equity inflows grew by 27.3% to US$ 30.9 billion, while FDI equity inflows to the services sector grew at a very high rate of 70.4% to US$ 16.4 billion. The rising trend was also continuing in the first seven months of 2015-16, with the FDI equity inflows in the services sector growing by 74.7% to US$ 14.8 billion, while total FDI equity inflows grew by 26.1% to US$ 27.1 billion.

As per data given by CSO, total revenue (exports plus domestic) of the Information Technology and Business Process Management (IT-BPM) sector for 2015-16 was expected to be US$ 143 billion including hardware and US$ 129 billion excluding hardware. The expected growth was 8.3% and 9.3%, including and excluding hardware, respectively over the previous year. Exports for both, including hardware and excluding hardware, was likely to record 10.2% growth to reach US$ 108 billion and US$ 107.6 billion, respectively. The domestic market, including hardware and excluding hardware was expected to grow at 2.9% to reach US$ 35 billion (excluding e-commerce) and 4.8% to reach US$ 22 billion over the previous year, respectively. E-commerce growth in 2015-16 was expected at 21.4% to reach US$ 17 billion.

What India needs is a targeted policy so that the issues are addressed properly and speedily and full potential in services sector is realized and higher dividend is received resulting in higher services growth and services exports, which in turn can help in pushing the economy to higher growth.

Investment

The Modi government has initiated various reform measures for simplification and rationalization of procedures and processes to attract more FDI. The impact thereof has started becoming visible. After the launch of the initiatives in September 2014, there was nearly 40 per cent increase in FDI inflows during October 2014 to June 2015 over the corresponding period of the previous year. According to Economic Survey 2015-16, during April-November 2015-16, total FDI inflows were US$ 34.8 billion as compared to US$ 27.7 billion during April-November 2014-15, showing a 26 per cent increase. The FDI equity inflows also increased from US$ 18.9 billion during April-November 2014-15 to US$ 24.8 billion during April-November 2015-16, showing a 31 per cent growth.

The priority area for the government has been the development of the infrastructure sector. A number of reforms have been initiated in this sector. Major infrastructure sectors such as power, road, railways, civil aviation, ports and telecommunication, performed better during 2014-15 as compared to 2013-14. During 2014-15, electricity generation was 1048.4 billion units as against a target of 1023 billion units, registering year-on-year growth of 8.4 per cent. Electricity generation during first three quarters of 2015-16 showed a growth of 4.4 per cent. A total of 3030 MW of grid-connected power generation capacity from renewable energy sources, like solar and wind, was added during this period, taking the cumulative generation capacity in India to more than 38,820 MW.

India's manufacturing infrastructure and capacity for innovation is poised to grow in a big way. New smart cities and industrial clusters are being developed in identified industrial corridors having connectivity, and new youth-focused programs through institutions dedicated to developing specialized skills are being launched.

A number of industrial corridors are being set up. A new National Industrial Development Authority (NIDA) is being created. It will coordinate, integrate and monitor the development of such corridors. Work on five smart cities in progress as a part of the Delhi-Mumbai Industrial Corridor: Dholera, Shendra-Bidkin, Greater Noida, Ujjain and Gurgaon. In the Chennai-Bengaluru Industrial Corridor, master planning for 3 new Industrial Nodes (i) Ponneri (TN), (ii) Krishnapatnam (AP), and (iii) Tumkur (Karnataka) is in progress. The north-eastern part of India is planned to be linked with other industrial corridors in cooperation with the government of Japan. Approval has been given to 21 industrial projects under the Modified Industrial Infrastructure Upgradation Scheme (MIIUS), wherein emphasis will be given on (i) use of recycled water, and (ii) central effluent treatment plants. With these programs of infrastructure development, there will be faster economic growth.

Captial Market

India's two major stock exchanges, Bombay Stock Exchange (BSE) and National Stock Exchange (NSE) had a market capitalization of US$ 1.71 trillion and US$ 1.68 trillion respectively as of February 2015, which, according to the World Federation of Exchanges, rank 11th and 12th largest in the world, respectively. A record 90 Indians with a combined net worth of $ 295 billion, featured in Forbes Billionaires List 2015, of which 28 made their appearance for the first time. India is also has fourth largest number of ultra-high-net-worth households that have more than 100 million dollars.

The infrastructure of Indian stock market has advanced and corporate governance has progressed faster than in many other emerging market economies. But in contrast to several developed countries and Asian economies, India's capital markets are still not very strong, which means that further reforms are needed to make India a world-class financial centre. Innovative products like securitized debt and fund products based on alternative assets are starting to break ground. There is need to increase domestic investors' knowledge regarding the merits and risks of capital market investing.

The Indian stock market turned out to be among the world's best performers in 2014 with the Bombay Stock Exchange (BSE) Sensex rising 29% from 21,140 on January 1 to 27,312 on December 19. However, for the year 2015, the S&P BSE Sensex ended 5% lower at 26,117.54 levels, while the Nifty50 closed 4% lower at 7,946.35 compared to their respective closing figures as on December 31, 2014.

According to *Business Standard*, the year 2015 was rather complicated for investors with corporate performance not meeting the market expectation. The momentum started to fade after the announcement of the budget in February 2015, and the actual earnings trajectory turned out to be flat or negative. Domestic politics also eluded market expectations as the dilution of political equity of the Modi government compounded following the state electoral results in Delhi and Bihar.

However, the silver lining for 2015 was the continued flows received by domestic institutions, particularly mutual funds, from retail participants who saw great opportunity in exploiting the valuation arbitrage created from the earlier run-up in the benchmark indices and large cap stocks. In year 2016 and 2017 equity market was likely to be driven more by real performance rather than by expectations. As of the end of June 2017, BSE was around 31000 and NSE around 9550.

Social Infrastructure

Social infrastructure plays an important role in improving the productivity of the population. Lack of access to affordable and quality health and educational facilities lowers the potential human capabilities. For fast and balanced economic development, we need to involve all sections of society, including the deprived and marginalized groups, like women and children, Scheduled Tribes, Scheduled Castes, the differently-abled and senior citizens.

Social infrastructure in India includes the education system in India, health care, the management of the education and health services in the country. The government looks after the social development in India by careful infrastructure planning and handling the social issues in close coordination with the states and agencies involved.

India has made considerable progress in education during the last two-three decades, but still there are inequalities in access and achievements across regions and populations. As per the Annual Status of Education Report (ASER 2014), the enrolment declined in government schools from 72.9% to 63.1% in rural areas. It was matched by a corresponding increase in enrolment in private schools.

There has been some improvement in the education of girls, as the Gender Parity Index (GPI) has become favourable at all levels of school education, except for Scheduled Caste students in higher education and Scheduled Tribe (ST) students at all levels of education, for which special efforts have to be made.

There is a need to improve the quality of education provided in schools to reverse the decline in enrolment in government schools and improve the educational outcomes in both public and private schools. An important contributor to improvement in the quality of education would be an increase in the percentage of qualified teachers. To foster education and skill development of its diverse population, including the marginalized sections, women and the differently-abled, and to provide quality health and other social services, the Government has identified the potential of technology platforms which can significantly improve efficiency in the system.

We need to upscale training and skill development to fill the skill gaps that exist in various productive sectors. Efforts are underway in this regard. For example, under the Pradhan Mantri Kaushal Vikas Yojana (PMKVY), aiming to offer 24 lakh Indian youth meaningful, industry-relevant, skill-based training, 4.38 lakh persons have successfully completed training throughout India.

Providing efficient health services in a vast and populated country like India is a big challenge. According to the World Bank's Universal Health Coverage (UHC) Index 2015, India's level of immunization is very low. High-risk patients like children and pregnant women require special preventive health care services.

Mission Indradhanush was launched in December 2014 with the aim of covering all those children who are either unvaccinated, or are partially vaccinated, against seven vaccine-preventable diseases by 2020. It has covered 352 districts of the country so far. The progress in sanitation has witnessed a spurt since the launch of the Swachh Bharat Mission. More than 122 lakh toilets have already been constructed in rural areas since the beginning of the Swachh Bharat Mission (Gramin). In order to improve the availability of drinking water in rural areas, the National Rural Drinking Water Programme initiated a new World Bank-supported project named the Rural Water Supply and Sanitation Project.

Employment Scenario

According to the fourth Annual Employment-Unemployment Survey conducted by the Labour Bureau during the period January-July 2014, the Labour Force Participation Rate (LFPR) was 52.5 for all persons. The LFPR of women is much lower than that of men in both rural and urban areas. A similar pattern is seen in the Worker Population Ratio (WPR). In our country, female participation in the labour force and employment rates are affected by economic, social and cultural issues. Moreover, the unpaid work by women is not accounted for by the conventional employment surveys. A special feature of the employment situation in India is the large share of informal employment and growth in informal employment in the organized sector. The share of informal employment in total employment has remained above 90% during the period 2004-05 to 2011-12. Central and State governments have initiated reforms in the labour markets to improve the situation.

Between 2004-05 and 2011-12, total employment in the country increased from 457.9 million to 472.4 million. The employment in the organized, non-agricultural sector, which includes all units with 10 or more workers if using power and 20 or more workers if not using power, increased from 28.8 million to 47.7 million, whereas employment in the unorganized sector rose from 185.4 million to 209.6 million. The organized sector employment stood at 6.3 per cent and 10.1 per cent respectively of total employment in 2004-05 and 2011-12. In absolute terms there were more who joined the unorganized sector's workforce than the number who entered the organized sector in this period. Even in 2011-12, as much as 86 per cent of workers in the private sector and 50 per cent in the public sector were in units that could be designated as unorganized, based on the size of employment.

Apart from agriculture, the sectors in which informal employment exists are manufacturing, construction and trade, both wholesale and retail.

Skill Development

In India a large number of workers are unskilled and they are mainly engaged in less productive informal sectors. According to the (National Skill Development Corporation (NSDC), there is a severe quality gap and shortage of trainers in the vocational education and training sector.

According to Economic Survey 2015-16, by the year 2017, the skill gap within the vocational training sector including both teachers and non-teachers will be to the tune of 2,11,000. The workforce requirement is projected to increase to 3,20,000 by 2022. The government has to take measures to bridge the skill gap in the vocational education and training sector to improve the employability of people. What we need is a multipronged policy approach to skill development.

In 2015 Prime Minister Narendra Modi launched a project named Skill India Campaign which included the launch of the National Skill Development Mission (NSDM) and unveiling of the new National Policy for Skill Development and Entrepreneurship 2015. The Mission has been developed to create convergence across sectors and States in terms of skill training activities. Further, to achieve the vision of 'Skilled India', the NSDM would not only consolidate and coordinate skilling efforts, but also expedite decision-making across sectors to achieve skilling at scale with speed and standards. It will be implemented through a streamlined institutional mechanism driven by Ministry of Skill Development and Entrepreneurship (MSDE). The main institutional mechanisms for achieving the objectives of the mission have been divided into three tiers, which will comprise a Governing Council for policy guidance at apex level, a Steering Committee and a Mission Directorate (along with an Executive Committee) as the executive arm of the Mission. Mission Directorate will be supported by three other institutions: National Skill Development Agency (NSDA), National Skill Development Corporation (NSDC), and Directorate General of Training (DGT)—all of which will have horizontal linkages with Mission Directorate to facilitate smooth functioning of the national institutional mechanism. Seven sub-missions have been proposed initially to act as building blocks for achieving overall objectives of the mission. They are: (i) Institutional Training, (ii) Infrastructure, (iii) Convergence, (iv) Trainers, (v) Overseas Employment, (vi) Sustainable Livelihoods, (vii) Leveraging Public Infrastructure.

According to the document on the framework of implementation of the NSDM, India is currently facing a severe shortage of well-trained, skilled workers. It is estimated that only 2.3% of the workforce in India has undergone formal skill training as compared to 68% in the UK, 75% in Germany, 52% in USA, 80% in Japan, and 96% in South Korea. In our country, even large sections of the educated workforce have little or no job skills, making them largely unemployable. Therefore, we must focus on scaling up skill training efforts to meet the demands of employers and drive economic growth. Over 54% of the country's population is below the age of 25, allowing it with an opportunity to provide a skilled workforce to fill the expected shortfall in the ageing developed world. If the mission is implemented in letter and spirit, India will be able to utilize this demographic dividend to take the economy to a high growth path.

Standard Training and Assessment Reward (STAR) scheme is likely to create a widespread positive impact on the skills ecosystem in India. Besides, under the Pradhan Mantri Kaushal Vikas Yojana aiming to offer 24 lakh Indian youth meaningful, industry-relevant, skill-based training, 4.38 lakh persons have successfully completed training throughout.

Human Development

India's human development index (HDI) for 2015 is 131 out of 188 countries. It puts India in the group of countries classed as "medium" in the list, as opposed to "low" in the 1990s. Factors like an increase in life expectancy and mean years of schooling in the past 25 years have contributed to this improvement. Other factors which have not let India come out better are regional disparities in education, health and living standards within India—or inequality in human development.

However, there is a prediction that things will improve further in future. According to Yuri Afanasiev, UN resident coordinator for India, "The success of national development programmes like Skill India, Digital India, Make in India and Beti Bachao Beti Padhao, aimed at bridging gaps in human development, will be crucial in ensuring the success of Agenda 2030. These programmes, and the long-running affirmative action measures, illustrate the government's commitment to identifying and mapping human development deficits, as well as taking action to achieve the Sustainable Development Goals."

According to the HDI Report (2016), "Between 1990 and 2015, India's life expectancy at birth increased by 10.4 years, mean years of schooling increased by 3.3 years and expected years of schooling increased by 4.1 years." India's Gross National Income, or GNI, per capita increased by about 223.4% during the period 1990 to 2015. This was mainly due to India adopting market reforms, attracting investment and devoting more resources to social development in the sectors of health and education.

HDI is an average measure of basic human development achievements in a country. Therefore, it "masks inequality in the distribution of human development across the population at the country level. "The 'loss' in human development as pointed out by HDI Report (2016) due to inequality is given by the difference between the HDI and inequality adjusted HDI, or IHDI. As the inequality in a country increases, the loss in human development also increases. So if India's HDI score for 2015 is 0.624, when this value is discounted for inequality, the HDI falls to 0.454, a loss of 27.2% "due to inequality in the distribution of the HDI dimension indices." We removing the inequalities should be at the top of our agenda for development if we are to show a perceptible improvement in our HDI ranking.

Table Inequality Adjusted Human development Index for 2015 is given in Table 2.7 below:

Table 2.7: Inequality-adjusted Human Development Index BRICs Countries (2015)

Country	Human Development Index (HDI)	Inequality adjusted (HDI)	Overall Loss (%)
Russia	0.804	0.725	9.8
Brazil	0.754	0.561	25.6
China	0.738	NA	NA
South Africa	0.666	0.435	34.7
India	0.624	0.454	27.2

Source: UN Human Development Report (2016)

Table 2.7 shows that India has the lowest rating among the BRICS countries. India's inequality-adjusted HDI is slightly better than South Africa but worse off than all other countries in this group. India's overall loss tot is lower than that of South Africa but higher than other members in the group. China being a communist country, inequality-adjusted HDI does to apply to it. India ranks lowest among BRICS nations: Russia (49), Brazil (79), China (90), South Africa (119) and India (131).

Technology will play a crucial role as an enabler of inclusiveness and provider of efficient services by preventing leakages. The government has introduced the gamechanging potential of technology-enabled Direct Benefits Transfers (DBT), namely the JAM (Jan Dhan-Aadhaar-Mobile), Number Trinity solution, which offers possibilities for effectively targeting public resources to those who need them most, and including all those who have been deprived in multiple ways. The subsidy regime has been overhauled to move to Aadhaar-DBT. This has paved the way for expenditure rationalization and is ensuring the removal of fake and duplicate entities from beneficiary lists, bringing substantial savings of public money. Aadhaar seeding in the beneficiaries' databases of the following six DBT schemes has seen significant rise as of the end of calendar year 2015:

(i) LPGDBTL—54.96%;
(ii) MGNREGS—54.10%;
(iii) Pradhan Mantri Jan Dhan Yojana (PMJDY)—42.45%;
(iv) Public Distribution System (Ration Card)—38.96%;
(v) National Social Assistance Programme (NSAP)—24.31% and
(vi) Employees' Provident Fund (EPF) Scheme—17.55%.

Riding on the technological platform that the Digital India Programme is expected to provide 'integration of various beneficiary' databases with Aadhaar, and appropriate process re-engineering is likely to bring substantial saving of effort, time and cost, and at the same time ensure full traceability of flow of funds from the Government to the beneficiary.

Climate Change and Sustainable Development

Climate change is a serious problem nowadays and what we need is sustainable development, rather than unbridled development in utter disregard of environment, which may prove catastrophic. Two landmark international events were held in the year 2015: (i) The climate change agreement under the United Nations Framework Convention on Climate Change (UNFCCC) adopted by 195 nations in Paris in December 2015, with the aim of keeping the rise in global temperature well below 2°C, which will set the world towards a low carbon, resilient and sustainable future; and (ii) The adoption of the Sustainable Development Goals (SDGs) in September 2015 which replaced the State of the Economy: An Overview 29 Millennium Development Goals (MDGs) and set the development agenda for the next 15 years with the aim of guiding the international community and national governments on a path of sustainable development.

India is wide awake to the challenges of climate change and environmental pollution. As one of the signatories of the climate change agreement under UNFCCC, it is committed to reduce the emission of greenhouse gases despite being at the threshold of fast economic development which calls for more and more utilization of resources.

The developing countries, including India, know that to destroy and overexploit natural resources will raise the short-term growth rate but the polluted environment will adversely affect the long-term future growth and the quality of life of the future generations as they will have smaller natural resource base and poor quality of environment.

The policymakers are going for growth strategy of no net loss of environmental assets so as to ensure sustainable development. If environmental resources are destroyed or depleted in one area, an equal or greater amount of environmental resources are replenished or regenerated to mitigate the effect.

Sustainable development requires a greater integration of economic and social progress and preservation of the environment. It requires to follow and support the Rio+20 Outcome Document which emphasizes the "rights-based, equitable, and inclusive processes that enhance sustainability at global, regional, national, and local levels".[8]

Indian Government has initiated a number of measures to ensure that the development is not environmentally destructive. It has been actively looking for clean technology and energy efficiency in its endeavor to pursue a low-carbon growth model. At several fora, Prime Minister Narendra Modi is reported to have shared his vision for "sustainable economic growth without compromising on environmental safety." Within a month of coming to power, the government initiated a multi-sector debate on reinvigorating the sacred River Ganges, which is arguably one of India's most polluted water bodies.[9]

Included in the measures initiated are an attempt to provide access to modern energy to the maximum number of people; enhancement of energy efficiency; protection of environment by increasing the share of renewable energy; cleaning the fossil fuel sources of energy.

Measures have also been taken to provide access to clean water supply to households including safe drinking water, improving water use efficiency and reducing water loss; conserve and manage water sources judiciously and efficiently; stopping the contamination and pollution of surface water and overuse of groundwater; managing wastewater; ensuring improved sanitation and hygiene; promoting green buildings; improving public transport in bigger cities; encouraging green cover and open spaces in cities; ensuring resource use; improving infrastructure of non-motorized transport; and promoting environmentally sound waste disposal, treatment, and recycling, among others. There is more and more use of biodegradable packings and carry bags instead of polythene.

Low Carbon Development

The concept of low carbon development was given in the UNFCCC adopted in Rio de Janeiro in 1992. It denotes low-emission development strategies (LEDS) and encompasses forward-looking national economic development plans and strategies that follow low-emission and/or climate-resilient economic growth (OECD, IEA 2010).

India's National Action Plan on Climate Change (NAPCC) highlights the co-benefit approach for low carbon activities that could in turn ensure energy security, reduced local pollution, and increased access to energy through distributed and decentralized forms of energy systems. At the fifteenth session of the Conference of Parties (COP-15) to the UNFCCC, India and China, along with their BASIC partners (Brazil and South Africa) made a significant contribution in drafting the 'Copenhagen Accord'. Under this Accord, India and China have pledged to reduce the emissions intensity of their GDP by 20–25% and 40–45% respectively by 2020 in comparison to their respective 2005 levels.[10]

The key question in this regard is whether India can bring about low-carbon development in its economic mix. It is not easy to readily shift to renewable energy because of a number of reasons. One, that such resources aren't enough in our country. For example, nuclear energy is not sufficient to cater to our huge demand. Although India entered a civil nuclear deal with America in 2005, there have been several roadblocks, and the generation of nuclear energy as envisaged is still a distant dream. Second, other renewable sources of energy such as solar energy, wind energy, tidal energy have not been developed in sufficient quantities in India. Electric energy has not been harnessed in a big way to meet the ever-increasing demand.

The shift to renewable energy in India requires huge capital investments. The country would need to depend on foreign fund inflows and technology assistance, especially with wind, solar and natural gas utilization to bear the burden of cost. A crucial step in realizing the objective of adopting low carbon development would be the reduction of cost of wind and solar storage technologies with technical progress. There is much substance in what Jeffrey David Sachs, an American economist and Director of the Earth Institute at Columbia University, says:

> We cannot combine growth and climate safety using existing technology. The only choice is a massive shift of technology. Some of those technologies exist but are not deployed. India at a very small cost could be deploying more renewable energy technologies than it does at present. Hydropower from Nepal and the Himalayas can be channelized and used. Globally, I feel, by 2030, new automobiles should be zero CO_2 emitting vehicles. They should be electric, fuel cell, advances biofuels but not internal combustion engines of the traditional sort. That is only 16 years from now. The question is moving as aggressively as possible towards right technologies.

Indian government has made climate change planning a priority, but not much headway has been made so far. The need to adopt ways and means fast is accentuated by the fact that India has, in recent years, experienced multiple extreme weather events, like devastating floods in Uttarakhand and Kashmir—areas which had never witnessed floods before, record-breaking heat, severe drought, etc. It is therefore necessary to prepare for and respond to new risks that are emerging across new regions.

Future Outlook of Indian Economy

India is one of the fastest growing economies in the world today. It is going through a good growth phase. It coped with the pressure of global financial crisis much better than other economies of the world excluding China. The inherent strong fundamentals that the Indian economy possesses were visible during that period. The recovery of global economy has been quite slow. The European debt crisis following the global slowdown made recovery even slower. India too felt the impact in terms of weaker exports due to decreasing global demand for its goods and services. Much has happened during the last few years, including the reduction of oil prices in the international market from around US$ 90 a barrel to around US$ 50 a barrel, the slowing down of the Chinese economy, and the change of central government in India and with it the changes in policy. The current decade is expected to play a crucial role in determining how Indian economy performs in future and whether the country goes on the right track to become a global power which many experts have predicted.

Dun & Bradstreet in "India 2020 Economy Outlook", states that the forecasts for the current decade can help us to prepare for the future challenges and seize opportunities that lie ahead. The report is segmented into five sections covering forecasts for key macroeconomic variables, growth prospects for some of the Indian states, potential growth drivers of the economy, major policy initiatives that would facilitate India's economic journey and growth concerns during the current decade.[11]

According to the above outlook, India is expected to be more than US$ 5 trillion (current market price) economy by 2020. The services sector will expand rapidly. The demographic dividend India is enjoying at present will lead to significant growth in private final consumption expenditure. A strong growth in domestic savings will support domestic investment. Although consumption will continue to be the major contributor to GDP during the current decade, its share is likely to decline gradually due to significant increase in the share of domestic investment.

The key drivers of the Indian economy in the current decade will be investments in physical, social and agricultural infrastructure. These investments will enable the economy to achieve 'inclusive growth' over the current decade. Infrastructure investment and an increasing working-age population are expected to bring a higher GDP growth by 2020. There will be an increased focus on infrastructure development in new townships and rural areas which will lead to higher economic growth.

India is a federation of states. Broadly speaking, the growth of the country is the sum total of the growth of the individual states. The so-called BIMAROU states (Bihar, Madhya Pradesh, Rajasthan, Odisha and Uttar Pradesh) have been a drag on India's economic growth owing to their large population and widespread poverty. These states, however, have vast natural resources and manpower and if these resources are used judiciously, they can contribute significantly to India's economic growth. According to "India 2020 Economy Outlook":

> Growth in the BIMAROU states is expected to gain traction, especially during in the second half of the current decade; their GSDP (gross state domestic product) contribution to incremental GDP would expand to 28% during FY16-FY20 as compared to 24% during FY11–FY15. Four of the five BIMAROU states expected to see double digit average growth during the current decade. Per capita income of Bihar and MP expected to almost triple by 2020, although remaining below national average.[12]

The developed states like Punjab and Haryana will continue to drive the country towards higher growth. States like Maharashtra, Gujarat and Andhra Pradesh will play a significant role in taking India's economy to strong growth. The central and state governments must create growth-enabling policies in agriculture, industry, services, and finance, generate more employment, and bring low interests regime to boost production to create an atmosphere of higher growth.

The International Monetary Fund (IMF) has forecast that India will be world's fastest growing major economy with 7.3% growth in 2015 and 7.5% in 2016, and expressed optimism about its future prospects ahead of China, which the IMF expects will grow 6.8% this year, followed by 6.3% in the next. The near-term growth prospects in India also remain favourable. The decrease in the current account deficit has lowered external vulnerabilities. The faster-than-expected decline in inflation has created space for considering modest cuts in the nominal policy rate, but the real policy rate needs to remain tight to contain inflation in the medium term as upside risks to inflation still remain, especially when GST has been implemented and because of higher tax on many items, there can be a rise in prices.

Table: 2.8: Global Outlook of Economic Growth

Country	Growth projected in July 2015	Growth projected in July 2016
India	7.3	7.5
China	6.8	6.3
Brazil	–0.3	–0.1
South Africa	1.4	1.3
Russia	–3.8	–0.6
U.S.	2.6	2.8
Eurozone	1.5	1.6
World Economy (IMF Projections)	3.1	3.6

Table 2.8 shows that India's economy will have a slightly higher rate of growth than that of China in 2015 and 2016, and much higher growth rate than the economies of other developing countries like Brazil, South Africa, and Russia. In comparison to India's growth rate of 7.3% and 7.5%, the US economy will grow only by 2.6% and 2.8% respectively. The Eurozone will grow only by 1.5% and 1.6% in 2015% and 2016% respectively. The world economy will grow by 3.1% and 3.6% for these years.

According to IMF, fiscal consolidation is necessary for India and it should be more growth-friendly. There should be tax reforms and a reduction in subsidies. India will also need to undertake structural reforms in education and labour to improve the country's competitiveness and increase productivity.

The priorities for India according to IMF should be easing supply constraints in the energy, mining and power sectors, transitioning to market-based pricing of natural resources to boost investment, addressing delays in the implementation of infrastructure projects and improving policy frameworks in the power and mining sectors. IMF has also stressed the need for enhancing financial sector regulations, increasing provisioning and strengthening debt recovery practices. If right policy measures are taken Indian economy will show robust growth in the coming years.

Notes

1. BRICS is the acronym for an association of five major emerging national economies: Brazil, Russia, India, China and South Africa. The BRICS members are all developing or newly industrialized countries, but they are distinguished by their large, fast-growing economies and significant influence on regional and global affairs.
2. CIA Fact Book, *Indian Economy*. The World Factbook, produced for US policymakers and coordinated throughout the US Intelligence Community, marshals facts on every country, dependency, and geographic entity in the world. We share this information with the people of all nations in the belief that knowledge of the truth underpins the functioning of free societies. The Fact Book provides information on the history, people, government, economy, energy, geography, communications, transportation, military, and transnational issues for 267 world entities.
3. Kelegama, Saman and Parikh, Kirit (2000). *Political Economy of Growth and Reforms in South Asia*. Second Draft. Sam Staley (2006).
4. Sam Staley (2006). "The Rise and Fall of Indian Socialism: Why India embraced economic reform."
5. *Economic Survey* 2004-2005 (p. 161), published by the Ministry of Finance, Govt. of India.
6. "Economy and the Plan—An Overview". Annual Report of Niti Aayog, 2014-15.
7. *India Today*. New Delhi, December 15, 2015.
8. The document called "The Future We Want" adopted at the UNFCCC Rio de Janeiro, Brazil (1992).
9. http://www.huffingtonpost.com/entry/sustainable-development-india
10. http://www.teriin.org/projects/locci/
11. http://www.dnb.co.in/India2020economyoutlook/e
12. *Ibid.*

3

Features of Indian Economy

India is the seventh-largest country by area, and the second-most populous country in the world (with over 130 crore people). In 2015, the Indian economy was the world's seventh largest by nominal GDP and third largest by Purchasing Power Parity (PPP). Following market-based economic reforms in 1991, India became one of the fastest-growing major economies and is considered a newly industrialized country. However, it continues to face the challenges of poverty, inadequate infrastructure, unemployment, regional disparities, etc.

According to the International Monetary Fund (IMF), the Indian economy in 2015 was nominally worth US$ 2.183 trillion and US$ 8.027 trillion by PPP. However, the country ranks 140th in the world in nominal GDP per capita and 129th in GDP per capita at PPP. Since 1991, it has slowly moved towards a free-market system by emphasizing both foreign trade and direct investment inflows. India's recent economic model is largely capitalist. The country has been a member of WTO since 1 January 1995.

As of 2011, India's 486.6 million workforce was the world's second-largest. The service sector makes up 55.6% of GDP, the industrial sector 26.3% and the agricultural sector 18.1%. India's foreign exchange reserves were US$ 379.3 billion as on 19 May 2017. Foreign exchange remittances which stood at US$ 62.7 billion in year 2016—the largest in the world—contributed to its economy by 25 million Indians working in foreign countries.

In 2011, India was the world's tenth-largest importer and the nineteenth-largest exporter. Averaging an economic growth rate of 7.5% for several years prior to 2007, India has more than doubled its hourly wage rates during the first decade of the new millennium. As of 2010, the country is placed 51st in global competitiveness, but it ranks 17th in financial market sophistication, 24th in the banking sector, 44th in business sophistication, and 39th in innovation, ahead of several advanced economies.

India's consumer market, world's ninth-largest, is expected to become fifth-largest by 2030. Driven by growth, India's nominal GDP per capita has steadily increased from US$ 329 in 1991, when economic liberalization began, to US$ 1,265 in 2010, and was estimated to increase to US$ 2,110 by 2016. According to a 2011 PricewaterhouseCoopers report, India's GDP at PPP could overtake that of the United States by 2045. During the next four decades, India's GDP is expected to grow at an annualized average of 8%, making it potentially the world's fastest-growing major economy.

The key factors in India's development have been young and rapidly growing working-age population; growth in the manufacturing sector because of rising education and engineering skill levels; and sustained growth of the consumer market driven by a rapidly growing middle class. However, as per World Bank, for India to achieve its economic potential, it must continue to focus on public sector reform, transport infrastructure, agricultural and rural development, removal of labour regulations, education, energy security, and public health and nutrition.

Despite fast development in many fields in India, its economy does not come in the category of developed economies. Indian economy at present has features of a developing economy, and a fast emerging economy. The main features of India's economy are discussed below.

Low Per-Capita Income

India's per capita income (nominal) was US$ 1,497 in 2013. The country was ranked at 120th out of 164 countries by the

World Bank. India's per capita income on PPP[1] basis was US$ 5,350, and the country was ranked 106th by World Bank.

Various states of India have significant disparities in their average income.[2] Bihar is by far the poorest state in India. Other low income states are Uttar Pradesh, Jharkhand, Jammu & Kashmir, Assam, Manipur and Nagaland. Goa had the highest income. Other high income states include Delhi, Haryana, Sikkim, Maharashtra, Tamil Nadu, Gujarat and Kerala.

In 2006, the National Council of Applied Economic Research of India completed a survey of 153 million people who belonged to middle income group. It used World Bank's definition of middle income families. Meyer and Birdsall and Tim Light used a different survey and estimated the number of middle Income population to be about 70 million in 2009-10. These groups as well as the World Bank estimated in their 2011 reports that if India's economy continues to grow per projection, the country's middle income group would double by 2015 over 2010 levels, and grow by an additional 500 million people by 2025. This would make it, with China, the world's largest middle income market.[3]

The IMF said it trimmed its 2016 forecast for India by one percentage point primarily because consumers were short of cash and could not spend much for some months after demonetization in November 2016.

As compared to other countries, income inequality in India is relatively small as measured by Gini-coefficient. India had a Gini coefficient of 32.5 in years 1999-2004. Its nominal Gini index rose to 36.8 in 2005, while real Gini after tax remained nearly flat at 32.6.[4]

It is widely acknowledged that India is one of the fastest growing economies in the world. According to *The Wall Street Journal*, India's growth slowed to 6.6% in 2016 from 7.6% in 2015. As per IMF's latest World Economic Outlook, China's economy grew by 6.7% in 2016. The fund expects India's expansion to bounce back to 7.2% in 2017 and accelerate to 7.7% in 2018. China, meanwhile, is projected to continue decelerating, to 6.5% in 2017 and 6.0% the year after.[5]

Infrastructure Development in India

Infrastructure is divided into two categories: (i) Physical infrastructure, and (ii) Social infrastructure.

Physical infrastructure refers to road, electricity, banking, transportation, communication, insurance, energy, etc. This infrastructure is related to development process and it is closely linked with GDP. Social infrastructure refers to education, health, housing, drinking water and sanitation. Social infrastructure is related to human resource development and it is not directly or indirectly related to GDP.

Infrastructure development is closely associated with economic development, as higher investment in infrastructure leads to greater output. India has relatively poor infrastructure which has proved a major roadblock in its fast development. Infrastructure bottlenecks are not only a medium-term worry, but can affect the country's near-term growth as well. It has been found that infrastructure companies always invest cautiously in India, partly because different states have different laws and taxation regimes. However, with the introduction of Goods and Services Tax (GST), this problem is likely to be addressed.

The primary reason for India's slow infrastructure development is poor implementation. The India Economic Summit 2014, Ministry of Statistics and Programme Implementation's 342nd flash report showed that out of 727 infrastructure projects on its monitor, 317 had no information on commissioning dates. Of the remaining 410 projects that had a schedule, only five were ahead of time, 123 were on time, and 282 were delayed.

India needs increased public infrastructure investment which will raise output in the short-term by boosting demand and in the long-term by raising the economy's productive capacity. In a sample of advanced economies, it was estimated that an increase of 1 percentage point of GDP in investment spending raises the level of output by about 0.4 per cent in the same year and by 1.5 per cent four years after the increase. In the emerging economies, the spending has to be more to augment the process of development.

In addition, the boost to GDP a country gets from increasing public infrastructure investment offsets the rise in debt, so that the public debt-to-GDP ratio does not rise. In other words, public infrastructure investment could pay for itself if done correctly. This is the reason the union government is pushing for PPP projects for public infrastructure projects to keep the debt to GDP ratio low.

Predominant Agriculture Sector

Another feature of India's economy is the predominance of agriculture sector. In India, agriculture provides employment to around 50 per cent of the workforce. Agriculture and allied sectors contribute only about 18 per cent of Gross Domestic Product (GDP). However, the share of income in agriculture is considerably less than the share of employment in agriculture which clearly reflects the relatively low productivity per labour unit in the agricultural sector. Predominance of agriculture is explained from the viewpoint of sectoral composition of national income and occupational pattern.

In contrast, the developed countries live mainly upon agriculture and extractive industries, like mining, fisheries and forests. In such countries the percentage of people actively engaged in agricultures ranges from 3 to 11 only.

Deficiency of Capital

Another feature of Indian economy is deficiency of capital. Like other developing countries, India is lacking in capital and thus cannot take up many projects of development or spend on building infrastructure to trigger development. Lack of capital does not allow it to introduce the latest technologies. Thus, the economy is slow to reach the level of technological advancement and remains internationally uncompetitive.

The CSO's Quick Estimates for 2009-10 placed gross domestic savings at 33.7 per cent of the GDP at current market prices. With private-sector savings more or less static, it was the savings of the public sector that went up from a revised level of 0.5 per cent in 2008-09 to 2.1 per cent in 2009-10. In the investment sphere the ratio of gross investment came down from

38 per cent in 2007-08 to around 36.5 per cent in 2009-10. Thus, the level of savings is very low and capital formation rate is also low. The major reasons of low level of capital formation in India have been (i) low inducement to invest, and (ii) low propensity and capacity to save.

In India, the capital availability per person is very low which results in low productivity and low per capita income. Low per capita income again results in low savings, low investment and low capital formation.

Some experts are of the view that considering the increasing foreign direct investment (FDI) inflow, India is not likely to be deficient in capital in future, at least not to the extent it was about five years ago.

In 2015, there was FDI of US$ 55 million to India. The Modi government has been rightly focusing on attracting more FDI. India's saving rate generates around 80% of what it needs to realize and sustain a GDP growth rate of 8%. But since the current saving rate is inadequate for financing that kind of financial growth, it has to depend on FDI. However, FDI as a source of capital in the present circumstances is not reliable for India because the global political situation is not as favourable as it was about ten years ago. There are many destabilizing factors like isolationist policy of the new American President, Donald Trump; the Brexit vote whereby, UK will no longer be a member of the European Union; China's unilateral and destabilizing actions like land reclamations by creating artificial islands in the busy South China Sea, and America's warnings to China to stop it; the continuing battles of Iraqi soldiers (backed by the US forces) with ISIS in civilian and military arenas; and Pakistan-China alliance against India, among others.

India cannot rely on foreign investments alone to propel its growth. India's domestic financial savings need to increase and become stable for the long-term financing of the economy. For this the country needs to restructure its financial sector so that the agents that allocate capital well are tapped and there is a flow of domestic financial savings for higher economic growth.

The Improving Level of Technology

India is not a technologically advanced country even more than half a century after achieving independence. In many parts, old methods of farming are still being used. Food production is consequently lower than that in the developed countries. Many industries lack in modern technology and there is low production.

But it would be wrong to say that India is technologically backward now. As a matter of fact, there has been technological upgradation across sectors. Significant achievements have been made in nuclear and space science, electronics and defense. The government is committed to making Science & Technology (S&T) an integral part of the socio-economic development of the country.

India has the third largest scientific and technical manpower in the world. It has 162 universities which together award 4,000 doctorates and 35,000 postgraduate degrees. The Council of Scientific and Industrial Research (CSIR) runs 40 research laboratories that have made some significant achievements. In the field of Missile Launch Technology, India is among the top five nations of the world.

S&T is now being used as an effective instrument for growth and change in India. It is being brought into the mainstream of economic planning in the major sectors, viz. agriculture, industry and services. The country's resources are used to derive maximum output for the benefit of society and improvement in the quality of life. About 85 per cent of the funds for S&T come directly or indirectly from the government. The S&T infrastructure in the country accounts for more than one per cent of the GNP.

S&T in India is entering new frontiers. There is visible advancement in the fields of atomic energy, space exploration, electronics, oceanography, biotechnology, IT, telecom, e-governance, as well as in primary, secondary and tertiary or services industries. There has been phenomenal development in the field of telecommunication in India during the last three decades. Mobile telephony has undergone a sea change due to Information Technology revolution in India. The use of internet has enabled people to make transactions of various types online. These include booking railway or air travel tickets, transferring money from one account into another, sending or receiving details required to buy or sell something, paying taxes or bills, and much more.

The era of modernization in India is thus viewed in several sectors, especially in the agriculture sector. Modern implements are being widely used. Use of fertilizers, pesticides, insecticides, and high-yielding varieties of seeds are being used by an increasing number of farmers. Even genetically-modified crops are being raised in many parts of India.

New technologies in the healthcare management systems which consist of electronic data storage, data maintenance and exchange are being adopted. The health care management process is much more streamlined in India and is effective.

However, it will be an exaggeration to say that India is a technologically advanced country. There are many fields in which either technology is not being used at all or old technology is being used. The country is at a stage where absorption of new technology is underway. Absorption of new technology have two major requirements: (i) availability of sufficient amount of capital, and (ii) training of adequate number of personnel. India still lacks in both. That's why adoption of new technology is taking time in India. It would be fair to say that Indian economy is marked by an improving level of technology.

Industrial Backwardness and Development

India had` been an industrially-backward country for over five decades after achieving independence. British rule had drained India of its wealth and left India without any industry worth the name. On the eve of independence, Indian economy was backward from industrial point of view, and there was deficiency of basic and heavy industries. Among heavy industries, there was Tata Iron and Steel industry. The production of machines in the country was negligible. Statistics reveal that in 1947 total production of iron & steel was just 9 lakh tonnes.

After independence it was an uphill task to set up more and more industries. Following a mixed economy and encouraging private industries paved the way for industrial development but it took a long period of time. There were other causes of industrial backwardness, like (i) environmental factors (terrain, relief, heavy rainfall, tough weather), (ii) economic (low resource development, bureaucratic bottlenecks, tough laws), (iii) cultural (low literacy, less skilled labour, low industrial temperament, low entrepreneurial initiative and poverty), (iv) infrastructural (shortage of basic infrastructure, like transport, communication, power generation, raw material, etc., and (v) demographic (large size of population, high rate of population growth, ethnic tension, regional conflicts, etc.).

However, there has been noticeable industrial development during the last two decades, especially after the economic reforms introduced during the early 1990s. These reforms brought foreign competition, led to privatization of certain public sector industries, opened up sectors hitherto reserved for the public sector and led to an expansion in the production of fast-moving consumer goods. In recent years, Indian cities have continued to liberalize, but excessive and burdensome business regulations remain a problem in some cities, like Kochi and Kolkata.[6] The manufacturing sector, in addition to mining, quarrying, electricity and gas, together account for about 28% of the GDP and employ 18% of the total workforce.

Under the policy of economic liberalization the license system for starting new industries was simplified. Maximum emphasis is now being given to the development of infrastructural facilities. States are granting concessions to attract capital and locate industries in backward areas.

Since India is a vast country and nearly 60% of its people live in villages, it is necessary to develop rural industries. Accordingly 76 items have been exclusively reserved for rural industries. These cover eight major heads of industries: (a) power loom, (b) handloom, (c) Khadi, (d) village, (e) sericulture, (f) handicraft, (g) coir industry, and (h) remaining industries. The 8th Five Year Plan proposed to give more emphasis to rural industrialization.

As of now, Indian economy is no longer an industrially backward economy but an industrially developing economy.

Low Enterprise and Initiative and the Changing Scenario

In India, enterprise and initiative are not high. Many people are inhibited by the social system which denies opportunities for creative faculties. In many parts of India, people adhere to orthodox views. The atmosphere in general is not favourable to enterprise, experimentation and innovation, owing to the force of custom, the rigidity of status, absence of intellectual curiosity and distrust of new ideas.

However, things are changing fast because of the following reasons: Firstly, with the spread of education, old customs and reservations are yielding place to new thinking and openness. Secondly, great advancement in communication technology in recent years has made people to get quick information about useful things. Thirdly, globalization has improved people's way of thinking and made them adopt new ideas. Fourthly, the government has brought a slew of measures which are changing the scenario. Under "Ease of Doing Business", the following concessions have been given, among others:

(i) Mine protecting projects are exempted from requirement of compulsory afforestation and Forest Rights Act (FRA) certificate for grant of forest clearance.

(ii) Industrial sheds and educational institutions have been exempted from environmental clearance.

(iii) Online submission of applications for environment/forest/wildlife clearances for transparent and expeditious decision-making.

(iv) NOC/Consent to establish is not required for getting an industrial electricity connection for setting up new industries and projects.

(v) All Sub-registrar offices have been digitized and records have been integrated with Land Records Department.

(vi) Department of Environment (DERC) has rationalized LT and HT tariff, thereby allowing LT connections up to 150 KVA.

(vii) Registration of VAT is being done without the need for field verification by VAT inspector through Delhi VAT Seva App.

(viii) One-stop access for investors to know about licenses/ approvals required from government agencies.

(ix) User-friendly features such as payment through net-banking, credit and debit cards, status tracking, SMS alerts, and help desk support have been enabled.

With these measures, new entrepreneurs will be encouraged to start new businesses.

The government has launched a Startup India campaign that is based on an action plan aimed at promoting bank financing for start-up ventures to boost entrepreneurship and encourage startups with jobs creation in the country. It was first announced by Prime Minister Narendra Modi in his 15 August 2015 address from the Red Fort. The focus of the campaign is on restricting the role of the states in policy domain, get rid of license raj and remove hindrances like the ones found in land permissions, foreign investment proposals, and environmental clearances. It was organized by the Department of Industrial Policy and Promotion (DIPP). Prime Minister Narendra Modi unveiled the action plan for startups in the country. He announced a self-certification scheme in respect of nine labor and environment laws and said there will be no inspection during the first three years of launch of the venture. Addressing the first conference of start-up entrepreneurs, Modi announced an action plan to boost such ventures which are seen as key to employment generation and wealth creation. The main features of the scheme are enumerated below:

(i) There is provision for self-certification to reduce the regulatory burden on startups and provide single window clearance.

(ii) A startup India hub will be created as a single point of contact for the entire startup ecosystem. This will enable knowledge exchange and access to funding.

(iii) A startup will be able to set up by just filling up a short form through a mobile app and online portal. There will be provision for mobile app through which startups can be registered in a day.

(iv) The government will also ensure a legal support for fast-tracking patent examination at lower costs. This will promote awareness and adoption of Intellectual Property Rights (IPRs) by startups and help them protect and commercialize IPRs.

(v) The government will set up a fund with an initial corpus of ₹ 2,500 crore and a total corpus of ₹ 10,000 crore over four years to provide funding support to startups. The fund would be managed by private professionals taken from the industry. Life Insurance Company (LIC) will be a co-investor in the fund.

(vi) A National Credit Guarantee Trust Company will be created for which there will be adequate budgetary allocation of ₹ 500 crore per year for the next four years.

(vii) At the time of launching the scheme, investments by venture capital funds in startups were exempt from this law. The same will be extended to investments made by incubators in startups.

(viii) There will be tax exemption to startups announced for three years.

(ix) There will tax exemption on investments above fair market value.

With all these measures, the enterprise initiative in India will improve in the time to come. Industrial sector will get a big boost.

Poverty and Income Disparities

Majority of people in India have low levels of income and live in poverty. Poverty in India is in fact a historical reality. Under the British colonial rule, poverty in India intensified, peaking in 1920s. Famines and diseases killed millions of people. After India's independence in 1947, there was some improvement as mass deaths from famines were prevented. Rapid economic growth since 1991, has led to sharp reductions in extreme poverty in India.[7] But even those who are living just above poverty line, like marginal farmers, landless labour and casual workers are living a fragile life.

According to World Bank's 2014 poverty calculation methodology and purchasing power parity, the world had 872.3 million people below the new poverty line, of which 179.6 million people lived in India. As of 2014, 58% of the total population was living on less than $ 3.10 per day. According to the Modified Mixed Reference Period (MMRP) concept proposed by World Bank in 2015, India's poverty rate for period 2011-12 stood at 12.4% of the total population, or about 172 million people. Rampant poverty means lack of educational and health facilities, poor hygienic living conditions, criminal environment, and lack of infrastructural facilities, which affect their life.

There are glaring income disparities in India. As of November 2016, India was the second-most unequal country in the world. The richest 1% of Indians own 58.4% of wealth. The richest 10% of the Indians own 80.7% of the wealth. This trend is going in the upward direction every year, which means the rich are getting richer and the poor are getting poorer. Thus, a large number of people in India are poor and a lot of government spending goes towards the uplift of the poor. In a country which is already short of capital, this is a drag and a big obstacle in India's march towards being a developed nation.

According to Global Wealth Report-2016 of Credit Suisse Research Institute, India is the second most unequal country in the world with the top one per cent of the population owning nearly 60% of the total wealth.[8] Inequalities of income distribution are to be observed both in the rural and urban sectors of the economy. Inequalities of income are to be seen in the form of unequal distribution of land in the agricultural sector and concentration of economic power in non-agricultural sector.

Growing income inequality in India has negatively impacted poor citizens' access to education, healthcare and other amenities necessary for good living. People working in unorganized sectors are the worst sufferers of economic inequality. Their wages are low, they have to work for long hours. They still lack basic services like drinking water and sanitation. One cannot expect them to participate meaningfully in economic development.

Reduction in Poverty: We must take note of the fact there has been reduction in poverty in India. The World Bank's Global

Monitoring Report for 2014-15 on the Millennium Development Goals says India has been the biggest contributor to poverty reduction between 2008 and 2011, with around 140 million or so lifted out of absolute poverty. Since the early 1950s, successive Indian governments have been initiating various schemes to help the poor acquire self-sufficiency in food production. One of the main reasons for record decline in poverty is India's rapid economic growth rate since 1991. Another reason proposed is India's launch of social welfare programs like Mahatma Gandhi National Rural Employment Guarantee Act (MGNREGA) and Midday Meal Scheme in government schools. The benefits of overall economic development in the country has percolated to poor people, albeit slowly and not to the desired level.

Unemployment and Underemployment

Unemployment is a situation when capable workforce willing to do job does not get work. Unemployment is a bane of most countries but its impact on developing economies like India's is more damaging. The developed countries like America which have unemployment are able to absorb this negative factor due to their large size of economy, other better indicators like higher level of exports, strong currency, better resource utilization skill, and also because they have far fewer constraints. But the developing countries which have low production are more affected by unemployment.

In India where a large population is barely able to subsist, unemployment immediately leads to poverty, hunger and low standard of living. From 1983 till 2011, unemployment rates in India averaged 9 per cent reaching an all-time high of 9.4 per cent in December 2010 and a record low of 3.8 per cent in December 2011.[9] In India, the unemployment rate measures the number of people actively looking for a job as a percentage of the labour force. The number of unemployed people in India decreased to 39963 thousand in 2009 from 39974 thousand in 2007. As can be seen there was no perceptible improvement in the unemployment situation during this period.

The more recent figures are not encouraging either. Unemployment rate in India shot up to a five-year high of

5 per cent in 2015-16, with the figure significantly higher at 8.7 per cent for women as compared to 4.3 per cent for men, says a report by Labour Bureau. According to the Fifth Annual Employment-Unemployment Survey at all-India level, about 77 per cent of the households were reported to be having no regular wage/salaried person.[10]

Since the size of India's population is very large, even a lower percentage of unemployment means millions of unemployed persons. Moreover, different forms of unemployment occur in India. People waiting for their first job come under frictional unemployment. Such kind of unemployment exists among people who are young or have just completed their education. Then there is seasonal unemployment, i.e. the one that is specific to certain seasonal industries like farming and tourism. There is disguised unemployment which means more people are engaged on a work than are required. Such employment is prevalent in agriculture sector in India. The worst type is the structural unemployment which occurs when there is a change in the structure of an economy. It is long-term unemployment and can be caused by various factors, including machines replacing humans, and change in consumer behaviour.

There are many causes of high unemployment in India. Not only the size of India's population is large, but the rate of growth of population is also very high. It is very difficult to create more and more jobs to accommodate such a huge population. A large number of people who seek employment lack skill and are not well-versed with the use of technology. According to India Skills Report launched in the 3rd CII National Conference on Skill Development, 34% were found employable out of about 1,00,000 candidates. The report not only captured the skill levels of talent pool but also brought out the hiring estimates across major Industry sectors in the country. As per the report's findings, the coming year would not see bullish hiring in any of the sectors. With the spread of education more and more people seek white collar jobs but such jobs are not available in number, so many remain unemployed for years. Because of the global economic conditions, Indian employers have posted less number of jobs in this job portal.

Employment is a driver of economic growth while unemployment is a drag. Realizing this, the Government has taken several steps to decrease the unemployment rates such as launching the Mahatma Gandhi National Rural Employment Guarantee Scheme (MGNREGS) which guarantees a 100-day employment to an unemployed person in a year.

The Government has also launched Skill Development Programme which will enhance the employability of those who get training to acquire some technical skill. The Government has also initiated National Career Service Scheme whereby a web portal named National Career Service Portal (www.ncs.gov.in) has been launched by the Ministry of Labour and Employment (India). Through this portal, job-seekers and employers can avail the facility of a common platform for seeking and updating job information. Both private vacancies and contractual jobs available in the government sector are available on the portal.

Agriculture is the most labour-absorbing sector of the economy. In recent years, there has been a decline in the dependence of population on agriculture, partly because of disguised unemployment. Some of the surplus labour in agriculture has moved to either secondary or the tertiary sector. In the secondary sector, small scale manufacturing is the most labour absorbing. In case of the tertiary sector, various new services are now being created, like biotechnology, Information Technology and so on. The Government has taken steps in these sectors for the disguised unemployed people.

All these measures will improve employment situation in the country but it will take some time, and much will depend how far India is able to control its population growth.

Standard of Living

Large sections of India's population have a low standard of living. They have no access to basic facilities like education, healthcare, and do not have money for minimum nutrition intake. The protein intake of average Indians is roughly half of that in developed countries. Around 30 per cent of Indian population suffers from malnutrition. They have no means to participate in the growth of the economy. Quantity of goods available per head of population is meager and the quality is invariably indifferent.

Standard of living in India varies from state to state. For instance, there is widespread poverty in rural areas of India, where medical care is either very basic or is unavailable, while cities boast of world class medical establishments. Similarly, there are mud houses in many villages, while cities have dwelling units will all the facilities of modern living. There is also occupational disparity which has a bearing on people's standard of living. Farmers, especially small and marginal farmers, are barely able to meet the basic needs of life. The same is the case with labour class. People in the salaried class live a mediocre life but are better placed than the small farmers and labour. Businessmen, upper middle class and the elites have a good standard of living and enjoy the luxuries of life.

But things are changing as India is marching towards being a developed economy. Being one of the fastest growing economies in the world, with a growth rate of 7.6% in 2015, India is marching fast towards becoming a large and globally important consumer economy. According to Deutsche Bank research estimates there are nearly 300 million people in India for all middle class.[11] A recent report says that if current trends continue, India's share of world GDP will significantly increase from 7.3 in 2016 to 8.5 per cent of the world share by 2020.[12]

According to National Council of Applied Economic Research (NCAER), India's middle class population was estimated to be 267 million in 2016, and by 2025-26, the number of middle class households in India is likely to more than double from the 2015-16 levels to 113.8 million households or 547 million individuals. Another estimate put the Indian middle class as numbering 475 million people by 2030.[13] It is estimated that average real wages will quadruple between 2013 and 2030.[14] All this will have a positive effect on the living standard of people in India.

Large Population and its Impact on Development

Large size of population in India has been a major factor in influencing its economy. India is the second largest populated country in the world having population of 238 million in 2001 and 1138 million in 2011. The country's population was estimated to be 13425 million as on June 2017. This large size and high rate of growth have negatively impacted India's economy.

It has reduced our rate of capital formation and diminished the availability of capital per head, reducing the productivity of its labour force. As a consequence, the income of labour has remained low and their capacity to save has been very low, adversely affecting capital formation.

The standard of living is determined by per capita income. The factors affecting per capita income in relation to population growth equally apply to the standard of living. A regular increase in population in India has lead to an increased demand for food products, clothes, houses etc., but as their supply cannot be increased due to the shortage of raw materials, skilled labour and capital, etc., the standard of living has been low or has not risen to the expected level.

With a rise in population, the number of jobseekers has been increasing regularly and for whom it may not be possible to provide employment. Despite all efforts to generate more employment many people have remained unemployed. Unemployment, underemployment and disguised employment are common features in India.

Increased population means more mouths to feed which, in turn, creates pressure upon the available stock of food. This is the reason there has been food scarcity in India, causing undernourishment of the people, lowering their productivity, and making India go for import of food grains straining the country's foreign exchange resources.

High rate of growth of population has adversely impacted India's agriculture. With land-man ratio getting disturbed, per capita availability of land for cultivation declined from 1.1 acre in 1911 to 0.6 acre in 1971 in our country which makes the size of holdings very small. According to NABARD, decreasing landholding has been the biggest challenge in Indian agriculture.

The decreasing landholding due to population growth has lowered the farmers' capacity to invest in agriculture leading to low yield. The small size of holdings makes adoption of modern technology means of irrigation and mechanization impossible. During the last 40 years our acreage has remained 140 million ha but the number of farmers has more than doubled despite the fact that many people engaged in agriculture have shifted to other occupations. There are many areas in our country which have remained uncultivable because of excessive salinity in soil or other deficiencies. These can be made cultivable by treating the soil.

A report from 2008 claimed India's population is growing faster than its ability to produce rice and wheat.[15] According to a review by World Bank, India can easily feed its growing population, plus produce wheat and rice for global exports, if it can reduce food staple spoilage, improve its infrastructure and raise its farm productivity to the level achieved by other developing countries such as Brazil and China.[16]

In the period July 2010 to June 2011, Indian agriculture accomplished an all-time record production of 85.9 million tonnes of wheat, a 6.4% increase from a year earlier. Rice output in India hit a new record at 95.3 million tonnes, a 7% increase from the year earlier.[17] There was an increase in the production of lentils and many other food staples. Indian farmers thus produced about 71 kilograms of wheat and 80 kilograms of rice for every member of Indian population in 2011.

In the year 2013, India exported $39 billion worth of agricultural products, which made it the seventh largest agricultural exporter worldwide, and the sixth largest net exporter.[18] This was done despite high local demand owing to a large population. India is the fastest growing exporter of agricultural products over a 10-year period, its $39 billion of net exports is more than double the combined exports of the European Union (EU-28).[19] It has become one of the world's largest suppliers of rice, cotton, sugar and wheat. India exported around 2 million metric tonnes of wheat and 2.1 million metric tonnes of rice in 2011 to Africa, Nepal, Bangladesh and other regions around the world.

However, when the monsoon is poor, there is a decline in food production and with a large population, and consequent high demand, the prices of food items tend to increase. India needs to control its population growth if it is to become a developed country.

Human Resources in India

It is however remarkable to note that despite having a large and increasing population, Indian economy has progressed well during the past three decades or so. The constraints of population size have not been able to stop it from being one of the fastest growing economies in the world.

Human resources are of utmost importance and they play an important role in the economic development. One of the features of developed countries like USA, UK, France and Japan is that they have good human resources, i.e. people with skill and scientific temperament. The situation in developing countries is reverse. A large number of their people are not skilled. Literacy rate is not to the desired level, and people are engaged in social problems rather than contributing to the economic development.

For a long time after achieving independence in 1947 India has been grappling with large population, low literacy rate, lack of technical skill, conservatism, orthodoxy, superstition, gender discrimination, poverty, exploitation of the poor, etc. India's human resources were thus not able to contribute meaningfully to economic development.

But things are changing and India is marching towards fast economic development in which our human resources are playing an important role. Literacy rate which was 18.33 per cent in 1951 reached 74.4 per cent as per 2011 census. Male literacy rate was 82.14 per cent and female literacy rate was 65.46 per cent. Indian people are gaining skills and a large number of them are tech-savvy. Technology is increasingly being used in manufacturing, trade, services, and communication.

There has been an Information Technology (IT) revolution in India. IT is an industry consisting of two major components: IT services and business process outsourcing (BPO). According to NASSCOM, IT sector increased its contribution to India's GDP from 1.2% in 1998 to 7.5% in 2012. The sector aggregated revenues of US$ 147 billion in 2015, where export revenue stood at US$ 99 billion and domestic revenue at US$ 48 billion, growing by over 13%. Prime Minister Narendra Modi started 'Digital India' project to give IT a secured position inside and outside India. He also called for a change in the old mindset of brain drain to brain gain in order to make the most of the huge human resource available with India. He said that India's biggest strength is its human resource with 65% of our population below the age of 35 years. In the coming years, India is only going to get younger, and we should use this wealth to evolve our development model.

According to Finance Minister Arun Jaitley, India's human resource as a part of service sector is the largest contributor to the country's economy. Services sector in India covers a wide variety of activities such as trade, hotel and restaurants, transport, storage and communication, financing, insurance, real estate, business services, community, social and personal services, as well as services associated with construction. This sector accounts for more than 60 per cent of output, about 30 per cent of exports and 30 per cent of total employment. India's share in global exports of commercial services increased in 2013 to 3.2 per cent from 1.2 per cent in 2000. Its ranking among the leading exporters in 2013 was sixth. India's major services exports are in computer services (45.8 per cent share), other business services (18.8 per cent share) including professional and consulting services (10.2 per cent share), technical and trade-related services (7.8 per cent share), R&D services (0.8 per cent share), travel (11.8 per cent share), transport (11.5 per cent share), and financial, insurance and pension services (5.8 per cent share). The sector contributed around 66.1 per cent of its Gross Value Added growth in 2015-16, thereby becoming an important net foreign exchange earner and the most attractive sector for Foreign Direct Investment inflows.[20] "India has the human resource to manage and contribute towards Indian economy which differentiates it from other developed countries," Jaitley said.

Human Development in India

India was placed at 130th position in the 2015 with 0.609 score in Human Development Index (HDI) among the 188 countries, and was in the medium human development category. In the 2014 report, the country's rank was 135 with a score of 0.586. Improvement in India's 2015 HDI from the previous year was attributed to rise in life expectancy and per capita income. India's life expectancy at birth increased to 68 years in 2014 from 67.6 in the previous year and 53.9 in 1980. Gross National Income (GNI) per capita increased to US$ 5,497 in 2014 from US$ 5,180 in 2013 and US$ 1,255 in 1980. India's Gross National Income (GNI) per capita increased by about 338 per cent between 1980 and 2014. The expected years of schooling remained stagnant at 11.7 since 2011. The mean years of schooling at 5.4 also did not change from 2010 to 2015. Gender Development Index (GDI) value of India was 0.795 in 2014. The female HDI value for India was 0.525 in contrast with 0.660 for males. In Gender Inequality Index (GII), India was placed at 130th position with value of 0.563 out of 155 countries as on 2014.

The top three countries in HDI are: Norway (1st rank), Australia (2nd) and Switzerland (3rd). India's neighbours had the following ranks in 2015: Sri Lanka (73 rank), China (90), Bhutan (132), Bangladesh (142), Nepal (145), Pakistan (147), and Afghanistan (171). BRICS nations have the following rank: Russia (50), Brazil (75), China (90), South Africa (116) and India (130).

The HDI is an average measure of basic human development achievements in a country measured by UNDP. It is an average of long-term progress in three basic dimensions of human development, viz. a long and healthy life, access to knowledge and a decent standard of living.

Demographic Dividend in India: Experts feel that in the near future, India will be the largest individual contributor to the global demographic transition. The International Monetary Fund Working Paper 2011 found that a substantial portion of the growth experienced by India since the 1980s is attributable to the country's age structure and changing demographics.[21] The U.S. Census Bureau predicts that India will surpass China as the world's largest country by 2025, with a large proportion of those in the working age category.[22] Over the next two decades the continuing demographic dividend in India could add about two percentage points per annum to India's per capita GDP growth.[23]

With a massive population of over 1.3 billion people, out of which nearly 400 million are between ages 10-24, India's demographics is a cause for envy to many nations which have an ageing population. However, to realize this massive potential demographic advantage, India needs to invest heavily in its human capital. In such a scenario, the emphasis should be given to entrepreneurship so that the country becomes a nation of job givers, not job seekers.

Dependence on Imports

India has an unfavourable balance of trade with many countries, which means that we import more goods than export. The country has to heavily depend on imports of many items. Armed forces of the country also depend on foreign imports. This is because there is advancement in warfare and high technology is used by countries like the US, France, and Russia which sell sophisticated military equipment to India. Besides, a number of consumer goods such as oil, medicines, electrical machinery, organic sewing machines, bicycles, etc. are imported from other countries.

In the pre-Independence period, India was forced to supply raw materials to Britain and import the manufactured goods. Industrialization at home was not permitted. The indigenous handicrafts suffered owing to competition from the British manufactured products as well as British traders located in India and abroad.

India had to change the colonial pattern of trade after achieving independence. In order to increase in the production capacity of the country heavy plants and machinery were imported. This was in the nature of development import. In order to maintain the productive capacity of the country, the objects like machines were imported, which was in the nature of maintenance import. These two types were necessary for our country to put it on the path of the economic development.

In the beginning India also needed to import lots of food grains because of low yield in our country and also to contain the inflation in these consumer goods. India was thus heavily dependent upon the imports. In comparison, exports were quite small. There was a pressure on the balance of trade. The imports were inelastic, and so the country needed to boost its exports to fight with the pressure of the foreign debt. In 1949-50, India's exports were worth ₹ 485 crore and the imports were worth ₹ 617 crore. The country had negative trade balance of ₹ 132 crore. With the passage of time both exports and imports increased and the trade deficit also increased. India has had a continuous trade deficit so far except only two years, viz. 1972-73 and 1976-77.

Post-liberalization, the devaluation of rupee and convertibility of Indian rupee in current account tried to create a favourable environment. There was some success initially, but trade deficit increased in the subsequent period. During the financial year 2015 16 (April-January), India's total export was US$ 217.7 billion, while total import during the same period was US$ 324.5 billion. The trade deficit stood at US$ 106.8 billion.

The merchandise trade had a 13.9% share in India's GDP in 1991-92. It rose to 27% in 2004-05, and further went up to 41% in 2013-14. In 2014-15, merchandise trade was 37.1% of GDP. In 2013, India's share in world merchandise exports was 1.7 per cent, and the aim was to take it to 4% of world trade in next five years.

Although India's imports exceed its exports, India has done well in maintaining and in case of some items, in increasing exports. According to India exports forecast 2016-20, exports in India were expected to be US$ 22,000 million by the end of the last quarter of 2016-17. In the long-term, India's exports are projected to be around US$ 28,900 million in 2020.

Regional Disparities

One of the major problems facing India's economy is that there are regional variations among the country's different states and territories in terms of infrastructure, business and employment opportunities, per capita income, poverty, education, health care facilities and socio-economic development. Some states have better infrastructure, more industry, less unemployment, more per capita income, higher literacy rate and better opportunities for development than others.

There are inter-state, intra-state and rural-urban disparities in India. Inter-state disparities or regional disparities refer to a situation where a per capita income, standard of living, consumption situation, industrial development, etc. are not uniform in different parts of a given region.

Intra-state disparities refer to disparities within the state. Intra-regional disparities are indicated by allocation of resources, quality of governance, agrarian structure, income, consumption patterns and estimates of poverty.

Rural-urban disparities are marked by lack of basic infrastructure in rural area, such as roads, electricity, water and sanitation facilities, schools and hospitals, etc. In contrast, these facilities are mostly available in urban areas. It is because of the absence of such facilities that rural areas lag behind urban areas in terms of the basic indicators of development—poverty, illiteracy, unemployment, etc.

Included in the better placed category of states in India are Tamil Nadu, Kerala, Maharashtra, Punjab, Gujarat, and West Bengal. The less developed states are Bihar, Madhya Pradesh, Rajasthan and Uttar Pradesh.

The difference in growth rate between the forward and backward states was 3.3% (6.3% and 3.0%) during 1990-91 to 1997-98.[24] Per capita income in India varies drastically. As of 2010, New Delhi had a per capita Income of US$ 3,020, whereas Bihar's per capita Income was paltry US$ 445.

These disparities have led to an unbalanced development of the country. Poor performance by some states in various parameters of development has not let India march towards fast economic development and therefore it is still placed in the category of developing countries.

Since India's independence, the Indian economy has been premised on the concept of planning, carried through the Five-Year Plans, developed, executed, and monitored by the Policy Commission up to 2013 and NITI (National Institution for Transforming India) Aayog since 2014. The Eleventh Plan completed its term in March 2012 and the Twelfth Plan is currently underway. Prior to the Fourth Plan, the allocation of state resources was based on schematic patterns rather than a transparent and objective mechanism, which led to the adoption of the Gadgil formula in 1969. Revised versions of the formula have been used since then to determine the allocation of central assistance for state plans. More assistance was given to the less developed states to bring about faster development and remove the hindrances that have been slowing down their growth.

The Five-Year Plans attempted to reduce regional disparities by encouraging industrial development in the interior regions. They also provided for the creation of adequate infrastructure to trigger growth. The aim was also to spread literacy and reduce gender gaps in literacy, make more use of technology, controlling the growth population, making efficient use of scarce resources to ensure rapid growth, combining public and private support to increase employment, reducing poverty, ensuring availability of primary health care facilities and other basic necessities, empowering the socially disadvantaged classes like Scheduled Castes, Scheduled Tribes and other backward classes, and developing self-reliance in terms of agriculture, among others. This has brought socio-economic development in the poor states, but since the more advanced states are better placed to benefit from them, with infrastructure like well developed ports, urbanization and an educated and skilled workforce which attract manufacturing and service sectors, regional imbalances have tended to persist in India.

The central government and state governments of backward states are also trying to reduce the disparities by offering tax holidays, cheap land, etc. and focus more on sectors like tourism, which can become a source of growth and are faster to develop than other sectors.[25] Therefore, though Indian economy has grown steadily over the last two decades, its growth has been uneven if we compare social groups, economic groups, geographic regions, and rural and urban areas.

India's Natural Resources and their Utilization

One major difference between the developed and the developing countries is that while the former utilize their resources judiciously, the latter lack in proper management of their resources. This makes a critical difference in the economies of both type of countries. Not every country is bestowed with rich mineral resources, but the developed countries which possess such natural resources have utilized them for their overall growth, for the development of people, securing employment and their livelihood, eradication of poverty and stabilizing their economies.

India is blessed with vast arable land and a good climate to grow every type of major crop in cereals, pulses, vegetables and fruits. We also have large water sources in the form of rivers, streams, lakes, etc. But our per-acre yield is less than that of most of the developed countries, and even some developing countries like China and Brazil. This is because a large number of our farmers are still using old methods of farming. Being poor, they cannot afford to buy inputs like high-yielding varieties of seeds, insecticides, pesticides, fertilizes, etc. They don't have modern farm implements and no provision to store their yield properly after harvest, which results in wastage of food grain. Transportation and marketing of yield is also not easy. When the rainfall is either inadequate or untimely, the yield is even lower. We have not developed our water resources to the potential.

People are making increasing use of technology in India but in many areas, particularly the rural areas, technology transfer is either lacking or is not proper. Rural artisans are not organized in India to get technology commensurate with their existing tools and skills. There is little technology that the poor can afford and handle. That's why development has not reached grassroots levels. An ideal organizational structure for better and efficient use of technologies is still at the development stage.

At one point, countries like Australia, Brazil, Canada, and South Africa were on par with India in terms of utilization of natural resources. Today, these countries have moved far ahead in economic development. Our slow progress is largely attributed to underutilization of our natural resources. For example, bauxite—a raw material for making aluminum—still remains underexplored and underutilized in India. Our country is blessed with the fourth-largest bauxite deposits in the world, about 3,000 million tonnes, but unfortunately we have still not witnessed the opening of any large bauxite mine.

There have been a series of mining scams in various ore-rich states of India, which generated controversy, relating to encroachment of forest areas, underpayment of government royalties, and conflict with tribals regarding land-rights. There was spill-over of the effects of legal mining into problems such as naxalism and the distortion of Indian democracy by mixed political and mining interests gained international attention.[26] The countries which have trade relations with India watched the situation closely.

All the 90 iron ore mines in Goa were shut down in 2012 after a government-led investigation into their operation and its impact on the environment. The ban in Goa followed a similar move in the Southern state of Karnataka in 2011. Although the ban was lifted subsequently, the recovery in the sector was gradual as the restrictions (2011-14) reduced India's iron ore exports by around 85% (100 m tonnes). It was not just the loss to miners, but thousands of ancillary industries associated with iron ore mining also suffered badly. Thousands of people lost their jobs. The biggest loss was to the economy which was over ₹ 25,000 crore.

We need a proper structure to create linkages between production, processing of materials and marketing. We have to lay more emphasis in research and development (R&D). We also need to make sure that technology is not limited to mere expansion of traditional technology but also adopting latest technology. This adoption should be widespread, not confined to some areas. We should also look for new technologies that help in increasing output, reducing capital requirement and saving foreign exchange.

Our public distribution system has many shortcomings. Corruption, poor quality of entitlements, wrong demarcation of below and above poverty households, bogus cards, poor performance of fair price shops are major drawbacks in the system followed by inadequate access to FPS, rural and urban bias, regional variability, too poor economic condition of beneficiaries to buy entitlements, unawareness of beneficiaries and FPS owners about PDS schemes, mortgaging of ration cards and logistics problems during transporting entitlements from central pool to FPS.[27] Due to these shortcomings people are deprived of the supply of quantity food grains in sufficient quantity. Even with an abundance of rich mineral reserves and resources, we are not able to capitalize them for our economic strength.

We must find ways and means by which our resources, including mineral resources are explored, mined and utilized in such a way that there is fast development across various sectors and in all the regions of the country. Wastage or overuse of resources has to be stopped, and people of all strata of society are benefited. We should also make sure that the sources like water and forests are replenished so that there is no shortage thereof in future and the cause of environment is also served.

Conclusion

India's economy is no longer underdeveloped. Today it is one of the fastest developing economies in the world with an average growth rate of approximately 7% over the last two decades. It is the seventh largest in the world by nominal GDP and the third-largest by purchasing power parity (PPP). The country is classified as a newly industrialized country, one of the G-20 major economies, and a member of BRICS. India's economy became the world's fastest growing major economy from the last quarter of 2014, replacing the People's Republic of China.

With sustained economic development, per capita income is increasing every year. There has been perceptible improvement in infrastructure development in India. Roads, bridges, marketing centres, etc. have come in large number. Power generation has increased, and services at airports, ports and other centres have improved. The agricultural sector is the largest employer in India's economy though its contribution to GDP has declined over the years (17% in 2013-14). However, India ranks second worldwide in farm output.

Gross Fixed Capital Formation in India has also steadied for the last three-four years. According to Trading Economics macro models, it was expected to be ₹ 8,350 billion by the end of the quarter ending 31st March 2017. In the long-term, India's Gross Fixed Capital Formation is projected to trend around ₹ 11,000 billion in 2020, according to our econometric models.[28]

The adoption and use of new technology is also being made more widely now than two decades ago. Industry, communication, health care, transportation, trade, banking, insurance, education, etc. are making use of technology and there is efficiency and accuracy in the delivery systems. India's service sector is one of the fastest growing in the world with annual growth rate of above 9% since 2001. It contributed 57% of GDP in 2012-13. India became a major exporter of IT services, BPO services, and software services with US$ 167 billion worth of service exports in 2013-14. It is also the fastest-growing part of the economy. The IT industry continues to be the largest private sector employer in India. India is also the fourth largest start-up hub in the world and had over 3,100 technology start-ups in 2014-15. The Industry sector has held a constant share of its economic contribution (26% of GDP in 2013-14). India's automobile industry is one of the largest in the world. It had an annual production of 21.48 million vehicles in FY 2013-14. India has US$ 600 billion worth of retail market in 2015 and one of world's fastest growing e-commerce markets.[29]

Poverty and income disparities have continued to exist in India, but due to poverty alleviation schemes and programmes by successive governments, millions have been lifted out of poverty. The benefit of economic development has reached the people, but slowly, and much more needs to be done in this regard.

Unemployment situation has not much improved in India. Although there is generation of more and more employment due to expansion of industry, services and trade, high growth rate of population, many people remain jobless for a number of years. With such a situation, it is not possible to control unemployment merely by creating more jobs. The government is encouraging self-employment so that there is less demand for jobs. The large size and high growth rate of population have also hindered India's march towards fast development. Large size of population is also India's demographic advantage because we have rather young population and the dependency ratio is low. But this demographic advantage will become demographic dividend only if there is more skilled population.

People's standard of living in India is also improving. Increase in literacy rate, spread of communication, including through social media, reduction in gender gap, influence of modern thinking, giving up of orthodoxy and superstitions have had a positive effect on the life of people.

India has an unfavourable balance of payments, but according to *Economic Survey* 2016-17, given the high elasticity of India's real export growth to global GDP, exports could contribute to higher growth, by as much as one percentage point in future and even more. India's exports appear to be recovering, based on an anticipated increase in global economic activity. This is expected to continue due to fiscal stimulus after Trump took over as the President of America.

IMF's January 2017 update of its World Economic Outlook forecast projected an increase in global growth from 3.1 per cent in 2016 to 3.4 per cent in 2017, with a corresponding increase in growth for advanced economies from 1.6 per cent to 1.9 per cent. This augurs well for India's exports. Further, a strong export recovery would have broader spillover effects to investment.

Steeper contraction in imports, compared to exports, during the first half of 2016-17 led to a sharp decline in trade deficit. From US$ 195.7 billion in 2012-13, US$ 147.6 billion in 2013-14, US$ 144.9 billion in 2014-15, US$ 130.1 billion in 2015-16, India's trade deficit decreased to US$ 49.5 billion in the first half of 2016-17. Despite slowing services exports, the decline in merchandise trade deficit helped improve the position of net exports of goods and non-factor services in the national accounts.

Regional imbalances have tended to continue in India. There are differences in per capita income, literacy rates, health and education services, levels of industrialization, etc. between different regions in the country. There are inter-state disparities, intra-state disparities, as well as rural urban disparities.

Concerted efforts are required to reduce these disparities. We need to identify backward areas in the country and give special attention to their development by preparing special plans and models of development suitable for such areas and allotting sufficient funds to implement those plans. There should be greater investment—public as well as private sector—in the backward areas. There is also need for ensuring equitable distribution of the gains of development to all the regions without any prejudice so that a balanced development takes place in the country. It is pertinent to mention here that regional disparities exist not just in India, but in many other countries and are a global phenomenon. In case of India such disparities are more pronounced and need to be reduced.

The long-term growth prospective of the Indian economy is positive because of its young population, low dependency ratio, healthy savings and investment rates, and increasing integration into the global economy. India's economy has the potential to become the world's 3rd-largest economy by the next decade, and one of the largest economies by mid-century. According to IMF, the Indian economy is the "bright spot" in the global landscape. India also topped the World Bank's growth outlook for 2015-16 for the first time with the economy having grown 7.6% in 2015-16 and was expected to grow over 7% in 2016-17.

India's industrial and foreign trade policies and FDI norms have had a deep influence on manufacturing. The Department of Electronics and Information Technology (DeITY), under the Industrial Approval Policy, has tried to cut the red-tape for electronics manufacturing by measures such as abolishing industrial licensing and eliminating reservation for public-sector enterprises. Permitting 100 per cent foreign investment in the electronics sector also seeks to expand the manufacturing sector in India. As the situation stands today, there is need for further reforms to make the situation more progressive and sustainable.

Many schemes and initiatives have been launched by the government to meet this vision. The Make in India initiative was started to give a boost to India's manufacturing sector cut down on red-tape. Stand-up India is aimed to promote entrepreneurship among women and dalits and involves loans ranging from

₹ 10 lakh to ₹ 1 crore for setting up any new enterprise. Digital India Initiative was launched to transform India into a digitally empowered society and knowledge economy. Micro Units Development and Refinance Agency (or MUDRA Bank) has been established to help small businesses, especially to access finance for development of micro units to encourage entrepreneurship in India and provide the funding to the non-corporate small business sector. Start-up Action Plan was launched to help start-ups. According to the National Association of Software and Services Companies (NASSCOM), India ranks third in the world in the number of technology start-ups and is among the fastest growing start-up ecosystems. There has been remarkable growth in the technology start-ups sector towards the creation of innovative start-ups.[30]

The features of Indian economy as detailed above show that it is a fast developing economy. In areas like Information Technology, India has been a global leader. In education, health care and transportation, fast development is being made. However, in some areas where India has not done well, concerted efforts are being made and the situation is improving. Still there are areas where much more needs to be done to put the economy on a higher growth path.

Notes

1. Purchasing Power Parity (PPP) is an economic theory that compares the currencies of different countries through a market "basket of goods" approach. According to this concept, two currencies are in equilibrium or at par when a market basket of goods (as per exchange rate) is priced the same in both the countries.
2. Ruddar Datt and K.P.M. Sundharam (2015). *Indian Economy*. pp. 471-72.
3. H. Kharas. "The Emerging Middle Class in Developing Countries" Brookings Institution. (World Bank Conference, 2011).
4. "Fact Sheet: Gini Coefficient": The World Bank, and Census and Statistics Department.
5. *The Wall Street Journal*. 16 January 2017.
6. Doing Business in India 2009. World Bank.
7. Bhagwati and Panagariya (2013). *Why Growth Matters: How Economic Growth in India Reduced Poverty and the Lessons for*

Other Developing Countries, Public Affairs. Public Affairs: New York.

8. "India second most unequal country in the world: Wealth Report." *Hindustan Times*. 24 November 2016.
9. Bureau of Labour Statistics, Indian Government (8 October 2010). "Report on Employment and Unemployment Survey." (2009-10)
10. *The Indian Express*. 29 September 2016.
11. Deutsche Bank Research: "The middle class in India."
12. "Report for Selected Countries and Subjects."
13. http://www.thehindu.com/business/Economy/average-wages-in-india-could-quadruple-by-2030-pwc-report/article5186360.ece
14. Labouring Brick by Brick: A Study of Construction Workers—www.sewa.org
15. Somini Sengupta. "The Food Chain in Fertile India, Growth Outstrips Agriculture". *New York Times*. 22 June 2008.
16. India Country Overview 2011. World Bank.
17. "India Allows Wheat Exports for the First Time in Four Years." Bloomberg. 8 September 2011.
18. "India's Agricultural Exports Climb to Record High." United States Department of Agriculture (2014).
19. *Ibid.*
20. http://www.aon.com/india/human-resources/
21. Shekhar Aiyar and Ashoka Mody. "The Demographic Dividend: Evidence From the Indian States", http://www.imf.org/external/pubs/ft/wp/2011/wp1138.pdf
22. http://www.washingtonpost.com/world/asia pacific/amid-population-boom-india-hopes-for-demographic-dividend-but-fears-disaster/2011/10/12/gIQA9I4nmL_story.html
23. Shekhar Aiyar and Ashoka Mody. *op. cit.*
24. Ruddar Datt and K.P.M. Sundharam. *op. cit.*, pp. 471-72.
25. D. Jeffrey Sachs; Nirupam Bajpai and Ananthi Ramaiah (2002). "Understanding Regional Economic Growth in India". Working Paper 88.
26. Jim *Yardley*. "Despite Swirl of Scandals, Indian Mining Bosses Thrive." *The New York Times*. 18 August 2010.
27. B. Mahalingam and D.P. Akash Raj. "Major Drawbacks of Public Distribution System in India—A Review."

    https://www.researchgate.net/publication/312053968_Major_Drawbacks_of_Public_Distribution_System_in_India—A_Review

28. http://www.tradingeconomics.com/india/gross-fixed-capital-formation/forecast
29. *Business Standard*. 6 February 2015.
30. http://alexis.org.in/indias-entrepreneurship-movement-need-for-social-entrepreneurship/

ANNEXURE

Issues in Infrastructure Financing in India

(Speech by Shri N.S. Vishwanathan, Deputy Governor RBI, 15 November 2016, at 6th National Summit organized by ASSOCHAM on "Infrastructure Finance—Building a New India", Mumbai.)

Let me quickly recall here some of the important measures that the RBI has taken to help flow of funds to infrastructure:

(i) In view of the fact that projects take long time to implement during which the interest cost is part of the project cost, the importance of a specified time for commencement of commercial operations is high. Taking into consideration the different reasons due to which project implementation can be delayed, extension of time for completion of projects has been allowed subject to certain conditions without change in classification of the loan. Limited cost overrun financing has also been allowed.

(ii) Banks are permitted to issue guarantees favouring other lending institutions in respect of infrastructure projects, provided the bank issuing the guarantee takes a funded share in the project at least to the extent of 5 per cent of the project cost and undertakes normal credit appraisal, monitoring and follow up of the project. In other cases, banks are precluded from issuing guarantees favouring other banks/lending institutions for the loans extended by the latter, as the primary lender is expected to assume the credit risk and not pass on the same by securing itself with a guarantee, i.e. separation of credit risk and funding is not allowed.

(iii) Normally promoters' contribution towards the equity capital of a company should come from their own resources and they should not normally grant advances to take up shares of other companies. However, banks have been permitted to extend finance for funding promoters' equity in cases where the proposal involves acquisition of shares in an existing company engaged in implementing or operating an infrastructure project in India, subject to certain conditions.

(iv) Banks have been allowed to structure loans flexibly, (what is called as the 5/25 scheme) so that the repayment schedule is aligned with the cash flows.

(v) Banks can raise funds from the market by way of infrastructure bonds, and the assets financed by such funds are exempted from the Priority Sector lending requirements and the funds raised are exempted from reserve requirements. More recently, we have allowed banks to raise such funds by way of masala bonds, as well.

(vi) An efficient bond market is an important requirement for raising funds for the infrastructure sector. This will de-risk the banks' balance sheets as well. We are taking several measures in this regard. As a part of this, we have allowed banks to provide credit enhancement for bond issuances, subject to certain conditions. In fact we have more recently allowed banks to jointly provide CE up to 50 per cent of the bond issue.

(vii) Cost of funds is an important element for infrastructure. At the same time, the financiers at the pre-construction stage need to be compensated for construction risk. Important measures like allowing setting up of IDFs, both as NBFCs and Mutual Funds, to take over the post construction assets from banks, allowing take out financing etc., have been taken.

(viii) We have allowed the debts due to the lenders in case of PPP projects to be considered as secured to the extent assured by the project authority in terms of the Concession Agreement, subject to certain conditions.

(ix) In view of certain safeguards such as escrow accounts available in respect of infrastructure lending, unsecured infrastructure loan accounts which are classified as sub-standard attract a provisioning of 20 per cent instead of the prescription of 25 per cent for other unsecured sub-standard accounts. To avail of this benefit of lower provisioning, the banks should have in place an appropriate mechanism to escrow the cash flows and also have a clear and legal first claim on those cash flows.

4

India's Demography

The 2011 census of India was the second census of the third millennium and the 21st century. It was also the 15th consecutive census in India. It was conducted in two phases, viz. the houselisting exercise and population enumeration. The houselisting exercise, which began in April 2010, provided the basis for uniform and precise frame to undertake population enumeration. It also involved collection of information about all buildings.

Information for National Population Register was also collected in the first phase. This was used to issue a 12-digit unique identification number to all registered Indians. The 2011 census was unique in the sense that it was for the first time that biometric information was collected. The motto of census 2011 was "Our Census, Our future". Spread across 29 States and 7 Union Territories, the census covered 640 districts, 5,767 tehsils, 7,933 towns and more than 600,000 villages. A total of 2.7 million officials visited households in 7,933 towns and 600,000 villages, classifying the population according to gender, religion, education and occupation.[1]

The cost of the exercise was approximately ₹ 2200 crore (US$ 330 million), which comes to less than $ 0.50 per person, well below the estimated world average of $ 4.60 per person.[2]

Information on castes was included in the census. It was the first time that such information was collected since 1931 during the British rule. It is believed that people in India often exaggerate their caste status to get a higher social status, but in the 2011 census it was expected that many people may downgrade their caste to gain government benefits.

The collection of data on caste also helped in knowing the exact population of Other Backward Class (OBCs) in India. The findings of the Socio Economic Caste Census 2011 were revealed on 3 July 2015 by Union Finance Minister Arun Jaitley.

Mandal Commission report of 1980 had stated that the OBC population in India was 52%, but the National Sample Survey Organization (NSSO) survey of 2006 quoted OBC population at 41%.

India's Population: Key Statistics

The population of the country as per the 2011 census was 1210.19 million of which 623.7 million (51.54%) were males and 586.46 million (48.46%) were females. The percentage growth in 2001-2011 was 17.64; males 17.19 and females 18.12. The 2001-2011 was the first decade (with the exception of 1911-1921) which actually added lesser population compared to the previous decade.

Uttar Pradesh (199.5 million) was the most populous State in the country followed by Maharashtra with 112 million. The percentage decadal growth rates of the following six most populous States declined during 2001-2011 compared to 1991-2001:

1. Uttar Pradesh (25.85% to 20.09%)
2. Maharashtra (22.73% to 15.99%)
3. Bihar (28.62% to 25.07%)
4. West Bengal (17.77 % to 13.93%)
5. Andhra Pradesh (14.59% to 11.10%)
6. Madhya Pradesh (24.26% to 20.30%)

During the decade 2001-2011, 25 States/UTs (with a share of about 85% of the country's population) registered an annual growth rate of less than 2% as compared to, 15 States/UTs (with a share of about 42% of country's population) during the period 1991-2001. Population in 15 States/UTs grew by less than 1.5 per cent per annum during 2001-2011, as compared to just four such States/UTs during the previous decade.

Child Population (0-6 Years)

The total number of children in the age-group 0-6 is 158.8 million as per 2011 census which is five million less than in 2001. Twenty States and Union Territories now have over one million children in the age group 0-6 years. On the other extreme, there are five States and Union Territories in the country that are yet to reach the one hundred thousand mark. The five states, Uttar Pradesh (29.7 million), Bihar (18.6 million), Maharashtra (12.8 million), Madhya Pradesh (10.5 million) and Rajasthan (10.5 million), have 52% children in the age group of 0-6 years. Population (0-6 years) 2001-2011 registered (–)3.08 per cent growth with (–)2.42 for males and (–)3.80 for females. The proportion of child population in the age group of 0-6 years to total population is 13.1 per cent while the corresponding figure in 2001 was 15.9 per cent. The decline has been to the extent of 2.8 points. Table 4.1 provides statewise figures of child population in the age group 0-6 years, by sex as per 2011 census.

Table 4.1. Child Population in India in the Age Group 0-6 (Males and Females)

State/UT Code	India/State/Union Territory#	Child population in the age Group 0-6		
1	2	3	4	5
	INDIA	**158,789,287**	**82,952,135**	**75,837,152**
01	Jammu & Kashmir	2,008,642	1,080,662	927,980
02	Himachal Pradesh	763,864	400,681	363,183
03	Punjab	2,941,570	1,593,262	1,348,308
04	Chandigarh#	117,953	63,187	54,766
05	Uttarakhand	1,328,844	704,769	624,075
06	Haryana	3,297,724	1,802,047	1,495,677
07	NCT of Delhi#	1,970,510	1,055,735	914,775
08	Rajasthan	10,504,916	5,580,212	4,924,704
09	Uttar Pradesh	29,728,235	15,653,175	14,075,060

State/UT Code	India/State/Union Territory#	Child population in the age Group 0-6		
10	Bihar	18,582,229	9,615,280	8,966,949
11	Sikkim	61,077	31,418	29,659
12	Arunachal Pradesh	202,759	103,430	99,329
13	Nagaland	285,981	147,111	138,870
14	Manipur	353,237	182,684	170,553
15	Mizoram	165,536	83,965	81,571
16	Tripura	444,055	227,354	216,701
17	Meghalaya	555,822	282,189	273,633
18	Assam	4,511,307	2,305,088	2,206,219
19	West Bengal	10,112,599	5,187,264	4,925,335
20	Jharkhand	5,237,582	2,695,921	2,541,661
21	Orissa	5,035,650	2,603,208	2,432,442
22	Chhattisgarh	3,584,028	1,824,987	1,759,041
23	Madhya Pradesh	10,548,295	5,516,957	5,031,338
24	Gujarat	7,494,176	3,974,286	3,519,890
25	Daman & Diu#	25,880	13,556	12,324
26	Dadra & Nagar Haveli#	49,196	25,575	23,621
27	Maharashtra	12,848,375	6,822,262	6,026,113
28	Andhra Pradesh	8,642,686	4,448,330	4,194,356
29	Karnataka	6,855,801	3,527,844	3,327,957
30	Goa	139,495	72,669	66,826
31	Lakshadweep#	7,088	3,715	3,373
32	Kerala	3,322,247	1,695,935	1,626,312
33	Tamil Nadu	6,894,821	3,542,351	3,352,470
34	Puducherry#	127,610	64,932	62,678
35	Andaman & Nicobar Islands#	39,497	20,094	19,403

Note: See General Notes

Sex Ratio

As per 2011 census, the overall sex ratio at the national level has increased by 7 points to reach 940 as against 933 in 2001. This is the highest sex ratio recorded since 1971 census and a shade lower than 1961. Increase in sex ratio was observed in 29 States/UTs. In three major States, viz. J&K, Bihar and Gujarat, there was a decline in sex ratio from 2001. With 1084, Kerala had the highest sex ratio, followed by Puducherry with 1038, while Daman & Diu had the lowest sex ratio of 618.

Table 4.2 shows a state-wise comparison of sex ratio of total population of India as per 2001 and 2011 censuses, sex ratio of child population of 0-6 year group, and sex ratio of people aged 7 and above. Kerala was the only State with a positive and the highest sex ratio of 1058 and 1084 females per 1000 males in 2001 and 2011 respectively. But the trend in the age group 0-6 years shows a declining trend, where sex ratio was 896 and 906 for in 2001 and 2011 censuses, respectively. In this State the sex ratio in the population ages 7 and above stands positive at 1072 and 1099 in 2001 and 2011. There are a number of States like Andhra Pradesh, Chhattisgarh, Assam, Bihar, Jharkhand, Karnataka, Maharashtra and Uttar Pradesh, where sex ratio in the 0-6 age group declined in 2011 from 2001. However, it increased in States like Gujarat, Haryana, Himachal Pradesh, Jammu & Kashmir, Mizoram, and Punjab.

It can be seen from Table 4.2 that sex ratio (0-6 years) as per 2011 census was 914. An increasing trend in the child sex ratio (0-6) was seen in Punjab, Haryana, Himachal Pradesh, Gujarat, Tamil Nadu, Mizoram and Andaman & Nicobar Islands. In all remaining 27 States/UTs, the child sex ratio showed a decline over 2001. Mizoram had the highest child sex ratio (0-6 years) of 971 followed by Meghalaya with 970. Haryana was placed at the bottom with ratio of 830 followed by Punjab with 846.

Table 4.2: Sex Ratio of Total Population and Child Population in the age group 0-6 and 7+ years: 2001-2011 (2001 and 2011 censuses)

State/ UT Code	India/States/Union Territory*	Sex ratio (females per 1000 males)					
		Total Population		Child Population 0 - 6		Population aged 7 and above	
		2001	2011	2001	2011	2001	2011
	INDIA	933	940	927	914	934	944
35	Andaman & Nicobar Islands*	846	878	957	966	831	868
28	Andhra Pradesh	978	992	961	943	981	997
12	Arunachal Pradesh	893	920	964	960	878	913
18	Assam	935	954	965	957	929	953

10	Bihar	919	916	942	933	914	912
04	Chandigarh*	777	818	845	867	767	812
22	Chhattisgarh	989	991	975	964	992	995
26	Dadra & Nagar Havel*	812	775	979	924	779	752
25	Daman & Diu*	710	618	926	909	682	589
30	Goa	961	968	938	920	964	973
24	Gujarat	920	918	883	886	927	923
06	Haryana	861	877	819	830	869	885
02	Himachal Pradesh	968	974	896	906	980	983
01	Jammu & Kashmir	892	883	941	859	884	887
20	Jharkhand	941	947	965	943	935	948
29	Karnataka	965	968	946	943	968	971
32	Kerala	1058	1084	960	959	1072	1099
31	Lakshadweep*	948	946	959	908	946	951
23	Madhya Pradesh	919	930	932	912	916	933
27	Maharashtra	922	925	913	883	924	931
14	Manipur	974	987	957	934	977	995
17	Meghalaya	972	986	973	970	971	989
15	Mizoram	935	975	964	971	930	976
13	Nagaland	900	931	964	944	890	929
07	NCT of Delhi*	821	866	868	866	813	866
21	Orissa	972	978	953	934	976	985
34	Puducherry*	1001	1038	967	965	1006	1047
03	Punjab	876	893	798	846	888	899
08	Rajasthan	921	926	909	883	923	935
11	Sikkim	875	889	963	944	861	883
33	Tamil Nadu	987	995	942	946	993	1000
16	Tripura	948	961	966	953	945	962
09	Uttar Pradesh	898	908	916	899	894	910
05	Uttarakhand	962	963	908	886	973	975
19	West Bengal	934	947	960	950	929	946

Source: Census 2011: Provisional Population Total – INDIA

Table 4.3 shows a comparison of India's total population in censuses of 2001 to 2011, along with decadal increase in population, growth rate, and sex ratio. The highest sex ratio of 972 females per 1000 males was in 1901, which declined to 930 in 1971, before improving marginally to 934 in 1981, but again declined to 927, its lowest ever, in 1991. In 2001 it was 933 and in 2011 it improved to 940. But it is still low. This reflects the orthodox beliefs prevailing in Indian society, whereby people prefer male child. Some people are guilty of female foeticide and infanticide. Measures are being taken to stop these crimes so that sex ratio improves. It is pertinent to mention here that women are as much important as men for socio-economic development of the country. If women are educated, and empowered, India can develop at a fast pace.

Table 4.3: Population, Growth Rate, Vital Rates and Sex Ratio (India 1901-2011)

Year	Population in Millions	Change in Population	Growth Rate (%)	Crude Birth Rate	Crude Death Rate	Sex Ratio (F/M) in 1000s
1901	238.4	–	–	45.8	44.4	972
1911	252.1	13.7	0.56	49.2	42.6	964
1921	251.3	-0.8	-0.03	48.1	47.2	955
1931	279	27.7	1.04	46.4	36.3	950
1941	318.7	39.7	1.33	45.2	31.2	945
1951	361.1	42.4	1.25	39.9	27.4	946
1961	439.2	78.1	1.95	41.7	22.8	941
1971	548.2	109.1	2.2	41.2	19	930
1981	683.3	135.1	2.22	37.2	15	934
1991	846.4	163.1	2.14	32.5	11.4	927
2001	1028.7	182.3	1.97	24.8	8.9	933
2011	1210.2	181.5	1.64	–	–	940

Source: Census 2011, Govt. of India

Literacy Rate

As per 2011 census, literacy rate was 74.04 per cent, as compared to 64.83 per cent in 2001, showing an increase of 9.21 percentage points. Percentage growth in literacy during the decade 2001-2011 is 38.82; males: 31.98% and females: 49.10%. Literates constituted 74 per cent of the total population aged seven and above and illiterates formed 26 per cent.

Anyone, above age 7 who can read and write in any language with an ability to understand was considered a literate. In censuses before 1991, children below the age 5 were treated as illiterates. The literacy rate taking the entire population into account is called "crude literacy rate", and taking the population from age 7 and above into account is known "effective literacy rate". In India, the effective literacy rate increased to a total of

74.04% with 82.14% of the males and 65.46% of the females being literate.

Table 4.4 shows the crude literacy rate in India from 1901 to 2011. In 1901, the literacy rate was abysmally low at 5.35 per cent. It progressed very slowly to reach 16.67 per cent in 1951 when the first census of India after Independence was conducted. It is quite clear that during the fifty years from 1901 to 1951, out of which the British ruled for 46 years, i.e. up to 1947, no effort was made to improve India's literacy rate. The British concentrated on prolonging their rule over India and exploiting its resources to their advantage. If we look at the picture fifty years later, i.e. 2001, we find that literacy rate reached 64.83 per cent, which bears testimony to the fact that after achieving Independence, the successive governments at the Centre and State levels made earnest endeavours and good results were achieved. As per 2011 census, the overall literacy rate in India was 74.04. As the literacy rate is improving, there are better chances of socio-economic development of the country.

Table 4.4: Literacy Rate in India

S.No.	Census Year	Total (%)	Male (%)	Female (%)
1	1901	5.35	9.83	0.60
2	1911	5.92	10.56	1.05
3	1921	7.16	12.21	1.81
4	1931	9.50	15.59	2.93
5	1941	16.10	24.90	7.30
6	1951	16.67	24.95	9.45
7	1961	24.02	34.44	12.95
8	1971	29.45	39.45	18.69
9	1981	36.23	46.89	24.82
10	1991	42.84	52.74	32.17
11	2001	64.83	75.26	53.67
12	2011	74.04	82.14	65.46

Source: https://en.wikipedia.org/wiki/2011_Census_of_India

Table 4.4 also shows the male and female literacy rates in India from 1901 to 2011. We notice a gap between male literacy and female literacy rate all along. Male literacy rate has been much higher than female literacy rate. In 1901, male literacy rate was 9.83 per cent, while female literacy was paltry 0.60 per cent. In 1951, the male literacy was 24.95 per cent, while female literacy rate was 9.45 per cent, which was quite low. Women at that time lead a passive life and were mostly confined to household work. Very few girls were sent to school. The British Government did nothing for the education of women. It was only after the achievement of Independence that attention was drawn towards education, particularly the education of women. The results are there to see. The female literacy rate reached 53.67 per cent in 2001 and 65.46 per cent in 2011.

Special efforts have been made to improve the literacy rate in villages and towns of India. State Governments have been directed to ensure an improved literacy rate in villages, where it is still poor. The steps taken by the Government to improve literacy rate in India include, (i) Free education programs to poor people living in villages and towns; (ii) Setting up of new school and colleges at district and State levels; (iii) Forming committees to ensure proper utilization of funds allotted to improve literacy rate; (iv) Bringing the Right of Children to Free and Compulsory Education Act or Right to Education Act (RTE, enacted 4 August 2009), which describes the modalities of the importance of free and compulsory education for children between 6 and 14 years of age in India under Article 21A of the Indian Constitution. However there is still much to do. We must also provide educational opportunity to girls from socially and economically disadvantaged communities of India, who traditionally have no access to schooling.

Table 4.5 shows the position of State-wise literacy rate in India. Some States like Kerala, Mizoram and Tripura have literacy rate well above national average, while States like Uttar Pradesh, Bihar, Madhya Pradesh and Rajasthan have a lower literacy rate than the national average. There is a need to improve the literacy rate in a balanced way in all the States and make female literacy rate at par with male literacy rate.

Table 4.5: Statewise Literacy Rate in India, Male and Female, 2011 Census

Sl. No.	States/Ut	Total Literates	Male Literates	Female Literates	Total Literacy Rate	Male Literacy Rate	Female Literacy Rate
	INDIA	**77,84,54,120**	**44,42,03,762**	**33,42,50,358**	**74.04**	**82.14**	**65.46**
01	Jammu & Kashmir	72,45,053	43,70,604	28,74,449	68.74	78.26	58.01
02	Himachal Pradesh	51,04,506	27,91,542	23,12,964	83.78	90.83	76.60
03	Punjab	1,89,88,611	1,06,26,788	83,61,823	76.68	81.48	71.34
04	Chandigarh#	8,09,653	4,68,166	3,41,487	86.43	90.54	81.38
05	Uttarakhand	69,97,433	39,30,174	30,67,259	79.63	88.33	70.70
06	Haryana	1,69,04,324	99,91,838	69,12,486	76.64	85.38	66.77
07	NCT of Delhi#	1,27,63,352	72,10,050	55,53,302	86.34	91.03	80.93
08	Rajasthan	3,89,70,500	2,41,84,782	1,47,85,718	67.06	80.51	52.66
09	Uttar Pradesh	11,84,23,805	7,04,79,196	4,79,44,609	69.72	79.24	59.26
10	Bihar	5,43,90,254	3,27,11,975	2,16,78,279	63.82	73.39	53.33
11	Sikkim	4,49,294	2,53,364	1,95,930	82.20	87.29	76.43
12	Arunachal Pradesh	7,89,943	4,54,532	3,35,411	66.95	73.69	59.57
13	Nagaland	13,57,579	7,31,796	6,25,783	80.11	83.29	76.69
14	Manipur	18,91,196	10,26,733	8,64,463	79.85	86.49	73.17
15	Mizoram	8,47,592	4,38,949	4,08,643	91.58	93.72	89.40
16	Tripura	28,31,742	15,15,973	13,15,769	87.75	92.18	83.15
17	Meghalaya	18,17,761	9,34,091	8,83,670	75.48	77.17	73.78
18	Assam	1,95,07,017	1,07,56,937	87,50,080	73.18	78.81	67.27
19	West Bengal	6,26,14,556	3,45,08,159	2,81,06,397	77.08	82.67	71.16
20	Jharkhand	1,87,53,660	1,11,68,649	75,85,011	67.63	78.45	56.21
21	Odisha	2,71,12,376	1,53,26,036	1,17,86,340	73.45	82.40	64.36
22	Chhattisgarh	1,55,98,314	89,62,121	66,36,193	71.04	81.45	60.59
23	Madhya Pradesh	4,38,27,193	2,58,48,137	1,79,79,056	70.63	80.53	60.02
24	Gujarat	4,19,48,677	2,39,95,500	1,79,53,177	79.31	87.23	70.73
25	Daman & Diu	1,88,974	1,24,911	64,063	87.07	91.48	79.59
26	Dadra & Nagar Haveli	2,28,028	1,44,916	83,112	77.65	86.46	65.93
27	Maharashtra	8,25,12,225	4,62,94,041	3,62,18,184	82.91	89.82	75.48
28	Andhra Pradesh	5,14,38,510	2,87,59,782	2,26,78,728	67.66	75.56	59.74
29	Karnataka	4,10,29,323	2,28,08,468	1,82,20,855	75.60	82.85	68.13
30	Goa	11,52,117	6,20,026	5,32,091	87.40	92.81	81.84
31	Lakshadweep	52,914	28,249	24,665	92.28	96.11	88.25
32	Kerala	2,82,34,227	1,37,55,888	1,44,78,339	93.91	96.02	91.98
33	Tamil Nadu	5,24,13,116	2,83,14,595	2,40,98,521	80.33	86.81	73.86
34	Puducherry	9,66,600	5,02,575	4,64,025	86.55	92.12	81.22
35	Andaman & Nicobar Islands #	2,93,695	1,64,219	1,29,476	86.27	90.11	81.84

Source: Indiafacts.in

Literacy and Economic Development

Literacy is key to economic growth of a country. Economic prosperity of a country entirely is dependent upon its economic resources, of which human resource is an important part. Human resource includes the population, its growth rate, skills and the working capacity of the labour force. All these factors can be enhanced by increasing the literacy rate of the population. India is endowed with rich natural resources like fertile land, minerals, ores, forests, etc. If the human resources are improved and are used effectively, the country can achieve high economic growth.

Friedrich Huebler, in his analysis on International Education Statistics, states that there is a correlation between GDP per capita and education. He studied factors like school net enrollment ratios (NER) against GDP per capita of 120 different countries, and found that countries with higher income levels had higher levels of school enrollment.

Literacy and Employment

Improved literacy rate can lead to higher economic growth only if there are commensurate employment opportunities. India has a large young population. Although literacy will play an important role in turning the young population into potential human capital, yet creating jobs to them will be a big challenge. It has been estimated that India will have 300 million more workers by 2025. What we need is to make strong policies to create more employment.

From 1983 to 2011, the average unemployment rates in India averaged 9 per cent reaching an all-time high of 9.4 per cent in December 2010 and a record low of 3.8 per cent in December 2011.[3] In India, the unemployment rate measures the number of people actively looking for a job as a percentage of the labour force. If strong and effective measures to create employment are not taken, then the number of unemployed people will only increase with the increase in the labour force. Thus, effective policies to create employment are a must for India as these will help in the increase in the labor productivity which otherwise might not be utilized and thus hampering India's growth in the long run.

We also have to bring tax reforms and take other supply-side policies as demand-side policies involve a lot of social-cost and hence will not suitable for long-run. Bringing down interest rates is absolutely necessary to boost production and enable to corporate sector to recruit more and more people. This will also be the right step in implementing the Government of India's initiative "Make in India", whereby many foreign companies will set up manufacturing units in India.

The statewise distribution of population in India along with key areas like males, females, literacy rate, rural and urban population, density of population, etc. as per 2011 census is given in Table 4.6. The table shows that Uttar Pradesh had the largest population with nearly 20 crore, of which 10.44 crore were males and 9.53 females. The sex ratio was 930 females per 1000 males. Literacy rate in UP was 67.8 per cent. The State had a high population living in villages, at 13.17 crore, and 3.45 crore living in urban areas. This shows that UP's major share of population has the occupation of agriculture. There is need to boost industry in the State. The State has the fourth highest density of population with 828 persons per sq. km., after Bihar (1102), West Bengal (1030) and Kerala (859).

Bihar has the third largest population in India at 10.41 crore, with 5.43 crore males and 4.98 females. The sex ratio at 918 is lower than the national average of 940. Literacy rate in Bihar is the lowest of all Indian States and Union Territories.

Madhya Pradesh stands sixth in terms of the size of population at 7.26 crore persons, out of which 3.76 crore are males and 3.50 crore females, and a sex ratio of 931. A large portion of the population in the State (4.44 crore) lives in rural areas and only 1.60 crore people live in the cities. This shows the agrarian nature of occupation of most of its people. The literacy rate at 69.3 per cent is lower than the national average of 74 per cent.

Rajasthan is the State that comes at number eight in terms of size of population at 6.85 crore, of which 3.56 crore males and 3.30 crore females. Sex ratio at 928 is quite low. The State has the second lowest literacy rate at 66.1 per cent.

Table 4.6. Population Distribution in India by States (2011 Census)

Rank	State/ Union Territory	Type	Population	%	Males	Females	Sex Ratio	Literacy	Rural Population	Urban Population	Area (km²)	Density (/km²)
1	Uttar Pradesh	State	199,812,341	16.5	104,480,510	95,331,831	930	67.68	131,658,339	34,539,582	240,928	828
2	Maharashtra	State	112,374,333	9.28	58,243,056	54,131,277	929	82.34	55,777,647	41,100,980	307,713	365
3	Bihar	State	104,099,452	8.6	54,278,157	49,821,295	918	61.80	74,316,709	8,681,800	94,163	1,102
4	West Bengal	State	91,276,115	7.54	46,809,027	44,467,088	950	76.26	57,748,946	22,427,251	88,752	1,030
5	Andhra Pradesh	State	84,580,777	6.99	42,442,146	42,138,631	993	67.02	55,401,067	20,808,940	275,045	308
6	Madhya Pradesh	State	72,626,809	6.00	37,612,306	35,014,503	931	69.32	44,380,878	15,967,145	308,245	236
7	Tamil Nadu	State	72,147,030	5.96	36,137,975	36,009,055	996	80.09	34,921,681	27,483,998	130,058	555
8	Rajasthan	State	68,548,437	5.66	35,550,997	32,997,440	928	66.11	43,292,813	13,214,375	342,239	201
9	Karnataka	State	61,095,297	5.05	30,966,657	30,128,640	973	75.36	34,889,033	17,961,529	191,791	319
10	Gujarat	State	60,439,692	4.99	31,491,260	28,948,432	919	78.03	31,740,767	18,930,250	196,024	308
11	Odisha	State	41,974,218	3.47	21,212,136	20,762,082	979	72.87	31,287,422	5,517,238	155,707	269
12	Kerala	State	33,406,061	2.76	16,027,412	17,378,649	1084	94.00	23,574,449	8,266,925	38,863	859
13	Jharkhand	State	32,988,134	2.72	16,930,315	16,057,819	948	66.41	20,952,088	5,993,741	79,714	414
14	Assam	State	31,205,576	2.58	15,939,443	15,266,133	958	72.19	23,216,288	3,439,240	78,438	397
15	Punjab	State	27,743,338	2.29	14,639,465	13,103,873	895	75.84	16,096,488	8,262,511	50,362	550
16	Chhattisgarh	State	25,545,198	2.11	12,832,895	12,712,303	991	70.28	16,648,056	4,185,747	135,191	189
17	Haryana	State	25,351,462	2.09	13,494,734	11,856,728	879	75.55	15,029,260	6,115,304	44,212	573
18	Delhi	UT	16,787,941	1.39	8,987,326	7,800,615	868	86.21	944,727	12,905,780	1,484	11,297
19	Jammu and Kashmir	State	12,541,302	1.04	6,640,662	5,900,640	889	67.16	7,627,062	2,516,638	222,236	56

Rank	State/ Union Territory	Type	Population	%	Males	Females	Sex Ratio	Literacy	Rural Population	Urban Population	Area (km^2)	Density ($/km^2$)
20	Uttarakhand	State	10,086,292	0.83	5,137,773	4,948,519	963	78.82	6,310,275	2,179,074	53,483	189
21	Himachal Pradesh	State	6,864,602	0.57	3,481,873	3,382,729	972	82.80	5,482,319	595,581	55,673	123
22	Tripura	State	3,673,917	0.30	1,874,376	1,799,541	960	87.22	2,653,453	545,750	10,486	350
23	Meghalaya	State	2,966,889	0.25	1,491,832	1,475,057	989	74.43	1,864,711	454,111	22,429	132
24	Manipur	State	2,570,390	0.21	1,290,171	1,280,219	992	79.21	1,590,820	575,968	22,327	122
25	Nagaland	State	1,978,502	0.16	1,024,649	953,853	931	79.55	1,647,249	342,787	16,579	119
26	Goa	State	1,458,545	0.12	739,140	719,405	973	88.70	677,091	670,577	3,702	394
27	Arunachal Pradesh	State	1,383,727	0.11	713,912	669,815	938	65.38	870,087	227,881	83,743	17
28	Pondicherry	UT	1,247,953	0.10	612,511	635,442	1037	85.85	325,726	648,619	479	2,598
29	Mizoram	State	1,097,206	0.09	555,339	541,867	976	91.33	447,567	441,006	21,081	52
30	Chandigarh	UT	1,055,450	0.09	580,663	474,787	818	86.05	92,120	808,515	114	9,252
31	Sikkim	State	610,577	0.05	323,070	287,507	890	81.42	480,981	59,870	7,096	86
32	Andaman and Nicobar Islands	UT	380,581	0.03	202,871	177,710	876	86.63	239,954	116,198	8,249	46
33	Dadra and Nagar Haveli	UT	343,709	0.03	193,760	149,949	774	76.24	170,027	50,463	491	698
34	Daman and Diu	UT	243,247	0.02	150,301	92,946	618	87.10	100,856	57,348	112	2,169
35	Lakshadweep	UT	64,473	0.01	33,123	31,350	946	91.85	33,683	26,967	32	2,013
TOTAL	India	28 + 7	1,210,854,977	100	623,724,248	586,469,174	943	73.00	833,087,662	377,105,760	3,287,240	382

Source: 2011 Census of India.

Rajasthan has a large size of its population (4.33 crore) living in rural areas, and only 1.32 crore of its people live in urban areas. The economy of the State is thus largely agrarian.

Odisha stands at number eleven in terms of size of population, with 4.20 crore people, out of which 2.12 crore were males and 2.08 females. Its sex ratio at 979 is higher than the national average but literacy rate of 72.9 was slightly lower than the national average of 74. Most of the population of the State lives in urban areas (3.13 crore) and only 55 lac people live in urban areas. This bears testimony to the agrarian nature of the State's economy.

Bihar, Madhya Pradesh, Rajasthan and Uttar Pradesh form the BIMARU States, i.e. the States that do not have healthy economies. Odisha has also been included in the list to make it BIMAROU. These five States together have a population of 48.72 crore which is roughly 40 per cent of India's total population of 121 crore as per 2011 census. Out of the total population in these States, 32.50 crore, i.e. 67 per cent of the total population live in rural areas. This shows that the economy of these States is based on agriculture. The farmers are poor with small land holdings. They use old methods of raising crops and depend largely on the monsoons for irrigation. Since the monsoons are uncertain, the farming in these States is mostly uncertain. When the rainfall is normal and uniform the crops are good, but when the rainfall is low there are droughts and very low yield. In case the rainfall is excessive, there are floods, damaging, or in the worst case scenario, destroying the crops. The farmers live in perpetual poverty. A large population in rural areas also means that the farmers are subsistence agriculture, i.e. they produce for their own consumption and very little for selling in the market. Rise in population also means that the landholdings are getting smaller with time, keeping the farmers in the poverty cycle. Literacy rate in these States is low, which means that people do not get many opportunities to bring a perceptible change in their lives. The poor economic growth of these States is a dampener on the growth of India's economy at large. If Indian economy is to grow at a high rate, we have to find ways and means to develop the economies of all the States, especially of the BIMAROU States.

Table 4.6 also gives us important data which can serve as an economic indicator. Maharashtra comes second in terms of the size of population with 11.24 crore persons of which males were 5.82 crore and females 5.41 crore. There was a near balance in male-female population which however is not reflected in the sex ratio of 929. The state is among the high-literacy states at 82.3 per cent. Maharashtra too has more people living in rural areas (5.58 crore) than in the cities (4.10 crore). But the State has the lower population density at 365 persons per sq.km. as compared to the national average of 382.

Density of Population

The density of population is defined as the number of persons per sq.km. It shows the concentration of population in a particular area. Table 4.7 shows that as per 2011 census, the density of population in India was 382 persons per sq.km. as compared to 325 persons per sq.km. as shown in 2001 census. Thus, on an average 57 more persons inhabited every sq.km. in 2011 as compared to a decade ago. Only Bangladesh has a

Table 4.7: Comparison of Density of Population (Censuses 1901 to 2011)

Census Year	Density (Per sq.km.)	Absolute Increase	%age Increase
1	2	3	4
1901	77		
1911	82	5	6.5
1921	81	-1	-1.2
1931	90	9	11.1
1941	103	13	14.4
1951	117	14	13.6
1961	142	25	21.4
1971	177[1]	35	24.6
1981	216[2]	39	22
1991	267[2]	51	23.6
2001	325[2]	58	21.7
2011	382[2]	57	17.5

Notes: 1. While working out the density of India, Jammu & Kashmir has been excluded as comparable figures of area and Population are not available for that State.

2. The density has been worked out on comparable data.

higher population density than India. In 1901, the density of population in India was only 77 persons per sq.km., which has increased steadily ever since. India has only 2.4 per cent of the world's surface area of 135.79 million sq.km., but it inhabits 17.5 per cent of world population. In contrast, America has 7.2 per cent of world's surface area, but has only 4.5 per cent of world population. Table 4.7 shows that absolute increase in density of population in India was 58 in 2001 and 57 in 2011. The percentage increase was 21.7 and 17.7 in 2001 and 2011, respectively.

Table 4.8 shows that NCT of Delhi had the largest density of population in India with 11,297 persons per sq.km. Chandigarh, with a population density of 9252 occupied the second place. The main reason of very high density of population in these cities is that a large number of people have migrated there due to better work opportunities and facilities. In States, Bihar has the highest population density of 1102 as per 2011 census as compared to 881 in 2001. This bears testimony to the rapid increase in the population of the State. West Bengal has the second highest population density of 1029 as per 2011 census as compared to 903 in 2001. Density of population in Uttar Pradesh also increased from 690 in 2001 to 828. States with lower population density than the national average of 382 are Maharashtra, Tripura, Karnataka, Andhra Pradesh (undivided), Gujarat, Odisha and Madhya Pradesh.

Table 4.8: Ranking of States and Union Territories by Density (Censuses 2001 and 2011)

Rank in 2011	States/Union Territory#	Density (per sq.km.)		Rank in 2001
		2011	2001	
1	2	3	4	5
	INDIA	382	325	
1	NCT of Delhi#	11,297	9,340	1
2	Chandigarh#	9,252	7,900	2
3	Puducherry#	2,598	2,034	3
4	Daman & Diu#	2,169	1,413	5
5	Lakshadweep#	2,013	1,895	4
6	Bihar	1,102	881	7

7	West Bengal	1,029	903	6
8	Kerala	859	819	8
9	Uttar Pradesh	828	690	9
10	Dadra & Nagar Haveli#	698	449	13
11	Haryana	573	478	12
12	Tamil Nadu	555	480	11
13	Punjab	550	484	10
14	Jharkhand	414	338	16
15	Assam	397	340	15
16	Goa	394	364	14
17	Maharashtra	365	315	17
18	Tripura	350	305	18
19	Karnataka	319	276	20
20	Andhra Pradesh	308	277	19
21	Gujarat	308	258	21
22	Odisha	269	236	22
23	Madhya Pradesh	236	196	23
24	Rajasthan	201	165	24
25	Uttarakhand	189	159	25
26	Chhattisgarh	189	154	26
27	Meghalaya	132	103	29
28	Jammu & Kashmir	124	100	31
29	Himachal Pradesh	123	109	28
30	Manipur	122	103	30
31	Nagaland	119	120	27
32	Sikkim	86	76	32
33	Mizoram	52	42	34
34	Andaman & Nicobar Islands#	46	43	33
35	Arunachal Pradesh	17	13	35

Source: censusindia.gov.in/2011

Note: While working out the density figures for Jammu & Kashmir for 2001 and 2011 censuses, the entire area and population of those portions of Jammu & Kashmir which are under illegal occupation of Pakistan and China have not been taken into account.

Another feature of India's density of population is that it is much higher in cities, especially the metropolitan cities and other large cities like State capitals and district headquarters. This has put a lot of pressure on the resources, existing infrastructure and the quality of life. The level of environmental pollution in cities like Delhi has reached alarming levels. Villages have a much lower population density than the cities. One of reason is the migration of a large number of people from rural to the urban areas, with adverse socio-economic consequences. For data on State-wise population in urban as well as rural areas see Table 4.6.

Religious Demographics

The religious data on India Census 2011 was released by Government of India in August 2015. The key points from the census report are listed below:

1. This is the first caste census done in independent India.
2. The last caste census in India happened in 1932.
3. Just 4.6% of all rural households in the country pay income tax.
4. The total households in the country—rural plus urban—stand at 24.39 crore.
5. Public sector-employed households made up 1.11% of the total.
6. Over 11% rural households possessed refrigerators.
7. As many as 20.69% rural households had either an automobile or a fishing boat.
8. About 94% of the rural households owned a house with 54% having 1-2 room dwellings.
9. Of all the rural salaried households, 5% earned salaries from the government while those employed in the private sector constituted 3.57% of the total households.
10. Landless ownership was 56% of the total rural population, with 70% of SCs and 50% of STs being landless owners.

Table 4.9 shows the percentage of people of main religious groups in India, decadewise from 1950 to 2011. Hindus the predominant religious group in India were 84.1 per cent of total population in 1950. But in 2011 the percentage decreased to 79.80. Muslims who were 9.8 per cent of total population in 1950 rose to 14.23 per cent. There was no significant change in the percentage of people of other communities during the last 60 years.

Table 4.9: Population Trends for Major Religious Groups in India (1951–2011)

Religious group	Population % 1951	Population % 1961	Population % 1971	Population % 1981	Population % 1991	Population % 2001	Population % 2011
Hinduism	84.1%	83.45%	82.73%	82.30%	81.53%	80.46%	79.80%
Islam	9.8%	10.69%	11.21%	11.75%	12.61%	13.43%	14.23%
Christianity	2.3%	2.44%	2.60%	2.44%	2.32%	2.34%	2.30%
Sikhism	1.79%	1.79%	1.89%	1.92%	1.94%	1.87%	1.72%
Buddhism	0.74%	0.74%	0.70%	0.70%	0.77%	0.77%	0.70%
Jainism	0.46%	0.46%	0.48%	0.47%	0.40%	0.41%	0.37%
Zoroastrianism	0.13%	0.09%	0.09%	0.09%	0.08%	0.06%	n/a
Other religions/ No religion	0.43%	0.43%	0.41%	0.42%	0.44%	0.72%	0.9%

Workers in India

Also called labour, workers in India refer to employment in the economy of India. In 2012, there were around 487 million workers, of which over 94 per cent worked in unincorporated, unorganized enterprises. The workers included a wide range from pushcart vendors to home-based diamond and gem polishing operations.[4] The organized sector included workers employed by the government, state-owned enterprises and private sector enterprises. In 2008, the organized sector employed 27.5 million workers, of which 17.3 million worked for government or government owned entities.

The organized sector or formal sector in India refers to licensed organizations, i.e. those who are registered and pay GST, income tax, etc. These include the publicly traded companies, incorporated or formally registered entities, corporations, factories, shopping malls, hotels, and large businesses. Unorganized sector, also called the informal sector or own account enterprises, implies all unlicensed, self-employed or unregistered economic activity, like owner-manned general stores, handicrafts and handloom workers, rural traders, farmers, etc.[5]

The unorganized occupational groups in India include small and marginal farmers, landless agricultural labourers, sharecroppers, fishermen, those engaged in animal husbandry, building and construction workers, leather workers, weavers, artisans, workers, in brick kilns and in saw mills, etc. There is a separate category based on the nature of employment such as those attached agricultural labourers, bonded labourers, migrant workers, casual labourers, etc. The distressed unorganized sector includes workers, like toddy tappers, scavengers, carriers of head loads, drivers of animal-driven vehicles, loaders and unloaders. Yet another category in the unorganized labour includes service workers such as midwives, domestic workers, barbers, vegetable and fruit vendors, newspaper vendors, pavement vendors, hand-cart operators, and the unorganized retail.[6]

The unorganized sector in India has low productivity and low wages. In 2006, India's unorganized sector accounted for over 94 per cent of workers, but it created only 57 per cent of the country's National Domestic Product. It was much less per worker than in the organized sector. One of reasons is high productivity gap as some of lowest income jobs are in the rural unorganized where population is large and poverty high. Agriculture and allied activities alone employ 52 per cent of labour in India. About 30 million workers are migrant workers, most of them being in agriculture. Local stable employment is not available for them.

As per current rate of growth of population in India about 13 million new workers are being added every year to the existing labour pool. India's economy has been adding nearly eight million new jobs every year, mainly in low paying, unorganized sector.[7] The remaining 5 million workers have to either take up poorly paid partial employment, casual labour or they remain unemployed.

Household Size

The household size refers to the number of persons residing in private households. Table 4.10 shows the ranking of Indian States according to household size, from the lowest to the highest. Tamil Nadu has the lowest household size at 3.5, followed by Andhra Pradesh with 3.9 and Goa with 4.2. Uttar Pradesh and

Jammu & Kashmir have the highest household size in India at 5.7, followed by Bihar and Jharkhand with a household size of 5.4. The average household size in India is 4.8. Large household size in India is the chief cause of poverty.

Table 4.10: Rank-wise Household Size in India

Rank	State	Household size
1	Tamil Nadu	3.5
2	Andhra Pradesh	3.9
3	Goa	4.2
4	Kerala	4.3
4	Tripura	4.3
6	West Bengal	4.5
6	Odisha	4.5
6	Sikkim	4.5
6	Nagaland	4.5
10	Himachal Pradesh	4.6
10	Karnataka	4.6
12	Assam	4.7
12	Gujarat	4.7
12	Maharashtra	4.7
15	Arunachal Pradesh	4.8
15	Mizoram	4.8
15	Whole INDIA	4.8
15	Chhattisgarh	4.8
18	Madhya Pradesh	5
18	Uttarakhand	5
18	Manipur	5
21	Meghalaya	5.1
22	Punjab	5.2
23	Rajasthan	5.5
24	Haryana	5.3
25	Bihar	5.4
25	Jharkhand	5.4
27	Jammu and Kashmir	5.7
27	Uttar Pradesh	5.7

Administrative Units

Census 2011 covered 35 States/Union Territories, 640 districts, 5,924 sub-districts, 7,935 towns and 6,40,867 villages.

In Census 2001, the corresponding figures were 593 districts, 5,463 sub-districts, 5,161 towns and 6,38,588 villages. There is an increase of 47 districts, 461 sub-districts, 2774 towns (242 statutory and 2532 census towns) and 2,279 villages in census 2011 as compared to Census 2001.

Overpopulation in India

India is an overpopulated country and ranks behind only China in terms of total population. Every year, India adds more people to its existing population than any other nation in the world. The population of some of its states is equal to the total population of many countries. For example, the population of Uttar Pradesh is more than the population of Brazil. The population of the second most populous state Maharashtra, which has a growth rate of 9.42%, is almost equal to the total population of Mexico. Bihar, third most populous state in India has more population than Germany.

The main reasons of India's rapidly growing population are poverty, illiteracy, high fertility rate, rapid decline in death rates or mortality rates and immigration from Bangladesh and Nepal. Alarmed by its increasing population, India has taken several measures to control the growth rate of population but has not met with success. As per current level of growth of population, India is likely to overtake China and become the most populated country in the world. A new UN study of global population trends predicts that India will overtake China to become the world's most populous nation by 2022. This new projection has India overtaking China's population six years earlier than previously predicted.

Decadal Growth Rate in Census 2011 India

The decadal growth rate is an important statistics obtained from census operations. It provides an overview of the percentage of total population growth in a particular decade. India showed a decadal growth of 17.64% for total population in 2011 from 2001, as compared to 21.15% in the previous decade, i.e. from 1991 to 2001. According to the Census of India, Ministry of Home Affairs, the decade of 2001 to 2011 is the 1st decade post Indian Independence, which added least number of people to the country's population. The percentage of decadal growth in the nation, for the first time, showed a decrease by 3.90%.

Among the total decadal growth rate, the rural areas of India grew at 12.18% whereas the urban areas of the country grew at the rate of 31.80% in the last census decade. The State of Bihar showed the highest decadal growth rate in between the years 2001 to 2011.

Decadal growth rate of India in Census 2011, at a glance

Decadal Growth Rate (2001-2011)		
Total:	18,14,55,986	(17.64%)
Male:	9,15,01,158	(17.19%)
Female:	8,99,54,828	(18.12%)

It is pertinent to mention here that although the rate of decadal growth has decreased in the last decade, yet the growth rate is very high because the size of population is large. Some States have contributed to the decrease of overall decadal growth rate as shown in Table 4.11.

Table 4.11: States Contributing to the Decrease of Overall Decadal Growth Rate

Name of State	Census 2001	Census 2011
Andhra Pradesh	14.59%	11.10%
West Bengal	17.77%	13.93%
Maharashtra	22.73%	15.99%
Madhya Pradesh	24.26%	20.23%
Uttar Pradesh	25.85%	20.09%
Bihar	28.62%	25.07%

It can be seen from Table 4.11 that even some of the most populated States like Uttar Pradesh, Bihar, and Maharashtra had a declining decadal growth rate. But they need to decrease it substantially to make an impact on the overall growth of population. The State-wise position of decadal growth rate in Census 2011 is given in Table 4.12.

Table 4.12: State-wise Position of Decadal Growth Rate in India (2011 Census)

Sl. No.	Name of State	Decadal Growth (2001 to 2011)	% of growth (2001 to 2011)
1	Andhra Pradesh	8455526	11.10%
2	Arunachal Pradesh	284643	25.90%
3	Assam	4513744	16.90%
4	Bihar	20806128	25.10%
5	Chhattisgarh	4706393	22.60%
6	Goa	110055	8.20%
7	Gujarat	9712611	19.20%
8	Haryana	4208517	19.90%
9	Himachal Pradesh	778609	12.80%
10	Jammu and Kashmir	2405226	23.70%
11	Jharkhand	6020409	22.30%
12	Karnataka	8280142	15.70%
13	Kerala	1546303	4.90%
14	Madhya Pradesh	12249542	20.30%
15	Maharashtra	15494345	16.00%
16	Manipur	427860	18.70%
17	Meghalaya	645185	27.80%
18	Mizoram	202441	22.80%
19	Nagaland	-9434	-0.50%
20	Odisha	5142698	14.00%
21	Punjab	3345237	13.70%
22	Rajasthan	12113824	21.40%
23	Sikkim	66837	12.40%
24	Tamil Nadu	9733279	15.60%
25	Tripura	471829	14.70%
26	Uttar Pradesh	33383556	20.10 %
27	Uttarakhand	1627403	19.20%
28	West Bengal	11171539	13.90%

It can be seen from Table 4.12 that as many as nine States have a decadal growth rate of over 20%. Eight States have a decadal growth rate between 15% and 20%. Only three States have a decadal growth rate of less than 10%. At these rates the growth of population will continue unabated, adversely affecting economic growth and putting severe burden on resources.

The position of decadal growth rate in India's Union territories is given in Table 4.13.

Table 4.13: Decadal Growth Rate in India's Union Territories (Census 2011)

Sl. No.	Name of U.T.	Decadal Growth (2001 to 2011)	% of growth (2001 to 2011)
1	Andaman and Nicobar Islands	23792	6.70%
2	Chandigarh	154051	17.10%
3	Dadra and Nagar Haveli	122363	55.50%
4	Daman and Diu	84707	53.50%
5	Delhi	2902728	21.00%
6	Lakshadweep	3779	6.20%
7	Puducherry	270119	27.70%

Table 4.13 shows that Dadra & Nagar Haveli and Daman & Diu have a very high decadal growth rate. Delhi too has a very high decadal growth but migration of a number of people to this city every year is also a major reason of increase in its population.

Effects of Large Population of India

India not only has a large population, but also a high rate of growth of population. The rapid rise in population, called population explosion, is responsible for many of the ills faced by the country. This is the main reason why India has not been able to match its rate of development with rising population. The major effects of India's large and growing population are mentioned below:

The decadal growth of Indian population is 17.64 per cent (as per 2011 census over 2001). The yearly growth rate is 1.8 per cent, which is very high considering the large size of the population. This is a major roadblock in the increase in per capita income to a satisfactory level.

A much larger investment is needed to raise per capita income than India has. This adversely affects the growth rate of the economy. In India, the capital output ratio is 4:1. It means that in order to stabilize the existing economic growth rate $(4 \times 1.8) = 7.2$ per cent of national income must be invested.

Composition of population in India hampers the increase in capital formation. High birth rate and low expectancy of life means large number of dependents in the total population. According to World Bank, the dependency ratio (% of working-age population) in India was 52.36 in 2013. Age dependency ratio is the ratio of dependents—people younger than 15 or older than 64—to the working-age population—those aged between 15 and 64. Data are shown as the proportion of dependents per 100 working-age population. In India, 35 per cent of population is composed of persons less than 14 years of age. Most of these people depend on others for subsistence. They are unproductive consumers. The burden of dependents reduces the capacity of the people to save. So the rate of capital formation is low. Table 4.14 shows a comparison of age dependency ratio in India for 1990, 2000, and 2010.

Table 4.14: Comparison of Age Dependency Ratio in India

	1990	2000	2010	
Birth rate; crude (per 1;000 people) in India	30.2	25.9	22.2	[+]
Death rate; crude (per 1;000 people) in India	9.7	9.0	8.0	[+]
Population ages 0-14 (% of total) in India	37.9	34.7	30.6	[+]
Population ages 15-64 (% of total) in India	58.3	61.1	64.5	[+]
Population ages 65 and above (% of total) in India	3.8	4.2	4.9	[+]
Age dependency ratio (% of working-age population) in India	71.5	63.8	55.1	[+]
Age dependency ratio; old (% of working-age population) in India	6.6	6.9	7.6	[+]
Age dependency ratio; young (% of working-age population) in India	64.9	56.8	47.4	[+]
Population growth (annual %) in India	2.0	1.7	1.4	[+]
Population; total in India	849515000.0	1053898107.0	1224614327.0	[+]

http://www.tradingeconomics.com/india/death-rate-crude-per-1-000-people-wb-data.html

The large size of India's population in India and its rapid rate of growth is the main cause of low per capita availability of capital. From 1950-51 to 1980-81, India's national income grew at an average annual rate of 3.6 per cent per annum. But per capita income had risen around one per cent which is very low.

The large size of population in India, and high growth rate of population have are the root cause of food problem. There has been a spectacular rise in crop production after the Green Revolution and the adoption of modern methods of farming, but as population goes on increasing, there is still shortage of food. People do not get sufficient quantity of food which affects their health and productivity. Low productivity in turn causes low per capita income and results in poverty. Shortage of food grains compels the under-developed countries to import food grains from abroad. So a large part of foreign exchange is spent on it. So development work suffers as has happened in India. So rise in population causes food problem.

In India we have a large labour force. But due to shortage of capital resources it is not possible to provide gainful employment to the entire working population. There is also disguised unemployment in rural areas in India, which means more people are engaged on a farm or field—usually members of the same family—than required.

Youth Unemployment Rate in India was 18.10 in 1012, which came down to 12.90 per cent in 2013. On an average, this rate averaged 15.50 per cent from 2012 until 2013. Youth Unemployment Rate in India is reported by the Labour Bureau of Government of India. Table 4.15 shows the youth unemployment rate in India. Table 4.16 shows that comparison of unemployment rate of 14 major countries including India. It can be seen that India has 9th highest youth unemployment in the list of countries. But considering the fact that we have the largest youth population in the world, the number of unemployed youth is very high.

The Rapid growth of population in India accounts for low standard of living. To millions, even the bare necessities of life are not available adequately. Internationally, an income of less than US$ 1.25 per day per head of purchasing power parity is defined as extreme poverty. By this estimate, about 32.7%

per cent of Indians are extremely poor. Income-based poverty lines consider the bare minimum income to provide basic food requirements. It does not account for other essentials such as health care and education.

Table 4.15: Youth Unemployment Rate in India

India Labour	Last	Previous	Highest	Lowest	Unit	
Unemployment Rate	4.90	5.20	9.40	4.90	per cent	[+]
Employed Persons	29650	28999	29650	17491	Thousand	[+]
Unemployed Persons	44.79	40.17	44.79	5.10	Million	[+]
Population	1238.89	1223.58	1238.89	359.00	Million	[+]
Retirement Age Women	60.00	60.00	60.00	60.00		[+]
Retirement Age Men	60.00	60.00	60.00	60.00		[+]
Labor Force Participation Rate	52.50	50.90	52.90	50.90	per cent	[+]
Wages	4.83	5.07	5.47	3.12	INR/Day	[+]
Wages In Manufacturing	6.25	6.55	6.97	3.92	INR/Day	[+]
Youth Unemployment Rate	12.90	18.10	18.10	12.90	per cent	

Table 4.16: Comparison of Youth Unemployment Rate of 14 Major Countries

Countries	Youth Unemployment Rate	Reference	Previous	Highest	Lowest	Unit	
Australia	13.68	Aug/15	13.81	20.22	7.61	per cent	[+]
Canada	13.50	Sep/15	13.10	20.70	10.40	per cent	[+]
Euro Area	22.30	Aug/15	22.20	24.60	14.90	per cent	[+]
France	24.50	Aug/15	24.30	26.20	14.50	per cent	[+]
Germany	7.00	Aug/15	7.00	15.60	5.70	per cent	[+]
India	12.90	Dec/13	18.10	18.10	12.90	per cent	[+]
Italy	40.70	Aug/15	40.40	43.70	18.40	per cent	[+]
Japan	5.50	Jul/15	5.60	10.90	4.00	per cent	[+]
Netherlands	11.20	Aug/15	11.30	17.70	6.60	per cent	[+]
South Korea	7.80	Aug/15	8.90	13.40	3.80	per cent	[+]
Spain	48.80	Aug/15	48.70	55.80	17.20	per cent	[+]
Turkey	19.10	Jun/15	18.70	25.00	14.90	per cent	[+]
United Kingdom	15.40	Jun/15	15.80	22.30	9.70	per cent	[+]
United States	11.00	Sep/15	11.00	19.50	7.80	per cent	[+]

Source: http://www.tradingeconomics.com/india/death-rate-crude-per-1-000-people-wb-data.html

Rising population has perpetuated poverty in India. People have to spend a large portion of their resources for bringing up of their wards. It results into less saving and low rate of capital formation. Hence improvement in production technique becomes impossible. There is low productivity of labour.

Population explosion has given rise to many social problems. Unemployment has led to the migration of people from rural areas to the urban areas causing the growth of slum areas. People live in most unhygienic and insanitary conditions.

Unemployment and poverty lead to frustration and anger among the educated youth. This leads to crimes like robbery, beggary, prostitution and murder, etc. The terrorist activities that we find today in various parts of the country are the reflection of frustration among educated unemployed youth. Overcrowding, traffic congestions, frequent accidents and pollution in big cities are the direct result of overpopulation.

The rising rate of population growth exerts pressure on land. The per capita availability of land goes on diminishing and the problem of sub-division and fragmentation of holdings goes on increasing, adversely affecting the economic development of the country.

Besides, common properties like forest and water are over-exploited. This results in deforestation and desertification with permanent damage to the renewable resources.

Population explosion in India has led to environmental degradation. Higher birth rate has brought more pollution, more toxic wastes, damaging the biosphere.

Our existing infrastructure has been put under great strain due to large size of population. Facilities like housing, transportation, health care, and education always fall short of the ever-increasing demand. Overcrowded houses, slums and insanitary localities, traffic congestion and crowded hospitals have become common features in every big city in India.

The large size of India's population requires large quantities of basic necessities of life such as food. For this, lands which are not high yielding have to be brought under cultivation. This raises the cost of production and consequent rise in the price of food, i.e. food inflation.

Increase in gross national product (GNP) has been greatly reduced in per capita terms in India because of rapidly growing population. The focus of policymakers is more on economic growth. Other important considerations of unequal distribution of income have been put on the back burner. The inequalities within the country have widened further.

National Population Policy 2000

Introduction

The overriding objective of economic and social development is to improve the quality of lives that people lead, to enhance their well-being, and to provide them with opportunities and choices to become productive assets in society.

In 1952, India was the first country in the world to launch a national programme, emphasizing family planning to the extent necessary for reducing birth rates "to stabilize the population at a level consistent with the requirement of national economy". After 1952, sharp declines in death rates were, however, not accompanied by a similar drop in birth rates. The National Health Policy, 1983 stated that replacement levels of total fertility rate (TFR) should be achieved by the year 2000.

On 11 May 2000, India's population reached 1 billion (100 crore), i.e. 16 per cent of the total world population, though the country occupies only 2.4 per cent of the globe's total land area. It was predicted that if trends continue, India may overtake China in 2045 to become the most populous country in the world. While global population increased threefold during the 20th century, from 2 billion to 6 billion, the population of India has increased nearly five times from 238 million (23 crore) to 1 billion in the same period. India's current annual increase in population of 15.5 million is large enough to neutralize efforts to conserve the resource endowment and environment.

India's population projections for 2011 and 2016 as per Technical Group on Population Projections, Planning commission were 117.89 crore and 126.35 crore respectively. But as per 2011 census, our population was 121.02 crore, far exceeding the prediction. In 2015, India's population was 128.69 crore.

As of June 2017 the country's population was 133.40 crore. This means that we have not been able to control the growth of population, which is an essential requirement for promoting sustainable development with more equitable distribution. However, it is as much a function of making reproductive health care accessible and affordable for all, as of increasing the provision and outreach of primary and secondary education, extending basic amenities including sanitation, safe drinking water and housing, besides empowering women and enhancing their employment opportunities, and providing transport and communications.

The National Population Policy, 2000 (NPP 2000) provides a policy framework for advancing goals and prioritizing strategies during the next decade, to meet the reproductive and child health needs of the people of India, and to achieve net replacement levels (TFR). It is based upon the need to simultaneously address issues of child survival, maternal health, and contraception, while increasing outreach and coverage of a comprehensive package of reproductive and child health services by government, industry and the voluntary non-government sector, working in partnership.

Objectives

The immediate objective of the NPP 2000 is to address the unmet needs for contraception, health care infrastructure, and health personnel, and to provide integrated service delivery for basic reproductive and child health care. The medium-term objective is to bring the TFR to replacement levels by 2010, through vigorous implementation of inter-sectoral operational strategies. The long-term objective is to achieve a stable population by 2045, at a level consistent with the requirements of sustainable economic growth, social development, and environmental protection.

In pursuance of these objectives, the following National Socio-Demographic Goals to be achieved in each case by 2010 were formulated:

National Socio-Demographic Goals for 2010

- Address the unmet needs for basic reproductive and child health services, supplies and infrastructure.
- Make school education up to age 14 free and compulsory, and reduce dropouts at primary and secondary school levels to below 20 per cent for both boys and girls.
- Reduce infant mortality rate to below 30 per 1000 live births.
- Reduce maternal mortality ratio to below 100 per 100,000 live births.
- Achieve universal immunization of children against all vaccine preventable diseases.
- Promote delayed marriage for girls, not earlier than the age of 18 and preferably after 20 years of age.
- Achieve 80 per cent institutional deliveries and 100 per cent deliveries by trained persons.
- Achieve universal access to information/counseling, and services for fertility regulation and contraception with a wide basket of choices.
- Achieve 100 per cent registration of births, deaths, marriage and pregnancy.
- Contain the spread of Acquired Immuno-Deficiency Syndrome (AIDS), and promote greater integration between the management of reproductive tract infections (RTI) and sexually transmitted infections (STI) and the National AIDS Control Organization.
- Prevent and control communicable diseases.
- Integrate Indian Systems of Medicine (ISM) in the provision of reproductive and child health services, and in reaching out to households.
- Promote vigorously the small family norm to achieve replacement levels of TFR.
- Bring about convergence in implementation of related social sector programmes so that family welfare becomes a people-centred programme.

If the NPP 2000 were fully implemented, India's population as projected by the Technical Group on Population Projections would have as under:

Table 4.17: Anticipated Growth in Population

(in million)

Year	if current trend continues Total Population	Increase in Total Population	and if TFR 2.1 is achieved by 2010 Total Population
1991	846.3	–	846.3
1996	934.2	17.6	934.2
1997	949.9	15.7	949.0
2000	996.9	15.7	991.0
2002	1027.6	15.4	1013.0
2010	1162.3	16.8	1107.0

Source: Ministry of Health and Family Welfare

The fact that our actual population has been much more than the above projections, bears testimony that NPP were not fully implemented and we need to bring a new national population policy and implement it properly.

India's Demographic Dividend

Demographic dividend refers to a period of two or three decades when fertility rates fall due to significant reductions in child and infant mortality rates. When women and families realize that fewer children will die during infancy or childhood, they begin to have fewer children to reach the number of offspring they desire to have. This further reduces the proportion of non-productive dependents.

The United Nations Population Fund (UNFPA) has defined demographic dividend as "the economic growth potential that can result from shifts in a population's age structure, mainly when the share of the working-age population (15 to 64) is larger than the non-working-age share of the population (14 and younger, and 65 and older)." It occurs when the numbers of people in the workforce are increasing as compared to the number of dependents and is thus is marked by a boost in economic productivity.

Such a drop in fertility rates is however not immediate. There is a time lag which produces a generational population bulge that surges through society. For some period of time this bulge is a burden on society and the dependency ratio goes higher. But after some time this group begins to enter the productive labour force. The dependency ratio declines with fertility rates continuing to fall and older generations having shorter life expectancies. This demographic shift initiates the demographic dividend.

India has a big competitive advantage in the shape of its demographic dividend. According to the United Nations population research, the countries of Asia, including India, and of Latin America have been the main beneficiaries of the demographic dividend during the last four decades. In comparison, the advanced countries of Europe, Japan and USA have an ageing population because of low birth rates and low mortality rates.

China's one child policy has reversed the demographic dividend it enjoyed since the mid-1960s.

In India, the falling birth rates in India have reduced the overall expenditure required to provide basic necessities for population under the age of 14 (which is yet to be productive). There is increased longevity which has ensured that a large proportion of the population is within the 15-59 age group, which is working population. Thus the dependency ratio (the proportion of non-working population on the working population) has decreased which is around 0.6 at present.

Demographic dividend is a favourable situation, but it requires focused policy action to utilize it and bring progress. Some experts feel that India is squandering this demographic opportunity, because its GDP growth has declined to below 6 per cent level from its peak of around 8 per cent. IIP data shows a fall in industrial output. High inflation has deterred savings and forced the households, and the balance of payments remains unfavourable. Moreover, the country has not been able to create enough jobs to absorb its large working force.

A recent survey by United Nations Economic and Social Commission for Asia and the Pacific (UNESCAP) has shown that there are no guarantees the demographic dividend will automatically translate to economic growth. There have to be appropriate "social and economic policies and institutions" to absorb the rapidly growing labour force. Other prerequisites include reforms in the health and education sector, financial inclusion and adequate employment opportunities to ensure that India's young population is used as a valuable asset.

In its 12th Plan discussions, the Planning Commission of India indicated that while the "demographic dividend" accounted for India having world's youngest workforce, the global economy is expected to face a skilled manpower shortage of around 56 million by 2020. Therefore, the demographic dividend that India has should be used not only to expand production of goods and services but also to meet the skilled manpower requirements of in India and overseas. It is pertinent to mention here that in order to reap the benefits of demographic dividend, the Eleventh Five Year Plan had called for the creation of a comprehensive National Skill Development Mission. Various strategies for the 12th Plan, included a focus on improved access to quality education, better preventive and curative health care, enhancement of skills and faster generation of employment. The demographic estimates of selected countries as on 2012 are given in Table 4.18.

Conclusion

India has a large population. Its growth rate of population is also very high. The large size of population has been one of the major reasons of backwardness, poverty of masses and slow socio-economic growth of the country. The Government at the Centre and State level are making policies and programmes for fast development, but the expected results are not achieved because of the large size of the population. Economic indicators do not show the desired level of progress. Per capita income does not increase much. Capital formation is hindered. Unemployment is widespread. There is a severe burden on resources. Demand for goods and services keeps on increasing but the output is unable to cope with it. There is distribution problem. Infrastructure is proving inadequate. India is predicted to be a superpower in

Table 4.18: Demographic Estimates for Selected Countries, 2012

Sl.No.	Country	Population (Million) 2010	Under 5 Mortality Rate	Infant Mortality Rate (Per 1000 Live Births)	Neonatal Mortality Rate (Per 1000 Live Births)	Life Expectancy At Birth (Years)	Population Annual Growth Rate (%)	Crude Birth Rate	Total Fertility Rate	Contraceptive Prevalence Rate (%)	Maternal Mortality Ratio Reported
1	Afghanisthan	31.4	149	103	45	48	2.6	44	6.3	23	1600
2	Bangladesh	164.4	48	38	27	69	1.0	20	2.2	53	190
3	China	1354.1	18	16	11	73	0.2	12	1.6	8569	32
4	Democratic People's Republic of Korea	24.3	33	26	18	69	0.4	14	2.0	54	77
5	India	1224.6	59 (As Per SRS)	44 (As Per SRS)	33 (As Per SRS)	65	1.1	22	2.5 (As Per SRS)	61	212 (As Per SRS)
6	Indonesia	239.9	35	27	17	69	0.8	18	2.1	79	230
7	Iran	74.0	26	22	14	73	0.7	17	1.7	54	25
8	Japan	126.5	3	2	1	83	-0.3	9	1.4	-	-
9	Malaysia	28.4	6	5	3	74	1.4	20	2.6	41	29
10	Mayanmar	48	66	50	32	65	0.6	17	2.0	48	320
11	Nepal	30.0	50	41	28	68	1.4	24	2.7	27	280
12	Pakistan	173.6	87	70	41	65	1.5	27	3.4	51	25
13	Philippines	93.3	29	23	14	68	1.5	25	3.1	80	160
14	Republic of Korea	48.2	5	4	2	81	0.2	10	1.3	-	-

Sl.No.	Country	Population (Million) 2010	Under 5 Mortality Rate	Infant Mortality Rate (Per 1000 Live Births)	Neonatal Mortality Rate (Per 1000 Live Births)	Life Expectancy At Birth (Years)	Population Annual Growth Rate (%)	Crude Birth Rate	Total Fertility Rate	Contraceptive Prevalence Rate (%)	Maternal Mortality Ratio Reported
15	Singapore	5.1	3	2	1	81	0.8	9	1.3	68	-
16	Sri Lanka	20.9	17	14	10	75	0.5	18	2.3	80	39
17	Thailand	69.1	13	11	8	74	0.3	12	1.6	80	12
18	Vietnam	87.8	23	19	12	75	0.7	17	1.8	71	69
19	Australia	22.3	5	4	3	82	1.1	14	1.9	-	-
20	Industrialized Countries	989.5	6	5	3	80	0.4	12	1.7	-	-
21	Developing Countries	5621.3	63	44	25	68	1.1	21	2.6	61	-
22	Less Developed Countries	832.3	110	71	34	59	2.1	34	4.2	33	-
23	World	6856.8	57	40	23	70	0.9	20	2.5	63	-

Source: The State of World Children, 2012 (UNICEF); - Data not Found

the coming decades, but the country's inability to contain its population has put a big question mark on the realization of that dream.

The only redeeming feature of India's population is its favourable age structure, viz. larger working population, i.e. in the age group of 15 and 64 years (64.9%) than the non-working-age share of the population, i.e. 14 and younger, and 65 and older (35.1%). This demographic dividend is a favourable situation, but we need to make good policies and implement them effectively to leverage it. Absorbing our rapidly growing labour force will be a huge task. Other prerequisites include reforms in the health and education sector, and financial inclusion.

Notes

1. C. Chandramouli (23 August 2011). "Census of India 2011—A Story of Innovations". Press Information Bureau, Government of India.
2. *Ibid.*
3. Bureau of Labour Statistics, Indian Government (8 October 2010). "Report on Employment & Unemployment Survey (2009-10)" (PDF).
4. Planning Commission of India (2007). "Labour Laws and Other Labour Regulations" (PDF). The Government of India.
5. Swaminathan (1991). "Understanding the informal sector: a survey" (PDF).
6. Nurul Amin (2002). "The Informal Sector in Asia from the Decent Work Perspective" (PDF). International Labour Office, Geneva.
7. Tripti Lahiri (April 2011). "India Passes 1.2 Billion Mark." *The Wall Street Journal.*

5

Agriculture and Food Security

Agriculture is the mainstay of Indian economy. As per Food and Agriculture Organization (FAO) world agriculture statistics, India is the world's largest producer of many fresh fruits and vegetables, milk, major spices, select fibrous crops such as jute, staples like millets, and castor oil seed. India is world's second largest producer of wheat, rice and major food staples. Demographically, agriculture is the broadest economic sector and plays a significant role in the socio-economic fabric of India. Overall, this sector has recorded satisfactory growth due to improved technology, better irrigation, higher quality inputs and better pricing policies. Livestock, poultry, fisheries and horticulture have surged ahead in production in recent years and are expected to have greater demand in the future. However, industrial and service sectors have expanded faster than agriculture sector, resulting in the declining share of agriculture in national accounts. Despite this structural change, agriculture still remains a key sector, providing both employment and livelihood opportunities to around 65 per cent of the total workforce in the country.

Importance of Agriculture

The importance of agriculture and allied sectors in the national economy can be best studied by analyzing the role of agriculture under separate headings:

Largest Provider of Employment

Agriculture provides employment and livelihood to a very high proportion of working population in India. As per the data provided by the Census of India, agriculture provided employment in absolute terms to 97 million persons in 1951, which increased to 402 million in 2001 (Table 5.1). In addition to those dependent on agriculture directly, a large number of people earn their living by working in occupations dependent upon agriculture, like storage, processing, and trade and transport of agricultural products. While in villages people earn from cultivation and allied agro-industries, a large number of labour force in towns and cities also find jobs in marketing, export and other activities linked with agriculture. According to National Sample Survey Office (NSSO), agriculture and allied activities remain the major source of livelihood for nearly half of the Indian population. The share of agriculture in employment is 48.9 per cent of the workforce. According to Ministry of Agriculture, over 58 per cent of the rural households depend on agriculture as their principal means of livelihood.

Table 5.1: Employment of Main Workers in Agriculture

(in million)

	1951	2001	2011
Total Population	361	1027	1210
Rural Population	299	742	833
Cultivators	70	128	178
Agricultural Labourers	27	107	125
Other Workers	43	167	178
Total Working Population	40	402	481

Source: Agricultural Statistics at a Glance.

Source of Large Supplies of Food and Fodder

Agricultural sector meets the need of food of the country's entire population. India has vast land plains and suitable climate to grow various types of crops such as cereals like wheat, rice, maize, soybeans, and barley, which are part of daily food of common Indian. India also produces dry fruits, roots and tuber crops, pulses, farmed fish, eggs, coconut, sugarcane and various types of vegetables. India is ranked among world's five largest producers of over 80% of agricultural produce items, including many cash crops such as tea, coffee and cotton. India is also one of the world's five largest producers of livestock and poultry meat.

Since India is a country with large population, we also have to import food grains and other food items. When there is low rainfall, or extensive damage is caused to standing crops due to untimely rain or hailstones, there is shortage of food, and prices tend to rise. Although imports of food grains have played a significant role in meeting the growing needs of rising population, yet the fact remains that the proportion of such imports has always been small. Except for 1966 and 1967, when food imports were higher than 10 per cent of the net availability of food grains in the country, in most of the years it was on an average less than 5 per cent. We also export many food items which are grown in abundance in our country.

The importance of agriculture in providing fodder to sustain livestock cannot be overemphasized. Various products given by livestock are the sources of nourishing food like milk, eggs, meat, etc. Products like wool and hides have high commercial value. A large number of farmers in India depend on animal husbandry for their livelihood. In addition to supplying milk, meat, eggs, wool and hides, animals, mainly bullocks, are the major source of power for both farmers and drayers. Thus, animal husbandry plays an important role in India's rural economy. Dairy farming provides supplementary employment and an additional source of income to many small and marginal farmers. Today, India has the world's largest dairy herd at over 304 million, and stands first in milk production, with 112.5 million tonnes of milk produced in 2009-10. India is also the third largest egg-producer in the world, at over 180 million eggs being produced every day or 65.7 billion eggs (2011-12). India is world's sixth largest producer of poultry meat.

Role of Agriculture in Foreign Trade

Agriculture contributes a considerable part to exports and is also an important segment of imports by the country. Exports of agricultural products have been quite large. Agricultural products, like tea, sugar, oilseeds, tobacco, spices, etc. constitute the main items of exports. These exports at present constitute 15 to 20 per cent of the total exports of the country.

While the majority of India's animal products are consumed domestically, exports are growing. India has emerged as a significant exporter of cotton, rice, meat, oil meals, spices, guargum meal and sugar. As per trade statistics given by World Trade Organization, the share of India's agricultural exports and imports in the world trade in 2013 and 2014 was 2.46% and 1.46%, respectively. Agricultural exports as a percentage of agricultural GDP increased from 7.95% in 2009-10 to 12.08% in 2014-15. Agricultural imports as a percentage of agricultural GDP also increased from 4.90% to 5.82% during this period. India is also the largest producer, consumer and exporter of spices and spice products. India's fruit production has grown faster than that of vegetables, making it the second largest fruit producer in the world. Agricultural export constitutes 10 per cent of the country's exports and is the fourth largest in terms of exported principal commodities.

India is the top global exporter of buffalo meat, and is also the fourth largest exporter of soybean meal, which is an important ingredient in commercial feed given to farmed animals. India's poultry production is also increasing, leading to expansion in export to countries in other parts of Asia and the Middle East. There are many small scale producers in the milk and cheese sectors, and the number of large, factory-style dairy operations is also increasing.

India exported US$ 39 billion worth of agricultural products in 2013, making it the seventh largest agricultural exporter worldwide and the sixth largest net exporter. Most of its agriculture exports serve developing and least developed nations. India has been the fastest growing exporter of agricultural products over a 10-year period, and its net exports are more than double the combined exports of the European Union. It has become one of the world's largest supplier of rice, cotton, sugar and wheat. India exported around 2 million metric tonnes of wheat and 2.1 million metric tonnes of rice in 2011 to Africa, Nepal, Bangladesh and other regions around the world.[1]

Table 5.2: Agriculture Sector: Key Indicators
(per cent change at 2011-12 prices)

Sl. No.	Item	2011-12	2012-13*	2013-14*	2014-15@
1.	Growth in GDP in Agriculture & Allied Sectors (at constant 2011-12 prices)	5.0#	1.5	4.2	(-)0.2
	Share of Agriculture & Allied Sectors in total GVA (at current 2011-12 prices)	18.5	18.2	18.3	17.4
	Share of Crops	12.1	11.8	11.9	10.9
	Share of Livestock	4.0	4.1	4.1	4.4
	Share of Forestry and Logging	1.5	1.5	1.4	1.2
	Share of Fishing	0.8	0.9	0.9	0.9
2.	Share of Agriculture & Allied Sectors in total Gross Capital Formation (GCF) (at current 2011-12 prices)	8.6	7.8	8.6	7.7
	Share of Crops	7.3	6.6	7.3	6.4
	Share of Livestock	0.8	0.8	0.8	0.8
	Share of Forestry and Logging	0.1	0.1	0.1	0.1
	Share of Fishing	0.4	0.4	0.5	0.5
3.	GCF in Agriculture & Allied Sectors as per cent to GVA of the sector (at current 2011-12 prices)	18.3	16.3	17.0	15.8

Source: CSO.

Notes: # at 2004-05 prices; * Second RE (New Series), @ First RE; GVA is Gross Value Added.

Share of Agriculture in GDP

According to the data provided by CSO, the share of agriculture in India's Gross Domestic Product (GDP) was 17.4 per cent in 2014-15 at 2011-12 prices. The Twelfth Five Year Plan (2012-13 to 2016-17) had envisaged a growth target of 4 per cent for agriculture and allied sectors, necessary for the Indian economy to grow at over 8 per cent. The growth rates in agriculture have been fluctuating at 1.5 per cent in 2012-13, 4.2 per cent in 2013-14, and (–) 0.2 per cent in 2014-15, as shown in Table 5.2. The growth in the agriculture, forestry and fishing sector was estimated at 1.1 per cent in 2015-16. The estimates of GDP for the second quarter (July-September) of 2015-16, agriculture, forestry and fishing sector reported a growth of 2.2% against the target of 4%. The shortfall in growth was due to the fact that 60 per cent of agriculture in India is dependent on monsoon, and there have been two consecutive drought years in 2013-14 and 2014-15. There was also shortage of capital formation in this sector. Moreover, volatility in market prices of agriculture produce altered and distorted the cropping patterns of some crops.[2]

Table 5.2 also shows that share of crops in India's agriculture & allied sectors in total GVA decreased from 12.1% in 2011-12 to 11.8% in 2012-13, 11.9% in 2013-14 and 10.9% in 2014-15. But the share of livestock increased and that of fishing remained steady. The share of Gross Capital Formation (GCF) in agriculture and allied sectors as a percentage of the sector went down from 18.3 in 2011-12, to 16.3 in 2012-13, before increasing to 17.0 in 2013-14 and then decreasing to 15.8 in 2014-15.

Performance of India's Agriculture—Production and Yield

India's food grains production during 2015-16 was estimated at 253.16 million tonnes, which was higher by 1.14 million tonnes over the production of 252.02 million tonnes during 2014-15. The area, production and yield of different crops is given in Table 5.3. The acreage under several crops declined substantially in 2014-15 compared to 2013-14 as per the Fourth Advance Estimates. The areas of gram and groundnut saw the largest decline at 20% and 15%, respectively, which resulted in decline in production of gram and groundnut by 27% and 32% in 2014-15 from the 2013-14 level. It is clear that the shift away from gram and groundnut has been in regions of relatively higher productivity, because the respective declines in output are much larger than the declines in the acreage. Only two crops, jowar and bajra, registered a higher percentage of yield in 2014-15 over the previous year. With scanty moisture and precipitation, there was delayed sowing, which is reflected in a decline in percentage change in area sown of the majority of crops (Table 5.3).

Table 5.3: Area, Production and Yield (2014-15*)

Group/Commodity	Area (million ha)	Percentage change in area	Production (million tonnes)	Percentage change in production	Yield (kg/ha)	Percentage change in yield
Foodgrains[a]	122.1	-3.1	252.7	-4.6	2070	-1.5
Rice	43.9	-0.2	104.8	-1.6	2390	-1.4
Wheat	31.0	-0.7	88.9	-7.3	2872	-6.6
Jowar	5.3	-9.0	5.1	-6.3	953	3.0
Maize	9.3	-1.8	23.7	-2.8	2557	-1.0
Bajra	7.1	-9.7	9.1	-1.4	1272	9.3
Pulses	23.1	-8.4	17.2	-10.8	744	-2.6
Gram	8.2	-19.9	7.2	-27.4	875	-9.4
Tur	3.7	-4.9	2.8	-15.5	750	-11.6
Oilseeds	25.7	-9.8	26.7	-18.9	1037	-10.0
Groundnut	4.7	-15.2	6.6	-32.2	1400	-20.0
Rapeseed and Mustard	5.8	-13.6	6.3	-20.7	1089	-8.3
Cotton[b]	13.1	11.8	35.5	-3.3	461	-13.3
Sugarcane	5.1	2.0	359.3	2.7	70#	0.0

Source: Directorate of Economics and Statistics, Department of Agriculture, Cooperation and Farmers Welfare.

Notes: *Fourth AE; # tonnes/ha; [a] : Includes cereals and pulses; [b] : Million Bales of 170 kg.

In order to get a clear picture of what improvement has been made in the average yields, we have to see the yearly data, as shown in Table 5.4.

Table 5.4: Average Yields of Major Crops in India (kg/ha)

Crop	Average yield 1970-71	Average yield 1980-81	Average yield 1990-91	Average yield 2000-01	Average yield 2010-11	Average yield 2013-14	Average yield 2014-15*
Rice	1123	1336	1740	1901	2239	2416	2390
Wheat	1307	1630	2281	2708	2989	3145	2872
Pulses	524	473	578	544	691	764	744
Oilseeds	579	532	771	810	1193	1168	1037
Sugarcane (tonnes/ha)	48	58	65	69	70	71	70
Tea	1182	1491	1794	1673	1712	2170	2170
Cotton	106	152	225	190	499	510	461

Source: Directorate of Economics & Statistics, Department of Agriculture, Cooperation and Farmers Welfare.

Note: * Fourth AE.

Table 5.4 shows that average yields of major crops had an impressive growth over the decades from 1970-71 to 1990-91. This was made possible with the introduction of high-yielding varieties of seeds (hybrid seeds). The increased use of chemical fertilizers and irrigation led to the increase in production needed to make the country self-sufficient in food grains, thus improving agriculture in India. The methods adopted include the use of high-yielding varieties (HYVs) of seeds and modern farming methods.

The increase in the production of wheat has brought the best results in fueling India's self-sufficiency. The increasing use of chemical pesticides and fertilizers also boosted the yield. The production of wheat and rice at 2872 kg/ha and 2390 kg/ha respectively, was double from its level of 1307 kg/ha and 1123 kg/ha respectively in 1970-71.

The average yield of pulses registered negative growth rate over the period 1980-81 over 1970-71 and 2000-01 over 1990-91. The introduction of Bt cotton resulted in a spurt in the yield of cotton during the period 2010-11 over 2000-01. In 2014-15, the yields in rice, wheat, pulses, and oilseeds showed a decline from their level of 2013-14. This was largely due to poor monsoon in many parts of the country.

International Comparisons

Per hectare yield of major crops in India is far lower than that of many other countries. Even our best performing States cannot match their production. For example, in case of chickpeas, per hectare yield is highest in Andhra Pradesh at 1,439 kilograms, but this is far lower than the average yield of Ethiopia which is 1,663 kilograms.

In paddy, the per hectare yield in Punjab, which is considered to be the highest in the country is around 3,952 kilograms, far lower than China's average yield of 6,661 kilograms. The yield of maize, in Tamil Nadu is around 5,372 kilograms, which is lower than the average yield of USA, which is 8,858 kilograms. The rapeseed yield in Gujarat, the best in the country, is around 1,723 kilograms, which is less than half of 3,588 of United Kingdom. According to Economic Survey 2015-16, China has an average cereal yield of above 5,800 kg per ha, while India has less than 3,000 kg/ha. USA has the largest average cereal yield of more than 7,000 kg/ha.

In order to increase the productivity in agriculture, we have to make more investment in key inputs, expand irrigated areas, improve efficiency in water use, mechanize operations of agriculture to lower costs and reduce wastage, develop improved varieties of seeds and address the concerns about introduction of genetically modified seeds, make efficient use of fertilizers and pesticides through improved practices, enhance credit access to farmers for investments at low rates, and develop more harvesting and storage facilities.

Important Factors Influencing Indian Agriculture

There are a number of factors that influence Indian agriculture. They are discussed below.

Irrigation

The all India percentage distribution of net irrigated area to total cropped area during 2012-13 was 33.9%. The percentage distribution of irrigated area to total cropped area varies in different states in India. Punjab, UP and Tamil Nadu have more than 50 irrigated area out of their respective total cropped area, while Bihar, MP, Gujarat, AP, and Karnataka have around 35% irrigated area out of their total cropped area. States like Assam, Sikkim, HP, Jharkhand, and Maharashtra have less than 30% irrigated area out of their total cropped area. The link between irrigated area and productivity is quite clear. Well irrigated states like Punjab and Haryana have higher yields than the states with lower irrigation facilities.

Irrigation infrastructure in India is comprised of a network of major and minor canals from rivers, groundwater well-based systems, tanks, and other rainwater harvesting projects for agricultural activities. The largest of these is groundwater system. Of the 160 million hectares of cultivated land in India, about 39 million hectares are irrigated by groundwater wells and an additional 22 million hectares by irrigation canals. About two-third of cultivated land in India is dependent on rainfall. When the monsoon is not normal, agriculture produce is adversely

affected. The improvements in irrigation infrastructure in the last 50 years have helped India improve food security, reduce dependence on rainfall, improve agricultural productivity and create rural job opportunities. Dams used for irrigation projects have helped provide drinking water to a growing rural population, control flood and prevent drought-related damage to agriculture. But a lot remains to be done keeping in view the ever-increasing demand for food in India due to high growth rate of population.

Depleting Water Table in India

The depleting water table in many parts of the world is an area of concern. As per data from NASA's Gravity Recovery and Climate Experiment (GRACE) satellites, groundwater is disappearing fast from the world and India is among the worst hit. Among the world's largest groundwater basins, the Indus Basin aquifer of India and Pakistan, which is a source of freshwater for millions of people, is the second-most overstressed with no natural replenishment to offset usage, said two new studies led by the University of California, Irvine (UCI), using data from GRACE satellites.

The recent NASA report on the status of groundwater depletion is both a cause of alarm as well as a trigger for action. The causes of groundwater depletion include wastage of rainwater which flows into the drains, regional variations in the major sources for recharging the aquifers, real estate boom in urban areas which has blocked the passage of rainwater and hindered its absorption in the soil, irregularity of monsoon which is sometimes inadequate to recharge aquifers, and indiscriminate use of water, adding to the exhaustion and lowering of water table.

The impact of groundwater depletion is varied on different segments. For instance, poor and vulnerable sections such as slum dwellers are more adversely affected due to lack of water for their basic needs, while those in arid areas such as Rajasthar are forced to use brackish water (having more salinity tha freshwater) for their use. Sectors of economy such as agricultu are most affected due to lack of water for irrigation. The regio growing crops like paddy which require intensive use of wa are adversely impacted and contribute poorly to the econon

The State-wise position of total crop area and the total crop area actually irrigated is given in Table 5.5, which underlines the fact that in many States the irrigation potential has not been realized. The table also shows how much area is equipped with groundwater irrigation and how much is canal irrigation equipped. It can be seen that more area is dependent on groundwater than on canals.

Table 5.5: State-wise Irrigation types, Capacity and Actual

State	Total crop area (2011) (million hectares)	Groundwater irrigation equipped crop area (2011) (million hectares)	Canal irrigation equipped crop area (2011) (million hectares)	Total crop area actually irrigated (2011) (million hectares)
Andhra Pradesh	14.3	2.5	2.7	4.9
Arunachal Pradesh	0.4		0.07	0.05
Assam	3.0	0.13	0.1	0.22
Bihar	6.4	2.2	1.3	3.5
Chhattisgarh	5.1	0.17	0.74	0.85
Goa	0.1		0.1	0.1
Gujarat	9.9	3.1	0.5	3.2
Haryana	3.6	1.99	1.32	3.26
Himachal Pradesh	1.0	0.02	0.09	0.11
Jammu & Kashmir	0.9	0.02	0.38	0.37
Jharkhand	3.2	0.11	0.13	0.24
Karnataka	12.2	1.43	1.33	2.38
Kerala	1.5	0.18	0.21	0.39
Madhya Pradesh	15.8	2.74	1.70	4.19
Maharashtra	19.8	3.12	1.03	3.36
Manipur	0.2		0.05	0.05
Meghalaya	0.3		0.06	0.06
Mizoram	0.1		0.01	0.01
Nagaland	1.1		0.1	0.07
Odisha	4.9	0.17	1.07	1.24
Punjab	4.0	3.06	0.94	3.96
Rajasthan	21.1	3.98	1.52	5.12
Sikkim	0.1		0.01	0.01
Tamil Nadu	6.5	1.61	1.43	2.66
Tripura	0.3	0.02	0.05	0.07
Uttar Pradesh	17.6	10.64	4.21	14.49
Uttarakhand	0.8	0.22	0.14	0.35
West Bengal	5.5	2.09	1.22	2.98
All India	159.6	39.43	22.48	58.13

Note: The all India total includes land area for Union Territories of India that is not shown in the above table.

There is need and scope for increasing the coverage of irrigated area across the country to increase productivity in agriculture.

According to Economic Survey 2015-16, achieving efficiency in the use of irrigation systems will be the main determinant of agricultural productivity in India. The conventional systems of irrigation have become non-viable in many parts of India due to increasing shortages of water, wastage of water through over-irrigation, and concerns of salination of soil as per Task Force on Agriculture (NITI Aayog, 2015). We can improve water use efficiency by adopting technologies like drip irrigation, sprinkler irrigation, etc. which are both economically and technically efficient.

One of the objectives of the Prime Minister's Krishi Sinchai Yojana (PMKSY) is to enhance on-farm Water-Use Efficiency (WUE) spatially and temporally to reduce wastage by promoting precision irrigation. According to National Committee on Plasticulture Applications in Horticulture (NCPAH), the case for greater spread of Micro Irrigation (MI) technology arises in the context of the successful outcomes seen in some of the major states that have adopted this technology. The adoption of sprinkler irrigation has resulted in 35 to 40 per cent saving of irrigation water in the cultivation of groundnut and cotton in Gujarat, Karnataka and Andhra Pradesh. The adoption of drip irrigation has resulted in 40 to 65 per cent savings in water for horticulture crops and 30 to 47 per cent for vegetables. These techniques need to be used in other areas/crops, wherever possible. There is a pressing need for equitable distribution of water to different segments with penalty on overuse, discontinuing the policy of providing free water and implementing reuse and recycling of consumed water, as well as adopting rainwater harvesting on a large scale.

Water Productivity

Water productivity refers to the crop yield per cubic metre of water consumption, including 'green' water (effective rainfall) for rain-fed areas and both 'green' water and 'blue' water (water diverted from water systems) for irrigated areas. In India, water productivity is very low and needs to be enhanced through tapping, harvesting and recycling water, adopting efficient on-farm water management practices, and resource conservation technologies. The overall irrigation efficiency of the major and medium irrigation projects in India is estimated at around 38 per cent. Efficiency of the surface irrigation system can be improved to around 60 per cent and that of groundwater from about 65-70 per cent to 75 per cent.

The new government has also emphasized the need for making efficient use of water. Prime Minister Narendra Modi has asked agricultural scientists to disseminate technologies to farmers in simple and acceptable manner and make "per drop, more crop" a mantra to promote farming through optimum utilization of water. He stressed the need to increase per hectare productivity by adopting short duration crop varieties. He also called for judicious mix of traditional wisdom and "new technologies" to improve soil health and fertility.

Second Green Revolution

Initiated by Norman Borlaug in 1978, the first Green Revolution depended on an increased use of irrigation, pesticides and fertilizers to boost agriculture growth. The insect-resistant, high yielding varieties of wheat and other cereals helped India embark on the road to achieving self-sustenance.

However, the practices and strategies adopted by the first Green Revolution are no longer sustainable. The increased irrigation has pushed the underground water to an alarmingly low level. The unrestrained usage of fertilizers and pesticides has proved detrimental to our environment. While the old technologies have run their course, the impetus provided by the first Green Revolution has slowed down which is being reflected in the low-key performance of our agriculture sector. There is an urgent need for laying a renewed emphasis on research to increase farm productivity.

The second Green Revolution can be defined as a change in agricultural production necessary to feed and sustain the growing population on Earth. In an effort to tackle sluggish long-term agricultural growth in India, there is a call for second Green Revolution with an entirely new approach, and a new set of technologies. This will involve precision agriculture, wherein farmers will make the most efficient use of vital inputs such as water and specific fertilizer by applying them in precise amounts. This will also prevent wastage of important inputs, and reduce the impact of agriculture on the environment.

The new government has called to reopen fertilizer plants in Sindri (Jharkhand) and Gorakhpur (Uttar Pradesh), and open new ones in West Bengal and take into account the fact that India's soil is diverse, and fertilizer requirements will vary greatly across the country. This is also known as nutrient stewardship which was overlooked by the earlier government subsidy programmes that only favoured urea for a long time. The second Green Revolution considers 4Rs of nutrient stewardship, viz. the right source, right rate, the right time and the right place. Testing of soil samples from agricultural fields is necessary to know which soil needs what type of fertilizer. For this, a vast network of 661 soil testing laboratories has been established in India. These include 120 mobile vans operating in 608 districts. Besides soil-testing, gadgets such as leaf colour charts and optical sensors are becoming popular with farmers to guide the application of urea—a nitrogen fertilizer—which, if used incorrectly, can affect groundwater reserves and contribute to emissions of the greenhouse gas, nitrous oxide.

Second Green Revolution also needs to address the problem of shrinking cultivable land and shortage of water for irrigation. Some of our water resources have dried, while many others have dwindled. Groundwater reservoirs have decreased in quality as well as quantity due to reckless extraction and flow of toxic material like chemical fertilizers and pesticides. We have to develop techniques which would deliver more crop for each drop of water as well as more yield per field of cultivated land. By suggesting the methods to address these problems our agro-scientists and irrigation engineers can help the farmers bring a water-efficient second Green Revolution.

Emerging Areas in Agriculture

The emerging areas in agriculture like horticulture, floriculture and organic farming trading have high potential of growth in India. The progress made in India is discussed below.

Horticulture

The total production and economic value of horticultural produce, such as fruits, vegetables and nuts doubled in India over the 10-year period from 2002 to 2012. In 2012, the production from horticulture exceeded grain output for the first time. The total horticulture produce reached 277.4 million metric tonnes in 2013, making India the second largest producer of horticultural products after China. India in 2013 produced 81 million tonnes of fruits, 162 million tonnes of vegetables, 5.7 million tonnes of spices, 17 million tonnes of nuts and plantation products (cashew, cacao, coconut, etc.), 1 million tonnes of aromatic horticulture produce and 1.7 million tonnes of flowers (7.6 billion cut flowers). During 2013-14, India exported horticulture products worth ₹ 14,365 crore (US$ 2.1 billion), which was nearly double the value of its 2010 exports.

The percentage share of horticulture output in agriculture is more than 33 per cent. The share of plan outlay for horticulture, which was 3.9 per cent during Ninth Plan (1997-2002) increased to 4.6 per cent during the Twelfth Plan (2012-17). Over the last decade, the area under horticulture grew by about 2.7 per cent per annum and annual production increased by 7.0 per cent. During 2013-14, the production of horticulture crops was about 283.5 million tonnes from an area of 24.2 million hectares. Out of the six categories—fruits, vegetables, flowers, aromatic plants, spices and plantation crops—the highest annual growth of 9.5 per cent was seen in fruit production during 2013-14. The production of vegetables increased from 58,532 thousand tonnes in 1991-92 to 1,67,058 thousand tonnes in 2014-15.

There was a sharp increase in acreage in horticulture crops compared to food grains during the period 2010-11 to 2014-15. The area under horticulture crops increased around 18 per cent compared to an expansion of area under food grains by 5 per cent during the stipulated period. As a result, the production of horticulture crops outpaced the production of food grain since 2012-13.

The Mission for Integrated Development of Horticulture (MIDH), was launched during the Twelfth Five-Year Plan with effect from 2014-15, for the holistic development of the horticulture sector, covering fruits, vegetables, mushrooms, spices, flowers, aromatic plants, coconut, cashew, cocoa and bamboo. Under this mission, the Government of India (GOI) initially contributed 85 per cent of the total outlay for developmental programmes in all the States. From 2015-16, the pattern of assistance was changed to be in the ratio of 60:40 between the Government of India and NHM States (18 States with poor infrastructure covered under National Rural Health Mission) and 90:10 for HMNEH States (North East and Himalayan States covered under Horticulture Mission For North East and Himalayan States).

According to Economic Survey 2015-16, since the start of the NHM, an area of 24.63 lakh ha has been covered under different horticulture crops. Besides, an area of 5.25 lakh ha of old orchards, has been rejuvenated. Over 12 lakh farmers have been trained under various horticulture activities, and nearly three thousand nurseries have been established for supply of quality saplings and other material to the beneficiaries.

Post-Harvest wastage

The post-harvest wastages and losses in horticulture are a matter of concern. According to a study conducted by the Central Institute of Post-Harvest Engineering and Technology (CIPHET), the wastage in various kinds of produce was very high and increased during the period 2010 and 2015. The wastage occurred at various levels of the value chain—at the levels of farmer, transporter, wholesaler and retailer. Wastage and losses occurred due to crop damage, improper harvesting techniques, poor packaging, poor transportation, poor handling, multiple handling, storage, grading sorting, and moisture loss at various stages of the value chain.

The study found that the biggest wastage happened during the transportation of horticulture products from the farm gate to the market. Even thereafter, there is wastage at every post-harvest stage—from the farm to the table. This needs to be minimized. Starting from the plucking, initial processing at the farm level, sorting and grading, transportation to the market, storage in the farm and subsequent levels, warehousing, which could be located near the market, there is loss of freshness, moisture, handling and other wastages. There is need to minimize the wastage at all stages, to enable farmers to get remunerative prices. This can be done by improving practices and facilities at each stage, including the transportation stage.

Plantation crops

The major plantation crops include coconut, arecanut, oil palm, cashew, tea, coffee and rubber. In India, tea, coffee and rubber are traditional plantation crops, which are grown mostly in the southern and north-eastern states. Besides meeting indigenous consumption demand, these crops also make significant contribution to our exports. India is the largest producer and consumer of tea in the world, accounting for around 27 per cent of world production and 13 per cent of the world trade.

India is the largest producer and consumer of cashew nuts. In 2011 the total production of cashew was around 0.57 million tonnes from an area of 0.24 million hectares. India accounts for about 65 per cent of global cashew exports. It exports cashew kernels to over 60 countries, the major ones of which are the US, the Netherlands, Japan, Spain, France, Germany, the UK as well as Middle East countries such as the UAE and Saudi Arabia. According to Ministry of Commerce, the overall exports of cashew for FY 2014-15 stood at US$ 887.5 million.

India is world's second largest tea producer in the world after China. In 2013, India's estimated tea production was 900 million kilograms, which accounted for around 23-24% of global tea production. The top five producer countries of tea are China, India, Kenya, Sri Lanka and Turkey. According to Tea Board of India, the production of tea for the period April 2015 to October 2015 was 946.97 million kg.

Coconut is grown in an area of 1.93 million ha with the production of 12,148 million nuts and productivity of 6,285 nuts per ha. India is the third largest producer of coconut and leads 90 coconut-producing countries of the world. It also occupies number one position in arecanut production. India is considered as a treasurehouse of valuable medicinal and aromatic plant species. The Government of India has identified and documented over 9,500 plant species considering their importance in the pharmaceutical industry. Out of these, about 65 plants have large and consistent demand in world trade.[3]

Coffee has made significant contribution to the Indian economy during the last 50 years. Although India contributes only 4 per cent of the world production, Indian coffee has created a niche for itself in the international market.

In India, rubber plantations are spread over 5.7 lakh hectares in 16 states. Production is dominated by small holdings which account for 88 per cent of the production as well as area with an average holding size of 0.5 hectare. High cost of production and stagnant productivity are the two major constraints in rubber plantation in India.

Floriculture

Floriculture or flower farming refers to the study of growing and marketing flowers and foliage plants. It includes cultivation of flowering and ornamental plants for direct sale or for use as raw materials in cosmetic and perfume industry and in the pharmaceutical sector. The production of planting materials through seeds, cuttings, budding and grafting is also included in floriculture.

In India, floriculture is an age-old farming activity having immense potential for generating gainful self-employment among small and marginal farmers. In recent years it has emerged as a profitable agri-business because the improved standards of living and growing consciousness among the citizens to live in environment-friendly atmosphere have led to an increase in the demand for floriculture products. The oil from the seeds of sunflower is said to be free from fats and therefore good for health. This has also led to the growing of sunflowers on a large scale. The floriculture industry in India is comprised of flower trade, production of nursery plants and potted plants, seed and bulb production, micro propagation and extraction of essential oils. It is estimated that the international demand for flowers is worth around ₹ 90,000 crore, but India's share in international market of flowers is negligible. However, there is a better scope in future owing to the shift in trend towards tropical flowers.

According to *Handbook on Horticulture Statistics* 2014, the total area under flower crops in 2012-13 was 232.70 thousand hectares. Total area under floriculture in India is second largest in the world and next only to that of China. Production of flowers was estimated to be 1729.2 MT of loose flowers and 76731.9 million (numbers) of cut flowers in 2012-13. The floriculture exports from India consist mainly of fresh and dried cut flowers.

Karnataka is the leading Indian state in floriculture with about 29,700 hectares under floriculture cultivation. Tamil Nadu and Andhra Pradesh in the South, West Bengal in the East, Maharashtra in the West, and Rajasthan and Haryana in the North are other States engaged in floriculture.

Notwithstanding an abundant and varied production base, India's export of floricultural products is not up to the mark. There are many constraints like non-availability of air space in major airlines. Trade-related challenges, like lack of proper infrastructure, high import tariff, low availability of perishable cargo carriers, higher freight rates and inadequate refrigerated and transport facilities also exist.

The Government of India has identified floriculture as an extreme focus area for exports considering the potential that this sector has in generating income and employment opportunities, promoting greater involvement of women and enhancement of exports. Things are expected to improve in the near future.

Genetically Modified (GM) Crops in Agriculture

Genetically modified (GM) crops, also called biotech crops, refer to plants used in agriculture, the DNA of which has been modified by using genetic engineering techniques. In such crops, a new trait is introduced to the plants, which does not occur naturally in the species. Production of pharmaceutical agents, biofuels, and other industrially useful goods, as well as for bioremediation, etc. are covered in GM crops.

Farmers worldwide have adopted GM technology. Between 1996 and 2013, the total surface area of land cultivated with GM crops increased by a factor of 100, from 4.2 million acres to (432 million acres). A 2014 meta-analysis concluded that GM technology adoption had reduced chemical pesticide use by 37%, increased crop yields by 22%, and increased farmer profits by 68%. This reduction in pesticide use has been ecologically beneficial, but benefits may be reduced by overuse.[4] Yield gains and pesticide reductions are larger for insect-resistant crops than for herbicide-tolerant crops. Yield and profit gains are higher in the developing countries than in the developed countries.

In 2010, about 10% of the world's arable land was planted with GM crops. According to the Economic Research Service, of the U.S. Department of Agriculture, in 2014, 94% of the planted area of soybeans, 96% of cotton and 93% of corn were genetically modified varieties in the US. The use of GM crops expanded rapidly in developing countries, with about 18 million farmers growing 54% of worldwide GM crops by 2013.[5]

Many controversies are associated with GM foods. According to John Paull, "GM foods are controversial and the subject of protests, vandalism, referenda, legislation, court action as well as scientific disputes. The controversies relate to a number of areas including consumers, biotechnology companies, governmental regulators, non-governmental organizations and scientists. The key areas are whether GM food should be labeled, the role of government regulators, the effect of GM crops on health and the environment, the effects of pesticide use and resistance, the impact on farmers, and their roles in feeding the world and energy production.[6]

Many scientists like Pamela Ronald and C. Bret are of the opinion that food from genetically modified crops is not inherently riskier to human health than conventional food. No reports of ill effects have been documented in the human population from GM food. GMO labeling is required in many countries, but the United States Food and Drug Administration (USFDA) does not require labeling. The USFDA does not recognize a distinction between approved GMO and non-GMO foods.

The proponents of GM crops have drawn attention to a number of advantages these crops give, like resistance to certain pests, diseases, avoidance of chemicals which are environmentally harmful, reduction of spoilage, or resistance to chemical treatments (e.g. resistance to a herbicide), or improvement in the nutrient profile of the crop. Some other advantages claimed by them are enumerated below:

(i) Some GM soybeans offer improved oil profiles for processing or healthier eating. Golden rice, developed by the International Rice Research Institute (IRRI), provides greater amounts of Vitamin A. The vitamin-enriched corn derived from South African white corn variety M37W, contains much more Vitamins A, and C. This serves the cause of nutrition.

(ii) The genetically modified cassava under development offers lower cyanogen glucosides. The USDA approved potato prevents bruising and produces less acrylamide when fried.

(iii) Many plants can tolerate non-biological stressors like drought, frost, high soil salinity, and nitrogen starvation.

(iv) The herbicides used in traditional grain and grass crops are highly toxic. In GM crops the plants can withstand spraying with glyphosate which reduces environmental and health risks, and gives an agricultural edge to the farmer.

(v) Some crops are engineered for resistance to multiple herbicides to allow farmers to use a mixture of two, three, or four different chemicals to combat growing herbicide resistance.

(vi) Papaya, potatoes, and squash have been engineered to resist viral pathogens, like cucumber mosaic virus which infects a wide variety of plants.

(vii) The introduction of Bt crops during the period between 1996 and 2005 is estimated to have reduced the total volume of insecticide active ingredient use in the United States by over 100 thousand tons. This represents a 19.4% reduction in insecticide use.

(viii) Algae is under development for use in biofuels. Modified jatropha offers improved qualities for fuel.

In recent years, GM crops have expanded rapidly in the developing countries. In 2013, approximately 18 million farmers grew 54% of worldwide GM crops in developing countries, of which the largest increase was in Brazil. GM cotton which started being grown in India in 2002, reached 1,10,000 km^2 in 2013.

According to the International Service for the Acquisition of Agri-Biotech Applications (ISAAA), India has the fourth largest area planted under genetically modified (GM) crops. Farmers in India planted a total 11.6 million hectares (mh) under transgenics in 2014, behind the corresponding areas for Argentina (24.3 mh), Brazil (42.2 mh) and the US (73.1 mh). The GM crop acreage in India is far more than that of China which has just 3.9 mh.

To feed the ever-increasing population, more and more food has to be produced from limited land water and other natural resources. We have to use new technologies to increase the yield in adverse biotic and abiotic stresses. The excessive use of chemicals like pesticides and insecticides has to be reduced for the sake of environment. GM crops are ideal to achieve all these aims. However GM foods should not be pushed into the Indian market without appropriate safety assessment to ensure that they do not increase health risks.

Allied Sectors: Animal Husbandry, Dairy, Poultry and Fishery

Agriculture and allied activities include agricultural products, livestock, forestry and logging, fishery. The Indian agricultural system is a mixed crop-livestock farming system. The livestock segment supplements farm incomes by providing employment, draught animals as well as manure. India ranks first in milk production, accounting for 18.5 per cent of world production, achieving an annual output of 146.3 million tonnes during 2014-15 as compared to 137.69 million tonnes during 2013-14.

The per capita availability of milk in India increased from 176 grams per day in 1990-91 to 322 grams per day by 2014-15.

This has taken India's average above the world average of 294. In India, dairying has become an important secondary source of income for millions of rural households engaged in agriculture. The success of the dairy industry has been built upon a number of factors, including "the integrated co-operative system of milk collection, transportation, processing and distribution, conversion of the same to milk powder and products, to minimize seasonal impact on suppliers and buyers, retail distribution of milk and milk products, sharing of profits with the farmer, which are ploughed back to enhance productivity and needs to be emulated by other farm producers."[7]

Besides making suitable policies, the Government's focus in poultry has been on enhancing commercial poultry production, and strengthening the family poultry system, which will also address livelihood issues. Egg production has shown an increasing trend over the years. Egg production was around 78.48 billion eggs in 2014-15, while poultry meat production was estimated at 3.04 metric tonnes. India's 2016 broiler production increased by approximately eight per cent to 4.2 million tons as demand rose from the growing middle class.

Production methods have changed in the last ten years, as producers have embraced the integrator production model. According to a report from the USDA's Foreign Agricultural Service, approximately 60-70 per cent of all operations use the integrator model, while the remaining are smaller backyard operations. The live poultry market constitutes 90 to 95 per cent of total sales since most consumers prefer freshly culled chicken meat. Consumption is growing and the 2016 total chicken meat consumption was 4.19 million tons, up by approximately, eight per cent over 2015.

Indian fisheries and aquaculture is an important sector of food production. It provides nutrition to Indian people, contributes to the agricultural exports and engages about 14 million people in different activities. With diverse resources—ranging from deep seas—to lakes in the mountains and more than 10% of the global biodiversity in terms of fish and shellfish species, India has shown continuous and sustained increments in fish production since independence. Marine aquaculture refers to the establishment of man-made enclosures to raise aquatic life, such as shell fish, finfish and sea weeds for the human consumption.

In India, many species of freshwater and marine organisms are being cultivated as they are highly productive and nutritious for consumption. It is the rapid expansion of intensive, commercial aquaculture that has brought the blue revolution in the country. Aquaculture has been recognized as a growth sector of economic importance in India and has attracted the attention of the private and public sectors. There is a rapidly growing awareness of the need to ensure the sustainability of the sector in the long-term.

Between 1990 and 2010, the Indian fish capture harvest doubled, while aquaculture harvest tripled. In 2008, India was the world's sixth largest producer of marine and freshwater capture fisheries and the second largest aquaculture farmed fish producer. India exported 6,00,000 metric tonnes of fish products to nearly half of the world's countries. The total fish production during 2014-15 was 10.16 metric tonnes—an increase of 6.18 per cent over 2013-14. Fish production during the first two quarters of 2015-16 also showed an increasing trend and was estimated at 4.79 MT. Sustained efforts to improve the sustainability of some aquaculture systems are required to get still better results in the medium and long-term.

The Government of India launched National Livestock Mission (NLM) in 2014-15 with an approved outlay of ₹ 2,800 crore during the Twelfth Plan for sustainable and continuous growth of the livestock sector. The objective of the mission is sustainable development of this sector, with a focus on improving availability of quality feed and fodder, risk coverage, effective extension, improved flow of credit, and organization of livestock farmers. As the protein items in India are expensive, growth rate of this sector is necessary to match the rising demand and add nutrition to Indian food consumption.

Agriculture Extension Services

Extension services are a common feature of the administrative structure of rural areas and these services have the responsibility, in partnership with the farmers, of directing programmes and projects for meaningful and perceptible change. These services constitute a key input which can improve productivity in agriculture by providing timely advisory services to farmers to adopt best practices, technology, meet with contingencies, and access and use market information. In India, there are multiple agencies offering agricultural advisory services, but the absence of functional autonomy, and rigid hierarchical structures result in lack of innovative methods and coordination failures at multiple levels.

In order to improve agricultural productivity, agriculture extension services have to be revitalized by making them more relevant, useful and timely. We need not take the form of implementing a new scheme or providing additional outlays in existing schemes. It needs to take the form of one-stop-shop, offering both hardware and software solutions to raise the incomes of farmers, especially small and marginal farmers.

The major aims of extension services should be to minimize wastage in inputs in all agricultural operations and also in the produce till it leaves the farm gate; enhance post-harvest processing/value added activities at the farm; support and highlight practices in inter and rotational cropping; and utilize all available inputs efficiently in the context of ground realities, soil and water conditions, and new seeds/crops. They should also share with the farmer, information on weather in order to improve the sowing, including time of sowing, enabling them to reap maximum yield, as well as forecasts about hailstones, rains and likely floods in order to minimize damage to crops.

Capital Formation in Agriculture and Allied Sectors

Capital formation refers to net additions of capital stock such as equipment, buildings and other intermediate goods. The Gross Capital Formation (GCF) in agriculture as a percent of total GCF showed a decline from 8.6 in 2011-12 to 7.4 in 2013-14 at 2011-12 prices. The revised data released by CSO reveals that the percentage share of GCF in agriculture and allied sector in the GVA (GDP) from agriculture also showed a decline from 18.3 per cent in 2011-12 to 15.8 per cent in 2014-15. Decrease in public sector investment was the main reason of decline in

GCF to GDP ratio in agriculture. This trend needs to be reversed because growth in agriculture depends on the investment rate in this sector. Both public and private sector must participate actively in effecting an increase in investment in agriculture, as can be seen from the percentage share of the public and private sectors in the GCF in agriculture and allied sectors.

New Initiatives in Agriculture Development

The Modi Government has taken several initiatives to stimulate growth of agriculture. It has begun to reorient public investment in ways that would raise productivity while using scarce resources efficiently. Emphasis on micro irrigation, soil cards, better seeds and improved extension programmes are all steps in this direction. Action is also under way to bring Green Revolution to the eastern states.

Agricultural produce is the biggest resource of economic activity and development in India. Agriculture and allied activities create a big base for agricultural machinery and other inputs. Any kind of industry which uses agricultural products as a raw material, directly adds to the list of products "Make in India (MII)".

The government is also focusing on targeted support for those who are vulnerable in agriculture, namely the small farmer and agricultural labourer. The Mahatma Gandhi National Rural Employment Guarantee Act (MGNREGA) brought by the previous government has the virtue of being reasonably well-targeted. The challenge for the new government is to build on this feature and use the programme to build assets such as rural roads, micro-irrigation and water management, while also shoring up rural incomes. The time is ripe for a more broad-based response to the challenges in agriculture and to ensure that agriculture grows at about 4 per cent on a sustained basis.

Agriculture and Food Security

Food security is totally dependent on agriculture. Over the years, India has made great strides in increasing agricultural productivity. Currently, the country feeds 17 per cent of the world's population on less than 3 per cent of the world's arable land. Its demographic pressures and limited land notwithstanding, India has made effective use of agriculture technologies and innovations, invested substantial resources and has become one of the biggest agricultural producers in the world.

According to FAO, the adoption of new technologies has been uneven throughout India. However, the country has accumulated valuable agricultural development experience and is now in a position to identify, scale up, and launch the agricultural development practices, technologies, and innovations in those parts where they had hitherto not been adopted. Diffusing the proven Indian agricultural innovations can contribute significantly to overcoming the challenges still present in India.

Under the US Government's global hunger and food security initiative, "Feed the Future", India is a strategic partner that focuses on developing, scaling, and transferring Indian agriculture innovations to benefit focus countries in Africa. The partnership engages a wide variety of public and private sector partners from India, Africa, and the US to address global agriculture development problems.

India's production of food grain has increased five-fold since the Green Revolution of 1970s. The agricultural sector has also made good strides in the production of high-value commodities like milk, livestock, aquaculture, fruits and vegetables, spices and plantation crops like tea, cashew and coffee. Agriculture in India has also benefited from government support for farmers in the form of fertilizer subsidies and other subsidies for technology adoption. Private sector participation has increased in the input markets, like those for fertilizers, seeds, and animal feed, as well as in output markets for crops produced such as basmati rice and wheat.

India's food supply is now largely self-sufficient, but the country's hunger and malnutrition levels are still very high. Restrictions like banning the movement of food grains from one state to another and from one district to another within the same state have proved to be a roadblock in the further growth of the sector. To meet the increasing demand for high-value commodities, a number of private companies are developing various models for working with farmers to enhance production and improve integration with local, regional, and international markets.

Challenges in Maintaining Food Security

Food security is not a one-time issue. We have to achieve it and maintain it for the foreseeable future and beyond so that there is no problem in the availability and supply of food in any part of the country. There are several constraints in achieving this level. The major ones are mentioned below.

Increasing productivity

Although India's food production has increased over the years, yet we need to increase productivity in agriculture. The per hectare crop yield in cereals like wheat, rice, maize, pulses and vegetables needs to be brought on par with that in the developed countries. This can be done by making our agriculture less dependent on the monsoon, strengthening the capacity of farmers to access and use information for problem-solving, using best practices in farming so that they can produce food grains not only for their consumption but also for marketing.

India's Twelfth Five-Year Plan (2012-17) lays emphasis on food security and also discusses ways to increase agriculture productivity. We need to adopt all those methods to achieve this goal.

Overcoming water deficit

India ranks fourth in the world in potential water resources. However, poor water management has led to water deficit in many parts of the country. Water wastage in households, overuse of water for irrigation and consumption, not taking care of our water resources, allowing rainwater to flow away instead of harvesting it, and water pollution, have led to water deficit in India. The water table is falling due to widespread pumping of water with the help of powerful diesel and electric pumps.

The solution lies in (i) making judicious and efficient use of water, (ii) replenishing our water sources, (iii) harvesting rainwater, (iv) recharging the aquifers to lift or at least maintain water table where it is still sufficient for irrigation, (v) desilting rivers so that there is no inundation and wastage of water,

(vi) adopting agriculture practices that need less water, and (vii) using seeds that are drought resistant. With these practices we will continue to have sufficient water for farming and our food production will increase.

Restoring soil fertility

India is hard pressed to grow more and more food to feed its ever-increasing population. Intensive farming often leads to exhaustion of soil fertility and decline of agricultural yields. According to *The Guardian*, approximately 40 per cent of the world's agricultural land is seriously degraded. India is among the countries where soil fertility is becoming low, as a result of which, per hectare yield is not up to the desired level.

To meet this challenge we need to (i) strengthen soil fertility by using minerals and fertilizers, (ii) get the soil tested to see what is lacking in the soil and replenish it accordingly, (iii) use crop rotation methods which means to grow different crops in succession on a piece of land to avoid exhausting the soil, (iv) use green manure which is also not environmentally harmful, and (v) leaving a piece of land fallow to allow it to recoup before the next crop, (vi) check soil erosion by taking precautions against flowing water and wind.

It is pertinent to mention here that the Government has launched Soil Health Card scheme under which soil cards are being issued to farmers. These cards carry crop-wise recommendations of nutrients and fertilizers required for individual farms to help farmers improve productivity through the use of required inputs. All soil samples are tested in the labs across the country and then the experts analyze the strengths and weaknesses of the soil and suggest measures to improve the soil. According to Ministry of Agriculture and Farmers Welfare, soil cards have been issued to eight crore farmers, as of June 2017, out of 14 crore target.

Another important step has been the launching of DD Kisan channel which is dedicated to agriculture and related sectors. It provides valuable information to farmers about inputs, new farming techniques, water conservation, and organic farming, among others.

Taking precautions against extreme events

Overnight floods as well gradually worsening droughts have an adverse effect on our agriculture, lowering our food production, and hence food security. The monsoons are highly unpredictable. They bring heavy rain in some areas and less than required rainfall in others. There are rare occasions when it is uniform throughout the country. It is a fact that weather pattern in India will not change to our relief. Therefore, food security in future will be linked to our ability to adapt agricultural systems to extreme events.

What we need to do is to equip ourselves for meeting abnormal precipitation and extreme events. This can be done by (i) making arrangements whereby water from excessive rain can be either diverted to a water body or stored by making ponds, tanks, etc., (ii) harvesting and storing rainwater, (iii) expanding canals network for irrigation in rain deficient areas, (iv) desilting our water bodies regularly so that they can accommodate more water. This will also prevent inundation and wastage of water, and (v) strengthening disaster management so that the effect of extreme events may be mitigated.

Combating climate change

Climate change is a change in the distribution of weather patterns when it lasts for an extended period of time. It also refers to a change in average weather conditions, or in the time variation of weather around longer-term average conditions. It is caused by factors such as biotic processes, variations in solar radiation received by the Earth, plate tectonics, and volcanic eruptions. Certain human activities have also been identified as significant causes of recent climate change, often referred to as global warming.[8]

Climate change has impacted our agriculture in various ways. It has brought changes in weather pattern. More rain is falling in fewer days and there are long intervals of dry period. There is heavy rain in some parts and less rain in others in the same season. There is decrease in the number of rainy days which is expected over much of India, along with an increase in heavy rainfall days in the monsoon season. The occurrence of floods, droughts and other such events has increased. Unprecedented floods in Uttarakhand in June 2013 and Kashmir in September 2014 bear testimony that weather pattern often results in devastating events. With global warming, the glaciers are melting at a faster rate and depleting these reservoirs of water. As the water runoff is increasing, many coastal areas are under the danger of being submerged. According to Krugman, "Glaciers aren't the only worry that the developing nations have; sea level is reported to rise as climate change progresses, reducing the amount of land available for agriculture."[9]

Increase in temperature also has adverse effect on some important crops. According to a forecast by International Rice Research Institute, there is a 20% reduction in yields over the region per degree Celsius rise in temperature. Rice becomes sterile if exposed to temperatures above 35 degrees for more than one hour during flowering and consequently produces no grain. The Universal Ecological Fund (FEU) of the US states that rising temperatures will adversely affect the world's food production and India would be hit the hardest. As a result, the crop yield in India, the second largest world producer of rice and wheat, would fall up to 30 per cent by 2020.

It has also been predicted that there will be 10 to 15 per cent increase in monsoon precipitation in many regions, and at the same time a decline of 5 to 25 per cent in precipitation in drought-prone central India and a sharp decline in winter rainfall in northern India. This will bring changes in output of wheat and mustard crops in North-western India. These predictions do not augur well for Indian agriculture which is highly sensitive to monsoon variability as 65% of the cropped area is rain-fed. The Intergovernmental Panel on Climate Change (IPCC) too has indicated that rice and wheat production of India will drop significantly because of climate change. Changes in temperature and precipitation could thus have a significant impact on India's food security. The following measures need to be taken in this regard:

(i) Carbon dioxide (CO_2) emissions must be reduced. For this we should make efficient use of energy. Dependence on fossil fuels like coal, petroleum, natural gas, etc. should be reduced by developing renewable energy generated from natural sources like water, wind, solar, biomass and geothermal.

(ii) We should adopt carbon-capture and storage (CCS) technology that removes and stores the CO_2 during the production of energy from fossil fuels. Experts feel that CSS technology may prove to be the bridging technology needed to serve our cause.

(iii) Reckless cutting of trees has harmed the environment more than anything else. We should prevent forest loss to reduce the threat of climate change. Forests are the largest storehouse of carbon, after coal and oil. When they are destroyed, by logging and by clearing forests for making roads, houses, factories, etc., massive quantities of CO_2 is released into the atmosphere. This must be stopped or atleast reduced to an acceptable level.

Fighting diseases affecting livestock and crops

Many diseases affect livestock like milch, draught and meat animals, poultry and piggery, as a result of which we suffer heavy loss in production. Sometimes there are epidemics like bird flu or swine flu and we have to cull thousands of birds and animals to check the spread of these diseases to healthy livestock.

Similarly, there are several crop diseases which either destroy the entire crop or reduce the yield considerably. This can have devastating effects on food availability especially if there are no contingency plans in place. For example, Ug99, a lineage of wheat stem rust which can cause up to 100% crop losses, is present in wheat fields in several countries in Africa and the Middle East and is predicted to spread rapidly through these regions and possibly further afield, potentially causing a wheat production disaster that would affect food security worldwide.[10]

Thus, our food security depends on how and to what degree we are able to fight and control livestock and crop diseases.

Augmenting agricultural research

In the longer run, growth in agricultural productivity can be sustained only through continuous technological progress. This calls for a well-considered strategy for prioritized basic research, which is now all the more urgent in view of mounting pressure on scarce natural resources, climate change and also lack of sufficient public research. New generation technologies based on rapidly evolving scientific developments will play a pivotal role in achieving new levels of productivity in agriculture. The country's large agricultural research system, which successfully launched the Green Revolution in the past, will now be called upon to address newer and more formidable challenges. In this endeavour, development practices which are not sustainable and are thus environmentally-destructive have no place whatsoever. The system needs to be thoroughly revamped and restructured in the light of the advice rendered by the high powered committees chaired by Dr. Swaminathan and Dr. R.A. Mashelkar, respectively.

In order to achieve greater progress in agriculture sector we need to learn from what has worked in our agricultural practices and what has not worked in terms of farmer participatory research. Researchers must find ways and means of making their findings more effective with greater participation of farmers, and support from institutions and the governments at the state and at the centre. The knowledge of new findings in research must be shared in such a way that it becomes accessible to farmers and those concerned with farming.

Developing genetic food

As already stated, genetically modified crops have several advantages over traditional crops. Besides, they are an excellent supplement to maintain food security. However, there are many misgivings about adopting GM crops or consuming GM food. As a result, we have not been able to develop GM crops to the desired level. We need to develop this technology further to grow more food. The genetic diversity of the crop wild relatives (wild plant species that are genetically related to cultivated crops) of wheat can be used to improve modern varieties to be more resistant to rust.

GM crops are as natural and safe as today's bread wheat, opined Dr. Borlaug, who also reminded agricultural scientists of their moral obligation to stand up to the anti-science crowd and warn policymakers that global food insecurity will not disappear without this new technology and ignoring this reality global food insecurity would make future solutions all the more difficult to achieve.[11]

However, we cannot ignore what agroecologists Miguel Altieri and Peter Rosset have to say about biotechnology. According to them, most innovations in agricultural biotechnology have been profit-driven rather than need-driven. Ecological theory predicts that the large-scale landscape homogenization with transgenic crops will exacerbate the ecological problems already associated with monoculture agriculture. Finally, that much of the needed food can be produced by small farmers located throughout the world using existing agro-ecological technologies. So what we need to do is to strike a balance between traditional crops and GM crops.

Replenishing more land for agriculture

Fast infrastructural and industrial development has been going on in India for the last few decades. Making of more roads, rails, bridges, etc. and setting up factories and industries has taken away large areas of land, including agriculture land. Many housing colonies have come up on the peripheries of cities encroaching upon agriculture tracts. Builders are purchasing agriculture land in areas surrounding big cities and making housing colonies. Many property dealers are also wooing farmers to sell their land as plots for houses. Thus every year more and more agriculture land is being put to non-agriculture needs. This is one of the major threats to India's food security.

Another apprehension that has been raised in the aftermath of the government promulgating an ordinance to amend the Land Acquisition Act is that farm land will be taken away for other purposes and given that, the acreage land used for farming will come down dramatically. However, the government has made it clear that agriculture land will not be acquired. This has assuaged farmers' fears to a large extent. The government has also said that the pieces of land which are barren and not being put to any use will be taken for industrial purpose. While this is a welcome step, efforts should also be made to replenish barren lands and make them fit for agriculture. Efforts need to be made at the grassroots level to make this happen.

Experts have also suggested the use of permaculture, the development of agricultural ecosystems intended to be sustainable and self-sufficient. It is a design methodology of creating food forests and biodiverse regions, leads to replenishment of nature and to maximize use of scarce space, and brings about increase in biodiversity.

Controlling the growth of population

Ever-increasing population is a major threat to food security in India. There has been an increase in food production, but due to large size of population, the demand remains high and the supply barely copes up. There is a growing pressure on environment, food supplies, land and energy resources. Controlling the growth of population has a key role to play in our food security.

The present government's new policies in agriculture complement the National Food Security Bill. The national food security mission addresses the problem of food security from the supply side by increasing food production. There is need to coordinate and harmonize these seemingly disparate programs. These policies need serious scrutiny in terms of their implementation, effectiveness and efficiency in achieving food security goals.

Notes

1. United States Department of Agriculture (2014). "India's Agricultural Exports Climb to Record High."
2. *Economic Survey*, 2015-16.
3. http://www.archive.india.gov.in/sectors/agriculture/index.php?id=24.
4. ISAAA (2013). Annual Report Executive Summary, Global Status of Commercialized Biotech/GM Crops: 2013 ISAAA Brief 46-2013.
5. *Ibid.*
6. John, Paull (2015). "The threat of genetically modified organisms (GMOs) to organic agriculture: A case study update", *Agriculture & Food*, 3: 56-63.
7. Press Information Bureau, Government of India, Ministry of Finance. (accessed on 22 March 2016).

8. America's Climate Choices: Panel on Advancing the Science of Climate Change; National Research Council (2010).
9. Paul Krugman, Loading the Climate Dice. July 22, 2012.
10. Robin McKie and Xan Rice. "Millions face famine as crop disease rages". *The Guardian* (UK). 22 April 2007.
11. Sateesh Kagale and Kevin Rozwadowski (October 2010). "Global Food Security: The Role of Agricultural Biotechnology Commentary." In *Plant Physiology* (Saskatoon, Saskatchewan: Saskatoon Research Centre, Agriculture and Agri-Food Canada,) 154: 1.

6

Food Inflation and Public Distribution System

Food inflation refers to the condition whereby there as an increase in wholesale price index of essential food items relative to the general inflation or the consumer price index. Food inflation in India has seen variations in recent times. After hitting 15.2 per cent in 2009-10, food inflation fell to 6.3 per cent in 2011-12. And then, it jerked up again, growing at 11.9 per cent and 12.4 per cent in 2012-13 and 2013-14, respectively. Persistent and elevated levels of food inflation have been a major concern of the government during the period 2010-11 to 2013-14. The CPI (IW)-based food inflation touched double digits and likewise WPI-based food inflation rose to a high of 9.3 per cent during the same period. The new combined monthly consumer price index (CPI) with base 2012 = 100, is now taken as the measure of headline inflation and is tracked by the Reserve Bank of India (RBI) to anchor its monetary policy.

Food inflation is not new to India. Some food item or the other has always been at very high price at any given time, making households complain. In 2008, it was food grains and food products; in 2010, it was fruits and vegetables, led by onions. After that, it was cereals and pulses again. However, the rising trend of 2010-11 to 2013-14 reversed from 2014-15 onwards and the economy has been experiencing sustained moderation in general inflation ever since. In July 2016 it was 8.35 per cent.

The position of inflation for 2012-13, 2013-14, 2014-15 and 2015-16 (provisional) under broad groups of food and beverages, fuel and light, non-food and non-fuel and only food is shown in Table 6.1 below:

Table 6.1: Inflation in CPI (Combined) Broad Groups (in per cent)

	Weights	Weights	2012-13	2013-14	2014-15	2015-16 (Apr-Dec) P
Base	2010	2012	2010	2010	2012	2012
Headline	100.0	100.0	10.2	9.5	5.9	4.8
Food and beverages	47.6	45.9	11.9	11.2	6.5	4.9
Fuel and light	9.5	6.8	8.5	7.4	4.2	5.5
Non-food non-fuel (core)	42.9	47.3	8.8	8.1	5.6	4.5
Food (CFPI*)	42.7	39.1	12.2	11.3	6.4	4.6

Source: CSO

Notes:* Consumer Food Price Index; P: Provisional

Table 6.1 shows that the inflation in food and beverages was 11.9% in 2012-13, 11.2% in 2013-14, but came down to 6.5% in 2014-15. The provisional figures for 2015-16 show food and beverages inflation at 4.8%. Table 6.1 also shows the consumer food price index (CFPI) which was 12.2% and 11.3% in 2012-13 and 2013-14, but came down to 6.4% and 4.6% (provisional) in 2014-15 and 2015-16 respectively.

The CFPI basket consists of different categories like cereals and products made from them, pulses, vegetables, fruit, milk and eggs, meat and fish. Food inflation remained high during 2010-11 to 2013-14. Supply-side constraints had been causing inflationary spurts from time to time, in particular in pulses, edible oils and fats, sugar and confectionery, and vegetables.

The year-wise position of inflation in CPI of these food groups for 2012-13 to 2015-16 is given in Table 6.2.

Table 6.2 shows that during 2012-13 the vegetable prices were very high, with the CPI at 20.6%. Oils & fats, cereals & products, and sugar & confectionary showed a CPI of 16.6%, 10.5% and 12.5% respectively for 2012-13. During 2013-14, the CPI for vegetables went still higher at 26.0%, while CPI for cereals increased to 13.2%. The prices of fruits also went up, with CPI for fruits going into the double figure, i.e. 11.2% from 7.5% in 2012-13. However, the CPI for oils and fats, and pulses came down to just 1.8% and 4.2% respectively. Only two groups, milk and its products, and fruits showed double digit inflation in 2014-15 at 10.3% and 13.9% respectively. Table 6.2 also shows provisional figures for food inflation for 2015-16.

Table 6.2: Inflation in CPI (Combined) Food Groups (in per cent)

	Weights	Weights	2012-13	2013-14	2014-15	2015-16 (Apr-Dec) P
Base	2010	2012	2010	2010	2012	2012
Food (CFPI)	42.7	39.1	12.2	11.3	6.4	4.6
Cereals and products	14.6	9.7	10.5	13.2	5.2	1.7
Meat and fish	2.9	3.6	12.2	12.1	6.3	5.9
Egg*	–	0.4	–	–	3.2	1.2
Milk and products	7.7	6.6	10.4	8.7	10.3	5.7
Oils and fats	3.9	3.6	16.6	1.8	2.4	3.9
Fruits	1.9	2.9	7.5	11.2	13.9	2.3
Vegetables	5.4	6.0	20.6	26.0	3.4	1.0
Pulses and products	2.7	2.4	12.3	4.2	7.9	29.6
Sugar and confectionery	1.9	1.4	12.5	-0.7	-0.4	-9.5
Spices	1.7	2.5	3.1	7.2	8.6	9.5

Source: CSO

Notes: P: Provisional; *Egg, which was part of the subgroup 'egg, fish and meat' in the 2010 series, has been treated as a separate subgroup in the 2012 series.

The CPI for pulses for this period is as high as 29.6%, which is quite alarming. The spike in pulse prices was mainly due to shortfall in production of *tur* and *gram*. In order to avoid further spikes in prices of pulses, the government has decided to build a buffer by procuring *tur* and *urad* and has initiated action to ensure timely imports. The prices of potato and onion were volatile during 2014-15 and 2015-16, yet overall inflation in vegetables remained low. But in other groups there is moderation in CPI. The prices of most protein-based food commodities such as egg, meat, fish, milk too eased significantly during April-December 2015-16.

According to *Economic Survey* 2015-16, supply-side constraints have been causing inflationary spurts from time to time, particularly in pulses, edible oils and vegetables. With deft and astute food management by the government, there has been significant moderation in wholesale and retail food inflation since 2014-15. The decline in food articles inflation during 2015-16 was mainly on account of a fall in the prices of cereals, vegetables, fruits, milk, egg, fish and meat. However, a spike in the prices of pulses on account of low domestic production kept food grain prices high.[1]

The position of food inflation as per wholesale price index (WPI), base 2004-05 is shown in Table 6.3 below:

Table 6.3: Inflation in WPI Food Groups (in per cent) (Base: 2004-05)

	Weights	2012-13	2013-14	2014-15	2015-16 (Apr-Dec) P
All food	**24.3**	**9.3**	**9.4**	**4.9**	**1.9**
Food articles	***14.3***	***9.9***	***12.8***	***6.1***	***3.0***
Food grains	4.1	14.6	9.1	4.0	6.7
Cereals	3.4	13.4	12.8	3.6	-0.3
Pulses	0.7	19.6	-5.5	5.9	39.5
Vegetables	1.7	17.2	40.2	-6.1	-4.3
Fruits	2.1	1.3	7.5	19.0	1.1
Milk	3.2	7.2	6.0	10.0	3.7
Egg, meat & fish	2.4	14.1	12.8	2.4	0.9
Condiments & Spices	0.6	-11.8	17.2	21.7	14.8
Food products	***10.0***	***8.1***	***3.2***	***2.4***	***-0.4***
Sugar	1.7	11.3	-2.4	-0.3	-13.2
Edible Oils	3.0	9.1	-0.8	-1.3	2.6

Source: Office of Economic Adviser, DIPP.

Note: P : Provisional.

The WPI series assigns less weight (24.3 per cent) to food items (food articles and food products) in its basket than the CPI. Table 6.3 shows that inflation in WPI food articles was high at 12.8 per cent in 2013-14, but declined to 6.1 per cent in 2014-15 and further to 3.0 per cent in April-December 2015-16. The decline in food articles inflation during 2015-16 was mainly on account of fall in the prices of cereals, vegetables, fruits, milk, egg, fish and meat. However, increase in the prices of pulses owing to low domestic production kept food grain prices high. Inflation in manufactured food products was low at 3.2 per cent in 2013-14, and it decreased further to –0.4 per cent in April-December 2015-16.

Fall in the prices of cereals, vegetables, fruits, milk, egg, fish and meat brought a fall in the WPI in 2015-16 (April-December). The prices of pulses on account of low domestic production kept food grain prices high and are still a bane for households and a challenge for the government.

Urban Sector and Rural Sector Inflation in India

Rural inflation is higher than urban inflation in India. This is apparent across categories like fuel and food. Structural bottlenecks are not letting rural Indians benefit fully from global deflation. This is seen in the greater use of non-oil based fuels that carry higher prices in rural homes. In case of food, benefits of cheaper imports are not reaching rural areas. The rural-urban output gap analysis depicts a steeper decline in the potential growth of rural India, which is driving core inflation higher. We need higher investment in rural infrastructure and reforms in agriculture to bring about a higher growth so that more supply contains inflation to 4% target set by the RBI.

According to *Economic Survey* 2015-16, the urban CPI basket has been experiencing lower inflation as compared to the rural consumer expenditure-based basket. As of December 2015, the headline inflation for the urban sector was 4.7 per cent as compared to 6.3 per cent for the rural sector. Urban consumers have been benefited by the meltdown in the global commodity prices, especially the fuel products. Consumption data from the NSSO suggests that rural India's fuel mix is more geared towards domestically produced firewood, chips and biogas inputs, which are not a part of the global deflation cycle. On the other hand, fuel products like LPG, petrol and diesel, which are more widely used in urban Indians have given them benefits from lower global prices.

The gap between rural and urban inflation in India has increased from the beginning of the year 2015. The difference is partly due to variation in the weights of items in the two baskets. The rural basket of the CPI assigns significantly larger weights to cereals, vegetables, meat, fish and pulses. Owing to supply side constraints coupled with a lack of a seamless common market for agri-products in the country, the prices of these commodities have been experiencing volatility.

Insufficient rain during the past years led to drought-like conditions in some parts of the country, making it necessary to import food products that are in short supply. However, people living in rural areas do not seem to have benefited as much from food imports as those of urban areas. The major reason seems to be lack of sufficient distribution channels required to supply the imported vegetables and oilseeds to rural areas. This means that rural India has some structural disadvantages vis-à-vis urban India such as lack of proper transportation and distribution channels. This calls for higher investment in rural infrastructure.

State-wise Inflation in India

In line with the overall trend of food inflation in India, the CPI-based general and food inflation also declined during 2015-16 from its level in 2014-15 in most of the states. The states like UP, West Bengal, Bihar, Kerala, Haryana and Punjab showed a more decline in food and beverages inflation than other states where such decline was small or marginal. There are states like Tamil Nadu, Andhra Pradesh, Telangana, and J&K, where CPI for food and beverages inflation showed a higher percentage in 2015-16 from their respective 2014-15 levels.

A number of factors can be attributed to this variation in food inflation trends in the states, like (i) difference in food supply and food consumption patterns in different states, (ii) difference in control systems to check bottlenecks such as hoarding in different states, and (iii) difference in demography, i.e. the level of income of people.

Reasons for High Food Inflation in India

The following reasons can be attributed to high food inflation in India:

(i) Our agriculture production has not risen over the years to meet the demand. This has been because of our overdependence on rain, which is uncertain, for irrigation; loss of crops due to untimely rain, hailstones, floods or drought; and our low per hectare yield.

(ii) Lack of sufficient storing and marketing facilities at the time of harvest, due to which there is wastage of produce.

(iii) Deficiencies in our Public Distribution System (PDS) due to which supply is not regular and sufficient in different parts of India.

(iv) Malpractices like hoarding and creation of artificial shortage by some traders to sell food items at high price to make more profit.

(v) Seasonal variation in the supply and price of fruits and vegetables.

(vi) Large size of India's population and high growth rate of population which creates more and more demand for food.

Food inflation can be contained only if the above issues are addressed. Price increases are due to both supply and demand factors. On the supply side, we have to shore up our agriculture, mainly by making efficient use of water and using best practices to increase our yield. On the demand side we have to (a) control the growth of our population, (b) compliment traditional crops with genetically modified crops, and (c) increase production in allied sectors such as meat and milk. Since the increase in onion prices has been due to poor functioning of the markets and speculative pricing by middlemen, we have to ensure that this does not become a recurring feature.

Outlook for Food Inflation

The cost of food in India increased 5.30 per cent in February 2016 over the same month in the previous year. Food inflation in India averaged 8.65 per cent from 2012 until 2016, reaching an all-time high of 14.72 per cent in November 2013 and a record low of 2.15 per cent in July 2015. The cost of food decreased by 1.5 per cent in May 2017 over the same month in the previous year. It was the first fall in food prices since the series began in 2012 led by pulses and vegetables. Food inflation in India averaged 7.51 per cent from 2012 until 2017. Food inflation in India is reported by the Ministry of Statistics and Programme Implementation (MOSPI), India.[2]

India Food Inflation—actual data, historical chart and calendar of releases as on March 2016 is shown in Table 6.4 below:

Table 6.4: Food inflation in India

India Prices	Last	Previous	Highest	Lowest	Unit	
Inflation Rate	5.18	5.69	11.16	3.69	per cent	[+]
Consumer Price Index CPI	125.90	126.30	126.60	86.81	Index Points	[+]
GDP Deflator	119.50	117.80	171.30	100.00	Index Points	[+]
Producer Prices	174.00	175.70	185.90	97.50	Index Points	[+]
Producer Prices Change	-6.40	-0.90	34.68	-11.31	per cent	[+]
Export Prices	300.00	312.00	312.00	100.00	Index Points	[+]
Import Prices	518.00	518.00	518.00	100.00	Index Points	[+]
Food Inflation	5.30	6.85	14.72	2.15	per cent	[+]
Cpi Transportation	111.30	111.10	113.10	103.20	Index Points	[+]
Inflation Rate Mom	-0.32	0.16	1.77	-1.00	per cent	[+]

Source: Ministry of Statistics and Programme Implementation (MOSPI), India.

Table 6.4 shows that food inflation that was as high as 14.72, came down to 6.85 and then 5.30 in March 2016. Since food inflation varies according to season and the produce of vegetables and fruits, it is likely to fluctuate. However, bottlenecks must be removed and distribution should be improved to ensure that such fluctuation is not high.

Minimum Support Price

Minimum Support Price (MSP) refers to market intervention by the Government of India to protect agricultural producers against any sharp fall in farm prices. MSPs are announced by the government at the beginning of the sowing season for certain crops on the basis of the recommendations of the Commission for Agricultural Costs and Prices (CACP). MSPs guarantee price for farmers' produce from the government. The major objectives are to support the farmers from distress sales and to procure food grains for public distribution. If the market price for the commodity falls below the announced minimum price owing to bumper production and the resultant glut in the market, the government agencies purchase the entire quantity offered by the farmers at the announced minimum price.

Historical perspective of MSP

Till the mid-1970s, government announced two types of administered prices, viz. (i) The Minimum Support Prices (MSPs) and (ii) Procurement Prices. The former served as the floor prices and were in the nature of a long-term guarantee for investment decisions of producers, with the assurance that prices of their commodities would not be allowed to fall below the level fixed by the government, even in the case of a bumper crop. Procurement prices, on the other hand, were the prices of kharif and rabi cereals at which the grain was to be domestically procured by public agencies, primarily the Food Corporation (FCI) for release through PDS. These prices were announced soon after the harvest began. Generally, the procurement price was lower than the open market price and higher than the MSP. In case of paddy, this policy of two official prices continued with some variation up to 1973-74. In the case of wheat it was discontinued in 1969 and then revived in 1974-75 for one year only. In 1975-76, the present system was evolved in which only one set of prices was announced for paddy and other kharif crops, and wheat being procured for buffer stock operations.

Factors that Determine MSP

Besides a comprehensive view of the entire structure of the economy in relation to the crop, the Commission for Agriculture Costs and Prices (Ministry of Agriculture), recommends that the MSP should make use of both micro-level data and aggregates at the level of district, state and the country, and consider a number of factors, which inter alia include the cost of production, changes in input prices, input-output price parity, market price trends, demand and supply, inter-crop price parity, effect on general price level, and international price situation.

Importance of MSP

MSP provides a safeguard to the farmers against the fall of the price of their produce below a certain level and prevents monetary loss to them if the price actually falls below it due to various reasons. The majority of Indian farmers are poor. If they do not get adequate remuneration for their produce, their condition will go from bad to worse. MSP prevents such a situation from arriving and plays an important role in bringing prosperity to the farmers. They are able to buy inputs for their next crop.

MSP serves a dual function of preventing distress sales by the farmers and procuring food grains for public distribution. In case the market price for the commodity falls below the announced minimum price, the government agencies purchase the entire quantity offered by the farmers at the announced minimum price. Since MSPs are fixed at incentive level, farmers can make capital investment for improved farming and adopt better technologies for higher yields. In the absence of such a guaranteed price, there is a concern that farmers may shift to other crops causing shortage in important produce like wheat rice and pulses.

Procurement at MSP

After the announcement of MSP for specific crop as per season, farmers are made aware of the procurement operations through advertisements like displaying banners and pamphlets. Procurement centres are opened by Government agencies, Food Corporation of India (FCI) and State Government, after mutual consultations. Factors like the amount of production, marketable surplus, convenience of farmers and availability of other logistics/ infrastructure like storage and transportation, etc. are taken into account for this.

In states like Bihar, Chhattisgarh, Odisha, Maharashtra, Karnataka, Jharkhand and Rajasthan, Co-operative Societies and Self-Help Groups are also engaged by the government agencies to work as aggregators of produce from farmers and bring the produce to purchase centres. This increases the outreach of MSP operations to small and marginal farmers. This aggregation by Co-operative Societies is in addition to the direct purchases from farmers. The Government of India has permitted the State Governments like those of Punjab and Haryana to engage regional moneylenders (arhatiyas) for procurement of food grains from the farmers on payment of commission. This helps in the procurement of maximum food grains directly from farmers by expanding the outreach of MSP benefit to farmers.

Shortcomings in MSP

Although the government announces MSP for 23 crops, effective MSP-linked procurement occurs mainly for wheat, rice and cotton. In case of sugarcane, there is an effective MSP-like arrangement whereby mills are legally obligated to buy cane from farmers at prices fixed by the government. But even in case of these crops MSP is restricted to a subset of farmers in a few states. There exist large gaps in the percentage of farmers who are even aware of the MSP policy. Most of the farmers are aware of MSPs in paddy and wheat, but very few farmers who grow pulses are aware of an MSP for pulses. Even for paddy and wheat only half or fewer of the farmers are aware of MSP in states like Gujarat, Maharashtra, Rajasthan, Andhra Pradesh and Jharkhand. There is a likelihood that procurement in these States may be happening in some districts, not in others.

Public procurement under MSP has focused mainly on wheat, rice and sugarcane, while other crops such as pulses and oilseeds have been ignored. This has resulted in buffer stocks of paddy and wheat to be above the required norms, but shortage and resultant price increase in pulses and edible oils.

In most of the states there is no procurement of a number of crops. The farmers have no option but to sell their produce to private traders below the MSP, which has resulted in a regional bias in farm incomes. These traders exploit the farmers' need and urgency to sell their crops and offer low prices.

MSP ignores the social returns and gives all the importance to private returns of production. Scientists have pointed out that there are some negative externalities associated with producing wheat, rice and sugarcane because of the use of chemical fertilizers (soil depletion and health hazards), water (falling water table), and from burning crops (pollution and adverse health consequences). On the other hand, there are social returns associated with production of pulses in the form of use of less water and fertilizers, fixation of atmospheric nitrogen naturally and help in keeping the soil porous and well aerated because of their deep and extensive root systems. These positive social benefits should be incorporated into MSP estimates. Farmers could also be assured a floor price for their crops through a "Price Deficiency Payment".[3] Removing these anomalies will make MSP more meaningful and effective.

PUBLIC DISTRIBUTION SYSTEM (PDS)

The Public Distribution System (PDS) in India was started as part of the strategy for poverty alleviation. It was one of the main constituents of government's strategy aiming to enhance food security, particularly to the economically weaker sections of the society. The PDS ensures the availability of the essential commodities like wheat, rice, sugar, edible oil and kerosene through a wide network of outlets or Fair Price Shops (FPS). At present there are 4.8 lakh PDS retail outlets in India.

The policy of PDS has been drawn primarily with the objective of providing food security to the poor and simultaneously fixing remunerative prices to the producers. In fact, the latter function was better served in the course of implementation of the PDS. This aims to ensure that the farmers may not resort to distress sale due to weak bargaining power and monopoly of market functionaries. The government through procurement operation provides Minimum Support Price to the producers to save them from market exploitation and to boost production as well. It also aims to build buffer stocks to ensure food security in case of scarcity situation.

The wide network of PDS is a major instrument of government, with the help of which it tries to implement food and economic policies for ensuring food security, particularly to the poor. This system largely aims to help the producers and consumers of food grains. It provides the Minimum Support Price (MSP) to the farmers as well as ensures the distribution of food grains to the consumers at affordable and subsidized prices throughout the country.

In the 1990s, when India adopted the policy of liberalization and globalization, the objective of expenditure reductions took priority over the welfare objectives, including the objective of providing food security to the poor. The existing PDS was characterized as inefficient, having more leakages, less benefit to the poor, and maladministration. The government shifted its operation to target-orientation and revamped orientation of PDS.

Origin of PDS

The PDS in the field of food grains in India dates back to the early years of World War II and the Bengal Famine in India. It was started as an emotional issue with an objective to help the common people. It was introduced as a measure to maintain the morale of the people in the context of war mobilization and food grains scarcity. Later it became an integral constituent of food and economic policy of the government that aimed to protect the vulnerable section of the society from the rising prices of essential commodities.

The PDS continues to be an essential plank of economic policy of the country even after independence. The policy on the food security of the fledgling Indian state had two essential components, namely the policy of increased agricultural production and the policy of food distribution system. The first one was clearly a vital component of the modernization of the Indian state. The second was more unambiguously a part of its welfare orientation. It is to achieve this goal that the system was assigned a significant role in the beginning of the planning era in India and to ensure efficient and equitable distribution of available food grains at reasonable prices. Over a period of time, the system evolved many measures regarding the procurement that included food grains price control, their procurement, building of buffer stocks by the FCI for stabilizing food grains prices and an even flow of the supplies by movement control through zonal system, fixation of producers' price to support their income. With the help of a wide network of Fair Price Shops (FPS), it now provides a protective umbrella to the vulnerable sections of the society by distributing food grains at concessional rates.

The FCI purchases food grains for the Central Pool at minimum support prices announced by the government and then it is released for Public Distribution System and other schemes at issue prices fixed by the government. The difference between issue prices and procurement prices constitutes food subsidy.

Handling, storage, interest, and administrative charges are also reimbursed to the FCI.

The PDS in India has been working efficiently for more than half-decade only because of the huge subsidy that is borne by the Government of India. The food subsidy was negligible until the end of the 1960s, but later it increased steadily. By the end of the mid-1990s, it rose to 50,000 million which constitutes 3 per cent of the total expenditure of the Central Government budget and about 0.5 per cent of the Gross Domestic Product (GDP).

Significance of PDS in India

The role and importance of PDS was realized as far back as the First Plan of 1951-56. The PDS was introduced with an objective to act as price support programme for the consumer during the food shortage of 1960s. As the food-items constitute a major portion of the consumption of workers, PDS helps in supplying wage-goods at prices lower than the market prices. At the same time the real wages of the workers are protected. The price level of several consumption goods is kept stable. Besides, the supply of food grains is also regulated by the PDS. It helps in overcoming the regional disparities in respect of food grains production which creates regional imbalances. For example, rice is the staple diet of the major proportion of the population, the difference in growth rates have often been very large as the Northern Region (Punjab, Haryana and Western Uttar Pradesh) achieved a much higher growth than the Southern Region (Andhra Pradesh, Karnataka, Tamil Nadu and Kerala). The Eastern Region (Eastern UP, Bihar, West Bengal, Odisha and Assam) registered a still lower growth of 0.8 per cent. The PDS helps in bridging this gap prevailing in various regions of the country. Thus, it maintains a balance between supply and demand as well as provides the non-inflationary way of development.

PDS helps in reducing food insecurity, particularly of those who are destitute with very little employment or earning. PDS ensures the supply of food grains at cheap rates, and thus provides a means of security to the poor. When PDS is made an integral part of some of the employment schemes of the poor, it becomes all the more important as payment of the workers in some such schemes made partly or wholly in food grains, protects their consumption level. Thus, PDS is one of the important tools to combat prevailing poverty and food insecurity in the country. PDS is of great help in providing security to the weaker sections of society who are vulnerable to the structural changes in the economy. The changes which promote an open and market-oriented economy have caused harm to the poor because a number of traditional occupations have been left open to the market forces.

Coverage of PDS

PDS ensures the distribution of essential items such as selected cereals, sugar, edible oils and kerosene at subsidized prices to holders of ration cards. It ensures the availability of essential commodities through its wide network. Through the PDS, the government regulates supply and distribution of essential commodities with a view to securing their equitable distribution and availability at fair prices. People living under Integrated Tribal Development Project (ITDP) are supplied food grains (wheat and rice) at special low prices. Rice, wheat, sugar and kerosene account for more than 80 per cent of the total PDS sales. Coarse cereals like *jowar* and *bajra*, which are largely consumed by the poor, account for about one per cent of total PDS sales. The share of pulses which is the major source of protein for the poor is also very low.

The Central Government is the pivot of the PDS. It procures and allocates or supplies the commodities to the states and the union territories, which are responsible for the allocation and distribution of food grains in their territories. Out of about five lakh Fair Price Shops in the country more than three-fourths are in rural areas and one-fourth in urban areas. On an average one Fair Price Shop is required to cover a population of 2000.

PDS and the Poor

One important question which needs to be probed is whether PDS has been successful in achieving its objectives. The history of PDS of the country reveals that its performance varies from state to state. Equally, PDS is grossly uneven in respect of its distribution of food grains across classes and regions. The socially and economically backward states of Bihar, Uttar Pradesh, Madhya Pradesh, Rajasthan and Odisha account for as much as 52 per cent of the population as well as the large proportion of the country's poor population, but these states receive only 20 per cent of central allocations of food grains. Thus, there is no relation between the incidence of poverty in a state and the scale of PDS supplies. Again, the PDS has evolved in such a way that the regional variations in it have nothing to do with the food grains deficits of the states or with the requirements of states.

This is evident from the studies conducted by Radhakrishna et al. on the basis of 42nd NSS round which reveals missed targeting in the distribution of food grains. In Kerala and Andhra Pradesh, PDS purchases were relatively high in all expenditure groups. The PDS purchases constituted 40-58 per cent of cereal consumption. Although the dependency of the very poor on PDS was as high as 58 per cent, yet the beneficiaries in the non-poor group constituted 40 per cent of the population as a result of the generalization of the scheme. The poor purchased 4.3 kg per month while the non-poor purchased 4.5 kg. Almost similar pattern could be observed in the urban areas. The same year monthly per capita purchases by the very poor and the non-poor in Andhra Pradesh were 2.3 to 2.5 kg and 2.2 to 2.6 kg in rural areas and urban areas respectively. In case of poor it constituted 22 per cent of the total cereal consumption of the poor in rural areas which was 17 per cent in the non-poor population. In urban areas, the PDS cereal purchases for the poor were 25 per cent against 19 per cent of the non-poor in urban areas during the same period.

Public Distribution System and Food Security

The main objective of PDS is to ensure food security through timely and affordable distribution of food grains to sections of population that live below the poverty line and are unable to pay market prices for their food. PDS involves procuring food grain at Minimum Support Price (MSP) by the Government, creating and maintaining food stocks, their storage, and timely distribution, making food grains accessible at reasonable prices to the poor sections of the population. A number of weaknesses in the PDS have been seen, which have led to leakages and a large number of targeted beneficiaries have been left out of the system. However, the FCI has maintained large stocks through offtake. The position of procurement, offtake and the stocks maintained by the FCI is given in Table 6.5.

Table 6.5 shows that the procurement of rice and wheat has increased from 38.7 MT in 2003-04 to 60.2 MT in 2014-15. The total offtake for wheat and rice was 49.3 MT in 2003-04, which increased to 55.9 MT in 2014-15. The stocks for wheat and rice taken together doubled from 20.7 MT in 2003-04 to 41 MT in 2014-15. Table 6.5 also shows that the best performance in procurement, offtake and stocks was in the year 2012-13 when monsoon was normal and produce was better than the earlier years.

Table 6.5: Public Distribution System—Procurement, Offtake and Stocks

(Million tonnes)

Year	Procurement			Offtake			Stocks		
	Rice	Wheat	Total	Rice	Wheat	Total	Rice	Wheat	Total
2003-04	22.9	15.8	38.7	25.0	24.3	49.3	13.1	6.9	20.7
2004-05	24.7	16.8	41.5	23.2	18.3	41.5	13.3	4.1	18.0
2005-06	27.6	14.8	42.4	25.1	17.2	42.3	13.7	2.0	16.6
2006-07	25.1	9.2	34.3	25.1	11.7	36.8	13.2	4.7	17.9
2007-08	28.7	11.1	39.9	25.2	12.2	37.4	13.8	5.8	19.8
2008-09	34.1	22.7	56.8	24.6	14.9	39.5	21.6	13.4	35.6
2009-10	32.0	25.4	57.4	27.4	22.4	49.7	26.7	16.1	43.3
2010-11	34.2	22.5	56.7	29.9	23.1	53.0	28.8	15.4	44.3
2011-12	35.0	28.3	63.4	32.1	24.2	56.3	33.4	20.0	53.4
2012-13	34.0	38.2	72.2	32.6	33.2	65.8	35.5	24.2	59.8
2013-14	31.8	25.1	56.9	29.2	30.6	59.8	30.6	17.8	48.4
2014-15	32.2	28.0	60.2	30.7	25.2	55.9	23.8	17.2	41.0

Source: Department of Food and Public Distribution.

Notes: *Procurement as on 18 January 2016; #Offtake up to November, 2015; @Stock as on 1 January 2016 and stock for the previous years are as on 1 April.

As per *Handbook of Statistics on Indian Economy 2016*, RBI, the procurement of rice and wheat in the year 2015-16 was 34.14 MT and 28.09 MT, respectively. The offtake for 2015-16 for rice and wheat was 31.82 MT and 31.84 MT, respectively. The stocks for rice and wheat for 2015-16 were 28.81 MT and 14.54 MT, respectively.

Issues in PDS

Although there has been improvement in the three main operations of PDS, many issues remain, as shown below:

(i) The costs for procurement, storage and distribution of food grains under PDS are high. There is scope for reducing costs and improving efficiency in PDS operations.

(ii) Only a small proportion of the public expenditure/ subsidy on PDS reaches the beneficiary. The corruption in the system must be removed.

(iii) The statistics show that there was an increase in procurement, offtake and stocks of rice and wheat during 2015-16 over 2014-2015. According to *Economic Survey* 2015-16, this suggests that notwithstanding an increased availability in the PDS and prevalence of high inflation in food grains, dependence on the PDS is reducing, which means that "there may be issues of availability, timely availability and quality of the PDS food grains".

The economic cost to the FCI of keeping food grains has been increasing over the years. The cost of agriculture production is increasing owing to high costs of inputs like fertilizers and high labour costs. This is pushing the MSPs high. Since the increase in the food subsidy bill is determined by the rate at which the MSPs for wheat and rice increase and the economic cost of handling grains, the amount of food subsidy is increasing. There are many incidental costs associated with procurement, like mandi charges and taxes, cost of gunny bags, commission of arhatiyas, mandi labour, forwarding charges, internal movement charges, storage charges, administration charges, etc. These, along with the increasing economic costs of handling food grains through procurement, distribution and storage, large procurement in recent years and the widening gap between the economic cost of food grains and the central issue price have been the major factors leading to the ballooning food subsidy.[4]

Food Subsidy in India

Subsidy is converse of tax and is an instrument of fiscal policy. Food subsidy in India is one of the largest food subsidy programmes in the world and has created a relatively effective social safety net.

The National Food Security Act (NFSA), 2013 aims to provide subsidized food grains to approximately two-thirds of India's population. It includes the Midday Meal Scheme (MMS), Integrated Child Development Services (ICDS) scheme and the Public Distribution System (PDS). It also recognizes maternity entitlements. The MMS and ICDS are universal in nature.

Under the provisions of the bill, beneficiaries of the Public Distribution System are entitled to 5 kilograms per person per month of cereals at the following prices:

Rice at ₹ 3 per kg.

Wheat at ₹ 2 per kg.

Coarse grains (millet) at ₹ 1 per kg.

Pregnant women, lactating mothers, and certain categories of children are eligible for daily free meals. The bill has been highly controversial. It was introduced into India's parliament on 22 December 2011, promulgated as a presidential ordinance on 5 July 2013, and enacted into law on 12 September 2013.

The food security bill has been criticized on some accounts. It has been stated that it will aggravate food price inflation as it will tilt supply towards cereals and away from other farm produce (proteins), which will raise food prices further. The government should address supply side constraints which are causing inflationary pressure in food and food products. According Vivek Kaul, the government's estimated cost of food security comes at 11.10% of the total receipts.[5] The CACP's estimated cost of food security comes at 21.5% of the total receipts. The Indian Ministry of Agriculture's Commission on Agricultural Costs and Prices warned that enactment of the bill could be expected to "induce severe imbalance in the production of oilseeds and pulses," and "...will create demand pressures, which will inevitably spill over to market prices of food grains. Furthermore, the higher food subsidy burden on the budget will raise fiscal deficit, exacerbating macro level inflationary pressures."[6] The Commission argued further that the bill would restrict private initiative in agriculture, reduce competition in the marketplace due to government domination of the grain market, shift money from investments in agriculture to subsidies, and continue focus on cereals production when shifts in consumer demand patterns indicate a need to focus more on protein, fruits and vegetables.

According to a report by Commission for Agricultural Costs and Prices (CACP), the swelling amount of subsidy has been the result of increasing economic costs of handling food grains through procurement, distribution and storage, large procurement in recent years and the widening gap between the economic cost of food grains and the central issue price. Table 6.6 below shows the amount of food subsidy from 2005-06 to 2015-16.

Table 6.6: Food Subsidy in India

Year	Food subsidy (₹ in crore)
2005-06	23071.00
2006-07	23827.59
2007-08	31259.68
2008-09	43668.08
2009-10	58242.45
2010-11	62929.56
2011-12	72370.90
2012-13	84554.00
2013-14	89740.02
2014-15	113171.16
2015-16*	105509.41

Source: Department of Food and Public Distribution
Note: *Figures as on 6 January 2016.

Table 6.6 shows that food subsidy, which was ₹ 23,071 crore 2005-06 increased to ₹ 62,929.56 crore in five years, i.e. in 2010-11, and further to ₹ 113171.16 crore in the next four years, i.e. in 2014-15. The amount of food subsidy as on 6 January 2016 was ₹ 1,05,509.41 crore. The major reasons are high PDS costs, increasing leakages, high administrative costs, corruption, and mismanagement. The amount of subsidy is very high and is hampering growth because it is a burden on the exchequer.

Additionally, subsidies bring distortions in the market and also pose a heavy burden on the government budget, especially during times when domestic or international prices are on the rise, when the Government has to resort to raising the MSPs of crops on a regular basis. However, the costs including opportunity costs of resources diverted for subsidy are high in terms of the public investments in agriculture which are foregone and which can improve productivity (*Economic Survey*, 2015-16).

Regional Difference in the Offtake of PDS Food Grains

The offake of food grains in PDS varies state to state. In some states it is even lower than the central allocation. It is the consequence of the upward revision of issue price that has caused the narrowing down of the gap between subsidized issue price and open market price. To some extent it is attributed to the State Government's persistence to implement subsidized PDS. According to a report by World Bank, the offtake in poorer states like Bihar and Odisha was substantially lower than central allocations, partly due to the narrow difference between the central issue price and open market price and partly because of weak fiscal capacity of these states in financing any additional subsidy in the form of lowering of issue prices. Besides, these states have not yet built effective institutional mechanisms to lift the quotas from FCI depots to fair price shops.

The higher per capita offtake of food grains was seen in some states, which reflects the social commitment of the states. Absence of adequate storage facilities in the states was the main reason why offtake was not as per expectations even in the bumper harvest years. In fact bumper harvest needs more storage facilities. There is also a need for higher lifting of allotments under the targeted PDS. The Centre wants creation of storage spaces in view of faster movement of food grains and higher consumption. Measures should also be taken to bring down wastage of food grains during procurement, storage and transportation.

Targeted Public Distribution System (TPDS)

The resolve of the government to reform and improve the PDS by focusing on the poor and needy sections of the society resulted in the launching of the Targeted Public Distribution

System in June 1997. It follows a two-tier subsidized pricing structure—families Below Poverty Line (BPL) and those Above Poverty Line (APL)—the former representing the poorest of the poor. The objective was to identify the persons/families living below the poverty line and issue a distinct ration card for selling specified cereal items through PDS outlets at specially subsidized rates, i.e. half the normal price under PDS. It was intended to benefit nearly seven crore poor families in the country for whom a quantum of 70 to 80 lakh tonnes of food grains was earmarked annually at the rate of 25 kg per family per month. It was started to make PDS more responsive to the needs of the poor.

The Central Government regulates the supply of food grains to the states for the BPL families. In case of additional demand from the states, the stocks in the Central Pool are made available at a price which is very close to the economic cost of FCI. According to a survey of 60 districts from 12 states comprising of 12000 households conducted for six months in two phases, the performance of the TPDS in terms of delivery of food to the targeted people was satisfactory in states such as Delhi, Uttarakhand and Rajasthan. In poor states like Bihar, Assam, Jharkhand and Madhya Pradesh, there were some roadblocks like issuing of excess card/unidentified families as well as inclusion/exclusion error among all the states, improper functioning of fair price shops, and corruption in the process of extricating the poor from those who are less needy.

Allocation under NFSA

In order to make food grains available to the people at cheaper rates, the government has enacted National Food Security Act (NFSA) under which food grains are to be provided to the States/UTs for distribution to the people at highly subsidized prices of ₹ 1/-, ₹ 2/- and ₹ 3/- per kg for coarse grains, wheat and rice respectively, based on Census 2011. As per the Act, up to 2/3rd population in the country will be covered under TPDS. Total estimated outgo of food grains under the Act is 614.4 lakh tons.

Allocation under existing TPDS

Meanwhile, the States/UTs which have not implemented NFSA so far are being provided food grains as per existing TPDS norms under which allocation of food grains is made @ 35 kg per family per month for Below Poverty Line (BPL), including Antyodaya Anna Yojana (AAY) families and @ 15 kg to 35 kg per family per month for Above Poverty Line (APL) families.

National Food Security Act 2013 and TPDS

The National Food Security Act, 2013 inter alia aims to streamline TPDS. Some relevant features of the Act are given below:

(i) Up to 75% of the rural population and 50% of the urban population will be covered under TPDS, with uniform entitlement of 5 kg per person per month.

However, since Antyodaya Anna Yojana (AAY) households constitute poorest of the poor, and are presently entitled to 35 kg per household per month, entitlement of existing AAY households will be protected at 35 kg per household per month.

(ii) Corresponding to the all-India coverage of 75% and 50% in the rural and urban areas respectively, state-wise coverage will be determined by the Central Government. State-wise coverage has been determined by the Planning Commission on the basis of 2011-12 NSSO Household Consumption Expenditure Survey data.

(iii) Food grains under TPDS will be made available at subsidised prices of ₹ 3/2/1 per kg for rice, wheat and coarse grains for a period of three years from the date of commencement of the Act. Thereafter prices will be suitably linked to Minimum Support Price (MSP).

(iv) In case, any state's allocation under the proposed legislation is lower than their current allocation, it will be protected up to the level of average offtake during last three years under normal TPDS, at prices to be determined by the Central Government. Existing prices for APL households, i.e. ₹ 6.10 per kg for wheat and ₹ 8.30 per kg for rice has been determined as issue prices for the additional allocation to protect the average offtake.

(v) Within the coverage under TPDS determined for each state, the work of identification of eligible households is to be done by States/UTs.

(vi) Provisions have been made for disclosure of records relating to PDS, social audits and setting up of Vigilance Committees in order to ensure transparency and accountability.

(vii) There is provision for penalty on public servant or authority, to be imposed by the State Food Commission, in case of failure to comply with the relief recommended by the District Grievance Redressal Officer. Based on the provisions of the Act, the requirement of food grains for TPDS and other welfare schemes is estimated to be 614.4 lakh tonnes. The estimated food subsidy for implementation of the Act at 2014-15 costs, is about ₹ 1,31,086 crore, which implies additionality of about 27,000 crore due to implementation of NFSA.

If the above provisions of the Act are implemented, TPDS will become more effective.

Farmers' Suicide in India

Farmers' suicide is a distressing phenomenon but stark reality that reminds us that something is wrong with our food security and food management. The news of farmers' suicide reaches us every now and then through newspapers and other media. The number of farmers' suicide is on the rise in the country.

According to the National Crime Records Bureau of India annual report 2012, 135,445 people committed suicide in India, of which 13,755 were farmers (11.2%).[7] Of these, 5 out of 29 states accounted for 10,486 farmers suicides (76%)—Maharashtra, Andhra Pradesh, Karnataka, Madhya Pradesh and Kerala.[8]

In 2012, the state of Maharashtra, with 3,786 farmers' suicides, accounted for about a quarter of the all India's farmer suicides total (13,754). From 1995 to 2013, a total of 296,438

Indian farmers committed suicide. During the same period, about 9.5 million people died per year in India from other causes including malnutrition, diseases and suicides that were non-farming related, or about 171 million deaths from 1995 to 2013. Around 2,590 farmers across Maharashtra committed suicide from January to October 2015—the highest number of suicides since 2001. In 2006, around 2,376 farmers ended their lives (*The Hindu* 21 December 2015). Official data obtained by *The Hindu* from 2001 to 2014 shows that over 17,276 farmers committed suicide due to issues ranging from crop failure, inability to repay loans, overdependence on market forces that mostly work in favour of traders.

Farmer suicides rates in Bihar and Uttar Pradesh—two large states of India by size and population—have been about 10 times lower than in Maharashtra, Kerala and Puducherry.[9,10] In 2012, there were 745 farmer suicides in Uttar Pradesh, a state with an estimated population of 205.43 million. In 2014, there were eight farmer suicides in Uttar Pradesh. In 2014, 5,650 farmers committed suicide in India. The number increased to 8,007 in 2015, a rise of 41 per cent.

Various reasons have been given to explain why so many farmers end their lives in India, like crop failure due to floods, drought, due to other reasons, like debt, food insecurity, use of genetically modified seeds, and government's economic policies. However, there is no consensus on what are the main causes. Studies reveal that victims are motivated by more than one cause, on average three or more causes for committing suicide.

A 2014 study found that the three specific characteristics associated with high risk farmers were "those that grow cash crops such as coffee and cotton; those with 'marginal' farms of less than one hectare; and those with debts of ₹ 300 or more". The study also found that the Indian states in which these three characteristics are most common had the highest suicide rates and also accounted for "almost 75% of the variability in state-level suicides".[11] The expressed reasons in order of importance behind farmer suicides were—debt, alcohol addiction, environment, low produce prices, stress and family responsibilities, apathy, poor states by rail, road and riverine modes to ensure availability of food grains for TPDS and OWS (other welfare schemes), and to maintain reasonable levels of buffer stocks at various strategic locations throughout the country.

The bulk of the movement is done through railways, with road and waterway transport undertaking about 10% of movement. About 25 lakh bags of 50 kg food grains each are transported every day from the procuring areas to the consuming areas, covering an average distance of 1500 km.

The FCI prepares an All India Movement Plan on a monthly basis keeping in view the quantity available in surplus states, quantity required by consuming states, likely procurement, storage capacity and monthly allocation as well as offtake.

An online tracking system for movement of food grains and depot management was launched in March 2016. It aims to provide various types of data regarding stock position, movement, quality and quantity online. It would also generate SMS alerts to depot officials, area manager and other decision-making authorities.

Buffer Stock Policy of the GOI

According to DFPD, the central government maintains buffer stock of food grains for (i) meeting the prescribed minimum buffer stock norms for food security, (ii) monthly release of food grains for supply through TPDS and other welfare schemes, (iii) meeting emergency situations arising out of unexpected crop failure, natural disasters, etc. and (iv) price stabilization or market intervention to augment supply so as to help moderate the open market prices.

The quarterly minimum buffer norms are given by Cabinet Committee on Economic Affairs, as on 1st April, 1st July, 1st October and 1st January of every financial year. Besides the buffer norms, the government has prescribed a strategic reserve of 30 lakh tonnes of wheat w.e.f. 01-07-2008 and 20 lakh tonnes of rice w.e.f. 01-01-2009.

Food grains stock in the Central Pool is comprised of stock held by FCI, DCP states and the SGAs for buffer as

irrigation, increased cost of cultivation, pressure by moneylenders, and crop failure.[12]

In Maharashtra, the state having the dubious distinction of having the highest number of farmer suicides, according to a survey conducted by Tata Institute, "government's lack of interest, the absence of a safety net for farmers, and lack of access to information related to agriculture were the chief causes for the desperate condition of farmers in the state".

Crop failure due to droughts is one of the major causes of farmers' suicide in India. Around 80 per cent of India's farmland depends on monsoon for irrigation. Inadequate rainfall can cause droughts, making crop failure more common. In regions that have experienced droughts, crop yields have declined, and food for cattle has become scarcer. Suicide rates in draught prone regions have increased. It is pertinent to mention here that global warming has changed the weather pattern all over the world, including India. More rainfall comes in less number of days followed by long durations without rain. Many parts go without sufficient rain even during monsoon. This has increased the worries of Indian farmers. What we need to do is to find alternative sources of irrigation and take up methods like drip irrigation and sprinkler irrigation. Quick clearing of weeds that compete with crops for minerals and water is necessary. Protecting the plants from diseases and insects is also required. Using seeds and growing crops that need less water will also be of great help.

Some studies have found a link between GM crops and farmer suicides. According to *New York Times*, Bt. cotton (*Bacillus thuringiensis* cotton) was claimed to be responsible for farmer suicides.[13] The Bt cotton seeds are very costly, nearly twice as much as ordinary ones. When the farmers in the cotton growing areas tried these seeds, they had to take larger loans from private moneylenders who charged exorbitant interest rates. When the crop failed, there were large debts and stress for the farmers. Some agriculture scientists claim that this Bt cotton theory made certain assumptions and ignored field reality.[14]

The action required in this regard is to adopt GM crops only after authentic findings on the basis of research are received. The problems encountered in getting a good crop must be solved. It is pertinent to mention here that GM crops are necessary for bringing and maintaining food security, because there are many advantages attached to these crops like avoiding use of chemical fertilizers which will help the cause of environment, less use of water, resistance to many plant diseases, etc.

Agriculture Marketing Reforms

The scheme for setting up of a National Agriculture Market (NAM) through an Agri-Tech Infrastructure Fund (ATIF) was approved by the Cabinet Committee on Economic Affairs (CCEA) in July 2015 with a budget of ₹ 200 crore, to be implemented during 2015-16 to 2017-18. It aims to implement NAM by setting up an appropriate common e-market platform that would be deployable in selected regulated wholesale markets in States/ Union Territories (UT) desirous of joining the e-platform.

There will be integration of State Agricultural Produce Market Committees (APMCs) with NAM. According to *Economic Survey* 2015-16, this needs certain "pre-requisites in the State AMPC Acts, namely (i) a single license to be valid across the state, (ii) single point levy of market fee and (iii) provision for electronic auction as a mode for price discovery. Only those states that have completed these three pre-requisites will be eligible for assistance under the scheme."

Proposals have been received from the following states for integration of their *mandis*: Gujarat 40, Maharashtra 30, Telangana 44, Jharkhand 19, Chhattisgarh 5, Madhya Pradesh 50, Rajasthan 25, and UT of Chandigarh 1. Almost all other states have shown their willingness to join the NAM.

Agriculture Trade Policy

The tariff protection and support accorded to agriculture sector remains higher than to the manufacturing and services sectors, because this sector is important for achieving the objectives of food security and price stability. The average tariff protection for agriculture is 36.4 per cent as against 9.5 per cent to non-agricultural products. India's trade policy is "responsive to the changing domestic situation of crop production, demand,

supply and most importantly retail prices" (*Econom* 2015-16). Such policy makes it necessary to revise customs duty of agricultural products frequently ac domestic conditions to protect the farmers and agricul value added industries.

Some policy changes made for the benefit of farm the following:

(i) Permitting export of edible oils in branded packs of up to 5 kg with a minimum expo US$ 900 per MT.

(ii) Permitting export of rice bran oil vid Notification dated 6 April, 2015.

(iii) Allowing export of Kabuli chana and 10,0 organic pulses per annum.

(iv) Permitting export of rice and wheat.

(v) Giving exemption to processed and/or v agricultural products from export restricti

(vi) Allowing export of cotton without any res

Although frequent policy changes are necess prevailing conditions, they create instability for inv the agro-processing industry. Some economists have such frequent changes should be done away with.

India has made good progress in agriculture crops like cotton, rice, meat, oil meals, spice, guargu sugar. According to trade statistics given by WTO, I of agricultural exports and imports in the world tra was 2.46 per cent and 1.46 per cent, respectively. Its exports as a percentage of agricultural GDP increase per cent in 2009-10 to 12.08 per cent in 2014-15. imports as a percentage of agricultural GDP also inc 4.90 per cent to 5.82 per cent during this period.

Movement of Food Grains

According to the Department of Food and Public I (DFPD), FCI undertakes transportation of food grain rice) from surplus states to the deficit states and als

well as operational requirements. Four months requirement of food grains for issue under TPDS and OWS are earmarked as operational stocks, and the surplus is treated as buffer stock. However, physically, both buffer and operational stocks are merged into one and are not distinguishable.

According to PDS web portal, the government treats the food stock over and above the minimum norms as excess stock and liquidates them from time to time through exports, open market sales or additional allocations to states. The buffer stock figures are normally reviewed after every five years.

Open Market Sale of Food Grains

Besides maintaining buffer stocks and making a provision for meeting the requirement of the TPDS and other welfare schemes FCI sells wheat and rice in the open market from time to time to enhance the supply of wheat and rice, especially during the lean season to maintain supply and to moderate the open market prices. FCI has switched over to e-auction for sale under Open Market Sale Scheme, which has brought transparency in operations. According to DFPD, the open market sale scheme conducts sale under the following three sub schemes:

(i) Sale of wheat to bulk consumers/private traders through e-auction.

(ii) Sale of wheat to bulk consumers/private traders through e-auction by dedicated movement.

(iii) Sale of Raw Rice Grade 'A' to bulk consumers/private traders through e-auction.

The responsibility of regulating the PDS is shared by central and state governments. The central government is responsible for procurement, storage, transportation, and bulk allocation of food grains, while state governments go for distributing the same to the consumers through the established network of Fair Price Shops (FPSs). While the PDS has been able to maintain supply of food grains throughout the country, some anomalies exist such as instances of consumers receiving inferior quality food grains in ration shops; corruption by some dealers, malpractices and illegal diversions of commodities, unsatisfactory regional allocation and coverage of FPS, etc.

The following measures are suggested to improve the current system of PDS: (i) strengthening vigilance squad to detect corruption; (ii) reducing the costs of procurement; (iii) improving efficiency in food grain movement; (iv) improving storage facilities, increasing capacity and reducing wastage. This will ensure better food supply and keep the prices in check.

Notes

1. *Economic Survey* 2015-16.
2. http://www.tradingeconomics.com/india/food-inflation?embed
3. NitiAayog 2014-15 Annual Report.
4. The Commission for Agricultural Costs and Prices (CACP), report.
5. http://everything.explained.today/National_Food_Security_Act,_2013/
6. Web site: National Food Security Bill, Challenges and Options, Discussion Paper No. 2. Ashok Gulati et al. Commission on Agricultural Costs and Prices, Ministry of Agriculture, Government of India. December 2012.
7. National Crime Reports Bureau, ADSI Report Annual–2012 Government of India, pp. xx and 242.
8. National Crime Reports Bureau, ADSI Report Annual–2014 Government of India, p. 242, Table 2.11.
9. Nagaraj (2008). "Farmers' Suicides in India: Magnitudes, Trends and Spatial Patterns". *Bharathi Puthakalayam*, pp. 16-25.
10. Mudit Kapoor and Shamika Ravi (2007)."Indian School of Business", Hyderabad; Shamika Ravi, "Suicides through the glass darkly". *The Indian Express* (4 December 2007).
11. Kennedy and King: "The political economy of farmers' suicides in India: indebted cash-crop farmers with marginal landholdings explain state-level variation in suicide rates." *Globalization and Health* 2014 10:16.
12. Dongre and Deshmukh. "Farmers' suicides in the Vidarbha region of Maharashtra, India: a qualitative exploration of their causes", *Journal of Injury and Violence Research*, Jan 2012; 4(1): 2-6.
13. "On India's Farms, a Plague of Suicide". *New York Times* (18 September 2006).
14. Glenn Davis Stone. "Field versus Farm in Warangal: Bt Cotton, Higher Yields, and Larger Questions". *World Development*, Volume 39, Issue 3, March 2011, pp. 387-98, doi:10.1016/j.worlddev.2010.09.008.

7

Industry in India

Industrialization can be defined as the process by which an economy is transformed from primarily agricultural to one based on the manufacturing of goods. Individual manual labour is often replaced by mechanized mass production, and craftsmen are replaced by assembly lines. The main features of industrialization include economic growth, more efficient division of labour, and the use of technological innovation to solve problems as opposed to dependency on conditions outside human control.

Rapid industrialization is important for a country's economy for generation of employment opportunities, utilization of all types of resources, promotion of education, training and research, improvement of the productivity of labour and balanced regional development.

Industry is more important for an economy than any other sector because of many reasons. It brings a rapid increase in the national income of the country; reduces the pressure of exploding population; has an unlimited scope and ability to create more and more jobs and absorb a large number of unemployed youths; it can use of waste material; make more use of capital and technologies; improve productivity of labour; remove regional disparities; and raise the standard of living of people, among others.

Industrialization has a major role to play in the economic development of the underdeveloped countries. Industrialization is linked with (i) increase in per capita income; (ii) growth in international trade; (iii) generation of more and more trade;

(iv) growth of infrastructure in the country; and (v) stimulation of growth of banking, insurance, commerce, shipping, air services, etc.

India's Industry Before Independence

India had no industry worth the name during the colonial period when the British ruled the country, first through the East India Company and then directly under British Government. The nature of foreign rule was exploitative. The British purchased raw material from India at cheap rates and processed it in England where they had set up factories, and then sold the finished goods in India and other parts of the world, making their own country richer and India and other colonies poorer. They discouraged the setting up of industry in India so that they may continue to get raw material from India and sell the manufactured goods to the Indian people.

The village and cottage industry, which was a traditional Industry in India, too suffered a lot during the British rule. The hand-made goods of India's rural artisans lacked polish and finish which only machines could provide. The handloom-made cloth by the Indian manufacturers was coarse and did not have the quality possessed by the machine-made cloth manufactured in the UK. But the British were not interested in setting up industry in India so that people may continue to buy the foreign goods. The local industries which used old methods and little use of machines suffered and the country remained industrially backward.

After winning the battle of Plassey in 1757, the East India Company (EIC) started dominating both economic and political power in the region and the country. Under pressure from the powerful rising English manufacturing interests, EIC dealt a severe blow to Indian industries that led to their final extinction—the phase of India's 'deindustrialization'. It employed the arm of political injustice on Indian products to strangulate the competitors with whom it could not contend 'on equal terms'.[1]

In 1813, the trading monopoly of the EIC was withdrawn, and the British policy of political domination and economic exploitation started. India was relegated to an importing country and was flooded with machine-produced goods. India was also forced to supply raw materials for triggering industrial revolution in UK. From a country of agriculturists and manufacturers, India was forcibly transformed into an agricultural colony of British manufacturing capitalism.

Some private industry developed in India during 1850 and 1914, but it was confined mainly to plantations like tea, jute and cotton. There was also some development in mining, especially coal. Most of these industries, except textile factories, were under European control. There were also attempts by EIC to develop iron and steel industry, but they proved futile. The credit for the development of large scale manufacture of steel in India must go to Jamshedji Tata and his son Dorabji. Tata Iron and Steel Company (TISCO) was set up in 1907.

Despite the inadequacy of domestic demand and high production costs, industries like woollen mills, breweries, and paper-making made some progress, but these industries were small in magnitude. Other such industries that operated were tanning, vegetable oil processing, leather goods manufacturing and glass making. However India's modern manufacturing industry could not develop on a sound footing before the World War-I. Shortage of capital, lack of management experience, absence of technical expertise, non-existence of a growing indigenous market, and, above all, general poverty, were the main reasons of slow expansion of Indian industries during this period. But at least the foundations of modern industries were laid.

However, during World War I, industries like cotton and jute progressed well. Steel industry also experienced substantial growth. Consumer goods industries like chemicals, cement, fertilizers, mineral acids, etc., for which India depended on foreign countries, also made some headway. But this progress was not long-lasting. There was tough foreign competition which demanded protection. Fiscal Commission was appointed in 1921 that brought in a policy of discriminating protection. This helped India's industry but could not bring economic development as such. In 1936, *The Economist* observed: "Although India has begun to modernize her industries, it can hardly be said that she is as yet being industrialized." The inter-war period saw an increase in the output of cotton goods, steel ingots, and paper. The number of factories in some other industries also increased.

During World War II, there was a faster development in India's basic and key industries. There was a near-cessation of imports due to war operations. As a result, industrial output of large scale industries increased and industrial diversification became possible. During 1938-39 and 1945-46, the general index of output of all large scale manufacturing activity (at 1938-39 prices) rose from 100 to 161.6 and that of factory employment increased from 100 to 159.[2]

During the pre-independence period, India did not have any capital goods industries worth the name. The import dependence of the Indian manufacturing sector was therefore huge. There was little technical skill and institutes offering technical education were very few.

Industrial Development in India after Independence

When India got its independence after a long period of subjugation, there was industrial backwardness. In order to make the economy, which was in shambles at that time, to stand on its feet, rapid industrialization was necessary. The result was that India made considerable progress in the industrial sector after achieving independence in 1947. During 1951-65 it had a steady growth rate of about 8 per cent. Although little was provided in the First Plan (1951-56) for industries, there was much by way of industrial development in the Second Plan and the Third Plan during 1956-61 and 1961-66, respectively. In addition to setting up several industries, the government took initiatives to provide resources and facilities for the private sector so as to enable them to start industries on their own or jointly with the government in the arena earmarked for the private sector. The other important factors that led to industrial development during this period were: firstly the existing entrepreneurial class invested considerably in establishing new set-ups as they realized better opportunities in the post-independence circumstances; secondly, restrictions on import, imposed by the government, helped remove the fear of foreign competition among the private entrepreneurs; thirdly, Indian industrial policy permitting, although conditionally, the entry of private foreign capital further helped in receiving foreign aid as loans on concessional terms. Such large funds in the form of foreign exchange enabled the country not only to overcome to some extent the balance of payments constraints on development, but also helped in purchasing equipments, machines and other inputs.

The period between 1965 and 1976, however, witnessed a slow growth in the industrial sector. In the 1960s, (1961-70) the average growth rate of industrial output was put at 5.5 per cent and in the seventies (1971-80) the average growth rate was about 4 per cent per annum. Thereafter, during 1980-85 the growth rate of industrial production was 5.5 per cent per annum. The above data reveal that the industrial sector showed a declining trend. Later, during the Seventh Plan (1985-90), the growth rate however picked up to an average of over 8 per cent per annum while in the Eighth Plan (1992-97) it again declined to 7.3 per cent per annum. In order to increase industrial production, the industrial policy was made more liberal and globalized and privatization was increased. The main objectives of the New Industrial Policy, 1991 were to increase industrial production, improve disequilibrium in balance of payments, get rid of the sick units of public or private sectors and control inflation by increasing production and regulating money supply, establish small, medium and large industries, abolish licensing system for all industries except 18, permit the use of foreign technology, and modify MRTP and FERA so that entrance asset limit could be abolished. The main focus of the New Industrial Policy, 1991 was to free the Indian industries from unnecessary and disadvantageous restrictions, to free growing entrepreneurial capacity, to provide proper control for market mechanism in resource allocation, get rid of costlier delays and inefficiency and uneconomical expenses, develop industrial structure based on technological dynamism and international competition, so that India could emerge as a main industrial power by the end of 20th century.

On account of industrial policy, structural changes in industrial production have taken place which is shown in Table 7.1.

Table 7.1: Index No. of the Structure of Industrial Production

(Base 1960=100)

Industry	1961	1965	1970	1975	1981-82	1987-88	1990-91	1991-92
1. Basic Industries	112.7	164.0	221.7	285.9	431.7	670.4	776.3	805.8 (614.9)
2. Capital Goods Industries	118.0	244.0	224.6	292.2	470.6	850.4	1112.9	1306.5 (1000.2)
3. Intermediate Goods Industries	105.8	140.2	158.8	180.5	235.5	336.8	391.7	415.4 (292.6)
4. Consumer Goods Industries	106.6	127.5	154.7	166.1	236.6	325.6	360.7	398.1 (273.4)

Source: Report on Currency and Finance, Vol. II, Various Issues.

Note: (i) Figures in brackets are calculated and show percentage figures.

(ii) Figures relating to 1975 onwards are converted with base 1960 = 100.

(iii) Figures up to 1975 are relating to Calendar year and figures after 1975 are relating to financial year. Hence, they are not comparable completely and do not show exact position.

Table 7.1 indicates that in 1961 consumer goods production index was 106.6, while that of intermediate goods was 105.8 which was lower than that of the former, but in 1991-92 this situation changed. Consumer goods production index became lower than that of intermediate goods, i.e. consumer goods production index in 1991-92 became 398.1, while that of intermediate goods was 415.4. Highest increase took place in the production of the capital goods. In this case, in 1991-92 as compared to 1961 production increased by 1007.2%. The second place was occupied by the increase in the production of basic goods industries. In 1991-92 its production increased by 614.9 per cent over 1961. During these periods the production of intermediate goods and consumer goods increased by 292.6 per cent and 273.4 per cent, respectively. Thus, it is obvious that due to industrial policy, the production of commodities has diversified and quantitative change have taken place. In addition, in industrial policy resolutions the development of basic industries and capital goods industries has always been given priority. Consequently, production has increased favourably in the same direction.

On account of industrialization of the economy, trade commodity composition has also changed. In India's imports, share of capital goods has increased. In 1960-61, the import of capital goods amounted to ₹ 356 crore which increased to ₹ 404 crore in 1970-71, ₹ 1,910 crore in 1980-81, ₹ 10,466 crore in 1990-91, ₹ 10,436 crore in 1991-92 and ₹ 13,123 crore in 1992-93. In India's exports, the share of manufactured goods has increased continuously. It was ₹ 291 crore in 1960-61 which increased to ₹ 772 crore in 1970-71, ₹ 3,747 crore in 1980-81, ₹ 23,736 crore in 1990-91, ₹ 32,693 crore in 1991-92 and ₹ 40,835 crore in 1992-93.

There was low annual growth rate of the economy of India before 1980, which stagnated around 3.5% from 1950s to 1980s, while per capita income averaged only 1.3%. Only four or five licences would be given for steel, electrical power and communications. A huge private sector emerged, while the state-owned enterprises made large losses. Licence raj established the "irresponsible, self-perpetuating bureaucracy that still exists throughout much of thc country".[3]

During 1980s the key strategy for developing the manufacturing sector in India was to develop large and heavy industries through central planning. It included import substitution, price controls and restrictions on private sector by means of licensing. There were controls on the foreign investment which limited the growth of the manufacturing sector. Rigid controls also led to underutilization of resources. Major industries during 1980s were consumer durables, export-oriented industries, modern technology-based industries, petroleum products, non-electric machinery, food and beverages, and intermediate goods. There was some loosening of controls towards the end of the decade due to which during the period from 1981-90 the manufacturing sector saw a total growth of 7.4 per cent. There was also increased public, private and foreign investment in the manufacturing sector.

Post-Liberalization Period

Liberalization of economic policies in India was initiated in 1991 with the aim of making the economy more market-oriented and expanding the role of private and foreign investment. There were specific changes like reduction in import tariffs, deregulation of markets, reduction of taxes, and greater foreign investment.

Liberalization has been credited by its proponents for the high economic growth recorded by the country in the 1990s and 2000s.

The key objective of the Industrial Policy Statement of 1991 was to maintain the growth of productivity, provide employment and optimally utilize the human resources. In 1991, 41% of FDI was allowed in certain selective industries. The FDI policy was revised up to 51 per cent. In as many as 35 high priority and technology-intensive industries, FDI was allowed through the automatic route. In 1997, 100% foreign investment was allowed in some industries, whereas investment ranging from 50% to 74% was allowed in 111 sectors of the economy. The process of reducing the protection for the small scale sector was also initiated by allowing foreign investment up to 24 per cent in the small scale sector. The limit on the share of foreign direct investment in individual Micro, Small and Medium Enterprises (MSMEs) was increased recently up to 100 per cent.

The major manufacturing industries post-1991 were automotive industry, computer hardware industry, textile industry, machine tools and parts industry, pharmaceuticals industry, light engineering industry, iron and steel, petroleum and refined product industry.

Liberalization also made it necessary to bring some structural changes in the manufacturing sector. Some measures in this regard were closures of old plants, sell-offs and relocation of factories. It also resulted in lay-offs due to adoption of technology which required less manpower.

However, it has enhanced production efficiency to face global competition and spurred innovation and product development. It also made people to acquire technical skills which has improved our human resources.

The Present Scenario

After liberalization, industry in India got a boost. There was increase in production of various types of goods. As per data given by NITI Aayog, the growth rate of GVA at basic prices was estimated to be 7.0 per cent, 7.8 per cent and 7.5 per cent during the first, second and third quarter of 2014-15 as against

7.2 per cent, 7.5 per cent and 6.6 per cent in the corresponding quarters of previous year, i.e. 2013-14. The GDP at market prices referred to as GDP (at constant 2011-12 prices) recorded a rise in growth rate from 5.1 per cent during 2012-13 to 6.9 per cent during 2013-14 and is expected to be at 7.4 per cent Advance Estimates (AE) in 2014-15.[4]

Table 7.2: Annual rate of growth of GVA by economic activity at constant (2011-12) basic prices in unit per cent.

No.	Item	2012-13*	2013-14#	2014-15@
1	Agriculture, forestry & fishing	1.2	3.7	1.1
2	Mining & quarrying	-0.2	5.4	2.3
3	Manufacturing	6.2	5.3	6.8
4	Electricity, gas & water supply & other utility services	4	4.8	9.6
5	Construction	-4.3	2.5	4.5
6	Trade, hotels, transport, communication and services related to broadcasting	9.6	11.1	8.4
7	Financial services, real estate, ownership of dwellings & professional services	8.8	7.9	13.7
8	Public administration & Defence & other services	4.7	7.	9
	Total GVA at Basic Prices	4.9	6.6	7.5
	Industry (2-5)	2.4	4.5	5.9
	Services (6-8)	8	9.1	10.6

Source: Central Statistics Office (CSO)

Note: *2nd Revised Estimates; #1st Revised Estimates; @ Advanced Estimates as on 09th February 2015.

Table 7.2 shows that manufacturing had 6.2 units per cent for the year 2012-13 and 5.3 units per cent and 6.8 units per cent during 2013-14 and 2014-15, respectively. Mining and quarrying which had a negative unit per cent at –0.2 during 2012-13 came in the positive territory at 5.4 unit per cent and 2.3 unit per cent during 2013-14 and 2014-15 respectively. Construction, which too was as –4.1 units per cent during 2012-13 showed positive units per cent of 2.5 and 4.5 during 2013-14 and 2014-15, respectively. Industry as a whole had a unit per cent of 2.4, 4.5 and 5.9 during 2012-13, 2013-14 and 2014-15 respectively.

There was a steady increase in growth rate of the industrial sector from 2.4 per cent in 2012-13 to 4.5 per cent in 2013-14 and was likely to grow at the rate of 5.9 per cent in 2014-15. But actually for the entire financial year 2014-15, industry grew by 5.6 per cent (CSO). This increase may be attributed to the rise in growth rates in 'electricity, gas & water supply & other utility services' and 'manufacturing' sector. The growth in the 'manufacturing' 'mining and quarrying', 'electricity, gas and water supply', and 'construction' was estimated to be 6.8 per cent, 2.3 per cent, 9.6 per cent and 4.5 per cent, respectively, during 2014-15 as compared to growth of 5.3 per cent, 5.4 per cent, 4.8 per cent and 2.5 per cent, respectively, in 2013-14.[5] The services sector grew by 9.2 per cent during 2014-15.

The Index of Industrial Production (IIP) which comprises mining, manufacturing and electricity showed 3.1 per cent growth during April-December 2015-16 as compared to 2.6 per cent during the same period of 2014-15 due to the higher growth in mining and manufacturing sectors. The mining, manufacturing and electricity sectors grew by 2.3 per cent, 3.1 per cent, and 4.5 per cent respectively during April-December 2015-16. The mining sector growth was mainly due to higher coal production. The manufacturing sector was propelled by the higher production by the industry groups like furniture; wearing apparel, dressing and dyeing of fur, motor vehicles, trailers & semitrailers; chemicals and chemical products; refined petroleum products & nuclear fuel.[6]

The growth in electricity was mainly due to higher growth in the generation of thermal and nuclear sector. In terms of use-based classification, consumer durable goods registered a remarkable growth at 12.4 per cent during April-December 2015-16. Basic goods and capital goods showed 3.4 per cent and 1.7 per cent growth with intermediate goods increasing by 1.9 per cent as shown in Table 7.3.

There was a cumulative growth of 1.9 per cent in eight core infrastructure supportive industries, viz. coal, crude oil, natural gas, refinery products, fertilizers, steel, cement and electricity that have a total weight of nearly 38 per cent, the IIP, during April-December 2015-16 as compared to 5.7 per cent during

April-December 2014-15. Month-wise performance of the eight core sectors shows that the production of coal and fertilizers has increased substantially, while that of crude oil, natural gas and steel has mostly been negative. Refinery products, cement and electricity have attained moderate growth. Crude oil and natural gas production declined because of a fall in production by Oil and Natural Gas Corporation (ONGC), Oil India Limited (OIL) and also private/joint venture (JV) companies. In electricity generation, while the thermal and nuclear sectors have registered higher growth, the hydro sector did not perform well.

While the overall IIP showed some recovery, there was variation in the performance of some of the major industries during April-December 2015. Some sectors like electricity, coal, fertilizers, cement and passenger cars showed positive growth, but sectors like steel and aluminium showed negative growth during April-December 2015.

Table 7.3: IIP-based Growth Rates of Broad Sectors/ Use-based Classification (in per cent)

	Weight	2013-14	2014-15	2014-15				2015-16			
				Q1	Q2	Q3	Apr.-Dec.	Q1	Q2	Q3	Apr.-Dec.
General	100.00	-0.1	2.8	4.5	1.3	2.0	2.6	3.3	4.8	1.5	3.1
Sectoral Mining	14.16	-0.6	1.5	3.0	0.5	2.1	1.8	0.4	3.1	3.3	2.3
Manufacturing	75.53	-0.8	2.3	3.9	0.4	1.1	1.8	3.7	4.7	0.9	3.1
Electricity	10.32	6.1	8.4	11.3	9.4	9.4	10.0	2.3	6.8	4.4	4.5
Use-Based Basic goods	45.68	2.1	7.0	8.7	7.0	8.3	8.0	4.7	4.4	1.3	3.4
Capital goods	8.83	-3.6	6.4	13.6	-0.5	3.2	5.1	2.0	13.4	-10.0	1.7
Intermediate goods	15.69	3.1	1.7	3.1	1.6	0.8	1.8	1.6	2.2	1.9	1.9
Consumer goods	29.81	-2.8	-3.4	-3.2	-5.4	-6.4	-4.9	2.5	2.7	6.8	4.0
Consumer durables	8.46	-12.2	-12.6	-9.5	-15.5	-20.9	-15.2	3.7	11.9	23.4	12.4
Consumer nondurables	21.35	4.8	2.8	1.4	2.3	3.2	2.3	1.7	-3.0	-1.6	-1.0

Source: CSO

Micro, Small and Medium Enterprises Sector

The Micro and Medium Enterprises (MSME) are classified into the following two categories:

(i) Manufacturing enterprises involved in the manufacture or production of goods relating to any industry specified in schedule of Industries (Development and Regulation) Act, 1951, or employing plant and machinery in the process of value addition to final product having a discrete name or character or use and defined in terms of investment in plant & machinery:

Micro Enterprise: does not exceed ₹ 25 lakh,

Small Enterprise: more than ₹ 25 lakh but less than ₹ 5 crore,

Medium Enterprise: more than ₹ 5 crore but less than ₹ 10 crore.

(ii) Service sector engaged in providing or rendering services and defined in terms of investment in equipment:

Micro enterprise: does not exceed 10 lakh rupees,

Small enterprise: more than 10 lakh but less than 2 crore rupees,

Medium enterprise: more than 2 crore but less than 5 crore rupees.

MSMEs play an important role of providing employment and industrialization of rural and backward areas, and thus reduce regional disparity. As supplementary units, MSMEs are harmonizing to large industries and contributing to socio-economic development. There are over 36 million units under MSMEs which are providing employment to over 80 million persons with 8% contribution to GDP. As per MSME Report 2014-15, the main industries in MSME sector are the following:

Retail trade (excluding vehicles and motor spare parts) and repairs of personal and household goods (39.85%),

Manufacturing of wearing apparels (8.75%),

Manufacturers of foods and beverages (6.94%),

Other services activities (6.21%),

Other business activities (3.77%),

Hotels and restaurants (3.64%),

Sales maintenance of motor vehicles and cycles (3.57%),

Furniture manufacturing (3.21%),

Textile (2.33%),

Fabricated metals except machinery and equipment (2.33%), and

Misc (19.4%).

According to MSME Report 2014, three sub sectors that show promising picture are: food processing (high potential because of agro linkage), textiles-innovation, and electronics-linkage with ITES.

Table 7.4: Performance of MSME, Employment and Investments

Sl. No.	Year	Total working enterprise (in lakh)	Employment (in lakh)	Market value of fixed Asset (₹ in crore)
1	2006-07	361.71	805.23	868,543.79
2	2007-08	377.36	842.00	920,459.84
3	2008-09	393.70	880.84	977,114.72
4	2009-10	410.80	921.79	1,038,546.08
5	2010-11	428.73	965.15	1,105,934.09
6	2011-12	447.64	1011.69	1,182,757.64
7	2012-13	447.54	1061.40	1,268,763.67
8	2013-14	488.46	1114.29	1,363,700.54

Source: Annual Report 2014-15, GOI, Ministry of MSME

Table 7.4 shows that the total number of working MSME enterprises in India has been increasing steadily and has risen by more than 20 per cent from 361.71 lakh in 2006-07 to 488.46 lakh in 2013-14. The number of employees too has increased by 309.06 in 2013-14 lakh from the 2006-07 level. The market value of assets in MSMEs has nearly doubled during the said period.

In order to know how and to what extent the MSMEs are contributing to the growth of the economy, we must calculate the contribution of the manufacturing output in India's GDP. Table 7.5 shows the percentage share of MSMEs in GDP in both the manufacturing sector and services sector, as well as the combined percentage of these two sectors. It can be seen that the share of manufacturing sector in our GDP has been declining steadily from 7.73 per cent in 2006-07 to 7.04 per cent in 2012-13. The growth value of output in manufacturing has been increasing to reach ₹ 1,809,976 crore in 2012-13 from ₹ 1,198,818 crore in 2006-07. This means that the percentage decline of the share of manufacturing sector in India's GDP is due to the fact that the total size of the GDP is increasing every year and the manufacturing is not rising at a rate high enough to register a higher percentage than before.

Table 7.5: Contribution of manufacturing output of MSME in GDP

Sl. No.	Year	Gross Value of Output of MSME Manufacturing Sector (in crore)	Share of MSME sector in total GDP (%)			Share of MSME Manufacturing output in total Manufacturing Output (%)
			Manufacturing Sector MSME	Services Sector MSME	Total	
1	2006-07	1198818	7.73	27.40	35.13	42.02
2	2007-08	1322777	7.81	27.60	35.41	41.98
3	2008-09	1375589	7.52	28.60	36.12	40.79
4	2009-10	1488352	7.45	28.60	36.05	39.63
5	2010-11	1653622	7.39	29.30	36.69	38.5
6	2011-12	1788584	7.27	30.70	37.97	37.47
7	2012-13	1809976	7.04	30.50	37.54	37.33

Source: Annual Report 2014-15, GOI, Ministry of MSME

As of 2015-16 the MSME sector has 3.6 crore units spread across the country, employing 8.05 crore people, and a contribution of 37.5 per cent to the country's GDP.

MSMEs in India are facing many problems, the major being absence of timely credit, lack of infrastructure inputs, limited capital skill, low managerial capability, low margins of profit and hence low return on investment (ROI), low productivity of our labour, inefficient marketing strategies, non-identification of new markets for goods produced by MSMEs, lack of innovation, lack of warehousing, and high competition, among others.

The sector has huge potential for helping address structural problems like unemployment, regional imbalances, unequal distribution of national income and wealth across the country. Owing to comparatively low capital costs and their forward-backward linkages with other sectors, MSMEs will play a crucial role in the success of the Make in India initiative.

Realizing the importance of the MSME sector, the government has undertaken a number of schemes/programmes like the Prime

Minister's Employment Generation Programme (PMEGP), Credit Guarantee Trust Fund for Micro and Small Enterprises (CGTMSE), Credit Linked Capital Subsidy Scheme (CLCSS) for Technology Upgradation, Scheme of Fund for Regeneration of Traditional Industries (SFURTI), and Micro and Small Enterprises Cluster Development Programme (MSECDP) for the establishment of new enterprises and development of existing ones. The government has taken some initiatives (See Appendix I) to address some core problems afflicting MSMEs, and better performance can be expected in future years.

PUBLIC SECOR AND PRIVATE SECTOR: THEIR ROLE AND INDUSTRY-WISE CONTRIBUTION

Public Sector

Since independence there has been progressive expansion in the scope of the public sector, owing to the adequate economic planning in India. The passage of Industrial Policy Resolution of 1956 and the adoption of socialist pattern of society as our national goal further added to the deliberate enlargement of the role of public sector.

The significant role of the Public Sector in the Indian economy cannot be overemphasized. In order to assess its role it would be desirable to use a few indicators, like employment, investment, value of output, national income generated, savings, capital formation and the capital stock.

Central Public Sector Enterprises (CPSEs) also called Public Sector Undertakings (PSUs) are those companies in which the direct holding of the Central Government or other CPSEs is 51% or more. They have played a significant role in India's growth process. As of 31st December 2015, out of 298 CPSEs under the administrative control of various ministries/departments, 235 were in operation and 63 under construction. Financial investment (paid-up capital + long-term loans) in all the CPSEs taken together stood at ₹ 10,96,057 crore as on 31 March 2015, showing an increase of 10.48 per cent over 2013-14. The net profit of profit making (157) CPSEs stood at ₹ 1,30,363 crore in 2014-15, while net loss of loss-making (77) CPSEs stood at

₹ 27,360 crore. ONGC Ltd., Coal India Ltd., NTPC Ltd., the National Mineral Development Corporation (NMDC) Ltd., and Power Finance Corporation Ltd. were the top five profit-making CPSEs during 2014-15, whereas Bharat Sanchar Nigam Ltd., Air India Ltd., Mahanagar Telephone Nigam Ltd., Hindustan Photo Films Manufacturing Company Ltd. and Mangalore Refinery and Petrochemicals Ltd. were the top five loss-making CPSEs. The government decided to sell off loss-making Air India, which has a debt burden of ₹ 50,00 crore.

CPSEs make a substantial contribution to the central exchequer by way of dividend payment, interest on government loans and payment of taxes and duties. Their gross internal source generation was ₹ 1,11,000 crore in 2008-09. Their contribution to the central exchequer was ₹ 2,20,981 crore in 2013-14, which declined to 2,00,584 crore in 2014-15. This was mainly on account of a decrease in their contribution to dividend, corporate tax and custom duty during that year. There was, however, an increase in their contribution to excise duty, dividend tax, sales tax and service tax.

Contribution of Public Sector to Export

CPSEs are an important contributor to the nation's foreign earnings as CPSE exports account for about 10 per cent of total merchandise export of the country. They are moving ahead to avail newer opportunities in the foreign capital market and has witnessed a steady increase in the mobilization of funds from the foreign market. Many CPSEs are undertaking joint venture abroad that has further improved the foreign exchange earning of the country.

The export performance of the public sector enterprises has been quite appreciable. Among the items exported from India, metal ores are in the second position. Even in the export of Indian handicrafts, light engineering goods, etc. the public sector has made huge strides. The State Trading Corporation (STC), Minerals and Metals Trading Corporation (MMTC), Hindustan Steel Ltd., Bharat Electronics Ltd., etc. have been promoting exports.

CPSEs mobilize savings through large network of banking and financial institutions. The profits of CPSEs are ploughed back into developmental activities of the country. Further, CPSEs contribute to the Government's exchequer through payment of tax and dividends.

The manufacturing sector constitutes the largest component of investment in CPSEs (45%) followed by services (35%), energy (12%), and mining (8%). Foreign investments are allowed in the CPSEs in all sectors. CPSEs face the same tax burden as the private sector, but avoid many hassles in procuring land and other regulatory issues, compared to private sector enterprises.[7]

There are two important categories of public sector employment. Firstly, government administration, defence and other services like health, education, research etc. and secondly, the economic enterprises owned by the Centre, State and Local Governments. There has been tremendous growth in providing direct employment by the public sector since independence.

Employment Generation

Public sector in India has generated millions of jobs. As per 2011 census, 150 lakh people were employed in the public sector. Overall, industry in India employs 22 per cent of the total work force. In the recent years, the biggest chunk of employment was in transport, storage and communications while manufacturing remained close to these sectors.

Those employed in agriculture and other allied activities reflect employment under Employment Guarantee Scheme rather than any usual productive activity. Overall, the public sector accounts for around 70 per cent of the total employment in the organized sector. Thus, the public sector has helped in the reduction of unemployment in the country. Besides direct jobs, this sector creates work for a large number of people like traders in goods, contractors, suppliers of raw material and providers of services and sellers of goods produced by CPSEs. This is important for a country like India where the population is large and there is need to create more jobs and work opportunities for a large number of people.

Share of Public Sector in Gross Domestic Product

There has been a steady advancement in the share in the public sector in net domestic product in the recent years, more particularly during the ongoing Tenth Plan period. Measured at current prices, public sector accounted for 7.5 per cent of NDP in 1950-51, which later in 1999-2000 rose to 24.0 per cent. In 2002-03 it declined to 23.6 per cent but again during 2004-05 it accounted for about one-fourth of national output. As of now it is around 20 per cent.

Share of Public Sector in Gross Fixed Capital Formation

Gross capital formation refers to annual flow of goods partly to meet the needs of depreciation of the capital stock and partly to increase the size of the total capital stock on a net basis. The amount of capital employed per unit of output in the public sector is far greater than in the private sector. It has made a significant contribution in improving gross fixed capital formation (GFCF), more particularly in the capital goods sector. During 2000-01 the growth rate of GFCF in the public sector was 1.3 per cent at 1999-2000 prices increasing to 3.9, 2.2, 13.7 and 8.6 respectively in the next four years consecutively. During 2010-11, capital formation by India's CPSEs was 24.6 per cent of total investment.

Balanced Regional Development

India is a vast country. Developing all areas equally or nearly equally is one of the aims of the government. However, regional disparities have continued to exist due to various reasons. Many CPSEs have contributed in removing regional imbalances to some extent. Many CPSEs have located their units in the backward areas of the country, which lacked basic industrial and civic facilities like electricity, water supply, skilled manpower, townships, transportation, warehousing. CPSEs have developed these facilities in such areas. This has led to a complete transformation in the socio-economic landscape of such areas. Steel plants at Durgapur, Bhillai and Rourkela, fertilizer plants at Sindri, etc. are a few examples.

Research and Development

The CPSEs are engaged in using high technology and heavy industries. Over a period of time they have built a strong base for self-reliance in technical skills, maintenance of operational sophistication and efficient use of new technology. For this they have to incur expenditure on research and development. This promotes research in the country, improves the quality of goods and services being produced and reduces cost. This also enhances our competitiveness in international market.

Import Substitution

Some CPSEs have started producing goods which were earlier imported from other countries. For example, Indian Drugs & Pharmaceuticals Ltd., Bharat Electronics Ltd., Bharat Heavy Electricals Ltd. and Hindustan Aeronautics Ltd. and Engineering Projects (India) Ltd. have produced goods which wc imported for local consumption. Public sector has thus saved valuable foreign exchange.

The public sector has undoubtedly entered into a wide spectrum of industries and products and its operations extending from basic and capital goods like steel, coal, copper, zinc and other minerals, heavy machinery, etc. to consumer goods like textiles, hotel services, etc. In areas like minerals, coal, petroleum products, hydro and steam turbines, its share is 100 per cent, while in other products it ranges between 50 to 95 per cent. It significantly mobilizes funds to cater the financial needs of the growing economy.

The expansion of the public sector was done with the objectives of removal of poverty, attainment of self-reliance, reduction in inequalities of income, expansion of employment opportunities, removal of regional imbalances, acceleration of the pace of agricultural and industrial development, reduction in concentration of ownership and prevention of growth of monopolistic tendencies by being an effective countervailing power to the private sector and making the country self-reliant in modern technology as well as finance. No doubt, the public sector has fulfilled its objectives to some extent but it is equally true that all the public enterprises are not functioning up to the mark. Factors affecting its performance need to be removed.

Problems Facing CPSEs in India

Although CPSEs have made very important contribution in many areas as shown above, its performance has not been on the expected levels. This is because there are many problems facing CPSEs in our country. Some major ones are given below:

(i) There has been faulty pricing. In the pre-reform period, the prices of goods and services produced by the CPSE in India were determined by the Government under administered price regimes (APR). This led to low profits and even losses in some CPSEs. In post-91 era, there was an increase in market competition which made the Government to dismantle the APR. In most cases and PSEs were given independence to fix their own price competitively. But by and large the Government continues to remain sensitive to the needs of the poor and thus does not let price level to rise. Any rise in price that tends to occur by market conditions is not allowed. For example, the prices of petroleum are not allowed to go high if there is a rise in the international price of crude oil. The social approach set prices in PSE bring lower returns and financial losses. The under recoveries by the oil marketing companies bear testimony.

(ii) There is too much political interference in the operational aspects of CPSEs. The appointments in the management, pricing of products, location of projects—all suffer from political influence. The decisions are guided by political considerations rather than economic factors, which ultimately harms the CPSEs.

(iii) The performance of public sector is also affected by faulty controls exercised over them. The Ministry of Finance exercises excessive financial control over the operations of public enterprises in India which are obligatory to submit to all the budgetary controls applicable to Government departments. The control over the operations and capital development plans of public enterprises by the Parliament often become rigid, thereby hampering the performance of the public sector. There is thus need to provide greater autonomy to this sector.

(iv) There has been lack of decision-making whereby CPSEs have often been unable to take advantage of opportunities that arise in the market. Dilly-dallying in adopting new technology, striking a deal, making innovations as per new conditions have been the reasons of low performance of many CPSEs.

(v) The public sector enterprises are overstaffed. This increases the cost of production and inefficiency in the organization.

(vi) There is little incentive for better performance. There are no penalties for delays, failures, lapses, etc. Job security has made the workers lethargic and inefficient. It has also been observed that the labour indiscipline has adversely influenced the performance of public sector enterprises recently. Besides, in many enterprises there has been surplus manpower and inadequate arrangement for training and education of workers as well as poor management-labour relation. More importantly, the unsatisfactory remuneration and incentives have compelled the efficient staff to switch over to private sector. The situation is grim and needs to be handled cautiously.

(vii) Most of the time, the CPSEs operate at less than their full capacity due to various reasons, like lack of raw material, erratic power supply, technical snags, like breakdown of a machine, etc. This results in lower than potential output, which in turn increases the cost of production as the fixed cost is distributed over small output.

As per the latest available data, 87 manufacturing units utilized 75 per cent of its total capacity, 32 units utilized 50 to 75 per cent and 47 functioned below 50 per cent utilization capacity. Thus, adequate measures must be taken to remove this deficiency.

The scenario however is changing rapidly with the adoption of new technology, improvement in the skill of workers in general, appointment of management experts at senior level positions.

Private Sector

Private sector is the part of the economy, and is sometimes referred to as the citizen sector, which is run by private individuals or groups, usually as a means of enterprise for profit, and is not controlled by the state (areas of the economy controlled by the state being referred to as the public sector).

Objectives of private sector enterprise are to (i) reduce political interference in the management of enterprise, leading to improved efficiency & productivity, (ii) provide adequate competition to the public sector, (ii) generate cash in order to fund the ever-increasing expenses, and (iii) reduce the concentration of economic power in the country. The government resorts to privatization with the multiple objectives which are as follows:

(i) Improve efficiency because the profit incentive makes the entrepreneurs work hard, achieve targets and expand business.

(ii) Make the business run on sound economic and business principles rather than other considerations. For example, private players are not reluctant in downsizing staff if it is redundant, rather than continue with it and bear costs.

(iii) Bring more investment in infrastructure. The public sector is often unwilling to invest in infrastructure improvements which will benefit the firm in the long-term because they are more concerned about projects that give a benefit before an election. The management in private sector has neither hesitation, nor such consideration. When the profits increase due to efficiency, there is more scope for investing in infrastructure.

(iv) Along with privatization of state owned monopolies there is also deregulation, which allows more firms to enter the industry and increase competitiveness of the market. This brings more efficiency and improvement in quality of the products being created. Increase in competition in the telecom sector, for instance has made the companies bring better products and offer better services.

The Scope and Growth of Private Sector in India

Private sector in India has been given sufficient scope to produce intermediate goods and machines since independence. Consequently, a wide range of industries producing chemicals, paints, plastics, machine-tools, ferrous and non-ferrous metals, rubber, etc. have come up, resulting in self-sufficiency in many consumer goods. Private sector plays a significant role in all important fields, namely agriculture, trade and industry.

Private sector is much more dominant in trading—both retail and wholesale. In the Industrial Policy Resolutions of 1948 and 1956, the Government allotted a specific role to private sector in the field of industries which enabled private sector to become more preponderant than public sector. While public sector was assigned a major role in the planned development of the country with industrial growth in the lead, private sector too was assigned a definite place in the mixed economy that became the basis of its functioning. An aspect of the growth of the private sector is the large increase in the presence of the foreign private companies with a sizeable segment of industries under their ownership and control. The entry of foreign companies or firms has taken rapid strides. It is either in the form of multinational companies or the Indian subsidiaries of foreign companies. Yet another form is that of collaborations between Indians and the foreigners. Advanced countries like the USA, the UK, Germany, Japan, Italy, etc. have come here and invested huge amount in varied areas like engineering, electronics, chemicals, computers, pharmaceuticals etc. The amount of foreign direct investment has indeed been large, more particularly in the recent years.

India has become one of the favourite spots for foreign investors. Indian Government is playing a proactive role in investment promotion through a liberal FDI policy. Due to a favourable policy regime and sound business environment there has been an increase in FDI flows into the country. With a view to liberalizing and simplifying the FDI policy to provide ease of doing business climate in the country that will also lead to larger FDI inflows, the Government has brought some reforms. Many sectors have been liberalized, including defence, construction, civil aviation, broadcasting, trading, private sector banking, plantation and credit information companies. During 2015-16, FDI policy in the pension sector has been revised to permit foreign investment up to 49 per cent, with 26 per cent under automatic route. Manufacturing of medical devices and white label ATM operations have been opened up to 100 per cent FDI under automatic route. Various reforms in the FDI sector have led to a significant increase in FDI inflows into India. During April-November 2015, total FDI inflows were US$ 34.8 billion as compared to US$ 27.7 billion during April-November 2014, showing a 26 per cent surge. FDI equity inflows also increased from US$ 18.9 billion during April-November 2014 to US$ 24.8 billion during April-November 2015, showing 31 per cent growth. There were FDI inflows into sectors like computer software and hardware, services, trading, automobile industry, construction (infrastructure) activities, chemicals (other than fertilizers) and telecommunications. FDI statistics of the last fifteen years reveal that the services sector has accounted for the highest inflows (17.6 per cent of total FDI inflows into India), followed by construction development (8.8 per cent), computer hardware and software (7.2 per cent), telecommunications (6.6 per cent) and the automobile industry (5.2 per cent).[8]

Table 7.6 shows that FDI inflows have increased in various segments of industry like services, computer software and hardware, trading, infrastructure activities, chemicals, hotels and tourism, etc. in 2015 over their levels in 2014. During the period April 2015-November 2016 (8 months) the total FDI inflows were US$ 5310.51 while the FDI inflows for the entire financial year 2014-15 were US$ 8131.51.

Table 7.6: Sector-wise FDI Inflows during April 2014 to November 2015

Sl.No.	Sector	Amount of FDI (in US$ million)		
		2014-15	2015-16	Percentage of total FDI
		Apr.-Mar.	Apr.-Nov.	Apr.-Nov. 2015-16
1	Services Sector (financial, non-financial and others)	4443.26	4102.47	16.5
2	Computer Software & Hardware	2296.04	4419.84	17.8
3	Trading	2727.96	2604.40	10.5
4	Automobile Industry	2725.64	1657.82	6.7
5	Telecommunications	2894.94	1062.91	4.3
6	Construction (Infrastructure) Activities	870.25	1368.96	5.5
7	Chemicals (Other than Fertilizers)	762.76	1157.37	4.7
8	Drugs & Pharmaceuticals	1497.74	321.37	1.3
9	Hotel & Tourism	777.01	865.25	3.5
10	Power	707.04	635.13	2.6
11	Mining	684.39	518.84	2.1
12	Petroleum & Natural Gas	1079.02	48.69	0.2
13	Non-Conventional Energy	615.95	440.64	1.8
14	Industrial Machinery	716.79	293.56	1.2
15	Others, excluding above-mentioned sectors	8131.71	5310.51	21.4

Source: DIPP

The growth of the private sector in India is marked by rapid increase in the diversification of the industrial products. Initially, the consumer goods industries were mainly earmarked for the private sector which, however, included a wide range from traditional goods like textiles to the modern products like motor cars, TV, fridge, etc. But, with the passage of time other types of industries also began to be included in the private sector. These industries include chemicals, engineering, cement, rubber and paper products, printing and publishing, etc. In other words, those industries which were earlier reserved for the public sector have been thrown open to the private sector except for a few like those of aircraft manufacture, heavy plant and machinery, etc.

In addition to its contribution to the industrial development in terms of output and diversification of products, private sector has some other plus points to its credit in its operations. This is apparently clear from the working of the public as well as private limited companies in the private corporate sector. It has exhibited fairly reasonable returns on sales, net assets, and its net worth. The profitability ratios like those of gross profits as percentage of sales, gross profits as percentage of total net assets, and profits after tax as percentage of net worth have been in the range of over 9-10 per cent for a number of years. These profitability ratios also compare well with those of the Indian branches of the MNCs and the Indian subsidiaries of the foreign companies.

The importance of the private sector in the Indian economy can be best assessed in terms of its contribution to national income and employment. As per the latest data available, the public sector contributes around 25 per cent of the net domestic product while the private sector contributes 75 per cent of net domestic product.

So far as its contribution to national employment is concerned, it provided employment to 84.21 lakh persons in 2002-03, which is considerably ahead than 73.95 lakh in 1981. The latest position of employment in the organized sector is given in Table 7.7.

Table 7.7: Employment in the Organized Sector (as on 31 March)
Sector Employment (in lakh)

Percentage change	2010	2011	2012	2011/2010	2012/2011
Public	178.62	175.48	176.09	(--)	1.8/0.4
Private	108.46	114.52	119.70	5.6	4.5
Total	287.08	289.99	295.79	1.0	2.0
Women	58.59	59.54	60.54	1.6	1.7

Source: Directorate General of Employment, Ministry of Labour and Employment.

Table 7.7 shows that employment growth in the organized sector, public and private combined, increased by 2.0 per cent in 2012 over 2011, as against a growth of 1.0 per cent in 2011 over 2010. The annual growth rate for the private sector was 4.5 per cent in 2012 as against a growth of 5.6 per cent in 2011.

The public sector registered a marginal growth of 0.4 per cent in 2012 against a decline of 1.8 per cent in 2011.

Cottage and Small Industries

Cottage industry is run in the home, usually with the help of family members. Simple implements are used and workers are not paid wages. In the small scale industry the male members of the family along with hired labour work together. Any firm employing less than 10 person are classified as small. Carpet making, utensils making, poultry farming, beekeeping, tailoring and furniture making are included in the cottage and small industry. In India there is a shortage of capital and technical skill. It is not possible to establish the heavy industries, but very easy to increase the number of small-scale industries. There are many advantages of cottage and small industries, such as the following:

(i) There is a shortage of manufactured goods in many areas in our country. Small scale industries considerably make up this shortage by producing goods for local consumption.

(ii) Due to increasing population in India, there is high rate of unemployment. Small scale industry which is labour-intensive mitigates the problem of unemployment to a large extent, especially in the semi-urban and rural areas where artisans also work and subsist.

(iii) Some of the goods produced in small scale industries like carpets and sports goods, utensils, etc. are sold in the international market. We earn a lot of foreign exchange by exporting these goods.

(iv) The waste of many bigger industries is a cause of pollution, and its disposal has been a major problem in India. The waste of large scale industries like cotton and steel can be used by the small scale industry. In this way we can save a lot of capital.

(v) Cottage industry in our country has engaged a large number of women. Thus, valuable human source is utilized for producing various types of goods. This also improves gender equality as women are able to earn some money by selling goods made by them.

(vi) Increase in the production of goods on small scale increases the income of the people. This removes inequalities and improves the standard of living of people.

(vii) The small scale industry is labour intensive, and labour is cheap in our country. Therefore the production of this industry is cheaper. Due to low prices people purchase more goods and there is market expansion.

(viii) Small scale industries do not require much capital. We can establish these industries with small capital. In India most of the people are poor, so they can start producing some type of goods with small capital.

(ix) One of the major causes of migration of people from poor, rural and backward areas in our country is that there is no work to earn a living. Small and cottage industries can check this migration if we expand these industries in such areas.

Small and cottage industries which form a part of private sector have an important role to play in industrial development. As these industries are labour intensive, they provide ample opportunities of employment. In addition, they ensure a rather more equitable distribution of income and wealth and assist in the effective mobilization of human and physical capital. In order to promote these industries the Government has adopted several measures like reservation of certain items for exclusive production in this sector, freedom licensing procedures, preference to small entrepreneurs, etc. It would not be an exaggeration to say that small and cottage industries would continue to remain and develop in the private sector.

Micro, Small and Medium Enterprises

Micro, Small and Medium Enterprises Development (MSMED) Act, 2006 defines the Micro, Small and Medium Enterprises (MSMEs) based on (i) the investment in plant and machinery for those engaged in manufacturing or production, processing or preservation of goods and (ii) the investment in equipment for enterprises engaged in providing or rendering of services.

The investment in plant and machinery is the original cost excluding land and building and other items specified by the Ministry of Small Scale Industries. The guidelines with regard to investment in plant and machinery or equipment as defined in the MSMED Act, 2006 are given below:

Nature of activity of the Enterprise	Investment in plant and machinery excluding land and building for enterprises engaged in manufacturing or production, processing or preservation of goods	Investment in equipment excluding land and building for enterprises engaged in providing or rendering of services (loans up to ₹ 1 crore)
Micro	Not exceeding ₹ 25.00 lakh	Not exceeding ₹ 10.00 lakh
Small	More than ₹ 25.00 lakh but does not exceed ₹ 500.00 lakh	More than ₹ 10.00 lakh but does not exceed ₹ 200.00 lakh
Medium	More than ₹ 500.00 lakh but does not exceed ₹ 1000.00 lakh	More than ₹ 200.00 lakh but does not exceed ₹ 500.00 lakh

The illustrative lists of enterprises that are engaged in providing or rendering services are:

Small road and water transport operators (original investment in vehicles up to ₹ 200.00 lakh under Priority Sector).

Retail trade (with credit limits not exceeding ₹ 20.00 lakh). Small business (whose original cost price of the equipment used for the purpose of business does not exceed ₹ 20.00 lakh). Professional and self-employed persons (whose borrowing limits do not exceed ₹ 10.00 lakh, of which not more than ₹ 2.00 lakh should be for working capital requirements, except in case of professionally qualified medical practitioners setting up of practice in semi-urban and rural areas, the borrowing limits should not exceed ₹ 15.00 lakh with a sub-ceiling of ₹ 3 lakh for working capital requirements).[9]

MSMEs have 3.6 crore units across the country, employing 8.05 crore people. In 2016, the sector had a contribution of 37.5 per cent to the country's GDP. The sector is very important as it has the potential for helping address structural problems like unemployment, regional imbalances, unequal distribution of national income and wealth in the country.

Since MSMEs have low capital costs and have established forward-backward linkages with other sectors, they can play an important role in the success of the Make in India initiative.

Realizing the importance of the MSME sector, the government has launched some programmes like the Prime Minister's Employment Generation Programme (PMEGP), Credit Guarantee Trust Fund for Micro and Small Enterprises (CGTMSE), Credit Linked Capital Subsidy Scheme (CLCSS) for Technology Upgradation, Scheme of Fund for Regeneration of Traditional Industries (SFURTI), and Micro and Small Enterprises Cluster Development Programme (MSECDP) for the establishment of new enterprises and development of existing ones. Some of the new initiatives brought by the government for the promotion and development of MSMEs, are mentioned below:

(i) Udyog Aadhar Memorandum (UAM): It was notified in September 2015 under section 8 of the MSME Development Act 2006, and is a significant step to promote 'ease of doing business' for MSMEs. Under this scheme, MSME entrepreneurs just need to file an online entrepreneurs' memorandum to get a unique Udyog Aadhar Number (UAN). The information sought is on self-certification basis and no supporting documents are required. This is a significant improvement over the complex and cumbersome procedure that was in place earlier.

(ii) Employment Exchange for Industries: It was launched in June 2015 in line with Digital India to facilitate employment to job seekers like an employment exchange for industries. As on 31st December 2015, more than 3.42 lakh job seekers have been registered on the portal.

(iii) Framework for Revival and Rehabilitation of MSMEs: This framework was notified in May 2015. In it, banks have to constitute a Committee for Distressed MSME enterprises at zonal or district level to prepare a Corrective Action Plan (CAP) for these units.

(iv) Scheme for Promoting Innovation and Rural Entrepreneurs (ASPIRE): It was launched in March

2015 and has the objective of setting up a network of technology centres and incubation centres to boost entrepreneurship and promote start-ups for innovation and entrepreneurship in rural and agriculture-based industry. Through this scheme, the government also intends to provide more credit to MSME sectors, particularly in rural areas, focusing on skill development, encouraging entrepreneurial activities with optimistic mindset among rural youth and creating job opportunities among rural women, for high, inclusive and sustained industrial growth.

Shortcomings in Private Sector

Despite the fact that private sector contributes significantly to the growth of Indian economy, there are some weaknesses in its functioning and there are some problems that it faces.

(i) *Inadequate Working*: First and foremost, most private enterprises, in their lust for profit, adopt undesirable practices which are against the consumers on one side and adversely affect the growth of medium and small-scale industrial units on the other. Besides, such practices often result in the generation of black money and corrupt business dealings.

Many of the leading business and industrial houses have become monopolistic and got concentration of wealth and economic power in their hands. The sector has also become too much dependent on the government for meeting its import requirements, output sale finances, etc. Private enterprises have been subject to frequent industrial disputes and industrial sickness.

(ii) *High Cost Economy*: Another serious drawback of the private sector is that its costs in general are large and the prices of products unduly high, mainly because of high costs of raw materials, components and the indirect taxes. For instance, in the case of imports, an importer has to pay basic duty, additional duty, and finally excise duty, apart from central sales tax on the final ex-factory gate cost and turnover tax.

(iii) *Promotion of Non-priority Industries*: The private corporate sector is charged for expansion of consumer goods industries having low priority such as cosmetics, air conditioners, perfumes, etc., which are mainly consumed by the elite class.

(iv) *Widespread Sickness*: Many sick and weak units constitute the private sector. The growing industrial sickness is evident in many lines of industrial and business activities, notably in textiles, engineering, chemicals, iron and steel, and paper. Factors responsible for industrial sickness are, inefficient and corrupt management, market fluctuations and inadequate marketing strategy, poor labour relations, and improper government policies.

(v) *Monopoly and Concentration of Power*: Some private enterprises have gained monopolistic power after the introduction of economic reforms in 1991. The dominance of some enterprises in terms of capital and assets is an economic and social problem because such enterprises operate on the principle of maximization of the monopoly profits rather than being production oriented. They have been found using the licensing system to prevent rivals from entering the sectors in which they were interested. This implies restriction of production, charging higher prices, and making monopoly profits.

(vi) *Industrial Disputes*: Smooth progress of the private sector is hampered by the recurring industrial disputes. Since independence, the nation has witnessed several strikes and lockouts that resulted in loss of valuable working days. Industrial disputes have risen mainly due to difference in the interests of capitalist owners and those of the workers. While the private capitalists aim at achieving maximum profits, the workers aim at securing higher wages and incentives. There is ample evidence that industrial relations in the private sector are much disappointing than those in the public sector. The losses caused by lockouts have a strong bearing on the developing economy as it requires optimum capacity utilization, more production, more employment, and more income.

In India the expansion of the private sector is being done with a view to giving a market-orientation to the economy. Since the Sixth Plan (1980-85) the private sector received due importance and showed sufficient expansion and a faster rate of growth. The private sector raised increasing amount of funds in the capital market and set up a series of joint ventures in foreign countries during this plan period.

Several first generation entrepreneurs ventured into business after the liberalization of India's economy in 1991. They collected capital from parents and relatives and borrowed from banks to start some venture and were able to establish themselves as entrepreneurs. Post-2008, some were trapped in the recession and a few others fell victim to regulatory activism. Due to ongoing business losses, their bank accounts turned into NPAs. Most of these enterprises can be revived if they get liquidity support from banks. But the prevailing NPA norms and credit policies don't permit the same.

In November 2016, when several small business, farmers and home loan borrowers found it difficult to service debt following cash crunch due to the withdrawal of ₹ 500 and ₹ 1000 denomination currency notes, the Reserve Bank of India (RBI) relaxed asset classification norms for banks, which allowed borrowers more time to repay. Now the government is bringing some banking reforms to deal with the NPAs of banks. The merger of some banks will be a part of such reforms. The responsibility of infrastructure and human development lies with the government. But private sector in India is also contributing in this regard to a large extent. Twelfth Plan (2012-17) envisaged that about 50 per cent investment in such development plan will be from private sector.[10]

MAJOR PRIVATE SECTOR INDUSTRIES

Engineering Sector

The Engineering Sector is a vast and diverse sector comprising a variety of industries, ranging from low-tech items such as castings, forgings, fasteners, to highly sophisticated microprocessors-based processed control equipment and diagnostic medical instruments. Industries like bearings, steel tyres and tubes also come under this sector. The products of this sector are largely used as inputs to the capital goods industry. The main features of a few of such industries are mentioned below.

Cement Industry

Cement makes an integral part of infrastructure industry. It is one of the most advanced industries in the country. India is the second largest producer of cement in the world. Since the decontrol of price and distribution of cement and introduction of other policy reforms, this industry has made sizeable progress in terms of capacity, production and technology. Cement production increased at a compound annual growth rate (CAGR) of 9.7 per cent in the period 2006 and 2013, producing 272 MT of cement. By 2020, the production capacity is projected to reach 550 MT. According to a report by the Department of Industrial Policy and Promotion (DIPP), cement and gypsum products attracted foreign direct investment (FDI) worth ₹ 13,370.32 crore (US$ 2.24 billion) between April 2000 and February 2014.

In India, the housing segment accounts for a major portion of the total domestic demand. In the 12th Plan there was a strong focus on infrastructure development and the Government plans to increase investment in infrastructure to an amount of US$ 1 trillion. The industry is expected to add a capacity of 150 MT during the Plan period.

India's cement demand is expected to reach 550-600 MT Per Annum (MTPA) by 2025. The housing sector is the biggest demand driver of cement, accounting for about 67 per cent of the total consumption in India. The other major consumers of cement, inter alia, are infrastructure at 13 per cent, commercial construction at 11 per cent and industrial construction at 9 per cent.

In order to meet the rise in demand, cement companies are expected to add 56 MT capacity by the year 2020. The cement capacity in India may register a growth of eight per cent by next year end to 395 MT from the current level of 366 MT. It was expected to increase further to 421 MT by the end of 2017. The country's per capita consumption stands at around 190 kg.

The Indian cement industry is dominated by a few companies. The top 20 cement companies account for almost 70 per cent of the total cement production of the country. A total of 188 large cement plants together account for 97 per cent of the total installed capacity in the country, with 365 small plants accounting for the rest. Of these large cement plants, 77 are located in the states of Andhra Pradesh, Rajasthan and Tamil Nadu.[11]

India has great potential for developing infrastructure and construction sector which can benefit the cement sector immensely. Some of the recent major government initiatives such as development of smart cities and housing for all by 2022, are expected to provide a major boost to the sector.

Expecting such developments in the country and aided by suitable government foreign policies, several foreign players such as Lafarge-Holcim, Heidelberg Cement, and Vicat have invested in cement sector in India in the recent past. Ready availability of raw material like limestone and coal for making cement has proved to be an important factor in aiding growth of cement industry in India.

Leather Industry

Leather is one of the most widely traded commodities globally. The growth in demand for leather is driven by the fashion industry, especially footwear. Apart from this, furniture and interior design industries, as well as the automotive industry also have big demand for leather. The leather industry has a place of prominence in the Indian economy due to substantial export earnings and growth.

Leather industry is a traditional industry of India. It spreads over both, organized and unorganized sectors. India has been very rich and skilled in this field since olden times. This industry is largely run by small-scale, cottage and artisan sectors which account for over 75 per cent of the total leather production in the country. In this sector, women and people from the weaker strata of society are predominantly involved. Women constitute more than 30 per cent of the total workforce employed in this sector.

Keeping in mind the strength and potentiality of this sector, government provided an outlay of ₹ 400 crore for implementation of various leather schemes during the Tenth Plan.

Indian leather industry accounts for around 13 per cent of the world's leather production of hides/skins. The country ranks second in terms of footwear and leather garments production in the world. India's leather industry has grown over the years and has transformed from a mere raw material supplier to a value-added product exporter.

Total leather and leather good exports from India stood at US$ 5.92 billion in FY 2015-16. During 2015-16, the major markets for Indian leather products were US (14.25 per cent), UK (12.24 per cent), Germany (11.5 per cent), Italy (6.9 per cent), Spain (5.6 per cent), Hong Kong (5.4 per cent), France (5.3 per cent), UAE (4.5 per cent), Netherlands (3.2 per cent), China (2.8 per cent) and Australia and Belgium (1.45 per cent each). At 47 per cent, footwear accounted for the lion's share of leather exports in the financial year 2015-16, followed by leather goods and accessories with 23 per cent share, finished leather with 18 per cent share, leather garments with 9 per cent share, and saddlery and harness with 3 per cent share.[12]

Paper and Newsprint Industry

The Indian paper industry, ranked among the 15 top global paper industries, plays an important role in the socio-economic development of the country. It accounts for about 1.6 per cent of world production of paper and paperboard, and contributes around ₹ 3000 to the national exchequer per year. The annual rate of paper industry in India is above 10 per cent. The per capita consumption of paper is considered as a benchmark of modernization of any country. The century-old paper industry has made sizeable progress with time. The newsprint and publishing paper consumption in India is 2 MT of which 1.2 MT is manufactured in India, while the remaining 0.8 MT is imported.

India's paper industry was delicensed in 1997, and foreign participation was allowed. Technology used in paper industry in our country ranges from tradional to modern. Paper made form hardwood and bamboo fibre is 40 per cent of total production, from agro waste and recycled fibre it is 30 per cent, and the remaining 30 per cent from grass and other resources. Paper industry in India employs 0.12 million people directly and 0.34 per cent people indirectly. Paper products include sheet paper, paper boxes, stationery, envelopes, greeting cards, napkins, tissues, and newspaper.

Rubber Industry

The rubber industry is a goods manufacturing industry. It is a delicensed industry under which major rubber goods such as tyres and tubes of all kinds, surgical gloves, prophylactics, conveyer and V-belts, hose pipes, sports goods, etc. are produced.

The global per capita rubber consumption is 3.2 kg, with China at 8 kg, developed nations at 14 kg, and India at a mere 1.16 kg. This shows high potential the rubber industry has as demand of rubber products in our country is likely to be high. At present, India is the third largest producer and fourth largest consumer of rubber in the world.

Rubber production in India is about 7 lakh tons per year, and is worth ₹ 3000 crore. Nearly 70 per cent of the total rubber production is in the form of ribbed smoked sheets. India also imports 50,000 tons of rubber annually. More than half of the rubber is used by tyre industry. There are around 6000 rubber producing units in India, of which 300 are large scale, 300 medium scale, and 5600 small scale and tiny units. A total of 4 lakh people are employed in these units, and make 35000 products, the major ones being automatic tyres, tubes, cycle tyres, footwear, rubber hoses, belts, etc. Rubber industry contributes ₹ 4000 crore to the national exchequer annually through taxes, duties, and other levies.

Fibre Industry

The fibre industry plays a prominent role in the textile industry. The industry comprises fibre and filament yarn manufacturing units of cellulosic origin. About 42 per cent of the total consumed raw material is manufactured by the man-made fibre industry.

Textile industry is a good source of foreign exchange. At present, India's export of textiles (including handicrafts, jute and coir) is about 20 per cent of total exports by the country. It is the largest foreign exchange earner for the country because the import content in textile goods is very little. After agriculture, it is the second most important sector in terms of employment generation in India. It contributes about 24.6 per cent to the gross export earnings of the country.

India is the second largest producer of fibre in the world. Cotton is the major fibre produced in India. Around 60% of the Indian textile Industry is cotton based. Other fibres produced include silk, jute, wool, and man-made fibres. The strong domestic demand and the revival of the economic markets by 2009 after the global recession led to huge growth of the Indian textile industry. In December 2010, the domestic cotton price was up by 50% as compared to the December 2009 prices. There was a projection of high production of textile (325 lakh bales for 2010-11). India's share of global textile trading has increased to 7 per cent in the last five years.

Man-made fibre includes manufacturing of clothes using fibre or filament synthetic yarns. It is produced in the large power loom factories, producing about 62% of the India's man-made fibre and provides employment to about five million people.

The cotton sector is the second most developed sector in India's textile industries. It provides employment to a large number of people but its production and employment is of seasonal nature. The handloom operators are mainly dependent on the SHGs for funds and have a share of 13% in the total cloth produced in India. As of 30 September 2013, there are 1962 cotton textile mills in India, of which about 80% are in the private sector and the rest in the public and cooperative sector. Apart from these, there are several thousand small factories with four to ten looms. Although India has a large share in world trade of cotton yarn, its trade in garments is only 4% of the world's total. This is due to the incompetency of local spinning and weaving mills to process yarn. There exist some large factories, but most of the production is fragmented in small units, which cater to the local market. This mismatch is a major drawback for the industry. As a result, many of the spinners export yarn, while apparel and garment manufacturers have to import fabric.

India is the 7th largest producer of the wool in the world. It produces 1.8% of the world's total wool.

India is the largest producer of raw jute and jute goods and the second largest exporter after Bangladesh. At present there are 88 jute mills in India, most of which are located along the banks of the Hooghly river, in a narrow belt (98 km long and 3 km wide), in West Bengal. The factors responsible for their location in the Hooghly basin include inexpensive water transport, good network of railways, roadways and waterways which facilitate movement of raw material to mills, abundant water supply, and cheap labour from the neighbouring states.

In 2010-11 the jute industry was supporting close to 4 lakh workers directly and another four lakh small and marginal farmers, who were engaged in the cultivation of jute.

India is the 2nd largest producer of silk in the world. It produces 18% of the world's total silk. The main types of silk produced in India are Mulberry, Eri, Tasar, and Muga. Since it is a labor-intensive sector, it engages many people.

Heavy Industry

The heavy industry includes heavy electrical industry, automotive industry and others that follows. These are described below.

Heavy Electrical Industry

The heavy electrical industry comprises industrial units manufacturing large plant and machinery required for power generation, transmission, and distribution. The products of the industry include transformers, switchgears, boilers, turbo-generators, and various types of turbines. These equipments are widely used in a number of sectors of the Indian economy such as multi-purpose power projects, including nuclear power stations, petrochemical complexes, chemical plants, integrated steel plants, non-ferrous metal units, etc. The industry has made great technological upgradation and is now ready to take up contracts for export markets.

Heavy electrical equipment industry is an important manufacturing sector, which caters to the need of energy sector and other industrial sectors. Major equipment like steam generators, turbo generators, turbines, transformers, switch gears and relays and related accessories are manufactured by this sector. The performance of this industry is closely linked to the power capacity addition programme of the country. For the 12th Plan targeted capacity addition was about 88000 MW corresponding to 9% economic growth.

Manufacturers of heavy electrical equipment have absorbed sub-critical technology up to a unit capacity of 660 MW and gearing up for adopting super-critical technology for unit size of 800 MW and above for thermal sets. Industry is also augmenting its installed capacity to meet future power capacity addition targets of the country. Gas turbines up to 260 MW unit capacity and Transmission and Distribution equipment up to higher voltage class of 1200 KV are also being manufactured by Indian industry.[13]

Iron and Steel Industry

The iron and steel industry is the backbone of industrial development in India. It is an integral part of infrastructural industry. India is the eighth largest steel producing country in the world. India produces 86.5 MT of steel annually, which is over 5 per cent of world production, making it the fourth largest producer of crude steel in the world. The domestic steel consumption in the country was 76.99 MT per cent in 2014-15, showing an increase of 3.9 per cent over 2013-14. Global steel consumption was estimated to increase by 0.5 per cent in 2015 and 1.4 per cent in 2016. The World Steel Association projected India's steel consumption to increase by 6.2 per cent in 2015 and 7.3 per cent in 2016. Steel imports increased from 5.45 MT in 2013-14 to 9.32 MT in 2014-15.[14]

India was the world's third-largest producer of steel in 2016. The domestic availability of raw materials such as iron ore and cost-effective labour are the main factors in the growth in the Indian steel sector. It has been a major contributor to India's manufacturing output. The steel industry in India is very modern with state-of-the-art steel mills.

In 2016, India's crude steel production grew by 7.4 per cent year-on-year to 95.6 MT. Total production of crude steel during February 2017 grew by 8.5 per cent year-on-year to 8.08 MT. India's steel exports grew 150.0 per cent year-on-year to 0.75 MT in February 2017, while steel imports declined 46 per cent year-on-year to 0.49 MT. Total consumption of finished steel grew by 3.4 per cent year-on-year to 76.22 MT during April 2016-February 2017.

India is expected to become the world's second largest producer of crude steel in the next 10 years, moving up from the third position, as its capacity is projected to increase to about 300 MT by 2025. Huge scope for growth is offered by India's comparatively low per capita steel consumption and the expected rise in consumption due to increased infrastructure construction and the thriving automobile and railways sectors.[15]

The Indian steel industry has entered into a new development stage from 2007-08, riding high on the resurgent economy and rising demand for steel.

Rapid rise in production has resulted in India becoming the 3rd largest producer of crude steel in 2015 and the country was the largest producer of sponge iron or DRI in the world during the period 2003 to 2015 and was the 2nd largest producer in 2016.

As per the report of the Working Group on Steel for the 12th Five Year Plan, there exist many factors which carry the potential of raising the per capita steel consumption in the country. These include among others, an estimated infrastructure investment of nearly a trillion dollars, a projected growth of manufacturing from current 8% to 11-12%, increase in urban population to 600 million by 2030 from the current level of 400 million, emergence of the rural market for steel currently consuming around 11 kg per annum buoyed by projects like Bharat Nirman, Pradhan Mantri Gram Sadak Yojana, Rajiv Gandhi Awaas Yojana among others.

At the time of its release, the National Steel Policy (NSP) 2005 had envisaged steel production to reach 110 million tonnes by 2019-20.

Steel industry was de-licensed and de-controlled in 1991 and 1992 respectively.

In 2015-16, production for sale of total finished steel (alloy + non-alloy) was 90.98 MT, registering a a decline of 1.3% over 2014-15. Production for sale of pig iron in 2015-16 was 9.23 MT, which was a decline of 4.8% over 2014-15.

India was the largest producer of sponge iron in the world during the period 2003-2015 and was the 2nd largest producer in 2016. The coal based route accounted for 89% of total sponge iron production in the country in 2015-16. Data on production for sale of pig iron, sponge iron and total finished steel (alloy/stainless + non-alloy) is given in Table 7.8.

Table 7.8: Indian steel industry: Production for Sale (in million tonnes)

Category	2011-12	2012-13	2013-14	2014-15	2015-16	April-Jan. 2016-17*
Pig Iron	5.37	6.87	7.95	9.69	9.23	7.85
Sponge Iron	19.63	14.33	18.20	20.38	14.53	12.39
Total Finished Steel (alloy/stainless + non-alloy)	75.70	81.68	87.67	92.16	90.98	83.01

*prov.

Source: Ministry of Steel, Government of India

Table 7.8 shows that the production of pig iron and sponge iron declined in the year 2015-16 from the previous year. In order to boost production, the government has approved the policy for providing preference to domestically manufactured iron & steel products on Government procurement. The policy seeks to accomplish the PM's vision of 'Make in India' with the objective of nation building and encouraging domestic manufacturing. The main points of the policy are given below:[16]

(i) It mandates to provide preference to domestically manufactured iron & steel products (DMI&SP), in Government procurement.

(ii) It provides a minimum value addition of 15% in notified steel products which are covered under preferential procurement.

(iii) The Ministry of Steel may review specified steel products and the minimum value addition criterion to provide flexibility.

(iv) It shows trust on each domestic manufacturer who shall provide self-certification to the procuring Government agency declaring that the iron & steel products are domestically manufactured in terms of the domestic value addition prescribed.

(v) It shall not normally be the responsibility of procuring agency to verify the correctness of the claim. In a few cases, the onus of demonstrating the correctness of the same shall be on the bidder when asked to do so.

(vi) In case a manufacturer is aggrieved, a grievance-redressal committee set up under the Ministry of Steel shall dispose of the complaint in a time bound manner.

(vii) There are provisions in the policy for waivers to all such procurements, where specific grades of steel are not manufactured in the country, or the quantities as per the demand of the project cannot be met through domestic sources.

Aluminum Industry

Aluminum has several properties. It is three times lighter than iron but is nearly as strong as steel. It is very flexible and corrosion resistant due to thin surface layer of aluminum oxide. It has been continuously finding new applications due to rising price competence, superior weight to strength ratio, corrosion resistance, formability, dampness etc.

On the industrial side, aluminum is extensively used in electrical power transmission, machinery and equipment, and construction. Housing makes heavy use of the lightweight material as a substitute for steel and wood in doors, windows and siding. On the consumer side, aluminum is used in a variety of retail products such as cans, packaging material, air conditioners, furniture and vehicles.

India is the second largest producer of aluminum in the world with a production of 3.96 MT in 2014-15, behind only China which produces 21.48 MT. India is the third largest aluminum consuming country with a consumption of 3.8 MT in 2014-15, lower than China with 22.09 MT and the USA with 5.5 MT. India's share in world aluminum consumption has increased from 3 per cent in 2008-09 to 7 per cent in 2014-15. World aluminum prices have dropped by 41 per cent from US$ 2,662/tonne in April 2011 to US$ 1,570/tonne in August 2015 and US$ 1,500/tonne in January 2016. During this period in India's imports as a proportion of total demand (sales plus imports) increased from 39.8 per cent in 2011-12 to 56.5 per cent in 2015-16.

The capacity utilization of the Indian aluminum industry has fallen drastically in the last one and a half years as international prices have gone down. The cost of production is higher than international prices. Huge capacity has been created in China and world growth has slowed down. The Indian capacity increased substantially in 2014-15 and 2015-16 (first half) but its utilization, which was nearly 100 per cent up to 2013-14, has declined to 50 per cent. India's cost of production of aluminum is increasing gradually even as world costs are static. The Indian aluminum industry will continue to face difficulty unless world prices increase, because in the short run it is not possible to reduce the cost of production. International aluminum prices, like other metal prices, are cyclical and though it is difficult to forecast when they will begin to move upwards, the trend is expected to change when world industrial growth improves.

According to Aluminum Sector Analysis Report the Indian aluminum demand is expected to remain robust following the steps taken by the government to boost industrial production and infrastructure. The demand is also expected to get a boost following the focus on smart cities and improvement prospects of business and construction industry. The other segments that are expected to see enhanced aluminum demand are automobile and food packaging industry. Rapid urbanization, as the country continues to develop towards a more consumer-focused economy, should augment consumer-driven demand and will help in sustaining strong growth in aluminum demand into the next decade. The global demand for primary aluminum is also expected to be robust and is likely to grow around 4.5% to around 59 million tonnes by 2016 and to 61 million tonnes by 2017.[17]

Automotive Industry

India's automotive industry is one of the largest in the world with an annual production of 23.96 million vehicles in 2015-16, registering a growth of 2.57 per cent over the previous year. It accounts for 7.1 per cent of the country's GDP. The two-wheeler segment, with 81 per cent market share, is leading the

Indian automobile market, catering to a growing middle class and a young population. The growing interest of companies in exploring the rural markets has further boosted the growth of the sector. The overall Passenger Vehicle (PV) segment has the market share of 13 per cent.

India is also a prominent auto exporter and has strong export growth prospects for the near future. During the financial year 2014-15, automobile exports grew by 15 per cent over the previous year. In April-October 2015, the overall automobile exports grew by 5.78 per cent. Passenger Vehicles (PVs), Commercial vehicles (CVs), Three Wheelers (3Ws) and Two Wheelers (2Ws) registered growth of 6.34 per cent, 17.95 per cent, 18.59 per cent and 3.22 per cent, respectively, in April-October 2015 over April-October 2014.

The industry produced a total 14.25 million vehicles including PVs, CVs, 3Ws, and 2Ws in April-October 2015, as against 13.83 in April-October 2014, registering a year-to-year marginal growth of 3.07 per cent. The sales of PVs grew by 8.51 per cent in April-October 2015 over the same period in the previous year. The overall CV segment registered a growth of 8.02 per cent in April-October 2015 as compared to same period last year. Medium and heavy commercial vehicles registered a very strong growth of 32.3 per cent.

The Government of India encourages foreign investment in the automobile sector and allows 100 per cent FDI under the automatic route.

The Government of India aims to make automobile manufacturing the main driver of 'Make in India' initiative, as it expects the passenger vehicles market to triple to 9.4 million units by 2026, as highlighted in the Auto Mission Plan (AMP) 2016-26.

The Automobile Mission Plan (AMP) for the period 2006-16, designed by the government is aimed at accelerating and sustaining growth in this sector. Also, the well-established Regulatory Framework under the Ministry of Shipping, Road Transport and Highways, plays a part in providing a boost to this sector.

Minerals

India has rich sources of a number of minerals. The mineral production in India for the period April-December 2015 increased by 3.1 per cent as compared to the same period of the previous year. This was due to increase in the production of bauxite, chromite, iron ore, limestone and phosphorite. There was also a rise in the production of coal by 4.6 per cent. The mining sector had been hit hard during 2011-12 and 2012-13, owing to legal issues in courts and environmental, regulatory and land acquisition issues. There was a notable turnaround in the mining and quarrying sector because of the initiatives taken by the Government, which are mentioned below:

1. The Government amended the Mines and Minerals Development and Regulation (MMDR) Act 1957 in January 2015 for promoting the mining sector. The salient features of the MMDR Act 2015 are:

   (a) The grant of mineral concessions through auction by competitive bidding, which is a transparent and non-discriminatory.

   (b) Transition provisions for extension of existing leases to obviate disruptions in supply of ore and to ensure regular supply of raw material to industry.

   (c) Assured tenure and easy transferability of mineral concessions granted through auction to attract private investments and FDI.

   (d) Stricter penalty provision to deter illegal mining.

   (e) District Mineral Foundation to be established in each mining affected district.

   (f) National Mineral Exploration Trust to be set up for impetus to exploration.

2. As per the MMDR Amendment Act 2015, the State Governments will conduct auction for grant of mineral concessions. The role of the Central Government is to prescribe the terms and conditions and procedures subject to which the auction shall be conducted, including the bidding parameters for the selection.

3. Under Pradhan Mantri Khanij Kshetra Kalyan Yojna (PMKKKY), an amount of ₹ 6000 crore per annum is to be spent on welfare schemes related to people and districts adversely affected by mining activities.

Petroleum and Natural Gas

Domestic annual production of crude oil has been around 37-38 million tonnes in the 2011-15 period. During April-December 2015, domestic production of crude oil was 27.9 MMT which was 0.8 per cent less than production of 28.2 MMT during the same period of the previous year. Gas production during April-December 2015 was 24.7 BCM against 25.397 BCM during the corresponding period of 2014-15, showing a decline of 2.8 per cent. Some of the issues relating to the sector include the absence of global gas market for benchmarking domestic gas prices in India; the network of gas pipelines is not expected to reach the deprived regions of the country; and there is no rationalization of LPG subsidy.

Exploration of Unconventional Resources

Coal Bed Methane (CBM)

The total available coal-bearing area in India is 26,000 sq.km., out of which CBM exploration has been initiated in about 17,000 sq.km. The estimated CBM resources in the country are about 92 trillion cubic feet (TCF), of which only 9.9 TCF have been confirmed so far. The current commercial production of CBM in India is about 1.0 million metric standard cubic metre per day (MMSCMD). The CBM production potential is likely to increase to 5.7 MMSCMD by 2019. In order to augment CBM gas production, CIL and its subsidiaries have been authorized to undertake CBM operations in coalmining areas held by them.

Shale Oil and Gas

Under the first phase of assessment of shale oil and gas, 50 Petroleum Exploration Lease (PEL)/Petroleum Mining Lease (PML) blocks have been awarded to ONGC and five to OIL. These blocks are located in Assam (6), Arunachal Pradesh (1), Gujarat (28), Rajasthan (1), Andhra Pradesh (10), and Tamil Nadu (9). ONGC has drilled 15 wells for shale gas exploration.

New and Renewable Energy

India has the medium term renewable energy potential of 8,96,602 MW, which includes the potential from solar (7,48,990 MW), wind (1,00,000 MW), small hydro (20,000 MW) and biomass (26,800 MW) power. Besides grid power requirement, renewable energy sources are also being used for distributed generation, lighting, pumping and motive power work in remote and far flung areas.

The generation of clean renewable energy in India has increased from Megawatts to Gigawatts. The target from various renewable energy sources has been increased to 175 GW by the year 2022. The major contributions are expected to be 100 GW from solar energy and 60 GW from wind energy. During April-December 2015, 3029.89 MW of grid-connected power generation capacity from renewable energy sources like solar and wind was added, taking the cumulative generation capacity to over 38,820 MW.

In addition, 74.68 MW equivalents decentralized systems have also been installed in the country for providing distributed generation, lighting, pumping and motive power requirements.

The government has taken some fresh initiatives to increase the generation of renewable energy, some of which are mentioned below:

(i) The budget for implementation of grid-connected rooftops systems over a period of five years up to 2019-20 under the National Solar Mission (NSM) has been scaled up from ₹ 600 crore to ₹ 5000 crore.

(ii) Under the Solar Parks Scheme, there is a provisions of setting up of 25 solar parks and ultra mega solar power projects with an aggregate capacity of 20,000 MW in the next five years in various states. The government has sanctioned 34 solar parks with capacity of about 22,000 MW in 22 states.

(iii) The government will set up 15,000 MW of grid-connected solar PV power projects under the NSM through NTPC Limited/NVVN (NTPC Vidyut Vyapar Nigam) in three tranches by the year 2018-19.

(iv) As on 31st December 2015, 1,21,524 solar pumps were sanctioned for irrigation and drinking water. By January 2016, 15,500 solar pumps had been installed.

(v) The National Offshore Wind Energy Policy 2015 is in place to exploit the 7600 km long coastline for development of offshore wind energy in the Indian Exclusive Economic Zone (EEZ).

(vi) Investments in renewable energy are on automatic route, i.e. automatic approval for up to 74 per cent foreign equity participation in a JV and 100 per cent foreign investment as equity is permissible with the approval of the Foreign Investment Promotion Board (FIPB).

Civil Aviation

The civil aviation industry in India is expanding fast, owing to factors like increasing private participation under Public Private Partnership (PPP), development of greenfield airports, restructuring and modernization of airports, increasing FDI in domestic airlines, increase in number of Low Cost Carriers (LCCs) cutting edge information technology interventions, and more regional connectivity.

There has been strong growth in traffic at Indian airports during 2015-16. During April-November 2014, 108.5 million domestic passengers and 35.2 million international passengers were handled at Indian airports. Domestic and international passenger traffic increased by 20.4 per cent and 7.8 per cent, respectively during April-November 2015, over the same period of the previous year.

International cargo throughput at Indian airports was 1.10 million MT, while domestic cargo throughput stood at 0.70 million MT. International and domestic cargo throughput increased by 5.8 per cent and 6.1 per cent, respectively in April-November 2015 as compared to the corresponding period of the previous year.

The Government released the National Civil Aviation Policy on 15 June 2016. The policy covers the broad policy areas, such as regional connectivity, safety, air transport operations, bilateral traffic rights, maintenance, repair and overhaul, air-cargo, etc. The broad key features of the NCAP are:

(i) Viability Gap Funding (VGF) for operation under Regional Connectivity Scheme (RCS).

(ii) Revival of un-served or under-served routes under RCS.

(iii) Introduction of a new Category 'Schedule Commuter Operator' under Commercial Air Transport Operations.

(iv) Rationalization of Category-I routes under Route Dispersal Guidelines (RDGs) on the basis of criteria given in NCAP 2016.

(v) The requirement of 5 years and 20 aircraft for international operation has been modified to 0 years and 20 aircraft or 20% of the total capacity (in terms of average number of seats on all departure put together) whichever is higher for domestic operations.

Indian Shipping Industry

Shipping industry is extremely important for India as around 95 per cent of the country's trade by volume and 70 per cent by value is done through maritime transport.

As on 2015, India has 12 major and 200 notified minor and intermediate ports. Cargo traffic, which recorded 1,052 million metric tonnes (MMT), was expected to reach 1,758 MMT by the end of 2017. India is the 16th largest maritime country in the world, with a coastline of about 7,517 km. The Government has allowed Foreign Direct Investment (FDI) of up to 100 per cent under the automatic route for port and harbour construction and maintenance projects. It has also facilitated a 10-year tax holiday to enterprises that develop, maintain and operate ports, inland waterways and inland ports.

During April-September 2016 the cargo traffic handled by India's major ports increased 5.1 per cent year-on-year to 315.4 million tonnes (MT). In terms of composition of cargo traffic, the largest commodity was P.O.L., i.e. petroleum, oil and lubricant (37.1 per cent), followed by coal (23.4 per cent), container traffic (19.6 per cent), other cargo (11.9 per cent), iron ore (5.66 per cent) and fertilizer and FRM (2.5 per cent).

The country's major ports handled a combined traffic volume of 586.29 million tonnes during April 2016-February 2017, up from 550.45 million tonnes during same period last year, while containerized cargo tonnage rose 3.7 per cent to 10.5 MT during August 2016. During April-June 2016, the ports had handled a combined volume of 2.12 million TEUs, which is roughly around 70 per cent of the country's overall container trade.[18]

There is a forecast of an investment of ₹ 180,626 crore (US$ 27.09 billion) for this industry in its 12th Five Year Plan. In addition, through The Maritime Agenda 2010-20, the Ministry of Shipping has set a target capacity of over 3,130 MMT by 2020, which would be driven by participation from the private sector. Non-major ports are expected to generate over 50 per cent of this capacity.[19]

Table 7.9 shows that the cargo traffic of Indian ports increased by 8.2 per cent to 1052.2 MT in 2014-15, with traffic at non-major ports increasing at a faster rate than at major ports. During April to September 2015, while cargo traffic at all ports increased by 1.1 per cent, major ports reported an increase of 4.1 per cent and non-major ports a decline of 1.0 per cent as compared to the corresponding period in 2014-15.

Table 7.9: Cargo Traffic at Ports (million tonnes)

Category	2013-14	2014-15 (P)	April-September	
			2014-15 (P)	2015-16 (P)
Major ports	555.49 (1.8)	581.33 (4.7)	287.74 (3.8)	299.58 (4.1)
Non-major ports	416.96 (7.5)	471.19 (13.0)	228.14 (11.8)	225.92 (-1.0)
All ports	972.45 (4.1)	1052.52 (8.2)	515.88 (7.2)	525.50 (1.1)

P - Provisional Inland Waterways Transport Sector

Source: Ministry of Shipping

Note: Figures in parenthesis indicate percentage growth over previous year.

Some of the major initiatives taken by the government to promote the ports sector in India are mentioned below:

(i) The Major Port Trusts Act, 1963 has been replaced by the Major Port Authorities Bill, 2016, which empowers major ports to perform with greater efficiency by having full autonomy in decision-making and by modernizing the institutional structure of major ports.

(ii) The Ministry of Shipping has undertaken the development of 37 national waterways (NWs) out of the 111 NWs declared under the National Waterways Act 2016.

(iii) India will collaborate with Germany for projects worth ₹ 1 trillion (US$ 15 billion), for enhancing port rail connectivity and identifying environment-friendly technology for scrapping of old vehicles.

(iv) The Ministry of Road Transport and Highways and National Highways Authority of India (NHAI) plan to take up 82 highway development projects under the Bharatmala project, which would help in improving connectivity to both major as well as minor ports in the country.

(v) The Ministry of Shipping plans to install 160.64 megawatts (MW) of solar and wind based power systems at all the major ports across the country by 2017, thereby promoting the use of renewable energy sources and giving a fillip to government's Green Port Initiative.

(vi) The Government plans to amend the current Model Concession Agreement (MCA), by providing a better allocation of risks between the government and private firms, thereby encouraging investments in the shipping sector.

(vii) The Government has set an ambitious target to convert 101 rivers across the country into waterways to promote water transport and propel economic growth.

(viii) The Government plans to establish two new major ports, at Sagar in West Bengal and at Dugarajapatnam in Andhra Pradesh. Prime Minister Narendra Modi has laid the foundation stone for the Fourth Container

Terminal of Jawaharlal Nehru Port at Mumbai. It is expected to more than double the existing capacity of the container terminal.

(ix) The Government has approved amendments in the National Waterways Bill, 2015, which will provide for enacting a legislation to declare 106 additional inland waterways, as the national waterways.

(x) A vision document for Coastal Shipping, Tourism and Regional Development has been prepared with a view to increasing the share of coastal/inland waterways transport mode from 7 per cent to 10 per cent by 2019-20. An action plan to achieve the objective has also been prepared and is being implemented. An ambitious programme has been drawn up to develop 78 lighthouses in the country as centres of tourism in the first phase under PPP. The identified lighthouses are in Gujarat, Maharashtra, Goa, Karnataka, Kerala, Lakshadweep, Tamil Nadu, Puducherry, Andhra Pradesh, Odisha, West Bengal and Andaman and Nicobar Islands.[20]

IT and ITeS Industry in India

The Indian IT and ITeS industry is divided into four major segments, viz. IT services, Business Process Management (BPM), software products and engineering services, and hardware. India is the world's largest sourcing destination for the information technology (IT). Over 65 per cent of the US$ 124-130 billion market is captured by India. The industry employs about 10 million as workforce. This industry has led the economic transformation of the country and enhanced other countries' perception about India's economy. India's cost competitiveness in providing IT services, which is approximately 3-4 times cheaper than that of the US, continues to be the mainstay of its Unique Selling Proposition (USP) in the global sourcing market. India is also gaining prominence in terms of intellectual capital with several global IT firms setting up their innovation centres in India.

The present market size and the outlook of India's IT and ITeS industry is given bellow.[21]

The Indian IT sector was expected to register a growth of around 12 per cent for financial year 2016-17. It is expected to triple its current annual revenue to reach US$ 350 billion by the year 2025.

Employees from 12 Indian start-ups, including Flipkart, Snapdeal, Naukri, and Ola have gone on to form more than 700 start-ups on their own, thereby expanding the Indian start-up ecosystem. India ranks third among global start-up ecosystems with over 4,200 start-ups. Total spending on IT by banking and security firms in India is expected to grow 8.6 per cent year-on-year to US$ 7.8 billion by the end of the year 2017. India's internet economy is expected to touch ₹ 10 trillion (US$ 146.72 billion) by 2018, which will be 5 per cent of the country's GDP.

The public cloud services market in India is slated to grow 35.9 per cent to reach US$ 1.3 billion according to IT consultancy, Gartner. Increased penetration of internet (including in rural areas) and rapid emergence of e-commerce are the main drivers for continued growth of data centre co-location and hosting market in India. The Indian Healthcare Information Technology (IT) market is valued at US$ 1 billion currently and is expected to grow 1.5 times by 2020. India's business to business (B2B) e-commerce market is expected to reach US$ 700 billion by 2020 whereas the business to consumer (B2C) e-commerce market is expected to reach US$ 102 billion by 2020.[22]

Some key initiatives taken by the Government to promote IT and ITeS sector in India are given below:[23]

(i) ₹ 10,000 crore (US$ 1.5 billion) have been allocated for BharatNet project under which it aims to provide high speed broadband to more than 150,000 gram panchayats by 2017-18.

(ii) PM Narendra Modi has launched the Bharat Interface for Money (BHIM) app, an Aadhar-based mobile payment application that will allow users to make digital payments without having to use a credit or debit card. The app has already reached the mark of 10 million downloads.

(iii) The Telecom Regulatory Authority of India (TRAI) will soon release consultation papers ahead of framing regulations and standards for the rollout of fifth-generation (5G) networks and Internet of Things (IoT) in India.

(iv) The Government of Gujarat signed 89 MoUs worth ₹ 16,000 crore (US$ 2.3 billion) in the IT sector, during Vibrant Gujarat Global Summit-2017.

(v) The Government of Telangana signed an agreement with network solutions giant Cisco Systems Incorporation, to cooperate on a host of technology initiatives, including Smart Cities, Internet of Things, cybersecurity, education digitization of monuments.

(vi) The Government of India has launched the Digital India program to provide several government services to the people using IT and to integrate the government departments and the people of India. The adoption of key technologies across sectors spurred by the 'Digital India Initiative' could help boost India's Gross Domestic Product (GDP) by US$ 550 billion to US$ 1 trillion by 2025.

Growth of telecommunications has been one of the key drivers of socio-economic development in India. The performance of the telecommunications sector during 2015-16 was quite encouraging. About 33.4 million new telephone connections were added during April to October 2015, as against 29.65 million new connections in the corresponding period of 2014-15. Overall tele-density in the country increased from 79.4 per cent at the beginning of the financial year to 81.5 per cent at the end of October 2015. The total broadband connections were nearly 121 million at the end of September 2015.

Gross Capital Formation in the Industrial Sector

India's Gross Capital Formation (GCF) at current prices was estimated at ₹ 42.76 lakh crore for 2014-15 as compared to ₹ 39.12 lakh crore during 2013-14.

However, the rate of GCF to GDP declined slightly to 34.2 per cent in 2014-15 from 34.7 per cent during 2013-14. The rate of GCF to GDP at constant (2011-12) prices also decreased from 36.2 per cent in 2013-14 to 35.9 per cent 2014-15. The rate of growth of GCF in industry showed a sharp rise from (–)3.7 per cent in 2013-14 to 3.6 per cent in 2014-15, depicting upward momentum of investment in industry.

Table 7.10 shows that the sector-wise shares of different industries in overall GCF are up in some type of industry and down in others. The share of electricity increased, while the shares of mining, manufacturing and construction declined.

Table 7.10: Per cent of GCF by Industry (at 2011-12 constant prices)

	2011-12	2012-13	2013-14	2014-15
Rate of growth of GCF in industry		2.8	-3.7	3.6
Sector-wise share in overall GCF				
(i) Mining	2.1	2.3	4.0	3.3
(ii) Manufacturing	19.2	18.4	17.4	16.9
(iii) Electricity	9.6	9.1	8.6	9.2
(iv) Construction	7.2	7.7	5.5	5.4

Source: CSO.

Credit Flow to the Industrial Sector

Growth in credit flow to the industrial sector, including mining and manufacturing, has slowed down in 2015-16 as compared to 2014-15 as shown in Table 7.10.

In the manufacturing sector, the credit flow declined to 2.5 per cent in 2015 (up to December) as compared to 13.2 per cent in 2014 (up to December). Credit flow to industries such as basic metal and metal products, chemical and chemical products and engineering industries increased. However, there was a sharp decline in industries like petroleum and nuclear fuel, cement and cement products, transport equipment and food processing industries.

The decline in credit flow to the petroleum sector was due to lower requirements by oil marketing companies as there was rationalization of fuel subsidies. In 2015-16, credit to micro and small industries, and large industries grew at 2.5 per cent and 6.6 per cent respectively. The credit flow to medium scale industries declined by 7.6 per cent during the said period. The position is given in Table 7.11.

Table 7.11: Growth of Credit to Industry by Scheduled Commercial Banks (in per cent)

Sectors	2014-15*	2015-16**
Industries	6.7	5.3
Manufacturing	13.2	2.5
Mining	3.9	–0.3
Manufacturing sub-sectors		
Food processing	12.4	–1.9
Textiles	2.8	2.1
Petroleum and nuclear fuel	–7.4	–10.4
Chemical and chemical products	–9.0	2.9
Cement and cement products	5.8	–1.1
Basic metal and metal products	7.3	8.8
All engineering	6.4	6.3
Transport equipment	5.0	–1.5
Other industries	–3.1	9.8

Source: RBI

Note: *End-December 2014 over end-December 2013. **End-December 2015 over end-December 2014.

Conclusion

India is tenth in the world in factory output. Manufacturing sector, mining, quarrying, electricity and gas together account for 27.6% of the GDP and employ 17% of the total workforce. Economic reforms introduced after 1991 brought foreign competition and led to privatization of certain public sector industries, which opened up sectors hitherto reserved for the public sector and facilitated expansion in the production of fast-moving consumer goods.

Post-liberalization, the Indian private sector was faced with foreign competition, including the threat of cheaper Chinese imports. It has since handled the change well, taking measures like squeezing costs, revamping management, focusing on designing new products and adopting latest technology. Narendra Modi and his government have taken many new initiatives to increase industrial production in India. This will make India an

Industrially advanced country in the time to come. Some of the new initiatives are given in the Appendices.

Notes

1. http://www.historydiscussion.net/british-india/industrial-development-in-india-during-the-british-rule/5979
2. *Ibid.*
3. Eugene M. Makar (2007). *An American's Guide to Doing Business in India.*
4. NITI Aayog Annual Report, 2014-15.
5. *Ibid.*
6. *Economic Survey*, 2015-16.
7. https://www.export.gov/article?id=India-Competition-from-State-Owned-Enterprises
8. *Economic Survey,* 2015-16.
9. http://www.kvb.co.in/msme/definition.html
10. http://news.steel-360.com/miscellaneous/role-private-sector-indias-prosperity/
11. *Outlook.* 1 February 2016.
12. Council for Leather Exports (CLE).
13. Department of Heavy Industry, Ministry of Heavy Industries and Public Enterprises, Government of India.
14. *Economic Survey*, 2015-16.
15. https://www.ibef.org/industry/steel.aspx
16. http://www.insightsonindia.com/2017/05/04/insights-daily-current-affairs-04-may-2017/
17. https://www.equitymaster.com/research-it/sector-info/aluminium/Aluminium-Sector-Analysis-Report.asp
18. Indian Ports Association, Ministry of Shipping, Media Reports, Press Releases.
19. *Ibid.*
20. *Economic Survey,* 2015-16.
21. Media Reports, Press Information Bureau (PIB), Department of Industrial Policy and Promotion (DIPP) Statistics, Department of Information and Technology, Union Budget 2017-18.
22. https://www.ibef.org› Industry
23. Press Information Bureau (PIB), Department of Industrial Policy and Promotion (DIPP) statistics, Department of Information and Technology, Union Budget 2017-18.

APPENDIX-I

New Initiatives of MSME Ministry

[Press Information Bureau (Government of India) and Ministry of Micro, Small and Medium Enterprises]

During the year 2015, Ministry of MSME launched various initiatives to improve the ease of doing business and to make Micro, Small and Medium Enterprises more globally competitive. These initiatives include ease of registration of the business in the form of Udyog Aadhar Memorandum, Framework to revive sick MSMEs, promoting innovation in rural entrepreneurship through ASPIRE scheme, fund for regenerating traditional industries, financial support in the form of credit guarantee and credit linked capital subsidy. Some of the programmes launched during the year include the following:

Udyog Aadhar Memorandum (UAM)

The Ministry in September-2015 under the MSME Development Act, 2006 has notified that every MSME unit shall file Udyog Aadhar Memorandum (UAM). This is a path breaking step to promote ease-of-doing-business for MSMEs in India as the UAM replaces the filing of Entrepreneurs' Memorandum (EM part-I & II) with the respective States/UTs. While some of the States/UTs had made the process online, either by themselves or through the portal created by this Ministry, several States/ UTs were still relying on the manual way of filing EM. The cumbersome filing of EM has now been dispensed with and the entrepreneurs in the MSME sector just need to file online, a simple one-page UAM on http://udyogaadhaar.gov.in to instantly get a unique Udyog Aadhar Number (UAN). The information sought is on self-certification basis and no supporting documents are required at the time of online filing of UAM.

The UAM can be filed online by individuals themselves in case they have an Aadhar Number. However, in all exceptional cases, including those of not having an Aadhar Number, the UAM can be filed in offline mode (i.e. on paper form), with the General Manager (GM) of the concerned District Industries Centre (DIC).

The UAM has emerged from the vision of Honorable Prime Minister of India shared with the nation through "Mann Ki Baat" telecast on 03-10-2014 and the recommendations for Universalization of Registration in the Report of the Kamath Committee on Financial Architecture of MSME sector. Wide-ranging consultation exercise has been done in the matter in the National Board of MSMEs and the Advisory Committee for MSME Act. It is expected that this simplified one-page memorandum to be filed online shall unlock the potential of MSMEs, besides improving our international ranking in Doing Business Index. Within a short time of three months, more than 95,650 UAMs have been filed in the country.

Framework for Revival and Rehabilitation of MSMEs

The existing mechanism for addressing revival, rehabilitation and exit of small enterprises is very weak in the country. The most recent Doing Business (DB) Report ranks India 137 out of the 189 economies for resolving insolvencies. It notes that resolving insolvency takes 4.3 years on average and costs 9.0% of the debtor's estate, with the most likely outcome being that the company will be sold as piecemeal sale.

Pending a detailed revision of the legal framework for resolving insolvency/bankruptcy, there was a felt need for special dispensation for revival and exit of MSMEs. The MSMEs facing insolvency/bankruptcy need to be provided legal opportunities to revive their units. This could be through a scheme for re-organization and rehabilitation, which balances the interests of the creditors and debtors.

The Framework for Revival and Rehabilitation of MSMEs has been notified in May 2015 under section 9 of the Micro, Small and Medium Enterprises Development Act, 2006. The salient features of the same are as follows:

- Identification of incipient stress,
- Committees for Distressed Micro, Small and Medium Enterprises,
- Corrective Action Plan (CAP) by the Committee with various Options,

- Restructuring Process,
- Prudential Norms on Asset Classification and Provisioning,
- Identification of Willful Defaulters and Non-Cooperative Borrowers.

Prime Minister's Employment Generation Programme (PMEGP)

PMEGP is the flagship programme of the government offering credit linked subsidy to establish new enterprises for generating continuous and sustainable employment opportunities in Rural and Urban areas of the country.

- An amount of ₹ 860.51 crore has been released by the MSME Ministry as margin money under PMEGP out of which ₹ 528.32 crore has already been disbursed by the banks.
- As many as 24,126 new enterprises providing employment to 170,983 persons have been benefited under the scheme.
- There is more than 50% increase over the previous year in terms of funds disbursed by the banks, number of projects with funds disbursed and the employment generated.

A Scheme for Promotion of Innovation, Rural Industry and Entrepreneurship (ASPIRE)

ASPIRE has been launched on 16-03-2015 with an objective to set up a network of technology centers, incubation centres to accelerate entrepreneurship and also to promote start-ups for innovation and entrepreneurship in rural and agriculture based industry with a fund of ₹ 210 crore.

- The planned outcomes of ASPIRE are, setting up Technology Business Incubators (TBI), Livelihood Business Incubators (LBI) and creation of a Fund of Funds for such initiatives with SIDBI.
- The 1st LBI was set up in April-2015 under ASPIRE within a month of launching the Scheme. The first batch of 107 youth has been trained and skilled through it.

- 19 LBIs have been approved till September 2015 and another 9 LBIs and 2 TBIs ready to be approved.

Scheme of Fund for Regeneration of Traditional Industries (SFURTI)

The objectives SFURTI are to organize the traditional industries and artisans into clusters to make them competitive and provide support for their long-term sustainability by way of enhancing the marketability of products, improving the skills of artisans, making provision for common facilities and strengthening the cluster governance systems.

- The guidelines of SFURTI have been revamped in 2015 and the scheme has taken giant strides in 2015. Funds to the tune of ₹ 62 crore have been sanctioned under the scheme in 2015 as against nil in 2014.
- As many 68 clusters have already been approved in 2015 itself against the target of 71 clusters during 12th Plan period with more than a year of the plan period to spare.

Lean Manufacturing Competitiveness Scheme (LMCS)

LMCS is being implemented across the country to enhance the competitiveness of manufacturing MSMEs. The objective of the scheme is to enhance the manufacturing competitiveness of MSMEs through application of various Lean Manufacturing Techniques [e.g. Total Productive Maintenance (TPM), 5S, Visual control, Standard Operation Procedures, Single Minutes Exchange of Dies or Quick Changeover (SMED), Value Stream Mapping, Just in Time, Kanban System, Kaizen, Cellular Layout, Poka Yoke].

- 188 new clusters identified and selected for LM (Lean Manufacturing) interventions.
- Lean Manufacturing interventions have been initiated in 359 Units.
- Organised 63 Awareness Programmes across the country.

Credit Guarantee Trust Fust for Micro and CGTMSE Scheme

CGTMSE was set up to strengthen credit delivery system and facilitate flow of credit to the MSE sector. The Credit Guarantee under CGTMSE seeks to reassure the lender that, in the event of a MSE unit, which availed collateral-free credit facilities, fails to discharge its liabilities to the lender; the CGMSE would make good the loss incurred by the lender up to 85 per cent of the credit facility.

- During the current financial year (April to October 2015), total number of proposals approved under the scheme was 2,31,774 involving a guarantee amount of ₹ 11,446 crore.

Credit Linked Capital Subsidy Scheme (CLCSS) for Technology Upgradation

CLCSS aims at facilitating technology upgradation of Micro and Small Enterprises (MSEs) by providing 15% capital subsidy (limited to maximum ₹ 15 lakhs) for purchase of Plant & Machinery. Maximum limit of eligible loan for calculation of subsidy under the scheme is ₹ 100 lakhs. Presently, more than 1500 well established/improved technologies under 51 sub-sectors have been approved under the Scheme.

- During the current financial year (April to October 2015), 1,195 units benefited and total subsidy released to the tune of ₹ 75.57 crore.

APPENDIX II

Make in India

With the objective of making India a global hub of manufacturing, design and innovation, the Make in India initiative, which is based on four pillars—new processes, new infrastructure, new sectors and new mindset—has been taken by the government. The initiative is set to boost entrepreneurship, not only in manufacturing but in relevant infrastructure and service sectors as well. An interactive portal http://makeinindia.com for dissemination of information and interaction with investors has been created with the objective of generating awareness about the investment opportunities and prospects of the country, to promote India as a preferred investment destination in markets overseas and to increase Indian share of global FDI. In addition, information on 25 thrust sectors, along with details of the FDI Policy, National Manufacturing Policy, Intellectual Property Rights and the proposed National Industrial Corridors including the Delhi Mumbai Industrial Corridor (DMIC), are available on the portal.

The Department of Industrial Policy and Promotion (DIPP), in consultation with various central ministries, state governments, industry leaders, and other stakeholders, has formulated a strategy for increasing the contribution of the manufacturing sector to 25 per cent of the GDP by 2020.

The Government of India has set up Invest India as the national investment promotion and facilitation agency. With the objective of promoting investment in the country, a full-fledged Investment Facilitation Cell has been set-up under the Make in India initiative, primarily to support all investment queries as well as to handhold and liaise with various agencies on behalf of potential investors.

As envisaged by the National Manufacturing Policy 2011, Make in India seeks to create 100 million additional jobs in manufacturing by 2022. The government is taking a number of steps to enhance the skills of workers/the unemployed in India in order to improve their employability. In order to tap the creative potential and boost entrepreneurship in India, the Start-up India, Stand-up India campaign has been announced. An innovation promotion platform called Atal Innovation Mission (AIM) and a techno-financial, incubation and facilitation programme called Self-Employment and Talent Utilization (SETU) are being implemented to encourage innovation and start-ups in India.

For supporting the financial needs of the small and medium enterprise sector and promote start-ups and entrepreneurship, the government has taken various steps through Make in India. The India Aspiration Fund has also been set up under the Small Industries Development Bank of India (SIDBI) for venture capital financing of newly set-up or expanding units in the MSME sector. SIDBI Make in India Loan for Small Enterprises (SMILE) has been launched to offer quasi-equity and term-based short-term loans to Indian SMEs with less stringent rules and regulations and a special focus on 25 thrust sectors of Make in India. Further, a Micro Units Development Refinance Agency (MUDRA) Bank has been set up to provide development and refinance to commercial banks/NBFCs/cooperative banks for loans given to micro-units. MUDRA Bank would follow a credit-plus approach by also providing financial literacy and addressing skill gaps, information gaps, etc.

8

Indian Public Finances

Public finance is a branch of economics which assesses the government revenue as well as government expenditure of the public authorities and the adjustment of one or the other to bring the desired effects. It is the study of the role of the government in the economy. Broadly speaking, the purview of public finance is threefold: governmental effects on efficient allocation of resources, distribution of income, and macroeconomic stabilization.

Since we study the finances of the government in public finance, it deals with the question how the government raises its resources to meet its expenditure. The effects of taxation, government expenditure, public borrowing and deficit financing on the economy are the subject matter of public finance. It also deals with fiscal policies which the country should adopt to achieve certain goals such as price stability, economic growth, and more equal distribution of income.

In the developed industrialized countries, the basic problem in the short run is to ensure stability at full employment level and in the long run to ensure steady rate of economic growth, while the developing countries face a more difficult problem of how to generate a higher rate of economic growth so as to tackle the problems of poverty and unemployment. In the developing countries like India, public finance also plays another important role, viz. that of promoting economic growth and maintaining price stability. Further, for developing countries mere economic growth is not enough. The composition of growing output and distribution of additional incomes need to be such that they ensure removal of poverty and unemployment. Public finance has not only to augment resources for development and to achieve optimum allocation of resources, but also to promote fair distribution of income and expansion in employment opportunities.

Indian Tax System

Taxes in India are levied by the Central Government and the State Governments. Some minor taxes are also levied by the local authorities like the municipality, for example, property tax. The authority to levy a tax is derived from the Constitution of India which allocates the power to levy various taxes between the Centre and the State. An important restriction on this power is Article 265 of the Constitution which states that "No tax shall be levied or collected except by the authority of law". Each tax levied or collected therefore has to be backed by an accompanying law, passed either by the Parliament or the State Legislature. In 2015-16, the gross tax collection of the Centre amounted to ₹ 14.60 trillion (US$ 230 billion).[1]

Economists believe that that tax policy of a developing country like India should be geared towards accelerating the rate of economic growth. Taxation must raise the level of savings. In the words of Dr. Raja J. Chelliah, it must "mobilize the economic surplus". A sound tax system must help in increasing the amount of economic surplus. Therefore, the general emphasis in tax system must be on curtailing the consumption standards. Further, whenever savings are promoted through tax system, they should also be diverted in desired channels.

In a developing country, the development process is always accompanied by growing inequalities. Therefore, as far as possible, a sound tax system must make an attempt to reduce these inequalities. Care should also be taken to ensure that tax rates are not unduly high which discourage the incentives to work, save and invest.

The development needs of developing countries are huge. Therefore, even the poorest have to pay some taxes, but as far as possible, the principle of ability to pay must be observed while collecting taxes from different individuals. A person's ability to pay can be measured in terms of that part of economic surplus accruing to him which he or she is not utilizing for productive investment. The greater the surplus a person has above his minimum necessary requirements, the greater should be his ability to pay taxes.

Another important objective of a sound tax policy in a developing economy is to check inflationary tendencies. High inflation is inherent in all developing countries. In the initial stages of economic development large investments are undertaken and there is always a time lag between investment and output. So there is price rise in the meantime. It is now generally believed that taxation can play a vital role in checking these inflationary tendencies. Taxes, direct as well as indirect, reduce the disposable income of the people and thus exercise restraints on demand. According to Taxation Enquiry Commission, "Taxes that fall directly on the large additional incomes, and commodity taxes that fall on the increase in general purchasing power resulting from inflation have a significant part to play in anti-inflationary policy." In a sound tax policy, the tax system is simple, nobody feels that he is being discriminated, tax evasion is almost non-existent, and tax administration is smooth and hassle free. If we carefully study the Indian tax system, the following features will emerge:

1. Higher Tax Rates: Contrary to common belief, India is one of the highest taxed nations in the world. Ever since the start of planning, the government has been imposing new taxes. The rates of existing taxes are sometimes raised to astronomical figures (97.5 per cent). Consequently, little is left as incentives to work, save and invest. People are now crying under the crushing burden of taxes—both direct and indirect.

Income Tax rates in India are too high. The tax rates are around 30%. Whatever profits one makes, 30% of that will go to income tax department. High rates are the cause of generation of black money. People do all wrong things to save money. If the tax rates are low, people will invest more money in the system and economy will boom. Realizing this, the Modi government has reduced income for those whose taxable income is up to

₹ 5 lakh w.e.f. financial year 2017-18. The new rates are given below:

Income Tax Slab For Individual Tax Payers & HUF
(Less Than 60 Years Old) (Both Men & Women)

Income Slab	Tax Rate
Income up to ₹ 2,50,000*	No Tax
Income from ₹ 2,50,000 – ₹ 5,00,000	5%
Income from ₹ 5,00,000 – 10,00,000	20%
Income more than ₹ 10,00,000	30%

Surcharge: 10% of income tax, where total income exceeds ₹ 50 lakhs up to ₹ 1 crore.

Surcharge: 15% of income tax, where total income exceeds ₹ 1 crore.

Cess: 3% on total of income tax + surcharge.

*Income Tax Exemption limit for FY 2017-18, is up to ₹ 2,50,000 for Individual and HUF other than those covered in Part (II) or (III)

Earlier the income tax rates for income up to ₹ 5 lakh was 10 per cent.

Even the new GST has high rates which in some cases is as high as 28 per cent.

2. Multiplicity of Taxes/Tax Bases: India has a broad-based and extensive tax structure. Its main feature is the existence of multiplicity of taxes. There are both Union Government taxes and State Government taxes. The tax structure includes both direct as well as indirect taxes.

All conceivable bases of taxes—both direct and indirect taxes—have been exploited. Direct taxes on income (from various sources, including interest and profits), wealth, property, (including land and houses), capital gains, gifts, etc. have been imposed. Then there is a multiplicity of indirect taxes imposed both by the Centre and the States such as export and import (custom) duties, tax on production (Union excise duty), tax on services, tax on the sale and purchase of goods, tax on the movement of goods from one State to another, entry tax on goods entering from one State to another and even entering a particular municipal area within the State, i.e. octroi, State excise duty, etc. VAT has been imposed by many States; but all other indirect taxes are still continuing. Apart from these, there are many other levies imposed at the local level. However, with the application of Goods and Services Tax, VAT has been removed.

A taxpayer has to pay income tax when he earns income, he has to pay wealth tax when he holds accumulated income, he has to pay gift tax when he transfers that income to others and has to pay estate duty (abolished recently) if he dies and leaves his accumulated income to his heirs. During 1957-58 to 1961-62 and 1963-64 to 1965-66, he had to pay expenditure tax if he spent more than the specified amount. This might appear taxation with vengeance. In the field of indirect taxes also, duties have been levied on the new items and increased on old items so as to tax more heavily those commodities which are consumed by the relatively well-to-do classes. Even commodities of mass consumption have not been spared.

The State Governments main taxes are land revenue, sale tax, state excise duties entertainment tax, stamp and registration duties etc.

It is pertinent to mention here that the government has brought Goods and Services Tax (GST), which will merge many individually-applied taxes into a single tax. It was introduced as The Constitution (One Hundred and First Amendment) Act 2016. GST is a comprehensive indirect tax on manufacture, sale and consumption of goods and services throughout India to replace taxes levied by the Central and State Governments. This will considerably reduce the multiplicity of taxes in India.

3. Revenue Surpluses or Deficits: Another important feature of Indian tax system has been excess of its collections compared with requirements till mid-seventies. There were surpluses on revenue account which were partly used to finance capital expenditure. It is only on capital account that our budgets were deficit. On both the accounts taken together, however, our budgets turned out to be deficit. However, since the mid-seventies because of increasing revenue expenditure, a chronic tendency of revenue deficit has been developed.

Despite the rising trend in tax revenue, the total revenue remained small when compared to developed countries. The tax GDP ratio generally remained in the range of just 8 per cent to 9 per cent in India as compared to 30 to 40 per cent in countries like Sweden, France, West Germany, UK, USA, etc.

4. Complicated Tax Structure: Successive governments have been imposing new taxes and raising the rates of existing taxes. Consequently our tax structure has become very complicated. Since a large number of people in our country are illiterate and numerous others have just basic education, they do not understand this complicated tax structure. This has led to various malpractices. Tax administration has become dishonest and corrupt. An average taxpayer has fallen victim to the corrupt tax officials who have earned huge amounts of black money. Sometimes tax administration, in collusion with the taxpayers, exploits the government treasury.

Both direct and indirect tax laws are highly complex, with a lot of loopholes which enable the people to avoid as well as to evade taxes. According to Prof. Kaldore, "There are definitional defects in India's tax system, which gives elaborate power to tax authorities to interpret tax laws according to their whims and fancies. This has generated widespread corruption in tax departments."[2]

5. Inequitable Tax Structure: Although we impose a large number of taxes, yet our tax structure lacks equity. According to Raja J. Chelliah, our tax system has neither horizontal equity nor vertical equity. By horizontal equity we mean that all taxpayers with the same level of income, regardless of the source of income, must pay the same amount of taxes. But we know that our agricultural sector pays fewer taxes than the industrial sector. In the industrial sector one has to pay direct taxes like income tax, corporation tax, etc. from which the agricultural sector is exempted. Even in case of indirect taxes, agricultural sector pays fewer taxes because it consumes only those commodities which it produces. Naturally, these commodities do not carry any tax burden, since they are not brought into the market.

According to Raja J. Chelliah even vertical equity is conspicuous by its absence from our tax structure. By vertical equity we mean persons having different levels of income must pay differently, i.e. persons with higher income must pay higher amount of taxes and persons with low income must pay lower amount of taxes. But this is not the case in India because of the predominance of indirect taxes which are regressive in nature.

6. Imbalance between Direct and Indirect Taxes: The main reason for our inequitable tax structure is the preponderance of indirect taxes. The documents on Long Term Fiscal Policy showed that the proportion of indirect taxes in total tax revenue had increased to as high as 82 per cent in the mid-sixties. Consequently, the ratio of direct taxes has declined to 18 per cent. In developed countries like USA, UK, Japan, etc. reverse is the case. The burden of indirect taxes as we know mostly falls on the poor. Consequently, inequality in the distribution of income has increased in India. It is a happy augury that in the post-reform period of 1990s, emphasis is now being shifted to direct taxes. Consequently, the ratio of direct taxes to total tax revenue is on the rise and presently this has reached nearly 24-25 per cent.

7. Anti-Inflationary Tax Structure: As already stated, inflation is in-built in the development process in a developing country. An ideal tax structure must cure this evil. Unfortunately, because of predominance of indirect taxes, our tax structure is not anti-inflationary. Rather it has kept inflation high.

8. Imbalance in the Tax Sources of States and Union: One of the negative features of our tax system is the increasing dependence of the States on the Union Government, for their resource requirements. It has been observed that of all the federations in the world, including USA, Australia, and Canada depend on the Central Government for funds. Indian Federation is the best in the sense that there is clear-cut division of resources between the Centre and the States. But while demarcating these resources, our Constitution makers appeared to have forgotten about the development needs of the States. While the States have to incur increasing amount of expenditure on such items as education, medical and public health, agriculture, industry, etc., they do not have sufficient resources. The elastic sources of revenue, like income tax, custom duty, excise duty, corporation tax, etc. are in the hands of the Centre. Consequently, the States have to look towards the Centre for more and more funds. The Central Government often discriminates one State from the other in the matter of allocating funds.

9. Apathy of the State Government to Exploit Resources: There are some State Governments that do not exploit the tax resources assigned to them in the Constitution. For example, taxes on agricultural income lie in the sphere of State Governments, but they do not levy these taxes because agriculturists constitute the biggest vote bank. During elections many tax concessions are announced by the Government so as to brighten the prospects of winning elections. Thus the State governments too are to be blamed for this failure.

10. Tax Evasion: Because of the structure of our tax system and the shortcomings inherent in it, considerable amount of tax evasion is generated by our tax system. It is almost impossible to ascertain correctly the extent of tax evasion in the country because of numerous difficulties involved in the process. Any such estimate can only be a guess and would involve an element of subjectivity. However, the Wanchoo Committee estimated that the extent of income tax evaded was ₹ 470 crore in sixties. Some conservative estimates show that black money has reached even the level of around 30 per cent of National Income. But after demonetization of currency notes of ₹ 500 and ₹ 1000 denominations a large portion of black money is claimed to have been unearthed. It has either been deposited in the banks or destroyed by those who had stashed it in their homes.

Tax Reforms in India

Taxes are inevitable and also necessary. In a free-market economy, the government has to provide public goods and services that are either too uneconomical to produce by private enterprise, (like health care and education for the under-privileged) or are too important (like defence, law and order, space exploration, etc.). The only way the government can finance the expenditure on these things is through taxes.

As stated above, tax laws in India tend to be complex. Instead of focusing on quietly raising revenue for the government, taxes have become an instrument used by governments for achieving political, socio-economic and even so-called moral goals. That's why we have higher taxes on liquor and cigarettes in India, which is termed as prohibitive taxation. With such a policy, taxation has ended up mis-allocating resources, creating a bloated bureaucracy and undermining the objective of fairness. Another problem is that our tax base in narrow and rates are high. According to World Bank Report on Doing Business in India, 2015, India is placed at a dismal 156 out of 189 countries in terms of ease of paying taxes. Most of tax officials are inclined to harassment rather than facilitation. That's why there has been a crying need of tax reforms in India.

In recent times, the UPA and now the NDA government have tried to implement reforms.

TAXATION POLICY SINCE 1991 AND ECONOMIC REFORMS

There was considerable scaling back in income, excise and trade taxes with the ushering in of economic liberalization and privatization of the 1990s. There were also attempts by the states to bring their sales tax in harmony with the policies made by the Central Government. The value added tax (VAT) was introduced by Dr. Manmohan Singh's government. This was the most important tax reform since the formation of the Indian Republic in January 1950. VAT is a type of general consumption tax which is collected incrementally, based on the surplus value, added to the price on the work at each stage of production, which is usually implemented as a destination-based tax, where the tax rate is based on the location of the customer.

Value-added taxation in India was introduced in India from 1st April 2005, as an indirect tax. The then existing general sales tax laws were replaced with the Value Added Tax Act, and associated VAT rules.

Some states like Gujarat, Tamil Nadu, Rajasthan, Madhya Pradesh, Chhattisgarh, Jharkhand, Uttarakhand, and Uttar Pradesh stayed out of VAT taxation system during the initial period but adopted it later. As of June 2014, VAT was implemented in all the states and union territories of India except Andaman and Nicobar Islands and Lakshadweep Island.

Although VAT was considered as the most desirable consumption tax for India since the early 1990s, some experts were of the opinion that it involved serious problems for the finances of regional governments. They also felt that implementing VAT in India during the current economic reforms would have paradoxical dimensions for Indian federalism. On one hand, economic reforms have led to decentralization of expenditure responsibilities, which, in turn, demands more decentralization of revenue raising power if fiscal accountability is to be maintained. On the other hand, implementing the VAT, to make India a single integrated market, would lead to revenue losses for the states and reduce their autonomy indicating greater centralization.[3]

It has also been pointed out that "political compulsions...led the government to propose an imperfect model of VAT" and it lacked both the removal of distortions in the movement of goods across states and the uniformity in the tax structure. Local or state level taxes like octroi, entry tax, lease tax, workers contract tax, entertainment tax and luxury tax were not integrated into the new regime, which goes against the basic premise of VAT, which is to have uniformity in the tax structure. The fact that no tax credit will be allowed for inter-state trade seriously undermined the basic benefit of enforcing a VAT system, namely the removal of the distortions in movement of goods across the states.[4]

Latest Reforms—Goods and Services Tax (GST)

Goods and Services Tax (GST) is considered a major tax reform policy in India. It was implemented from 1st July 2017. Most of the economists are very positive about it and feel that in time it will improve the tax structure, simplify it and increase the revenue of the State Governments as well as Central Government as this system is broad-based and leaves no scope for businessmen and traders to avoid it.

It has merged various tax stages into one and replaced VAT. Earlier, when a product was manufactured, the centre would levy an excise duty on the manufacture, and then the state will add a VAT tax when the item was sold to the next stage in the cycle. Then there would be a VAT at the next point of sale.

Earlier, in indirect taxes, the tax liability was passed on to someone else. The shopkeeper paid VAT on his sale, and passed on the liability to the customer. So, in effect, the customer paid the price of the item as well as the VAT on it so the shopkeeper could deposit the VAT to the government. This happened because the shopkeeper had paid a tax when he bought the item from the wholesaler. In order to recover that amount, as also to make up for the VAT that he had to pay to the government, he passed the liability to the customer who had to pay the additional amount. There was no other way for the shopkeeper to recover whatever he paid from his own pocket during transactions and therefore, he had to pass on the liability to the customer. GST addresses this problem as it has a system of Input Tax Credit which allows sellers to claim the tax already paid by them, and thus the final liability on the end consumer is decreased. The main features of GST are given below:

1. It has introduced a single taxation system in the entire country for all goods and services, and reduced the number of indirect taxes.
2. It is a transparent tax. A business house can show the tax applied in the sales invoice, and the customer will know exactly how much tax he/she is paying on the product bought or service consumed.
3. It has brought down the cost of doing business as there are no hidden taxes. Exports from India are likely to become more competitive.
4. GST has also helped in the diversification of income sources for Government other than income tax and petroleum tax.
5. Under GST, the tax burden is likely to be divided equally between manufacturing and services. This can be done through lower tax rate by increasing tax base and reducing exemptions.
6. It has benefited people as the prices of many goods and services have come down. This has increased consumption and helped the companies in terms of increase in sales.
7. With the introduction of GST, many multiple taxes like octroi, central sales tax, state sales tax, entry tax, license fees, turnover tax, etc. are no longer present as they have been merged in GST.

8. There are four tax slabs of 5%, 12%, 18% and 28%. Luxury and demerit goods will be taxed at 28% plus cess.
9. Since India has a federal structure of government, it has opted for dual GST – SGST and CGST, administered by State and Centre respectively.
10. All services have been fitted into four different rates, which are 5%, 12%, the standard 18% and the luxury rate of 28%. Travelling on metro, local train, religious travel, Haj yatra will all be exempt from GST. Healthcare and education have been exempted from the service list. Most service structures will remain as they are. This implies that services will become cheaper in some segments.

The following taxes have been bound together by the GST:

Central Excise Duty, Service Tax, Countervailing Duty, Special Countervailing Duty, Value Added Tax (VAT), Central Sales Tax (CST), Octroi, Entertainment Tax, Entry Tax, Purchase Tax, Luxury Tax, Advertisement Taxes, and taxes applicable on lotteries.

Introduction of Goods and Services Tax (GST) is a significant step in the reform of indirect taxation in India. Amalgamating several Central and State taxes into a single tax will mitigate cascading or double taxation and facilitate a common national market. The simplicity of the tax will lead to easier administration and enforcement. From the consumer point of view, the biggest advantage would be in terms of a reduction in the overall tax burden on many type of goods from their previous level, free movement of goods from one state to another without stopping at state borders for hours for payment of state tax or entry tax and reduction in paperwork to a large extent.

Direct Taxes and Indirect Taxes

Direct taxes are taxes that are recovered directly from the taxpayer, not through somebody else. The taxpayer gives tax directly to the government as per his tax liability. Income tax and corporate tax are examples of direct tax. Direct taxes are considered to be progressive because they are based on the ability to pay, and thus they help in reducing income and wealth inequalities.

On the other hand, indirect taxes are collected by the government from an intermediary and are applied on the manufacture or sale of goods and services. Sales tax, value added tax, service tax, excise duty and custom duty, and now Goods and Services Tax, fall under the category of indirect tax.

Indirect taxes are considered regressive because every consumer, whether rich or poor, pays the same tax which is included in the price of the goods and/or services purchased. The indirect taxes hit the poor more than the rich because the poor spend all or major share of their income on consumption. However, in order to protect the low income group, low taxes are levied on items of general consumption, like food items, and high tax is levied on luxury items like cars, ACs, etc. Indirect taxes also serve a social purpose by charging more on prohibitive items like liquor and cigarettes. Indirect taxes are easier to collect with less administrative costs.

Income Tax

The Constitution of India gives power to the Central Government to levy a tax on any income other than agricultural income which is defined in Section 10 (1) of the Income Tax Act, 1961. The Income Tax Law consists of The Income Tax Act, 1961, Income Tax Rules, 1962, Notifications and Circulars issued by Central Board of Direct Taxes (CBDT), Annual Finance Acts and Judicial pronouncements by the Supreme Court and High Courts.

The government imposes tax on taxable income of individuals, Hindu Undivided Families (HUFs), companies, firms, association of persons, body of individuals, local authority and any other artificial judicial person. Levy of tax is different on each person. The Indian Income Tax Department is administered by CBDT which is part of the Department of Revenue under the Ministry of Finance, Govt. of India. Income tax is a key source of funds that the government uses in various projects of development and to serve the public.

The Income Tax Department is the biggest revenue mobilizer for the Government. The total tax revenues of the Central Government increased from ₹ 1,392.26 billion (US$ 22 billion) in 1997-98 to ₹ 5,889.09 billion (US$ 91 billion) in 2007-08. The data regarding total income tax collection, corporate tax collection and other direct tax collection during the financial years 2009-10 to 2015-16 is given in Table 8.1. It shows that income tax collection which was ₹ 132,833 lakh crore in 2009-10, reached ₹ 286,801 lakh crore in 2015-16.

Table 8.1: Direct Tax Collections (in ₹ lakh crore)

Financial Year	Corporate Tax	Income Tax	Other Direct Tax	Total
2009-2010	244725	132833	505	378063
2010-2011	298688	146258	1049	445995
2011-2012	322816	170181	990	493987
2012-2013	356326	201840	823	558989
2013-2014	394678	242888	1030	638596
2014-2015	428925	265772	1095	695792
2015-2016	454419	286801	1075	742295

Source: https://thewire.in/.../new-data-indicates-that-direct-tax-share-in-economy-is-at-decade-

The salient features of Income Tax India are enumerated below:

1. For the assessment year 2016-17, individuals earning an income up to ₹ 2.5 lakh were exempt from Income Tax.
2. Only about 1% of the national population, called the elites or upper class, fall under the 30% slab. The middle class fall under the 5%, 10% and 20% slabs.
3. As per Income Tax Act, 1961, income tax is on income under the following five heads: (i) income from house property, (ii) income from business and profession, (iii) income from salaries, (iv) income in the form of capital gains, and (v) income from other sources.
4. In terms of the Income Tax Act, 1961, a person includes the following (i) individual, or a body of individuals, (ii) Hindu Undivided Family, (HUF), (iii) association of

persons, (iv) company, (v) firm, (vi) local authority, and (vii) artificial judicial person not falling in any of the preceding categories.

5. Income tax rate is prescribed every year by parliament in the Budget. The rate may or may not be changed by the parliament.
6. Indian income tax is progressive, which means that the rate increases as the income of the taxpayer increases. In other words, a higher tax is collected from the taxpayers who earn more and lower taxes from taxpayers earning less. Income tax is divided into slabs. As the income of the taxpayer crosses a benchmark income, a higher tax is charged to him. Progressive tax is based on the premises that those who earn more should contribute more to the development of the nation. They can bear more burden than the people with less income.

Corporate Tax

Also called corporation tax, or company tax, corporate tax is a direct tax imposed on the income or capital of corporations or analogous legal entities. Many countries impose such taxes at the national level, and a similar tax may be imposed at state or local levels. Partnerships are generally not taxed at the entity level. In India, corporate tax may apply to the flowing: (i) corporations incorporated in the country, (ii) corporations doing business in India on income from India, (iii) foreign corporations who have a permanent establishment in India, and (iv) corporations deemed to be resident for tax purposes in India.

The company income subject to tax is determined much like taxable income for individual taxpayers. Generally, the tax is imposed on net profits. The operating earnings are calculated by deducting expenses, including the cost of goods sold, and depreciation from revenues, and then the prevalent rates are applied to meet the legal obligation the business has. Rules surrounding corporate taxation vary greatly around the world and must be voted upon and approved by the government to be enacted.

In some jurisdictions, rules for taxing companies may differ significantly from rules for taxing individuals. Certain corporate acts, like reorganizations, may not be taxed. Some types of entities may also be exempt from tax. Countries may tax corporations on its net profit and may also tax shareholders when the corporation pays a dividend. Where dividends are taxed, a corporation may be required to withhold tax before the dividend is distributed.

In India the companies are allowed to reduce taxable income by certain necessary and ordinary business expenditures. All current expenses required for the operation of the business are fully tax deductible. Investments and real estate purchased for the intent on generating income for the business are also deductible. A body corporate can deduct employee salaries, health benefits, tuition reimbursement and bonuses. In addition, it can reduce its taxable income by insurance premiums, travel expenses, bad debts, interest payments, sales taxes, fuel taxes and excise taxes. Tax preparation fees, legal services, bookkeeping and advertising costs are also used to reduce business income.[5]

Double Taxation

Double taxation refers to the way taxes are imposed on corporate shareholders and on corporations. While the company or corporate is taxed on its earnings, the shareholders are also taxed on the dividends they receive from those earnings. In other words, when corporations pay out dividends to shareholders, those dividend payments incur income-tax liabilities for the shareholders who receive them, even though the earnings that provided the cash to pay the dividends were already taxed at the corporate level.[6]

Another form of double taxation is tax applied to shareholders who are also employees as well as to owners of the corporation. The owner of a body corporate receives salary as an employee, which is taxed at the prevailing income tax rate. In addition, the owner is also a shareholder. If the company pays dividends on the profits of the corporation, the owner must pay the tax on those dividends on his/her personal tax return. Thus, there is a double taxation. It is pertinent to mention here that double taxation exists only in corporates, not on other type of businesses like partnerships, proprietorships, firms, etc. which are "pass through" entities, and in whose case the income of business is passed through the owners who pay taxes by means of their individual income tax returns.

Advantages of Corporate Taxation

Paying corporate taxes is considered beneficial for business owners as compared to paying additional individual income tax, because while arriving at corporate tax liability, medical insurance for families as well as fringe benefits, including retirement plans and tax-deferred trusts are deducted. It is easier for a corporation to deduct losses. A corporation may deduct the entire amount of losses, while a sole proprietor must provide evidence regarding the intent to earn a profit before the losses can be deducted. Moreover, the profit earned by a company may be left within the company which can allow for tax planning and potential tax advantages in future.

Expenditure Tax

In a developing economy a direct tax on the basis of aggregate consumption or aggregate expenditure is often recommended in order to promote savings in the economy.

The early advocates of expenditure tax, like J.S. Mill, based their case on the 'double taxation' of savings involved in the levy of income tax. On equity grounds too, the expenditure tax was preferred because the principle of taxing income confers differential benefit on property owners as against those who derive their income from personal labour and who cannot treat the whole of their income as 'spendable' as the capitalists can. Moreover, since taxable income from property can be converted into capital gains in numerous ways, income was considered a defective measure of taxable capacity as it could be manipulated by taxpayers.

Professor Nicholas Kaldor, who vehemently argued in favour of substituting income tax by expenditure tax, favoured it in the context of Keynesian framework also. To him the expenditure tax provides a more efficient instrument for controlling the economy in the interests of economic stability and progress than taxes levied on income. However, this line of thinking has only a limited validity in relation to the developing countries like India because economic fluctuations in these countries occur at relatively lower level of output.

The proposal to adopt expenditure tax in India was first made by Professor Kaldor in the mix-1950s when he was invited to suggest some reforms in the Indian tax structure. It was almost at the same time (1955) that he published his book entitled *An Expenditure Tax*. His mind was naturally preoccupied with finding a suitable economic environment in which he could test his ideas. Consequently, expenditure tax came to be levied in India in 1957 only to be abolished in 1962. It was reintroduced in 1964 and abolished again in 1966.

It will not be out of place to mention here that in the context of British economy, Kaldor himself was fully aware of the difficulties inherent in the replacement of personal income tax by expenditure tax. He, therefore, suggested the substitution of expenditure tax in place of surtax—a tax on exceptionally higher incomes. However, surtax was merged with the general income tax with effect from 1970. Thus, it appears that the record of expenditure tax is not very encouraging. As at present, there is only one country in the world (Sri Lanka) that levies a personal expenditure tax. In many developing as well as developed countries, Kaldor's work received more attention for its careful analysis of concepts of income than for its arguments in favour of tax on expenditure. In India also, although his personal view for levying an expenditure tax was considered administratively complex, yet the income tax base has been sufficiently widened to include gifts, capital gains, notional income from owner-occupied houses, etc. This has made replacement of personal income tax by expenditure tax almost redundant.

It may be stated that the replacement of income tax base by expenditure base has two constituents: (i) personal income tax, and (ii) corporate tax. As regards replacement of personal income tax, the main task is to make a choice between the two forms of tax so as to step up the rate of savings in the economy. As things are now, there does not appear to be much scope for increasing the aggregate rate of savings. Personal income tax is already sufficiently conducive to savings. Currently, the rate of savings of the upper income groups in the non-corporate sector is quite high. This has been brought about either by direct concessions on current savings or indirect concessions on interest, income and wealth. There are already loud protests that such concessions are promoting inequalities as they act as stimulant for accumulation of wealth by the richer classes who have a higher propensity to save. Thus, total exemption of all savings from income tax would clearly be inequitable.

It may be mentioned here that expenditure tax was suggested for India when there was no tax on capital gains, and when notional income from self-occupied property was excluded from personal taxation. Presently, we include not only such gains but also casual earnings like lottery wins within the net of income tax. As such, the need for expenditure tax is less than obvious.

Administratively also, the expenditure tax is too complex to be handled by the country's tax administration and revenue intelligence system. At present, 80 to 90 per cent of income tax revenue is collected by way of advance tax or deduction of tax at source, i.e. on the principle of PAYE (pay as you earn). How will the expenditure tax handle this aspect? For proper administration of expenditure tax, we would need additional data on stocks, opening balances of all types of assets, including borrowing, lending, bank accounts, etc. This would create additional problems of an unknown magnitude. Further, expenditure needs of different families are different, depending upon such factors as the number of dependents, the number of aged and chronically sick persons, etc. To tackle this issue, Kaldor proposed that the tax administration should work out the aggregate family expenditure on per capita basis to be used as some sort of index. The crux of the problem here is, would it not add to the burden of tax administration and make the tax structure still more cumbersome? We had earlier dispensed with such concessions in the 1970s so as to make our tax structure less complicated.

The second constituent in the scheme of replacing income tax by expenditure tax is the corporate tax. It is here that there appears to be some scope for experiment. It is an open secret that the corporate sector of the economy tends to inflate its expenditure in order to reduce the level of corporate as well as personal income. Many perquisites, which do not fall within the purview of their salary, are given to the directors and other executives in order to reduce the level of corporate profits. Oftentimes, even family expenditure on conveyance and entertainment is debited to the firm. Thus, expenditure tax on firms—it would be better to call it cost-based tax—may be worth trying. But even here a number of safeguards have to be provided for. In a labour surplus economy, it is just possible that the firms may reduce the use of labour in order to reduce their aggregate cost. Further, industries like mining where labour input is exceptionally high would be discriminated against capital-intensive low-cost industries. Therefore, different yardsticks will have to be applied to arrive at the aggregate taxable expenditure of different firms. Anyway, the problem of reforming corporate tax is a different one and should not be mixed up with that of personal income tax.

The main conclusion that follows is that there is hardly an effective substitute for personal income tax. The objectives which we want to realize through expenditure tax in an indirect manner can be directly achieved through the existing income tax structure. It is only in the case of corporate tax that there is some scope for replacing it with the expenditure tax. The problem is one of reforming the corporate tax and not of levying expenditure tax in lieu of tax on income for all categories of taxpayers.

The Expenditure Tax Act, 1987 governs all taxation-related processes associated with the chargeable expenditure that an individual incurs in certain hotels or restaurants. This act provides that for tax expenditure to be charged, the following two criteria need to be are fulfilled: (i) the charges are incurred in a hotel where the room rent is ₹ 3,000 (per day), or more; and (ii) the charges are incurred in a restaurant. In case of room rent charges in hotels, the Assessing Officer of the Income Tax Department has been given the power to deem whether the breakup of charges has been stated in the correct manner.

Other respective charges such as those for food, drinks, and other services cannot be used to cover up the actual charge of the room rental, etc. If there are discrepancies in this regard, the

Assessing Officer will decide what amounts need to be charged under the various headings in the itemized breakup of the bill.

Under the Expenditure Tax Act, 1961, chargeable expenditure denotes any payment made to (or expenditure incurred in) the hotel which is connected to the provision of accommodation (residential, or otherwise), and accommodation in the hotel on hire or lease.

Chargeable expenditure does not include payments made in any shop/office which is not owned or managed by the person who carries on the business of a hotel; expenditures incurred by way of taxation under any act, including this one; and any expenditure incurred in Indian currency that was acquired on the conversion of foreign exchange into Indian currency.

Expenditure tax is collected from the person running the business (hotel and/or restaurant) as the case may be, when he or she provides the services that result in chargeable expenditure.

Taxation of Agriculture

India ranks second in the world in farm output. As of 2013, agriculture and allied sectors like forestry and fisheries accounted for 13.7% of the GDP and engaged about 50% of the workforce. Although the economic contribution of agriculture to India's GDP is steadily declining because the country's economic growth has become broad-based, yet agriculture is the broadest economic sector demographically, and plays a key role in the overall socio-economic fabric of India. According to *CIA Factbook*, sectorwise Indian GDP composition in 2014 was as follows: Agriculture (17.9%), Industry (24.2%) and Services (57.9%).

According to Ministry of Statistics and Programme Implementation, the contribution of agriculture sector in Indian economy is much higher than world's average (6.1%). Contribution of Industry and Services sector is lower than world's average 30.5% for Industry sector and 63.5% for Services sector.

The mobilization of resources from agriculture has come to occupy a place of central importance in the current theory of economic development. In most of the countries the channeling of resources from agriculture has been considered responsible for their take-off. The examples of Japan since 1868, USSR since 1917 and China since 1948 have proved how agriculture plays a dynamic role in the economic development.

Japan was the first Asian country, which despite its traditional form of agriculture, primitive methods of cultivation and very small size of landholdings, succeeded in bringing a striking phase of agricultural development with the help of revenue derived from agricultural taxation. In Japan, land tax siphoned off much of the surplus generated within agriculture and was the principle source of revenue for the government. Resources extracted by the government by way of land taxes were applied to economic development including the provision for service to the agricultural sector.

In Japan a substantial increase in agricultural production was attained by the adoption of increased irrigation facilities, improved seeds, advanced knowledge, etc. Thus, the dynamic nature of the Japanese society and greater efforts taken to enhance the agricultural production yielded quick results. It was all due to this that the required surpluses from the agricultural sector were siphoned off in an indirect way by the imposition of heavy land tax which amounted to 63.7 per cent of the aggregate tax yield in 1868, 93.2 per cent in 1873 and 83.2 per cent in 1877.

In the erstwhile USSR, inadequate agricultural production was a major impediment in the process of industrialization. But the enforcement of collectivization largely changed the picture. The basic reasons for the introduction of collectivization were political rather than economic. As far as political reasons were concerned, the Soviet Government wanted to set up a socialist society by nationalizing all lands. Insofar as economic reasons were concerned, the transition of the Soviet village to large agricultural farms meant a great revolution in economic relations in the whole way of life of the peasantry. Collectivization put an end for ever to the exploitation of the peasants by large farmers (Kulaks). Also all the advantages of large scale farming could be reaped by the introduction of collective farms, which were required to hand over a significant proposition of their produce to the government at a price which was much below the market price.

Similarly the rate of capital formation in China was closely related to the extent of tax, primarily in the form of tax in kind, imposed on the peasants. In addition to the taxes payable in kind, the peasants were bound to sell a large quantity of cereals and certain other agricultural goods to the State. This was a form of disguised taxation.

Thus, for promoting economic development in less developed countries, heavier taxation of agriculture is generally recommended. Some studies have used the argument of existence of inter-sectoral inequality as the basis for building a case for additional taxation on Indian agriculture. As Ved P. Gandhi puts it, "There is inter-sectoral inequality in India in favour of the agricultural sector, which must be corrected on grounds of equity between sectors either by additional taxes, on the agricultural sector or by reducing the taxes levied on the non-agricultural sector."

In India, land revenue is the major source of agricultural taxation, though a few States also levy a tax on agricultural income. Land revenue is assessed at a flat rate, i.e., the rate of tax does not vary with the area of land or income therefrom. The levy varies with grades of land, as it is related to net produce. But this is not satisfactory as land of equal fertility can be used to raise different crops. The result is that the burden of land revenue could be comparatively heavy in cereal growing tracts than on land where commercial crops are grown. Further, the burden of land revenue was comparatively low in the permanently settled areas as the State demand had remained fixed. This led to inequity between permanent and temporary settled areas. In brief, the system of land taxation in India is not based upon any satisfactory criterion of ability.

The Taxation Enquiry Commission (1953-54) suggested the following steps to improve the system of land revenue:

1. Disparities in the rates of land revenue in different States should be removed and a uniform rate be adopted as a standard method for cultivation in each State.
2. Rate of land revenue should be revised at an interval of time (say 10 years) and the revision should be based on the price-index of agricultural produce.

3. Rates may be revised any time if a situation of exemption occurs.
4. Local bodies such as panchayats and district boards should be authorized to levy surcharges to meet the local financial needs.
5. Fifteen per cent of land revenue collected from each local area should be given to the local bodies of the area.

In 1972, Government of India appointed a committee under the chairmanship of Professor K.N. Raj (commonly known as the Committee on Taxation of Agricultural Wealth and Income), to investigate the question of agricultural wealth and income taxes from all angles.

The main recommendation of the Raj's Committee which received widespread attention was the replacement of land revenue by Agricultural Holding Tax (AHT).

The AHT was to be imposed on the rateable value of land, which was to be determined not on the assessor's actual income, but on what he ought to earn from this operational holding, i.e. on the basis of productivity of land. For the determination of AHT land has to be divided into homogeneous regions according to soil and climate conditions. Norms of output per acre (i.e. productivity norm) are to be determined for each year for each such region or district on the basis of actual yields, for the previous 10 years. The value of the output so estimated has to be multiplied by the average harvest prices of the preceding three years. This amount has to be used to calculate the rateable value for the purpose of calculating the AHT. The figure has to be revised every year to account for the changing developments. Further, in order to find out the rateable value for the purpose of tax calculation, costs of cultivation are to be deducted from the gross value of output. On this reduced gross value, a further rebate of 20 per cent, subject to a maximum of ₹ 1000, is to be allowed to account for the vagaries of nature, i.e. failure of monsoons. There was a further provision that if the total yield during any year is half of the average yield during the previous 10 years, then the rateable value should be treated as zero or non-taxable.

Agricultural Income Tax

The income earned from agricultural land is exempt in India from taxes under Section 10(1) of the Income Tax Act 1961. Agricultural income is computed in the same manner as business income.

If someone suffers losses in agriculture, these losses can be set off against the agricultural profits for the next 8 years.

If the income you earn is only from agriculture then it is fully tax exempt. For example, if you earn 4 lakhs per annum the income you earn is fully tax exempt under agriculture, there is no need to file Income Tax return.

If you have agricultural income along with other sources of income you would have to pay income tax on these other sources of income.

Niti Aayog, a Government of India policy think-tank established by the Narendra Modi Government in January 2015, to replace the Planning Commission which followed the top-down model, has strongly backed taxing agricultural income above a certain threshold and removal of exemptions on personal income tax as part of a strategy to expand the tax base and prevent evasion. According to the Aayog, the blanket relief on agricultural income was aimed at protecting farmers, but it is being misused by many non-farmers who declare agriculture as their source of income to evade tax.[7]

One member of the Aayog suggested that instead of using agriculture income for one particular year, we should average it over a three-year period or maybe over a five-year period as agriculture income is subject to annual fluctuations; barring that threshold should be the same.

Taxing agriculture has been a controversial issue in our country and the recommendations by the *Economic Survey* a few years ago met with stiff opposition, and there was widespread criticism of the recommendations from various quarters. Finance Minister Arun Jaitley stated that government has no plan to tax agricultural income. But this too has been criticized by some economists as it showed that the government is ignoring the linkages between the agriculture and non-agriculture sectors which, among other things, allows for tax evasion. They feel that India's policymakers need to treat agriculture on par with other sectors, which means not just taxation but also removing multiple regulatory obstacles which limit opportunities for farmers.[8]

Any serious campaign to widen the tax base and curb black money should address what income tax department reports have shown: agricultural income is used as a conduit to avoid tax. A tax on agricultural income will bypass most of India's 90 million agricultural households as their average income is way below the threshold income. One way to proceed could be to act on a proposal of the last tax administration reforms committee, which suggested a high threshold of ₹ 50 lakh annually. To facilitate this move, state governments will have to be enlisted to follow the relevant constitutional procedure. This should be feasible with BJP in power in almost half of India's states.

A move to tax agriculture income should be packaged with steps to help farmers. For instance, sudden export bans on a commodity when international prices are soaring amounts to imposing a cap on farmer incomes. In the same vein, restrictions on movement within India distort agricultural trade. Agricultural products too need a common market and farmers should be freed of shackles which tie them to designated wholesalers. The NDA Government must use its political mandate to fundamentally transform agriculture.

As things stand today it is unlikely that the government will bring any legislation to tax agricultural income. There are many reasons for that. Firstly, most of our farmers are poor. If the government puts agricultural income above a certain threshold, under tax net, not many farmers will be required to pay tax, and the amount of revenue going to the government will not be much. Secondly, income from agriculture is not stable. There will be years when farmers earn no income and are barely able to subsist. So it will be unfair to tax farmers when their income is high and leave them to fend for themselves when they grapple with tough farming conditions like poor monsoon, drought, flood, or crop failure due to some other reasons. Thirdly, there is no foolproof method of assessing actual income from farming. If left to the farmers to show their income, tax evasion will continue as before. Fourthly, since as a sector, agriculture has not done well for several years now, farmers need support in the form of income-tax exemption. Fifthly, since farmers form a large vote bank, government can ill afford to tax agriculturists. Many economists feel that it is time for the government to rise above political considerations and see what is best for the economy of the country. Since Modi has taken many bold decisions, it is expected that his government will do something to tax agriculturists whose income is high and take other measures to stop tax evasion where people show their other income as agricultural income.

REVENUES OF THE CENTRAL GOVERNMENT

Tax and Non-Tax Revenue Receipts

Revenue is any income that does not generate a liability. Therefore any borrowing from any source is not a revenue as it creates the liability to repay. On the other hand, if an institution gets a money as grant or donation, it is a revenue as it is not to be repaid.

Taxes are the most important revenues of the governments. Revenue receipts are of two types, tax revenues and non-tax revenues. Tax revenues are either from direct taxes or indirect taxes. Direct taxes are taxes paid directly to the government by the persons on whom it is imposed. Income Tax, Gift Tax, Wealth Tax and Property Tax, etc. are direct taxes. Indirect taxes are taxes collected by an intermediary (like retail store) from the person who bears the ultimate economic burden of the tax (such as a consumer). Sales tax, Value Added Tax (VAT), Goods and Services Tax (GST) are examples of indirect texts. The revenues of the Central Government include the following:

Taxes on income other than agricultural income (List I, Union List, Entry 82).

Duties of customs including export duties (List I, Union List, Entry 83).

Excise duties on tobacco and other goods manufactured or produced in India except (i) alcoholic liquor for human consumption, and (ii) opium, Indian hemp and other narcotic drugs and narcotics, but including medicinal and toilet preparations containing alcohol or any substance included in (ii). (List I, Union List, Entry 84).

Corporation Tax (List I, Union List, Entry 85).

Taxes on capital value of assets, exclusive of agricultural land, of individuals and companies, taxes on capital of companies (List I, Union List, Entry 86).

Estate duty in respect of property other than agricultural land (List I, Union List, Entry 87).

Duties in respect of succession to property other than agricultural land (List I, Union List, Entry 88).

Terminal taxes on goods or passengers, carried by railway, sea or air; taxes on railway fares and freight (List I, Union List, Entry 89).

Taxes other than stamp duties on transactions in stock exchanges and futures market.

Taxes on sales or purchase of newspaper and advertisement therein.

Taxes on sale or purchase of goods other than newspapers, where such sale or purchase takes place in the course of inter-State trade or commerce.

Taxes on the consignment of goods in the course of inter-State trade or commerce.

All residuary types of taxes not listed in any of the three lists of Seventh Schedule of Indian Constitution.

At present, the largest amount of tax revenues of Central Government comes from Corporate Tax, followed by Income Tax, then Union Excise Duties, Customs and then Service Tax. The collection of service taxes has increased over the last few years.

The major components of receipts of the Central Government are given in Table 8.2.

Non Tax Revenue

Non-tax revenue includes those revenue receipts which are not generated by taxing the public. These include the following: (i) money which the government earns as dividends and profits from its profit-making public enterprises (PSUs), (ii) interest,

Table 8.2: Central Government Receipts—Major Components

(₹ Billion)

Year	Tax revenue	Direct tax	of which		Indirect tax	of which		Non-tax revenue	of which	Revenue receipts (2+9)	Capital receipts	Total receipts (11+12)
			Personal income tax	Corporation tax		Excise duties	Customs duties		Interest receipts			
1	2	3	4	5	6	7	8	9	10	11	12	13
1972-73	34.43	7.52	1.37	5.58	26.91	17.57	8.57	10.80	7.13	45.23	24.64	69.87
1973-74	39.00	8.48	2.13	5.83	30.52	19.71	9.96	11.14	7.36	50.14	28.76	78.90
1974-75	50.97	11.42	3.62	7.09	39.56	25.28	13.33	13.45	7.76	64.42	27.74	92.16
1975-76	60.10	14.80	4.80	8.62	45.30	29.88	14.19	18.54	9.34	78.64	41.49	120.13
1976-77	65.81	16.86	5.42	9.84	48.95	31.93	15.54	19.87	11.05	85.68	49.58	135.26
1977-78	70.60	17.42	3.27	12.21	53.19	33.35	18.24	24.78	14.41	95.38	50.35	145.73
1978-79	85.68	18.42	4.71	12.56	67.26	41.28	24.24	24.06	14.27	109.74	62.85	172.59
1979-80	85.67	19.50	4.75	13.92	66.17	34.81	29.24	25.42	13.60	111.09	54.20	165.29
1980-81	93.58	18.93	4.38	13.11	74.65	37.23	34.09	30.15	17.95	123.73	79.18	202.91
1981-82	115.42	25.18	4.59	19.70	90.24	41.81	43.00	34.82	22.15	150.24	88.49	238.73
1982-83	130.17	27.23	4.38	21.85	102.94	45.67	51.19	44.17	28.52	174.34	117.01	291.35
1983-84	154.41	31.31	5.27	24.93	123.10	61.65	55.83	42.70	26.68	197.11	144.06	341.17
1984-85	176.51	33.75	6.97	25.56	142.76	66.25	70.41	58.15	39.63	234.66	164.21	398.87
1985-86	211.40	36.98	6.65	28.65	174.42	73.31	95.26	68.95	45.95	280.35	193.15	473.50
1986-87	243.19	40.23	7.19	31.60	202.96	81.64	114.75	87.64	53.53	330.83	215.72	546.55

Year	Tax revenue	Direct tax	of which		Indirect tax	of which		Non-tax revenue	of which	Revenue receipts (2+9)	Capital receipts	Total receipts (11+12)
			Personal income tax	Corporation tax		Excise duties	Customs duties		Interest receipts			
1987-88	280.15	41.00	6.03	34.33	239.15	94.23	137.02	90.22	57.55	370.37	254.08	624.45
1988-89	337.51	60.21	14.92	44.07	277.30	109.22	158.05	98.40	69.81	435.91	298.78	734.69
1989-90	383.49	60.28	10.88	47.29	323.21	130.96	180.36	139.47	84.74	522.96	300.20	823.16
1990-91	429.78	69.03	12.50	53.35	360.75	141.00	206.44	119.76	87.30	549.54	389.97	939.51
1991-92	500.69	101.03	16.27	78.53	399.66	160.17	222.57	159.61	109.33	660.30	385.28	1045.58
1992-93	540.44	120.75	18.31	88.99	419.69	163.67	237 76	200.84	124.87	741.28	361.78	1103.06
1993-94	534.49	125.22	13.55	100.60	409.27	172.24	221.93	220.04	150.78	754.53	554.40	1308.93
1994-95	674.54	184.09	34.68	138.22	490.45	210.64	267.89	236.29	157.97	910.83	686.95	1597.78
1995-96	819.39	222.87	43.18	164.87	596.52	221.76	357.57	281.91	184.19	1101.30	583.38	1684.68
1996-97	937.01	253.74	47.15	185.67	683.26	234.63	428.51	325.78	221.06	1262.79	615.44	1878.23
1997-98	956.72	271.72	35.89	200.16	685.00	255.16	401.93	382.14	253.23	1338.86	990.77	2329.63
1998-99	1046.52	321.20	57.60	245.29	725.32	285.81	406.68	448.33	300.76	1494.85	1300.64	2795.49
1999-00	1282.71	414.36	91.31	306.92	868.36	349.44	484.19	532.11	338.95	1814.82	1157.07	2971.89
2000-01	1366.58	496.51	237.66	251.77	870.07	497.58	341.63	559.47	328.11	1926.05	1341.84	3267.89
2001-02	1335.32	477.03	221.06	251.33	858.28	544.69	283.40	677.74	355.38	2013.06	1625.00	3638.06
2002-03	1585.44	616.12	277.79	338.93	969.32	623.88	313.98	722.90	376.22	2308.34	1805.31	4113.65
2003-04	1869.82	765.90	307.65	457.06	1103.92	702.45	345.86	768.31	385.38	2638.13	2113.33	4751.46
2004-05	2247.98	959.44	354.43	602.89	1288.54	772.41	418.11	811.93	323.87	3059.91	2003.91	5063.82

Year	Tax revenue	Direct tax	of which		Indirect tax	of which		Non-tax revenue	of which	Revenue receipts (2+9)	Capital receipts	Total receipts (11+12)
			Personal income tax	Corporation tax		Excise duties	Customs duties		Interest receipts			
2005-06	2702.64	1206.92	452.38	751.87	1495.72	866.42	466.45	768.13	220.32	3470.77	1795.49	5266.26
2006-07	3511.82	1697.38	627.07	1067.01	1814.44	926.51	628.19	832.05	225.24	4343.87	1444.82	5788.69
2007-08	4395.47	2315.74	865.63	1446.60	2079.72	961.78	753.82	1023.17	210.60	5418.64	1979.78	7398.42
2008-09	4433.19	2481.52	869.85	1607.97	1951.69	818.72	692.17	969.40	207.17	5402.59	2998.63	8401.22
2009-10	4565.36	2716.23	945.32	1767.97	1849.13	843.83	602.23	1162.75	217.84	5728.11	4530.63	10258.74
2010-11	5698.68	3135.01	1024.41	2091.15	2563.67	1102.22	975.98	2186.02	197.34	7884.71	4024.28	11908.99
2011-12	6297.64	3433.10	1182.24	2274.11	2864.54	1162.26	1056.14	1216.72	202.52	7514.37	5689.18	13203.55
2012-13	7418.77	3965.85	1404.38	2555.70	3452.92	1412.45	1158.90	1373.54	207.61	8792.32	5821.52	14613.83
2013-14	8158.54	4558.29	1694.08	2857.42	3600.25	1379.75	1210.59	1988.70	218.68	10147.24	5638.94	15786.18
2014-15	9036.15	5005.31	1883.36	3114.53	4030.85	1537.09	1279.94	1977.66	237.34	11013.81	4844.48	15858.29
2015-16	9475.08	4701.46	1818.35	2883.05	4773.63	2190.00	1274.82	2585.76	231.42	12060.84	6013.92	18074.75
2016-17	10541.01	5284.18	2140.33	3143.80	5256.83	2471.42	1405.39	3229.21	296.20	13770.22	5878.43	19648.65

Source: RBI Handbook of Statistics on Indian Economy

Notes: 1. Data for 2015-16 are Revised Estimates and Data for 2016-17 are Budget Estimates.

2. All the tax revenues in this table are net of State Government's share and amount assigned to National Calamity Contingency Fund (NCCF).

3. Capital Receipts for 2002-03, 2003-04 and 2004-05 include receipts under the State Debt Swap Scheme.

4. Capital Receipts and Total Receipts of 2007 include an amount of `343.09 billion which represents the Reserve Bank's surplus transferred to the Central Government on account of transfer of its stake in SBI to the Central Government.

5. Capital Receipts and total receipts exclude Draw-Down of Cash balances.

which the government earns on the money lent by it to external or internal borrowers; the money which the government receives out of its fiscal services such as stamp printing, currency printing, medal printing, etc., and (iii) money which the Government earns from its general services like power distribution, irrigation, banking services, insurance, and community services, etc. which form part of the government business; money, which accrues to the government as fees, fines, penalties, etc., (iv) grants the government receives from the external sources.[9]

Revenues of the State Government in India

Taxes the items contained in the State List of the seventh Schedule of the Constitution. These include the following:

Land revenue, including the assessment and collection of revenue, the maintenance of land records, survey for revenue purposes and records of rights, and alienation of revenues (List II, Entry 45).

Taxes on agricultural income (List II, Entry 46).

Duties in respect of succession to agricultural land (List II, Entry 47).

Estate duty in respect of agricultural land (List II, Entry 48).

Taxes on land and buildings (List II, Entry 49).

Taxes on mineral rights (List II, Entry 50).

Excise duties for following goods manufactured or produced within the State (i) alcoholic liquors for human consumption, and (ii) opium, Indian hemp and other narcotic drugs and narcotics (List II, Entry 51).

Taxes on entry of goods into a local area for consumption, use or sale therein (List II, Entry 52).

Taxes on the consumption or sale of electricity (List II, 53).

Taxes on the sale or purchase of goods other than newspapers (List II, Entry 54).

Taxes on advertisements other than advertisements published in newspapers and advertisements broadcast by radio or television (List II, Entry 55).

Taxes on goods and passengers carried by roads or on inland waterways (List II, Entry 56).

Taxes on vehicles suitable for use on roads (List II, Entry 57).

Taxes on animals and boats (List II, Entry 58).

Toll taxes (List II, 59).

Taxes on profession, trades, callings and employments (List II, Entry 60).

Capitation taxes (List II, Entry 61).

Taxes on luxuries, including taxes on entertainments, amusements, betting and gambling (List II, Entry 62).

Stamp duty (List II, Entry 63).[10]

It can be seen from Table 8.3 that the total revenue receipts were just ₹ 99.31 billion during 1977-78, of which tax receipts were ₹ 61.55 billion and non-tax receipts ₹ 37.76 billion. Total revenue receipts reached ₹ 20,118.90 during 2015-16, of which tax receipts were ₹ 14,177.30 billion and non-tax receipts were ₹ 5941.59 billion. This shows the expansion of tax base of states in India. Grants from the centre which were just ₹ 18.38 billion in 1977-78 increased to ₹ 4072.84 billion in 2015-16. The central government gives grants to the states to fund their projects of development, meet emergencies like floods, etc. Some states are given more grants than the others so that regional disparities are bridged. Some grants are based on revenue sharing policy, while others are circumstantial or need-based.

Service Tax

Service tax is levied by Central Government on services that are provided or are agreed to be provided. It does not include services covered under negative list and is governed by the Place of Provision of Services Rules, 2012. It is collected as per Point of Taxation Rules, 2011 from the person liable to pay it. According to Service Tax Rules, 1994, the person liable may be a service provider or service receiver or any other person made so liable. The service provider collects the tax on services from service receiver and pays the same to government of India. It is thus an indirect tax. At present some services are exempt from tax as per Mega Exemption Notification 25/2012-ST, as

Table 8.3: Pattern of Receipts of the State Governments

(₹ Billion)

Year	Total Revenue Receipts	Tax Receipts	of which		Share in Central Taxes	of which		Non-tax Receipts	of which		Total Capital Receipts	Total Receipts (2+12)
			Sales Tax	State Excise Duties		Income Tax	Union Excise Duties		Interest Receipts	Grants from the Centre		
1	2	3	4	5	6	7	8	9	10	11	12	13
1977-78	99.31	61.55	24.14	5.70	18.06	6.76	11.20	37.76	4.90	18.38	31.00	130.31
1978-79	116.47	69.23	27.73	5.83	19.53	7.00	12.42	47.24	6.21	24.73	50.52	166.99
1979-80	136.29	90.77	32.11	6.98	34.08	8.63	25.34	45.52	6.97	20.83	41.05	177.34
1980-81	162.94	104.05	38.88	8.24	37.89	10.03	27.74	58.88	8.24	26.23	54.73	217.67
1981-82	184.55	124.94	48.93	11.15	42.60	10.22	32.20	59.61	8.17	27.26	56.95	241.50
1982-83	211.25	141.19	54.96	13.43	46.33	11.32	34.85	70.07	9.92	33.82	67.96	279.21
1983-84	240.14	157.61	62.61	15.69	50.08	11.70	38.23	82.53	11.71	40.93	89.66	329.80
1984-85	274.25	181.14	70.60	18.39	58.55	12.67	45.70	93.11	12.66	47.62	109.93	384.18
1985-86	334.24	218.11	84.29	20.52	72.60	17.64	54.78	116.13	13.65	63.23	131.31	465.55
1986-87	382.26	250.96	96.40	24.21	83.84	21.69	62.05	131.31	16.88	69.85	128.92	511.18
1987-88	440.00	289.82	111.85	28.67	96.60	25.20	71.33	150.19	19.47	82.75	158.06	598.06
1988-89	504.21	331.37	131.22	30.81	107.36	27.76	79.60	172.84	23.87	96.60	170.37	674.58
1989-90	565.35	390.93	150.60	38.64	130.97	39.38	91.59	174.42	26.34	85.05	200.86	766.21
1990-91	664.67	445.86	176.67	47.95	142.42	39.89	102.53	218.81	24.03	126.43	246.93	911.60

Year	Total Revenue Receipts	Tax Receipts	of which		Share in Central Taxes	of which		Non-tax Receipts	of which		Total Capital Receipts	Total Receipts (2+12)
			Sales Tax	State Excise Duties		Income Tax	Union Excise Duties		Interest Receipts	Grants from the Centre		
1991-92	805.36	526.04	210.64	54.39	168.48	49.85	118.63	279.32	53.20	152.26	272.38	1077.73
1992-93	910.90	604.48	233.49	62.65	205.80	61.82	143.98	306.43	39.38	177.59	300.73	1211.63
1993-94	1049.97	682.69	272.27	70.09	223.95	78.28	145.67	367.28	47.21	211.76	284.89	1334.86
1994-95	1203.03	788.32	318.83	74.39	248.85	85.65	163.20	414.72	53.45	199.11	431.90	1634.93
1995-96	1345.07	908.02	367.04	81.80	290.48	112.04	178.43	437.05	57.86	208.74	428.05	1773.12
1996-97	1500.41	1036.04	421.12	83.58	350.38	134.89	215.49	464.36	81.66	229.49	420.11	1920.51
1997-98	1668.20	1186.99	468.13	107.56	404.11	181.71	222.40	481.21	77.77	238.53	589.07	2257.27
1998-99	1727.87	1253.28	510.03	128.61	394.21	153.33	240.86	474.60	73.39	234.80	853.63	2581.51
1999-00	2029.27	1432.72	599.55	144.66	441.21	182.19	259.02	596.55	89.93	301.77	1019.25	3048.52
2000-01	2325.09	1643.14	699.76	154.79	507.34	–	–	681.95	109.61	372.89	1097.05	3422.14
2001-02	2494.22	1754.15	731.81	165.04	522.15	–	–	740.07	84.15	426.02	1157.14	3651.36
2002-03	2736.74	1934.74	821.55	182.68	566.55	–	–	802.00	87.61	451.70	1408.66	4145.39
2003-04	3091.87	2211.17	931.72	189.28	670.80	–	–	880.74	77.48	508.36	2056.41	5148.28
2004-05	3635.12	2605.77	1115.54	210.96	785.50	–	–	1029.35	86.48	563.22	2001.48	5636.60
2005-06	4310.21	3063.32	1287.69	250.36	940.24	–	–	1246.90	93.80	767.50	1646.07	5956.28
2006-07	5305.56	3728.41	1535.73	293.16	1202.93	224.77	261.82	1577.14	118.25	944.51	1430.49	6736.05
2007-08	6237.48	4379.48	1734.22	341.27	1514.02	317.96	287.51	1857.99	126.37	1086.22	1419.87	7657.35

Year	Total Revenue Receipts	Tax Receipts	of which		Share in Central Taxes	of which		Non-tax Receipts	of which		Total Capital Receipts	Total Receipts (2+12)
			Sales Tax	State Excise Duties		Income Tax	Union Excise Duties		Interest Receipts	Grants from the Centre		
2008-09	6946.57	4829.83	1983.27	409.90	1610.52	327.77	286.41	2116.75	163.56	1299.23	1966.34	8912.92
2009-10	7681.36	5280.75	2206.44	483.75	1650.14	372.74	203.01	2400.62	152.94	1509.72	2394.97	10076.33
2010-11	9353.47	6801.98	2788.38	591.69	2194.89	447.09	305.46	2551.49	156.25	1634.97	2382.28	11735.75
2011-12	10985.31	8129.87	3450.63	717.82	2555.92	511.96	287.26	2855.44	185.82	1864.17	2693.85	13679.17
2012-13	12520.24	9460.81	4038.49	826.25	2915.30	628.40	330.00	3059.43	241.18	1886.82	3053.14	15573.38
2013-14	13691.87	10306.92	4539.38	813.82	3182.73	706.51	367.64	3384.95	272.15	2059.52	3188.60	16880.47
2014-15	18058.26	11830.86	5218.53	941.60	3662.16	842.33	379.35	6227.40	243.43	4617.50	4056.37	22114.63
2015-16	20118.90	14177.30	5943.32	1092.62	4855.19	1128.77	507.49	5941.59	190.39	4072.84	4383.34	24502.24

Source: RBI Handbook of Statistics on Indian Economy.

Notes: 1. Data for 2014-15 relate to Revised Estimates while 2015-16 are Budget Estimates.

2. Data relate to 29 State Governments.

3. Data for capital receipts prior to 1991-92 are adjusted for remittances (net).

4. Regarding share in Central tax revenue, see Notes on Tables.

5. Capital receipts include Public Accounts on a net basis.

Also see Notes on Tables.

amended up-to date. In case of some services, service tax is charged at abated rate as per Notification No. 26/2012-ST as amended up-to-date. As of 1st June 2016, service tax rate has been consolidated at 14% + 0.5% + 0.5 % = 15% of value of services provided or to be provided. It is now consolidated rate as education cess and secondary higher education cess are subsumed with 2% of "Swachh Bharat Cess (0.50%)" has been notified by the Government.

The service tax is important for accelerating the growth process in the economy as it helps agriculture and industry. Services constitute a very heterogeneous spectrum of economic activities. Today services cover wide range of activities such as management, banking, insurance, hospitality, administration, communication, entertainment, wholesale distribution, and retailing, including R&D (Research and Development) activities. Service sector is now occupying an important stage of the economy so much so that in the contemporary world, development of service sector has become synonymous with the advancement of the economy.

Broadly defined, the service sector includes all economic activities whose output is not a physical product. This sector encompasses the major areas of trade, finance, insurance, communications, public utilities, transportation, government administration, healthcare, education, business (accountants, consultants) and personal service. There are three sectors in an economy, viz. primary sector, secondary sector and tertiary sector or service sector. Primary sector includes agriculture, forestry and fisheries. Secondary sector includes mining, manufacturing and electric supply and construction. Tertiary sector or service sector covers trade, transport, communication, finance, real estate and community, social and personal services.

Economists say that as the economy develops, the share of primary sector in GDP declines, and that of secondary and tertiary sector increases. The growth of service sector and its contribution to income and employment generation are indicators of economic development.

From 15 November 2015, the effective rate of service tax plus Swachh Bharat Cess, post introduction of Swachh Bharat

Cess, was 14.5 per cent. Currently, Swachh Bharat Cess and Krishi Kalyan Cess would also be levied on all services on which service tax is being levied and therefore, the service tax (including Swachh Bharat Cess and Krishi Kalyan Cess), applicable from 1st June 2016 has become 15 per cent.

The collections of service tax from 1993-94 to 2012-13 are given in Table 8.4. It shows that the collections which were ₹ 254 crore in 1993-94 reached ₹ 132,518 crore in 2012-13.

Table 8.4: Collection of Service (1993-94 to 2012-13)

Financial Year	Revenue Rupees (in crores)	Number of services	Number of Assessees
1993–1994	254	2	2568
1994–1995	407	3	3943
1995–1996	862	6	4866
1996–1997	1059	6	13982
1997–1998	1586	18	45991
1998–1999	1957	26	107479
1999–2000	2128	26	115495
2000–2001	2613	26	122326
2001–2002	3302	41	187577
2002–2003	4122	52	232048
2003–2004	7891	62	403856
2004–2005	14200	75	774988
2005–2006	23055	84	846155
2006–2007	37598	99	940641
2007–2008	51301	100	1073075
2008–2009	60941	106	1204570
2009–2010	58422	109	1307286
2010–2011	71016	117	1372274
2011–2012	97509	119	1535570
2012–2013	132518	Negative List Regime	1712617

According to RBI, service tax collections rose 21.6 per cent in April-August, which reflected the increase in service tax rates (inclusive of education cess) effected in June 2015. Direct taxes—accounting for 42 per cent of total tax collection—were subdued through April-July.[11]

Value Added Tax (VAT)

Although VAT has been subsumed in GST, it is necessary to know its main features. VAT was introduced in India as an indirect tax from 1 April 2005. The then existing general sales tax laws were replaced with the Value Added Tax Act (2005) and associated VAT rules.

The states of Gujarat, Tamil Nadu, Rajasthan, Madhya Pradesh, Chhattisgarh, Jharkhand, Uttarakhand and Uttar Pradesh opted to stay out of VAT taxation system during the initial introduction of VAT but adopted it later. VAT was implemented in all the states and union territories of India except Andaman and Nicobar Islands and Lakshadweep Island on 2 June 2014.

VAT was meant to bring about simple and uniform domestic trade taxation, and was considered to be a panacea for all the ills from which India's commodity taxation was suffering, particularly the increasing compliance cost, both on the part of the Government and the taxpayers, and cascading effect of taxes which discouraged specialisation.[12]

VAT was preferred because unlike excise duty it was levied not only at the production stage but also at different stages of value addition. In modern days, when many durable commodities are sold for prices which include service, warranty and installation charges, VAT would fetch considerably more revenue than general sales tax. Having uniform rate structure throughout the country, it was thought to encourage the free flow of internal and inter-state trade, besides promoting optimum allocation of resources and plugging the artificial channels of distribution of goods which were a consequence of non-uniform commodity taxation. It was thought that having no cascading effect of taxes, it would improve the production efficiency.

The implementation of a broad-based federal VAT was considered as the most desirable consumption tax for India since the early 1990s, but it was found that it involved serious problems for the finances of regional governments. The economic reforms led to decentralization of expenditure responsibilities, which, in turn, demanded more decentralization of revenue raising power if fiscal accountability is to be maintained, but at the same time, implementing the VAT, to make India a single integrated market, also led to revenue losses for the states and reduced their autonomy, indicating greater centralization.[13]

It was also found that the local or state level taxes like octroi, entry tax, lease tax, workers contract tax, entertainment tax and luxury tax are not integrated into the new regime, which goes against the basic premise of VAT, which is to have uniformity in the tax structure. The fact that no tax credit will be allowed for inter-state trade seriously undermines the basic benefit of enforcing a VAT system, namely the removal of the distortions in movement of goods across the states.[14]

Now the government has brought a single, country-wide indirect tax system to replace all existing consumption taxes. This new system is known as Goods and Services Tax (GST), and is based on the standard OECD VAT model, that aims to be neutral on taxable persons, and will be levied on the supply of goods and services, with potential reduced rate and exempt supplies for essential supplies such as foodstuffs and public transport. Imports will be subject to GST, but exports are exempt.

State Level Reforms

On the recommendation of the Eleventh Finance Commission (EFC), Government of India implemented a scheme called the 'States Fiscal Reforms Facility (2000-01 to 2004-05) to incentivize the states to undertake fiscal reforms. Under this scheme, which came to an end on March 31, 2005, all the 28 states had submitted their medium term fiscal reforms programme and all but the Government of Goa entered into memorandum of understanding with Government of India, individually. As on March 31, 2005, an amount of ₹ 7,217 crore was released to states from incentive fund on the basis of improvement in revenue deficit as a proportion of revenue receipts. States (excluding NCT Delhi), in aggregate, have registered an improvement of 17.95 percentage points in the ratio of revenue deficit to total revenue receipts during EFC award period (2000-01 to 2004-05), over the base year 1999-2000.

According to the recommendations of the 14th Finance Commission (valid for 2015 to 2020), the states' share in net proceeds from tax collections be will be 42% as compared to 32% recommend by the 13th Finance Commission. Revenue deficit is to be progressively reduced and eliminated, while fiscal deficit to be reduced to 3% of the GDP by 2017-18. There is a target of 62% of GDP for the combined debt of centre and states.

There would be a basic grant and a performance grant. The ratio of basic to performance grant would be 90:10, with respect to panchayats, and 80:20 in the case of municipalities. Total grants would amount to ₹ 2,87,436 crore for a five-year period from April 1, 2015 to March 31, 2020. Of this, ₹ 2,00,292.20 crore is to be given to panchayats and ₹ 87,143.80 crore to municipalities.

For the year 2015-16, transfers will be to the tune of ₹ 29,988 crore. The percentage share of states will continue as before and follow the current mechanism, to the tune of ₹ 55,097 crore. After the implementation of GST, disaster relief will be given according to the recommendations of the 15th Finance Commission.

There will be a total of ₹ 1,94,821 crore on account of expenditure requirements of states, tax devolution and revenue mobilization capacity of the states. These will be given to 11 states.

PUBLIC EXPENDITURE IN INDIA

Public expenditure is an essential part of the welfare states. It is sometimes also divided into plan and non-plan expenditure or development and non-developmental expenditure. Since independence, public expenditure has gained a significant place in the country to pull the economy out of turmoil. Public expenditure regulates the economic activities and helps to attain the long-run and short-run objectives of economic development. This is the reason why there is a continuous upward trend in both revenue and expenditure of the Indian Government. Actually, the government has been widening its activities in social and economic spheres to bring economic growth as early as possible. Even in the post-reform period, public expenditure on social sector has been on the rise. The government cannot leave the provisions like education, medical and public health, social security and poverty alleviation programmes in the hands of the private sector.

Broadly, public expenditure in India can be classified into two parts: Expenditure on Revenue Account, and Expenditure on Capital Account. These are explained below.

Expenditure on Revenue Account of the Central Government

Generally, major heads of revenue expenditure shown in the budget of the Central Government are defence services, civil services, grants-in-aid, interest payments, fiscal services and economic services. Revenue expenditures are generally met out of the revenue receipts of the government like tax revenue and non-tax sources. However, since 1980s an unhealthy trend has developed whereby even capital account receipts like borrowings and disinvestment proceeds are used for meeting revenue expenditure needs.

(i) **Defence Expenditure:** According to Adam Smith: "Defence is more important than opulence." Therefore, it is the most important item for every government. For national wealth to save against external aggression and internal disorder, defence expenditure is must. It is constantly increasing as the modern warfare instruments are becoming costlier and more sophisticated.

(ii) **Civil Services:** Before independence, the aim of the government was the maintenance of law and order whereas after independence, it was sought to change from "law and order state" to "welfare state". Thus, expenditure in this sector has been rising continuously. It includes expenditure on general administration, justice, election and on the Office of Comptroller and Auditor General. Besides, other types of expenditure are on Secretariat and attached offices of Ministries of Education and Social Welfare, Health and Family Welfare, etc.

(iii) **Grants-in-Aid to States:** State Governments cannot work properly without the help of Central Government as the expenditures of State Governments have gone up because of the fact that most of the welfare programmes fall within the jurisdiction of the states, whereas all elastic and growing sources of revenue rest with the Central Government.

(iv) **Interest Payments:** These include expenditure on the payment of interest on the outstanding debt. In recent years, these payments have shown a rising trend on account of the fact that the government borrowed extensively in the past, which has necessitated the interest payment now.

(v) **Fiscal Services:** Collection of taxes and other duties also entail huge public expenditure. Directorate of Customs and Excise Duties, and Directorate of Income Tax are the two major departments of the Central government involved in the collection of taxes.

(vi) **Economic Services:** After Independence, it has become the foremost need of the government to spend on economic services to develop the economy at a rapid speed. It includes the expenditure on Department of Commerce, Shipping and Transport, Irrigation, Energy, Chemicals and Fertilizer, Company Affairs and Electronics, Industry, Agriculture, etc.

Expenditure on Capital Account

Expenditure on capital account consists of expenditure for the acquisition of assets such as land, buildings, machinery, equipments, etc. Expenditure on renewals and repairs of machinery, increase in food grain stocks and inventories, commuted pensions, etc. also constitute capital account expenditure.

Here, we must remember that revenue and capital account expenditure is known as economic classification. As already mentioned this economic classification can be converted into economic and functional expenditure depending upon the break-up of total expenditure into various functions like civil, fiscal, economic, etc. performed by the government.

The year-wise position of expenditure of the Central Government under major heads from 1977-78 to 2016-17 is given in Table 8.5. Three main heads under revenue expenditure are defence expenditure, interest payments, and subsidies. Three main heads under capital expenditure are loans and advances, capital outlay, and defence expenditure. Table 8.5 shows a

Table 8.5: Major Heads of Expenditure of the Central Government

(₹ Billion)

Year	Revenue expenditure	of which			Capital expenditure (7+8)	Loans and advances	of which		Total expenditure (2+6)
		Defence expenditure	Interest payments	Subsidies			Capital outlay	Defence expenditure	
1	2	3	4	5	6	7	8	9	10
1977-78	91.08	23.86	16.46	12.87	63.98	41.55	22.43	2.48	155.06
1978-79	106.82	26.14	19.84	14.75	80.84	56.66	24.18	2.54	187.66
1979-80	118.03	30.94	22.92	18.21	71.59	47.20	24.39	2.62	189.62
1980-81	144.10	32.78	26.04	20.28	83.58	52.85	30.73	3.26	227.68
1981-82	154.08	38.44	31.95	19.41	98.57	56.58	41.99	4.85	252.65
1982-83	187.42	44.94	39.38	22.62	120.49	73.84	46.65	5.27	307.91
1983-84	222.51	51.89	47.95	29.02	132.83	80.53	52.30	6.42	355.34
1984-85	276.91	63.24	59.74	40.38	159.41	91.94	67.47	7.37	436.32
1985-86	339.24	70.21	75.12	47.96	187.42	110.87	76.55	9.67	526.66
1986-87	408.60	91.79	92.46	54.51	220.56	127.97	92.59	12.98	629.16
1987-88	461.74	88.61	112.51	59.80	220.87	127.93	92.94	31.07	682.61
1988-89	541.06	95.58	142.78	77.32	250.05	147.50	102.55	37.83	791.11
1989-90	642.10	101.94	177.57	104.74	286.98	168.90	118.08	42.22	929.08
1990-91	735.16	108.74	214.98	121.58	317.82	196.52	121.30	45.52	1052.98
1991-92	822.92	114.42	265.96	122.53	291.22	177.23	110.43	49.05	1114.14
1992-93	927.02	121.09	310.75	108.24	299.16	162.97	133.85	54.73	1226.18
1993-94	1081.69	149.78	367.41	116.05	336.84	204.54	130.89	68.67	1418.53
1994-95	1221.12	164.26	440.60	118.54	386.27	237.36	148.91	68.19	1607.39
1995-96	1398.61	188.41	500.45	126.66	384.14	243.16	140.99	80.15	1782.75
1996-97	1589.33	209.97	594.78	154.99	420.74	278.78	141.96	85.08	2010.07
1997-98	1803.35	261.74	656.37	185.40	517.18	341.93	175.26	91.04	2320.53

Year	Revenue expenditure	of which			Capital expenditure (7+8)	Loans and advances	of which		Total expenditure (2+6)
		Defence expenditure	Interest payments	Subsidies			Capital outlay	Defence expenditure	
1998-99	2164.61	298.61	778.82	235.93	628.79	440.37	188.41	100.36	2793.40
1999-00	2490.78	352.16	902.49	244.87	489.75	249.38	240.37	118.55	2980.53
2000-01	2778.39	372.38	993.14	268.38	477.53	230.08	247.45	123.84	3255.92
2001-02	3014.68	380.59	1074.60	312.10	608.42	342.84	265.58	162.07	3623.10
2002-03	3387.13	407.09	1178.04	435.33	745.35	316.68	291.01	149.53	4132.48
2003-04	3620.74	432.03	1240.88	443.23	1091.29	287.68	341.50	168.63	4712.03
2004-05	3843.29	438.62	1269.34	459.57	1133.31	289.10	523.38	319.94	4982.52
2005-06	4393.76	482.11	1326.30	475.22	663.62	113.37	550.25	323.38	5057.38
2006-07	5146.09	516.82	1502.72	571.25	687.78	85.24	602.54	338.28	5833.87
2007-08	5944.33	542.19	1710.30	709.26	1182.38	112.98	1069.40	374.62	7126.71
2008-09	7937.98	733.05	1922.04	1297.08	901.58	141.07	760.51	409.18	8839.56
2009-10	9118.09	906.69	2130.93	1413.51	1126.78	156.47	970.31	511.12	10244.87
2010-11	10407.23	920.61	2340.22	1734.20	1566.05	249.85	1316.19	620.56	11973.28
2011-12	11457.85	1030.11	2731.50	2179.41	1585.80	207.37	1378.43	679.02	13043.65
2012-13	12435.14	1112.77	3131.70	2570.79	1668.58	208.00	1460.58	704.99	14103.72
2013-14	13717.72	1243.74	3742.54	2546.32	1876.75	191.98	1684.78	791.25	15594.47
2014-15	14669.92	1368.07	4024.44	2582.58	1966.81	292.18	1674.63	818.87	16636.73
2015-16	15476.73	1432.36	4426.20	2578.01	2377.18	265.13	2112.05	814.00	17853.91
2016-17	17310.37	1627.59	4926.70	2504.33	2470.23	278.77	2191.46	863.40	19780.60

Source: Budget documents of the Government of India.

Notes:
1. Data for 2015-16 are Revised Estimates and data for 2016-17 are Budget Estimates.
2. Capital Expenditure for 2002-03, 2003-04 and 2004-05 include repayments to National Small Saving Fund (NSSF) amounting to ₹ 137.66 billion, ₹ 462.12 billion and ₹ 362.75 billion respectively, apart from loans and advances and capital outlay.
3. Total Expenditure, Capital Outlay and Capital Expenditure for 2007-08 include an amount of ₹ 35531 crore, on account of transactions relating to transfer of RBI's stake in SBI to the Central Government.

large increase in expenditure of the Central Government under various heads. Defence expenditure, interest and payments, and subsidies, which were ₹ 23.86 billion, ₹ 16.46 billion, and 12.87 billion respectively in 1977-78, reached ₹ 1627.59 billion, ₹ 4926.70 billion, and ₹ 2504.33 billion respectively in 2016-17.

The three main heads under capital expenditure saw a steady increase from 1977-78 to 2016-17. Capital expenditure went up from Rs. 63.98 billion in 1977-78 to ₹ 2470.23 billion in 2016-17. Total expenditure increased from ₹ 155.06 billion in 1977-78 to ₹ 19780.60 billion in 2016-17.

PUBLIC DEBT IN INDIA

Public debt, also called government debt refers to a part of the total borrowings by the Central Government including market loans, special bearer bonds, treasury bills and special loans and securities issued by the RBI. It also includes the outstanding external debt. The total borrowings by the Central Government, consisting of the public debt and these other borrowings are known as "net liabilities of the Government".

After the achievement of independence, borrowings from the public were used for financing economic development of the country. The Planning Commission made ambitious targets and therefore the government had to raise large sums from the market and small savings schemes. In recent years, the government has been borrowing to meet its expenditure. Most of government debt is held in long-term interest-bearing securities like national savings certificates, rural development bonds, capital development bonds, etc.

The government debt is of two types, internal and external. The internal debt, which is the major component of public debt of the Central Government has the following components:

Market Loans: These are loans raised by the government in the open market by the sale of securities, etc. These securities usually have a maturity period of 12 months or more at the time of issue and are generally interest bearing.

Bonds: These are debt investments in which the government loans money to an entity—typically corporate or governmental—

which borrows the funds for a defined period of time at a variable or fixed interest rate. Bonds are fixed-income securities and are one of the three main generic asset classes, along with stocks or equities and cash equivalents.

Treasury Bills: These are short-term debt obligations backed by the government with a maturity of less than one year. They have various maturities and are issued at a discount from par. Treasury bills can have maturities of just a few days up to the maximum of 52 weeks, but common maturities are one month, three months, or six months. The longer the period of the bill, the higher the interest rate the bill gives.

Special Floating and Other Loans: These are in the nature of India's contribution towards share capital of international financial institutions like IMF, World Bank, and Regional Development Banks. These are non-negotiable, non-interest bearing securities. The Government of India is liable to pay the amount at the call of these institutions.

Special Securities Issued by RBI: The government obtains temporary loans for a period of maximum 12 months from RBI and issues special securities, which are non-negotiable and non-interest bearing. Such securities provide short-term funds to the government.

Ways and Means Advances: It is a mechanism used by the RBI under its credit policy by which it provides to the states banking with it to help them to tide over temporary mismatches in the cash flow of their receipts and payments. These debts are purely temporary in nature and are usually repaid within three months.

Securities against Small Savings: These are national small savings that have been converted into the Central Government securities under the new accounting system from the year 1999-2000.

External debt denotes the liabilities of the government, the public sector, the private sector and financial institutions to overseas parties. It can be broadly divided into two groups, i.e. long-term debt and short-term debt.

Long-term debt consists of the following:

Multilateral Borrowings: These are debts from multilateral institutions like International Development Association (IDA), International Bank for Reconstruction and Development (IBRD), Asian Development Bank (ADB), etc.

Bilateral Borrowings: These are debts from sovereign countries with whom sovereign and non-sovereign entities enter into one-to-one loan arrangements. Japan and Germany are the two major bilateral creditors for India.

Loans from IMF, World Bank, etc.: These are loans taken by a country from IMF or World Bank which it has to repay.

Short-term Debt: Short-term debt includes all debt having an original maturity of one year or less and interest in arrears on long-term debt.

Besides the above, there are some other liabilities of the government, as mentioned below.

Other Internal Liabilities

The government does not include liabilities under Public Debt. However, the government is liable to make repayment of these liabilities. These include the following:

Small Savings: In recent years, small savings have increased due to rising money income in the economy.

The Government of India has launched a number of small savings instruments like Gold Bonds, Kisan Vikas Patras, Indira Vikas Patras, etc.

Provident Funds: Provident funds are divided into two categories (i) Employee Provident Funds meant for employees; (ii) Public Provident Funds meant for general public.

Other Accounts: These include Postal Insurance and Life Annuity Fund, Borrowings against Compulsory Deposits, Income Tax Annuity Deposit, Special Deposit of Non-Government Provident Fund and Outstanding Amount.

Reserve Funds and Deposits: These are of two types, interest bearing and non-interest bearing.

The position of India's internal and external public debts is given in Table 8.6 below:

Table 8.6: Internal and External Pubic Debt

(₹ in crore)

	31st March 2015	31st March 2016
Internal debt and other liabilities	60,84,267.76	66,89,231.43
Of which, under Market Stabilization Scheme	—	20,000.00
External debt	1,94,286.21	2,05,459.56
Total	62,78,553.97	68,94,690.99

Source: Budget 2015-16

Deficit Financing in India

Deficit financing refers to the budgetary situation where expenditure is higher than the revenue. The excess expenditure is financed either by printing of currency or through borrowing. These days, most of the governments, whether of developed or developing countries are having deficit budgets. These deficits are often financed through borrowings. Hence, fiscal deficit is an indicator of deficit financing.

In India, the size of fiscal deficit is the leading deficit indicator in the budget. As per 2015-16 budget estimate, fiscal deficit was estimated to be 3.9% of the GDP. Deficit financing is very useful in the developing countries like India because of shortage of revenue and development expenditure needs.

Indicators of deficit in the budget are the following:

(i) Budget deficit which equals total expenditure less total receipts,

(ii) Revenue deficit equals revenue expenditure less revenue receipts,

(iii) Fiscal Deficit equals total expenditure less total receipts except borrowings,

(iv) Primary deficit equals fiscal deficit less interest payments,

(v) Effective revenue deficit equals revenue deficit less grants for the creation of capital assets,

(vi) Monetized fiscal deficit equals the part of the fiscal deficit that is covered by borrowing from RBI.

Fiscal Deficit in India

During the period April-December 2016, India's fiscal deficit reached 93.9 per cent of the budget target. It was 87.9 per cent of the budget target during the same period in the previous year. In value terms, the April-December 2016 fiscal deficit stood at ₹ 5.01 lakh crore or 93.9 per cent of the year 2016-17 budget estimates. In the corresponding period a year ago, it was 87.9 per cent of the 2015-16 budget estimates. For the year 2015-16, fiscal deficit was pegged at 5.33 lakh crore or 3.5 per cent of GDP.

As per data released by Controller General of Accounts (CGA), tax revenue was ₹ 7.52 lakh crore, or 71.4 per cent of the full year budget estimate of ₹ 10.54 lakh crore.

Total receipts from revenue and non-debt capital of the government during April-December 2016 was ₹ 9.68 lakh crore or 67 per cent of the budget estimates. Government's plan expenditure during the period was ₹ 4.10 lakh crore which was 74.6 per cent of the budget estimates for the full year. During the same period a year earlier, it was 74.4 per cent of the budget estimates.

Total expenditure, plan and non-plan was ₹ 14.69 lakh crore, 74.3 per cent of government's full year estimate of ₹ 19.78 lakh crore. Revenue deficit during April-December 2017 stood at ₹ 3.54 lakh crore or 100 per cent of budget estimates for 2016-17.[15]

India's fiscal deficit in the period April 2016-February 2017 reached ₹ 6.06 lakh crore or 113.4 per cent of budget estimates for 2016-17, as against 107.1 per cent of budget in the same period of last year. Tax revenue during the period was ₹ 8.85 lakh crore, or 81.3 per cent of the estimates, while total receipts, from revenue and non-debt capital, during the first eleven months of 2016-17, were 11.47 lakh crore, or 77.5 per cent of the estimates for the entire year 2016-17. Total expenditure during the April-February period was ₹ 17.53 lakh crore, or 87 per cent of the entire year's estimate. Of the total expenditure, money spent on plan was over ₹ 4.81 lakh crore, while non-plan expenditure came to more than ₹ 12.71 lakh crore. The revenue deficit during the period April 2016-February 2017 was over ₹ 4.44 lakh crore, or 142.8 per cent, of the estimates. The government had set the target of restricting the deficit for the year at 3.5 per cent of the GDP or to ₹ 5.34 lakh crore.[16]

Fiscal Deficit of States

According to India Ratings and Research (Ind Ra) estimates, the aggregate fiscal deficit of Indian states will increase marginally to 3.3 per cent of GDP in the financial year 2017-18 from its forecast of 3.2 per cent. The states' debt/GDP ratio increased marginally to 24.3 per cent in 2017-18 from 24 per cent forecast.

Net borrowing of states is expected to increase to ₹ 3.7 lakh crore in financial year 2017-18 from its forecast of ₹ 3.5 lakh crore for the previous year. However, as a percentage of GDP, states, net market borrowing is likely to moderate to 2.2 per cent in financial year 2017-18 from 2.3 per cent in 2016-17.

On the expenditure side, Ind Ra expects the aggregate capital expenditure/DTP ratio of states to remain stable at 3.4 per cent in 2017-18 which is same as in the year 2016-17.

Factors Responsible for Fiscal Deficit

Fiscal deficit denotes net borrowings by the government. It may look harmless like borrowings by companies. But there is a basic difference. Companies borrow to invest productively and earn an income which would be more than the rate of interest they have to pay, Governments, on the other hand, borrow mostly to fund consumption. Consequently, there are no assets against and no income from the outlays. Interest becomes a dead burden. To pay the interest, the governments have to borrow once again. That is what has increased public debt of the centre and the states. The problem affects the whole economy. The diversion of public savings to government consumption reduces private investment and consequently pulls down rate of growth. Had the budgets been balanced, there would have been enough resources for a 10 per cent growth instead of 7 to 8 per cent, which would have generated more employment and improved the income of the people further.

The real cause of the problem lies in the fact that the Central and State Governments are more interested in populist measures

The macroeconomic costs of unjustified subsidies are reflected in persistent large fiscal deficits. In addition, unduly high levels of subsidization, as seen in corresponding low user charges, cause serious micro-economic distortions. The main manifestations include excessive demand for subsidized services, distortions in relative prices and misallocation of resources. These are visible in the case of certain input based subsidies.

There should be more reforms to reduce subsidies, limiting them to areas where there is dire need for fast and balanced development of the country. The overall scale of subsidies should be reduced by laying more emphasis on creating infrastructure and opportunities to grow without the assistance of subsidies. Subsidies should be allowed only for well defined economic objectives, not as populist measures to build vote bank. It must be ensured that the impact of subsidies is maximum on the target population at minimum cost. There should be periodic reviews of subsidies to see if they are necessary, and whether can be reduced or even disheveled.

Notes

1. "Tax Collection in 2015-16". *The Times of India.* 3 August 2016.
2. http://www.accountingnotes.net/taxation/tax-structure/10-main-features-of-indian-tax-structure/10090
3. "Consumption Tax Trends 2008 VAT/GST and Excise Rates, Trends and Administration Issues: VAT/GST and Excise Rates, Trends and Administration Issues." *OECD Publishing.* 2008: 115.
4. Chanchal Kumar Sharma (2005). "Implementing VAT in India: Implications for Federal Polity". *Indian Journal of Political Science* 66(4): 915-34.
5. http://www.investopedia.com/terms/c/corporatetax.asp#ixzz4iRzWipFW
6. www.investopedia.com/terms/d/double_taxation.asp
7. *Times of India.* 26 April 2017.
8. *Ibid.*
9. https://www.gktoday.in/blog/tax-and-non-tax-revenue-receipts/
10. *Ibid.*
11. https://rbi.org.in/scripts/PublicationsView.aspx?id=16691

12. R.K. Bansal and J.R. Gupta. *Economic Aspects of Sales Tax*, Atlantic Publishers, 1985.
13. "Consumption Tax Trends 2008 VAT/GST and Excise Rates, Trends and Administration Issues: VAT/GST and Excise Rates, Trends and Administration Issues." *OECD Publishing*. 2008: 115.
14. Chanchal Kumar Sharma (2005). "Implementing VAT in India: Implications for Federal Polity". *Indian Journal of Political Science* 66(4): 915-34.
15. *The Economic Times*. 31st January 2017.
16. *Business Standard*. 31 March 2017.